NAZI YOUTH

in the
WEIMAR
REPUBLIC

Studies in Comparative Politics

Peter H. Merkl, *editor*

NAZI YOUTH
in the
WEIMAR
REPUBLIC

Peter D. Stachura

introduction by
Peter H. Merkl

CLIO BOOKS

Santa Barbara, California

Oxford, England

© 1975 by Peter D. Stachura

Library of Congress Catalog Card Number 74-14196
ISBN Clothbound Edition 0-87436-198-2
ISBN Paperbound Edition 0-87436-199-0

American Bibliographical Center—Clio Press, Inc.
2040 Alameda Padre Serra
Santa Barbara, California

European Bibliographical Center—Clio Press
Woodside House, Hinksey Hill
Oxford OX 1 5BE, England

Designed by Liz Maynard
Composed by Computer Typesetting Services
Printed and bound by R. R. Donnelley and Sons Co.
in the United States of America

To

MY MOTHER &
FATHER

CONTENTS

List of Abbreviations

I. Political Organisations

BDAJ	: Bund deutscher Arbeiterjugend
BDM	: Bund deutscher Mädel
DAP	: Deutsche Arbeiterpartei
DDP	: Deutsche Demokratische Partei
DJ	: Deutsches Jungvolk
DNVP	: Deutschnationale Volkspartei
DSP	: Deutsche Staatspartei
DVP	: Deutsche Volkspartei
GDJB	: Grossdeutsche Jugendbewegung
GSRN	: Gruppe Sozialrevolutionärer Nationalisten
HJ	: Hitlerjugend
KGRNS	: Kampfgemeinschaft Revolutionärer Nationalsozialisten
KPD	: Kommunistische Partei Deutschlands
NSABJ	: Nationalsozialistische Arbeiter-und Bauernjugend
NSDAJ	: Nationalsozialistische Deutsche Arbeiterjugend
NSDAP	: Nationalsozialistische Deutsche Arbeiterpartei
NSDStB	: Nationalsozialistischer Deutscher Studentenbund
NSJB	: Nationalsozialistische Jugendbewegung
NSJBO	: Nationalsozialistische Jugendbetriebszellen-Organisation
NSKK	: Nationalsozialistisches Kraftfahrerkorps
NSS	: Nationalsozialistischer Schülerbund

RJF	: Reichsjugendführung
SA	: Sturmabteilung
SPD	: Sozialdemokratische Partei Deutschlands
SS	: Schutzstaffel
Uschla	: Untersuchungs-und Schlichtungsausschuss

2. Archives

BA	: Bundesarchiv
BA:ZSg	: Bundesarchiv:Zeitgeschichtliche Sammlung
Bay.HSA:ASA	: Bayerisches Hauptstaatsarchiv: Allgemeines Staatsarchiv
Bay.HSA:GSA	: Bayerisches Hauptstaatsarchiv: Geheimes Staatsarchiv
Bay.HSA:SAOB	: Bayerisches Hauptstaatsarchiv: Staatsarchiv für Oberbayern
BDC	: Berlin Document Center
FSGNS	: Forschungsstelle für die Geschichte des Nationalsozialismus
LASH	: Landesarchiv Schleswig-Holstein
SAB	: Staatsarchiv Bremen
SAK	: Staatsarchiv Koblenz

3. Newspapers, Journals, Documentary Collections

Amer.Hist.Rev.	: American Historical Review
HJZ	: Hitler-Jugend-Zeitung
Inter.Mil.Trib.	: International Military Tribunal
VB	: Völkischer Beobachter
VZG	: Vierteljahrshefte für Zeitgeschichte.

Preface

The role played by politicised youth during the rise and short-lived victory of German nazism is difficult to exaggerate. No other phenomenon, except for the impact of World War I, explains as well the attraction and virulence of the brown shirt movement—and, by implication, the ensuing disasters of war, totalitarian government, and genocide that eventually overcame Europe in the years that followed. The emergence of youth as a political factor in recent German history began with the sudden growth of youth organisations during the two decades preceding the war. Initially, those organisations were rather apolitical in form, such as the bourgeois *Wandervogel* and the Socialist and Catholic youth organisations. After 1918, however, the organised youth cultures turned to political activism. That shift can be partially explained by the outer violence and inner fears vicariously experienced by youngsters having older brothers or fathers at the front. The effect of absent fathers in a formerly patriarchal society also was felt, as was the demise of the monarchy, the revolutionary upheavals, and counterrevolutionary repression by the Free Corps. All of these factors contributed to the politicisation of Weimar youth.

Whatever the causes, the symptoms of politicisation and political activism were unmistakable. Dr. Stachura admirably analyses the youth culture of that period: the *Bündische* youth of liberal, *völkisch,* or nationalist-military persuasion, the Socialist and Communist youth, and the various religious youth groups. Each group represented a unique subculture in which different processes of political socialisation inducted young people into a sociopolitical community of faith. In spite of the intensity of the specific socialisation patterns which were often reinforced in the home and school environment there was an astonishing mobility among youth groups. Young men frequently wandered through four or five groups and sometimes changed from one political camp to another before outgrowing the youth group phase. The Theodore Abel Collection of pre-1933 vitae, for example, contains numerous cases of such pilgrimages which terminated only when the respondents acquired girl friends or married.

The youth groups, like the adult *Männerbünde* of the Weimar Republic, tended to be sexually segregated. They derived their romanticism from group life, comradeship, and youthful adventure. Dr. Stachura shows that membership in youth groups was frequently culminated by recruitment into the Hitler Youth, the young storm troopers (SA), and other paramilitary groups, e.g., the *Jungstahlhelm*, *Wehrwolf*, the republican *Reichsbanner*, and the Communist Red Front. These groups had in common a militantly political stance and were often involved in political demonstrations, street violence, and meeting hall battles.

Street violence in the early thirties plagued the Weimar Republic; it involved hundreds of clashes and thousands of dead and wounded every year. The antagonists and the victims generally were young stormtroopers, Communists, and policemen. The authorities vainly attempted to keep Nazi and Communist demonstrations separate or to suppress them altogether. The impetuous youth in both movements invariably managed to join in a series of bone-cracking, blood-spattering confrontations until the frightened bourgeoisie finally sought "law and order" from Adolf Hitler.

Plainly, the seeds of violence and the gruesome result can be largely attributed to the youth of the Weimar generation. My research on the Abel Collection reveals that budding Nazi stormtroopers tended to show a penchant for violence early in life while still belonging to harmless *Wandervogel* or religious groups. I also have found that pre-1933 Nazis were unlikely to play violent roles unless they were involved in violence or were members of fighting organisations by the age of eighteen. Some Nazi violence during the early years of the Weimar Republic was obviously attributable to battle-hardened veterans of World War I and the Free Corps. By about 1928, however, a new generation of violent youth too young to have served in the war or to have suffered its effects at home began to occupy centre stage. The first postwar "generation of 1902" (said to have been shattered without the help of cannonballs) was replaced by a generation born in 1908 and later. Members of this later generation itched to march for a cause—they were spoiling for a fight. Dr. Stachura catalogues and describes the ideological rationalisations involved and their appeal to youth.

This book therefore treats a crucial and neglected aspect of Weimar history and society. The author's perceptive analysis of the early Hitler Youth and the whole youth climate in the Weimar Republic is an important contribution to understanding the fateful evolution of Weimar politics to the appointment of Hitler. Dr. Stachura's well-researched study illuminates the internal dynamics of the Nazi youth movement and of the party itself, including the early flirtation with quasi-socialistic goals. Unfortunately, the pluralistic factionalism characteristic of German youth and the party provided a deceptive picture of the unifying storm that eventually swept most Germans into the same ideological torrent. German youth who emphatically repudiated the existing system were left few viable alternatives other than the Nazi movement. The Communist youth movement—an attractive competitor at the time—awaits the attention of another Dr. Stachura. Step by step other groups and individuals, especially those in the bourgeois camp, were drawn into Hitler's fighting movement during its *Kampfzeit* ("time of battle") from 1929–33.

In retrospect it is almost incomprehensible that this particular youth cohort was so combative. It is also difficult to understand how Hitler's NSDAP became a self-styled advocate of youth, despite its defiant slogan "Step aside, you old ones," which it threw into the face of the Weimar gerontocracy. In the meantime, of course, the current generation has witnessed another youthful upheaval, the student riots around the world in the late 1960s which challenged anybody over thirty, indeed the whole adult establishment. In either case there are no adequate explanations for the differing behaviour of one generation in comparison to that of a preceding one; we don't know why high school and university students in the 1960s were so radically different from those of the "quiet fifties." Sociologists and psychologists have never fully elucidated the wellsprings of youthful emotion and politicisation characteristic of the period 1968–70. We know, however, that in some years locusts are born bigger and stronger, more capable of plaguing whole regions. The years 1908–15 may well have been the birth "years of the locust" for German youth, and perhaps the same was true, more recently, of the young people born in 1947–52.

It is perhaps more appropriate to compare the Nazi youth generations born just before World War I to the lemmings, the little brown rodents which periodically embark on migrations ending in their own death. In their fervour a great many Nazi youth perished in the final suicidal plunge of World War II. Understanding the causes of that tragedy need not imply forgiveness, notwithstanding the French adage *tout comprendre c'est tout pardonner*. On the contrary, understanding may enable us to resist such phenomena while there is still time. In any case, the historical profession, the other disciplines of social

science, and the general reader with an interest in contemporary politics and recent history are all deeply indebted to Dr. Stachura for
having filled a notable gap in our understanding of our era.

PETER H. MERKL

University of California
Santa Barbara

August 1974

Acknowledgements

In the preparation of this study, I have become indebted to a considerable number of individuals and institutions in both the United Kingdom and in the Federal Republic of Germany. It is a pleasure to record my gratitude for the assistance and expertise provided by the staffs of the various archives and libraries whose resources I have used. I would like to mention in particular Dr. Werner Jochmann and Dr. Henning Timpke of the Forschungsstelle für die Geschichte des Nationalsozialismus in Hamburg; Dr. Hector of the Landesarchiv Schleswig-Holstein; Dr. Schwebel of the Staatsarchiv Bremen; Frau Kinder of the Bundesarchiv in Koblenz; Dr. Maruhn of the Staatsarchiv Koblenz; Dr. Hemmerle, Dr. Puchner, and Dr. von Rehlingen of the Bayerisches Hauptstaatsarchiv in Munich; Herr Hans Wolf of the Archiv der deutschen Jugendbewegung at Burg Ludwigstein, Witzenhausen; Mr. Wheaton B. Byers of the Berlin Document Center; and Mrs. M. Johnson of the Institute of Contemporary History and Wiener Library, London.

I am grateful to Professor K. O. Freiherr von Aretin of the Institut für Europäische Geschichte in Mainz for granting me a scholarship to study in the intellectually stimulating atmosphere of the Institut for a period of six months in 1970–71, and for allowing me a further stay in 1972. Of the staff there, Herr Lacher, Fräulein von Reden, Herr Claus Scharf, and Dr. Hans-Jürgen Schröder especially deserve my thanks.

The Deutsche Akademischer Austauchdienst and the Cassel Educational Trust contributed to the financing of my research in Germany in 1972.

I learned much from conversations and discussions at different stages with Professor Michael Balfour, who supervised my doctoral thesis; Professor Kurt Tauber; and Nicholas J. Ryschkowsky, Ewald Dalhke, Hans Dehmel, James Diehl, Wayne Davis, and Robert Hoffmann. I also wish to thank Herr Hartmann Lauterbacher for submitting to a series of interviews. Regretfully, Herr Baldur von Schirach declined to offer me that facility. The endeavours of Mr. Lalit Adolphus on my behalf I appreciate very much.

I owe a special word of thanks to Dr. Volker R. Berghahn who besides giving me the benefit of detailed and incisive criticisms of my manuscript was always generous in his encouragement and advice. Dr. Wolfgang Horn also read the manuscript and made useful comments. I need hardly add, however, that the responsibility for any deficiencies is entirely mine.

Finally, the interest shown by my whole family throughout the writing of this work was an indispensable factor of support.

PETER D. STACHURA

Introduction

Despite the rapidly expanding volume of literature dealing with national socialism during the "years of struggle" before 1933, most of the writing has been devoted either to the background in the pre- and post-1918 period in Germany which made the appearance and development of national socialism possible, or alternatively, to the organisational, propagandistic, and leadership structure of the Nazi party itself.[1] A more recent trend has been to analyse the nature and evolution of the party at a regional or local level, which is useful in allowing a detailed insight into the workings of a mass movement in microcosm.[2] A conspicuous and interesting aspect of the ascent of national socialism which has received comparatively scant attention, however, is that of the national socialist youth movement in general, and the Hitler Youth in particular.

During the Third Reich, the Hitler Youth occupied a position of fundamental importance in the lives of millions of young Germans. At a very impressionable age, German youth became susceptible to the teachings of national socialism, and it was that generation which the Hitler Youth had inculcated with the national socialist *Weltanschauung* (ideology) which furnished the most convinced and fanatical followers of the Führer, Adolf Hitler. The Hitler Youth's political significance during the Hitlerian era as the institution principally responsible for ensuring the younger generation's loyalty towards the state is, therefore, incontestable. Several works have attempted to describe this development, in varying degrees of depth (A. Klönne's *Hitlerjugend. Die Jugend und Ihre Organisation im Dritten Reich* and W. Klose's *Generation im Gleichschritt*) while some others have looked at the Hitler Youth's assault on certain sections of German youth after 1933.[3]

None of these, however, have dealt adequately with the formative years of the Hitler Youth. The few accounts written in Germany before 1945, though sometimes helpful in providing a point of detail, are obviously too tendentious in their interpretation to be a trustworthy guide.[4] H. C. Brandenburg's book, *Die Geschichte der HJ*, does concentrate on the period prior to 1933, but unfortunately leaves unanswered too many basic questions regarding organisation, ideology, and political orientation to be wholly satisfactory. Hence, the present study, which has evolved from my doctoral thesis, "The Development and Organisation of the Hitler Youth, 1930–1933" (University of East Anglia, 1971), is concerned with an analysis of the early history of the Hitler Youth as a constituent member of the national socialist movement. The intention is to make clear that these early years were vital to the Hitler Youth and decisive for its later growth. Although it was only when Hitler became chancellor of the Reich that the wider, practical implications of the Hitler Youth's ambitions were realised, many of the far-reaching decisions which shaped its character were taken before 1933.

A recently published monograph on the Nazi party emphasises the central and dominant role of Hitler and the emotional, pseudo-religious reverence surrounding him in the organisational development of the party.[5] This book, *Nazi Youth in the Weimar Republic,* will show that Hitler's influence and his conception of how his movement should progress also extended at crucial moments to the Hitler Youth, whose history in consequence must always be seen within the broader context of national socialism. The origins of the Hitler Youth in an assorted variety of national socialist or at least pronational socialist youth organisations before it was founded in 1926 will be explained with the purpose of setting the background in due perspective. Thereafter, by posing questions pertaining to its ideological outlook, sociological composition, organisational machinery, leadership, and strength, the Hitler Youth's role within the movement will be elucidated. In this respect, the relationship between the Hitler Youth and both the party and SA will be taken into consideration.

The Hitler Youth's credentials vis-à-vis the groups of the German youth movement and other political youth associations will be investigated in order to clarify its status in the historical development of the youth movement. There is a relatively large and well-documented literature on most major features of the youth movement, including its growth in the Weimar Republic. But these works have taken only superficial account of the Hitler Youth's position, mainly because the latter's political style effectively debarred it from being recognised as a full-fledged member.[6] On the other hand, even works delineating the specific dealings between the Hitler Youth and the youth movement do not tell us very much of substance about the intrinsic character which made the Hitler Youth so different from the vast majority of contemporary groups.[7]

Finally, archival material on the Nazi party is richer than that available for the Hitler Youth, and moreover, students of the party are able to call upon a considerable number of memoirs written by former associates of Hitler[8] as well as up-to-date documentary collections.[9] But a further, technical reason for justifying a study of the earlier phase of the Hitler Youth is that due to loss and destruction during the last war, the bulk of primary sources are for the pre-1933 period. The deficiencies and generally poor quality of secondary material for the Hitler Youth has meant that most of this book is based on these primary sources.

Koblenz

October 1974.

Notes: Introduction

1. For example: D. Orlow, *The History of the Nazi Party 1919–1933* (Pittsburgh, 1969); D. K. Bramsted, *Goebbels and National Socialist Propaganda 1925–45* (London, 1965); and J. Nyomarkay, *Charisma and Factionalism in the Nazi Party* (Minneapolis, 1967).

2. W. S. Allen, *The Nazi Seizure of Power. The Experience of a Single German Town 1930–35* (London, 1965); J. Noakes, *The Nazi Party in Lower Saxony 1921–33* (Oxford, 1971); W. Maser, *Die Frühgeschichte der NSDAP* (Frankfurt, 1965); H. Gordon, *Hitlerputsch 1923. Machtkampf in Bayern 1923–24* (Frankfurt, 1971); R. Heberle, *Landbevölkerung und Nationalsozialismus. Eine soziologische Untersuchung der politischen Willensbildung in Schleswig-Holstein 1918 bis 1932* (Stuttgart, 1963); and G. Pridham, *Hitler's Rise to Power. The Nazi Movement in Bavaria, 1923–1933* (London, 1973). There are also a number of doctoral dissertations on the NSDAP in Hesse, Hamburg, and Düsseldorf (see Bibliography).

3. D. von Lersner, *Die Evangelischen Jugendverbände Württembergs und die Hitler-Jugend, 1933–34* (Göttingen, 1958); H. Roth, ed., *Katholische Jugend in der NS-Zeit* (Düsseldorf, 1959); L. D. Walker, *Hitler Youth and Catholic Youth 1933–36* (Washington, 1971); M. Priepke, *Die Evangelische Jugend im Widerstand gegen das Dritte Reich von 1933 bis 1936* (Frankfurt, 1960); and A. Klönne, *Gegen den Strom* (Hannover, 1957).

4. H. Bolm, *Hitler-Jugend in einem Jahrzehnt. Ein Glaubensweg der niedersächsischen Jugend* (Brunswick, 1938); G. Usadel, *Entwicklung und Bedeutung der NS-Jugendbewegung* (Berlin, 1935); and B. von Schirach, *Die Hitler-Jugend. Idee und Gestalt* (Leipzig, 1934).

5. W. Horn, *Führerideologie und Parteiorganisation in der NSDAP* (Düsseldorf, 1972).

6. For example, H. Pross, *Jugend. Eros. Politik* (Bern, 1964); and W. Z. Laqueur, *Young Germany: A History of the German Youth Movement* (London, 1962).

7. E. M. Jovy, "Jugendbewegung und Nationalsozialismus" (Ph.D. diss., University of Cologne, 1952); and U. Schmidt, "Die Jugendbewegung und Ihre Nachwirkungen in die Hitler-Jugend" (Unpublished manuscript, Bielefeld Hochschule, 1960).

8. For the Hitler Youth, there are the memoirs of B. von Schirach, *Ich Glaubte an Hitler* (Hamburg, 1967), and of M. Maschmann, a former high-ranking official of the girls' branch of the Hitler Youth (the *Bund deutscher Mädel*), *Account Rendered* (London, 1964), but they are not of any notable value.

9. Among them, E. Deuerlein, *Der Hitler-Putsch. Bayerische Dokumente zum 8/9 November 1923* (Stuttgart, 1962); W. Hofer, ed., *Der Nationalsozialismus: Dokumente 1933–45* (Frankfurt, 1957); W. Jochmann, *Nationalsozialismus und Revolution. Ursprung und Geschichte der NSDAP in Hamburg 1922–33. Dokumente* (Frankfurt, 1963); H. A. Jacobsen and W. Jochmann, *Ausgewählte Dokumente zur Geschichte des Nationalsozialismus* (Bielefeld, 1966); and A. Tyrell, *Führer befiehl . . . Selbstzeugnisse aus der "Kampfzeit" der NSDAP. Dokumentation und Analyse* (Düsseldorf, 1969).

NAZI YOUTH

in the
WEIMAR
REPUBLIC

Chapter 1

The Early National Socialist Youth Movement, 1922–26

For the nations of Europe, the year 1918 was of special significance because it inaugurated a new age of political, social, and economic instability. Particularly in Germany, political happenings of paramount importance came suddenly and quickly: the unexpected military collapse, the abdication of Kaiser Wilhelm II, and the November revolution. The revolution, which was intrinsically the outcome of many unsolved problems in the Bismarckian-Wilhelmian system, sharpened by the war-weariness and distress of wide sections of the population, seemed to mark a new era in German history. Above all, the introduction of parliamentary government appeared to indicate a fresh beginning.

But the triumph of liberal democracy was more apparent than real. Pillars of the old imperial order, the army, bureaucracy, the judiciary, the Junker aristocracy, big business, and the universities, were left largely untouched. It was in fact these very groups of the antidemocratic counterrevolution which helped Adolf Hitler destroy the Weimar Republic in 1933. In short, the German revolution of 1918–19 was abortive and too replete with improvised compromises. Moreover, the harsh Treaty of Versailles, the fallacious but widespread Dolchstoss ("stab-in-the-back") legend, and the uncooperative policy

1

pursued by the victorious Allies added to the unpropitious circumstances in which the republic was conceived.

Despite many other preoccupations at this chaotic time, the political parties of the Weimar Republic readily appreciated the advantages of having a youth group affiliated with the party structure; it would especially provide a prepared nucleus of support among the younger generation. The period immediately after 1918 was therefore characterised by an almost frenetic establishment of party youth organisations.[1] But there was a mutual commitment: more youths than ever before became organised because they wished to join a group with whose interests they could identify. This expansion of youth activity was certainly prompted to a considerable degree by the state of flux and bewilderment which German youth shared with the rest of the population. The uncertainty which the rapidity and totality of the German collapse had provoked was instrumental in directing youth's search for a new basis of life. The parties, understanding this feeling only too well, manifested a solicitude for the allegiance of the younger generation that was quite extraordinary in view of adult apathy toward the young before 1914. There were two important developments coinciding with this state of affairs, the first of which relates to the German youth movement.

The independent youth movement dates from the foundation of the *Wandervogel, Ausschuss für Schülerfahrten* (Committee for Schoolboy Excursions) on 4 November 1901 in Berlin.[2] In some ways, the *Wandervogel* was a manifestation of the perceptible mood of boredom and restlessness affecting much of Europe at the turn of the century, and also an indication that the solid and contented appearance of Wilhelmian Germany was little more than a facade which concealed latent tensions beneath the surface.

The *Wandervogel's* immediate genesis reflected a rejection of accepted standards and institutions by the German liberal bourgeoisie, which was communicated by parents to the youths. The movement was linked to the fascination for avant-garde trends in the arts and sciences and to the aspirations for a richer life and broader freedoms which inspired and accompanied the emergence of modern mass society around 1900. Moreover, since the bourgeois class had materially benefited most of all from Germany's rapid economic expansion after 1871, bourgeois youth now took their comfortable homes and well-being for granted and began to direct their criticism against the generation which had given them their prosperity. In these circumstances, this kind of confrontation between generations is often unavoidable. Only by 1900 had middle-class youth for the first time both the opportunity and inclination to challenge the adult world. The *Wandervogel* arose when it did, therefore, because only then did the pattern of

German economic growth and sociological development make it possible for a section of the younger generation to express its disenchantment with the older generation.

Under the leadership of Karl Fischer, the *Wandervogel* resented the monotonous routine, restraints, and conventions imposed on young Germans by the conservative-minded adult generation. It wanted youth to be able to lead their own lives, and demanded at least a partial release from the tutelage of the parental home, school, and the whole system of authority which the *Wandervogel* claimed did not understand, or even try to understand, the problems peculiar to youth. The traditionally lowly status of youth in German society was to be contested. The *Wandervogel* aimed to assert youth's longing to be recognised as an entity in itself, and to find an awakened sense of purpose in a society it felt had become too harsh, complex, and materialistic. But the *Wandervogel* possessed no clearly formulated programme to solve these problems, and instead channelled its protest through a hazy form of escapist romanticism which yearned for a return to the simplicities of unadulterated Nature and the uncomplicated, rustic life.

The *Wandervogel's* attraction was by no means universal, and throughout its history it remained a mainly Protestant, urban, middle-class phenomenon, with its deepest roots in northern and middle Germany. Activities were composed of rambling, hiking, camping, folk dancing, discussions, and the singing of old folk songs, which in 1909 were published in the *Wandervogel's* most famous songbook, the *Zupfgeigenhansel*.[3] The movement's organisational structure lacked centralisation, however, and this along with the petty jealousies of certain leaders explains why it soon disintegrated into a host of warring factions.[4] The rupture and dissension in its development inevitably meant that the youth movement, which had approximately 60,000 members in 1914, never realised its full potential.[5]

Although the movement was initially nonpolitical and unreceptive to the strident nationalism and militarism of the older generation, right-wing *völkisch* ideas were later propagated extensively in *Wandervogel* circles. Consequently, despite official policy prohibiting racial or religious discrimination in the movement, anti-Semitism was embraced by many members.[6] Another aspect of the *Wandervogel* which did arouse a good deal of public controversy was the serious problem of homosexuality.[7] In its quest to rediscover the genuineness of Nature, the *Wandervogel* came to hold the concept of male physical beauty in high esteem, and this outlook may help explain the wide prevalence of homosexuality within its ranks.

World War I, which had been greeted by German youth with as much enthusiasm as any other section of the nation, resulted in the death of thousands of *Wandervogel* members at the front, many of them at the Battle of Langemarck in 1914,[8] and as the youth movement absorbed more leftist ideas, the fabric of the *Wandervogel* had been destroyed by 1918. All but its most naive admirers then realised that a radical transformation in both the concept and practice of the youth movement was necessary. The *Wandervogel* was now out of date and incompatible with the postwar situation; a different era clearly had to evolve that would satisfy the needs of youth desperate for change. The original *Wandervogel* principles were now generally considered too unrealistic and romantic, and only a small number of revived *Wandervogel* groups continued to cultivate the old tradition. Those who nonetheless wished to remain within the free youth movement organised themselves anew during the second phase of the youth movement from 1918 to 1923.

From the beginning, however, profound differences arose, and a definite cleavage between the political left and right severely weakened the movement. The *Jungdeutsche Bund,* racialist, nationalist, and anticommunist, became the leading representative of the right wing for a time, while the more liberal factions, which supported the November revolution, grouped in the *Freideutsche Jugend.* But each stream was divided into many cliques and neither succeeded in attaining a cohesive front. In 1923, the *Freideutsche Jugend* finally disintegrated, signifying the conclusion of this strife-torn and indecisive phase of the youth movement. The absence of good, clear-headed leadership and of precise objectives were the principal reasons for this failure. After 1923, the *Bündische Jugend,* a generic term for a conglomeration of youth organisations, emerged as the heir of the independent German youth movement.

The postwar politicalisation of youth, with its newly awakened political sensitivity, indubitably facilitated the attempts of the parties to enlist their organised support. German youth had become more conscious of political events and simultaneously more cognisant of their own capacity to help influence these events. This frame of mind was in clear contrast to the pre-1914 political indifference of the majority of youth and represented one of the most significant changes brought about by the war and its aftermath. The demand by youth to fill the spiritual vacuum created by the war with a substantive meaning allowed the political parties to compete more vigorously than before for the services of youth. Hence, in 1918, the German National Peoples' party (DNVP) founded the *Bismarckjugend;* in 1919, the German Communist Party (KPD) set up the *Kommunistische Jugendverband Deutschlands,* while the Social Democrats (SPD) established the *Sozialistische Arbeiterjugend;* in 1920, the Centre Party officially took the *Windthorstbund* under its wing; and finally, the

Hindenburgjugend became the youth auxiliary of the German Peoples' Party (DVP).

The parties' interest in the younger generation was noticeably lacking in the National Socialist German Workers' Party (NSDAP) and its predecessor, the German Workers' party (DAP). Indeed, the National Socialists' early disinterest in youth reveals a surprising paradox, for during the years of struggle before 1933 *(Kampfzeit)*, and to a lesser extent in the Third Reich, national socialist propaganda ceaselessly proclaimed the NSDAP to be the "party of youth," and was fond of depicting the *Machtergreifung* as a spontaneous upsurge of young Germany under Hitler's leadership against the Weimar Republic. The apathy of the National Socialists made them comparative latecomers in the pursuit for youth's support; the *Jugendbund der NSDAP* was not created until 1922. This disinterested attitude was a crucial factor in the relative fragmentation and ineffectiveness of the national socialist youth movement before the foundation of the Hitler Youth in 1926. It is perhaps significant that the NSDAP's twenty-five-point political programme of February 1920 made no provision for attracting the very young.[9] Youths under eighteen years of age who supported the party before 1922 were obliged to join the SA, where they were expected to display the same toughness as fully mature men.

The NSDAP was only one of the numerous political splinter groups which arose in Bavaria soon after the war. Although the origins of the first National Socialist political party may be traced to pre-1918 Bohemia, the direct predecessor of the NSDAP was the anti-Semitic and nationalist German Workers' Party, founded by Anton Drexler and Karl Harrer in January 1919.[10] Hitler became a member in 1919 while still serving in a political educational unit of the army. The DAP would have remained a nonentity in the crowded Munich political scene had he not instilled it with his brilliant organisational, oratorical, and propagandistic talents. Hitler became so indispensable to the party (renamed the NSDAP in 1920) that following increasing disagreement with the leadership, he was able to effect his first political *Machtergreifung* in July 1921 with that curious mixture of dissimulation, pertinacity, and intimidation which he was to employ on other occasions of party crisis before 1933. Hitler assumed dictatorial powers, replaced the existing democratic administrative framework with a new structure based on the authoritarian *Führerprinzip,* and introduced into important positions his own faithful group of followers, including Hermann Esser, Alfred Rosenberg, Dietrich Eckart, Gottfried Feder, and Max Amann.

The NSDAP grew as part of the extensive, but uncoordinated, nationalist front of resentment against Germany's defeat, the Versailles

Treaty, democracy, communism, and the Jews, a standpoint nourished by profound economic and social suffering. The NSDAP, like most other right-wing groups, drew most of its early support from the shattered middle and petty bourgeoisie. The party programme was nonetheless designed to appeal to the broadest sections of the nation. As an ideological treatise, the twenty-five points were significantly unoriginal, incorporating ideas which had already been canvassed by *völkisch,* anti-Semitic, anti-Marxist, and Pan-German nationalist movements before and after 1918. Never during the course of his career did Hitler allow the programme to restrict his actions, for he remained consistently devoted to only one tenet, *völkisch* anti-Semitism.

The *Jugendbund der* NSDAP 1922–23

The postwar situation was as turbulent in Bavaria as it was in Berlin. In rapid succession, Bavaria experienced Kurt Eisner's socialist republic, Johann Hoffmann's social democratic government, a soviet workers' regime, and another brief spell of Hoffman until March 1920. The repercussions were important, for subsequently and until early 1924, Bavarian politics showed a marked propensity to right-wing extremism. Bavaria became the haven of scores of nationalist, *völkisch,* and paramilitary organisations, most of which were dedicated to destroying the infant republic. The NSDAP and its youth movement were among these organisations bidding for support in an uneasy, contentious atmosphere.

The generally accepted date of the official foundation of the first national socialist youth group, the *Jugendbund der* NSDAP, is March 1922. Yet there is evidence to suggest that the leader of the group, an unemployed youth, Gustav Adolf Lenk of Munich, actually attempted to establish a youth affiliate of the NSDAP in 1920–21 at the direction of the party chairman, Drexler. According to Lenk's account, he and his father attended a meeting of the NSDAP in the *Stadtkeller* in Munich on 12 September 1920. On finding that he could not join the party because he was under eighteen years of age, Lenk enquired if there was a party youth group that he could join in the meantime. There was no youth group, but because Lenk was willing to create one, Drexler gave him an official commission to do so. Although Hitler vaguely referred to the foundation of a youth association at an NSDAP rally in 1921, Lenk, a member of the party since 16 February 1921, failed to carry out his commission.[11]

The matter was deferred until an NSDAP meeting in Munich on 24 February 1922 at which Hitler himself took the initiative for a second attempt at setting up a youth organisation, and formulated the rather long-winded proclamation which appeared in the *Völkischer Beobachter* on 8 March 1922:

> To German Youth!
> A youth association of the National Socialist German Workers' Party has been established in which all young followers of our cause, who because of their age are ineligible for membership of the Storm Section, will be grouped and organised. The association has its own statutes, and will instruct its members in the same spirit as in the party. We believe that the name of the association alone is sufficient guarantee that in it our youth will find the best preparation for the difficult tasks of the future. On their shoulders rests the future of the Fatherland. The *Jugendbund der* NSDAP will therefore ensure that their shoulders are strong enough to bear this giant burden.
> We demand that National Socialist youth and also all other young Germans, without distinction of class or occupation, aged 14 to 18 years, who have the need and misery of our Fatherland at heart, and who want to join the ranks sometime later of our party and the Storm Section as fighters against the Jewish enemy, the sole creator of the present ignominy and misery, join the *Jugendbund der* NSDAP. We demand that the youth organisations which are not affiliated to any of the great political movements also join, in order to strengthen the German United Front against the common enemy, and to create a powerful Storm Bloc.[12]

The establishment of the *Jugendbund* followed the reorganisation of the NSDAP after Hitler's coup in July 1921. The youth committee that was then set up constituted one of six subcommittees responsible to the Hitler-dominated central *Aktionsausschuss* (Action Committee). Hitler, probably with some persuasion from Lenk, was at last aware of the unsatisfactory practice of youths being grouped with men in the SA, and he believed that the time was now opportune to have a separate organisation for them.[13] It was agreed that the *Jugendbund* would be a means of ensuring due publicity for the movement among the younger generation while at the same time presenting a challenge to other right-wing organisations for the loyalty of nationalist-minded youth.

On the other hand, Lenk wanted the *Jugendbund* to enjoy relative autonomy from both the NSDAP and SA and thus to be able to grow as an authentic youth organisation. This aim conflicted, however, with the viewpoint of Hitler and the SA that the *Jugendbund* should provide in the final analysis a future reservoir of party and SA members (as the proclamation of 8 March 1922 explicitly stated). The difference was resolved at the *Jugendbund's* inaugural meeting on 13 May 1922 in the *Jägerstube* of the *Bürgerbräukeller* in Munich when Lenk was formally appointed leader, but made responsible to the SA commander, Johann Ulrich Klintsch. Moreover, because it was a party unit, the *Jugendbund* was not given an individual legal identity. Since this outcome was not what Lenk had hoped for, some tension existed between the *Jugendbund* and SA from the very beginning. The seventeen youths who attended the meeting were addressed by Lenk and Hitler, who brought an "unforgettable evening" to a close by exhorting the youths "to carry the banner to freedom and to victory. It is you who will have to endure this struggle; you must learn to fight, therefore, so that Germany will be freed of her tormentors."[14]

The first statutes of the *Jugendbund,* drawn up by Lenk and approved by Hitler, had been published in March 1922 and had defined the group's objectives. The *Jugendbund* aimed at gathering youth "on a purely *völkisch* basis," to fight for the *"völkisch* idea," to teach "love of homeland, love of *Volk,* joy in honourable, open struggle, and a healthy physical activity, high regard for everything of moral and civilised goodness," and finally, "contempt for the Jewish-Mammonist ideal." The group did not recognise "class, position or occupational differences because this . . . runs contrary to old concepts of togetherness, and to the blood community of all German national comrades" *(Volksgenossen).* "The *Jugendbund* . . . does not segregate apprentices from intermediate-grade schoolboys *(Mittelschüler)* or the latter from secondary schoolboys; it means clearly and unequivocally: Germans on one side, non-Germans on the other side." Members were to be Aryan Germans between the ages of fourteen and eighteen years; foreigners and Jews were specifically excluded. The *Führerprinzip* was copied from the party, and every member had to swear allegiance to the Führer, the eleven statutes of the *Jugendbund,* and the NSDAP political programme.[15]

The outstanding feature of the *Jugendbund's* statutes was the emphasis on *völkisch* ideas; indeed, the group was, like the NSDAP before 1923, a *völkisch* nationalist movement above all. At the same time, however, it was heavily influenced by the progressive development of the SA from a party political troop to a paramilitary organisation *(Wehrverband).* The clear organisational and ideological affinity between the *Jugendbund* and SA at this early date foreshadowed something of the nature of the Hitler Youth-SA relationship later.

As in the NSDAP, Munich was the focal point of the *Jugendbund* and its activities, but branches *(Ortsgruppen)* were quickly founded in other parts of the Reich. Hence its pattern of development indicates that the *Jugendbund* was not merely a Munich or even a Bavarian phenomenon (see Appendix I). Under Lenk's direction from the

Reichsführung in the Corneliusstrasse 12, the NSDAP headquarters at this time, the local branches were grouped into *Landesverbände*, a process that continued to the eve of the Hitler putsch (see Appendix II). Many branches had only a few members, but Lenk's success in arousing interest in his group over scattered areas of Germany despite the paucity of financial resources at his disposal deserves recognition.[16]

The *Jugendbund* was divided into three sections; *Jungmannschaften* for boys aged fourteen to sixteen years; the *Jungsturm Adolf Hitler* for those between sixteen and eighteen years; and a girls' section. The uniform consisted of a windjacket, white shirt, blue cap bearing a silver swastika on the top part with a black, white and red cockade on the lower part, boots, and an armband in black, white and red stripes bearing a black swastika against a white square background.[17]

Because of the difficulty in collecting a respectably sized membership as well as organisational problems, the *Jugendbund* did not make its first public appearance until the nationalist rally in Coburg on 14–15 October 1922, when Lenk led his contingent of youths past Hitler and other right-wing leaders.[18] At the SA flag dedication ceremony during the first full NSDAP party rally in Munich in January 1923 Hitler solemnly consecrated the first pennant of the *Jungsturm Adolf Hitler*. The pennant showed a golden anchor and swastika on a white foundation, the anchor signifying that German youth was rooted to the national socialist movement. At this meeting, Lenk reported that after ten months, the *Jugendbund* had 39 local branches and approximately 1,200 members, but this evidence of growth must be seen within the context of the setback sustained by the NSDAP at the end of 1922.[19]

The acute problems which had afflicted Germany since the termination of the war showed little sign of being alleviated between 1920 and 1922. The problem of controlling inflation was already critical, while the antirepublican campaign of the extreme right and left continued unabated. The government was under severe pressure, and the scope of the political crisis had been enlarged by the Reichstag elections of June 1920 in which the Weimar coalition parties irretrievably lost their majority. The hostility of the right had been underlined by the Kapp putsch and a series of political assassinations. In fact, it was in response to the widespread revulsion at the murder of Foreign Minister Walther Rathenau that the Law for the Protection of the Republic, promulgated shortly afterwards, was applied to prohibit many radical rightist groups. The NSDAP was consequently banned in Prussia in November 1922 and shortly in all German states except Bavaria.

The *Jugendbund* held its first national congress in the *Hackerbräukeller,* Munich, on 13–17 May 1923, the anniversary of its inaugural meeting. Representatives from the organisation in Germany joined with delegates from Austria and the Sudetenland in proclaiming their loyalty to national socialism, and in dedicating themselves to fulfilling their self-appointed "mission among German youth."[20] Shortly afterwards, the first newspaper of the group, *Der Nationale Jungsturm, Nachrichtenblatt der Nationalsozialistischen Jugendbundes,* was published; from 12 August, however, it appeared as a weekly youth supplement in the *Völkischer Beobachter* under the new title, *Nationalsozialistische Jugend.*[21] The last public appearance of the *Jugendbund* was on 2 September 1923 at the Sedan Day Rally in Nuremberg which was attended by a cluster of nationalist organisations, including the NSDAP. There was an attendance of 80,000, and Lenk led 900 youths in the march.[22]

The internal situation in Germany deteriorated during 1923. In addition to the ruinous inflation and governmental crisis, exacerbated by the SPD's refusal to form a coalition with the middle-class parties, French Premier Raymond Poincaré decided to occupy the Ruhr in January 1923 in retaliation for a default in Germany's reparations payments. As a result, it appeared more than once that the republic was on the verge of collapse. However, the appointment of Gustav Stresemann as chancellor in August inaugurated a brighter epoch. Stresemann wisely called off the campaign of passive resistance against the French in the Ruhr and resumed reparations payments to France and Belgium. The nationalists used Stresemann's policies as a pretext for more venomous attacks against the "November Criminals," and the Bavarian extremists prepared for the long-awaited "March on Berlin." The groundwork was provided by the government crisis between Bavaria and the Reich in the autumn of 1923, and the whole situation was further confused by communist uprisings in Saxony, Thuringia, and Hamburg.

By 1923, the NSDAP, now firmly under Hitler's autocratic will, had fashioned a sound organisational structure, and with a membership of 55,000, the party was the dominant group of the Bavarian right. Hitler hoped to use the Reich government's preoccupations to further his own political ends. He led the NSDAP into the *Deutsche Kampfbund,* an association of right-wing formations, in which he possessed political control. The ultimate consequence of the plotting and intrigue, which also involved high-ranking members of the Bavarian police and state government, was the abortive national socialist insurrection in Munich on 8–9 November 1923.

The *Jugendbund* did not participate in this affair, although individual members, including Lenk and his brothers, Karl and Walter, were active as messengers and demonstrators. On the march to the *Feldherrnhalle, Jugendbund* member Kurt Neubauer was one of the sixteen national socialists shot dead. Lenk had actually prepared a proclamation in the *Völkischer Beobachter* calling for a mobilisation of his group, but it appeared too late in the newspaper on 9 November.[23]

The failure of the uprising humiliated the NSDAP leadership. Hitler was arrested two days later at Ernst Hanfstaengl's home in Uffing; Hess and Göring fled to Austria and most other rebel leaders were rounded up and arrested. General State Commissioner for Bavaria, Gustav von Kahr, whom Hitler had previously tried to win over to his plans, prohibited the NSDAP, SA, and *Jugendbund* on 9 November; other states quickly followed the example so that soon the movement was no longer legal in any part of the Reich.[24] This date was enshrined in the national socialist "calendar of honour," and in later years of triumph, even after the outbreak of World War II, Hitler would return to pay homage to the martyrs of the movement. But in 1923, November 9 marked the end of the first phase of the NSDAP and its youth organisation.

Adolf Lenk was a purposeful leader, but he never succeeded in stamping his personality on the *Jugendbund*. The shortage of time at his disposal is not adequate reason. Because of his narrow and characteristically Bavarian outlook and limited education, Lenk failed to understand the complexities of building up his group on a sound national basis; he entertained grandiose ideas about its future development that were totally divorced from reality. On the other hand, it must be acknowledged that Lenk was not given meaningful assistance from the NSDAP, an anomaly which was later an important feature of the relationship between the Hitler Youth and the party. Lenk's work was, therefore, of only ephemeral value.

In the same way as the NSDAP now broke up into various *völkisch* parties, the national socialist youth movement splintered into a host of *völkisch* nationalist groups.[25] Lenk sought to make a fresh beginning immediately; on 15 November, he founded the *Vaterländischer Jugendverband Grossdeutschlands* (Patriotic Youth Association of Greater Germany), but the police authorities, realising that it was a mere cover for the illegal continuation of the *Jugendbund,* banned it in December 1923, and had Lenk committed to prison the same month.[26] Upon his quick release, he became engaged in the organisation of the *Grossdeutsche Jugendbewegung* (Greater German Youth Movement) which he established in Munich in April 1924, but he was again arrested for leading an illegal association on 25 November 1924. Lenk was freed from Landsberg Prison on 20 December 1924, the same day as his Führer, who had served only nine months of a five-year sentence for high treason imposed by a Munich court on 1 April of that year. Undeterred by the recent setbacks, Lenk endeavoured to organise the *Deutsche Wehrjugend* independently of the

NSDAP in March 1925, but the venture proved unsuccessful. The same year, broken in spirit, ill, and having been convicted and fined in June 1924 for embezzling stamps from the *Eher-Verlag,* the national socialist publishing concern, Lenk retired from the youth movement altogether.[27]

Lenk might well have passed into oblivion had not the Hitler Youth sought after 1933 to clarify the origins of the national socialist youth movement. In so doing, however, the Hitler Youth began a controversy that lasted until at least 1937. At first, *Reichsjugendführer* Baldur von Schirach acknowledged the part played by Lenk and his *Jugendbund.* In a letter to Lenk on the occasion of a *Jugendbund* reunion in June 1934, von Schirach wrote: "The Hitler Youth will never forget you old fighters, since it was you who laid the foundation stone for the future of National Socialism."[28] He went on to express the debt owed by the Hitler Youth "to you early fighters of the national socialist youth movement."

The attitude of the Hitler Youth later changed quite dramatically, however, as correspondence between Lenk and the staff leader of the *Reichsjugendführung, Obergebietsführer* Hartmann Lauterbacher, indicates. Lauterbacher explained in a letter dated 3 November 1936 that: "From a historical viewpoint, the Hitler Youth has not developed from your association. The *Reichsjugendführer* has therefore refrained from recognising your association."[29]

In a further note to Hitler Youth leaders, Lauterbacher wrote:

> A certain Adolf Lenk of Munich has sent invitations for a Comrades' Social *(Kamaradschaftsabend)* of the so-called *"Jungsturm Adolf Hitler"* on 9 November 1936 to . . . leaders of the Hitler Youth. The leadership corps of the Hitler Youth is not to participate in this meeting. I stress that the Hitler Youth does not on principle recognise this *Jungsturm* as a forerunner. 1926 is the year when the Hitler Youth was founded.[30]

The matter did not end there. Lenk complained to the Führer's deputy, Rudolf Hess, on 31 March 1937 and sought his assistance. Hess in turn agreed to make enquiries on Lenk's behalf. In a reply to Hess on 8 June 1937 von Schirach confirmed that the Hitler Youth would not extend recognition to the *Jugendbund* because Hitler had given his name only to the national socialist youth movement in 1926, and also because he feared that if the *Jugendbund* were recognised, other youth groups would inevitably follow suit and claim to be precursors of the Hitler Youth.[31] The attitude now adopted by von Schirach was in complete contradiction to that expressed in his letter to Lenk in June 1934.

At this juncture, the Youth Movement Department of the party archives *(Hauptarchiv der NSDAP)* intervened, and on 27 October

1937 it issued a report supporting Lenk's case "since the *Jungsturm* was founded on the order of the Führer and since it was the only youth organisation of the NSDAP"; von Schirach's stated objections to Lenk's group were repudiated. The report opined that the real reason for the attitude of the *Reichsjugendführer* was his disapproval of Lenk's personal character, mentioning his conviction for petty larceny in 1924. The report also added that because Lenk had been inactive during the *Kampfzeit*, he was now clearly an opportunist hoping to benefit by the victory of national socialism.[32]

It was obvious therefore that Lenk was persona non grata as far as the Hitler Youth was concerned. But it would be unsatisfactory to explain von Schirach's antagonism to the *Jugendbund* and Lenk on purely personal grounds; in a wider sense, his attitude reflected the Hitler Youth's own pretensions which were boosted in 1936 when it was formally accorded the status of a state youth organisation *(Staatsjugend)* (see Epilogue). Forerunners who might impinge on this exalted position were therefore unwelcome. There is no indication of von Schirach's reaction to the report, but documentary evidence proved beyond a shadow of doubt that the *Jugendbund* was indeed a predecessor of the Hitler Youth.

The National Socialist Youth Development in Saxony, 1922–26

As mentioned previously, the *Jugendbund der NSDAP* was not confined to Bavaria and soon spread to north Germany. Among the branches established in 1922 was one in Plauen (Saxony) where a group of eight youths under the leadership of a law student, Kurt Gruber, came together.[33] Gruber, who later became the first leader of the Hitler Youth, was born in Plauen on 21 October 1904, joined the NSDAP in May 1923, and joined again on 10 June 1925 (membership number 7270). He was in a better position to reinvigorate national socialist youth activities in Saxony when he was appointed by Lenk to succeed Alexander Bettschneider in October 1922 as leader of the Saxony unit of the *Jugendbund*. A brief glimpse of Hitler for the first time at the German Sports Festival in Munich on 15 July 1923 apparently convinced Gruber of the worthiness of the cause.[34]

After the 1923 *Verbot* (prohibition), the Plauen group continued under the innocuous cover name of *Wandersportverein Vogtland,* which in 1924 had between forty and fifty members. The same year, Gruber's group was heartened when the *Deutsche Jugendbund* of Markneukirchen (Saxony) joined it. Later in 1924, Gruber affiliated his group with Lenk's *Grossdeutsche Jugendbewegung*. Lenk's southern part of the organisation failed within a few months but Gruber enjoyed considerable success in Saxony. He held a youth meeting on 12–13 July 1924 in Jocketa (Plauen), and shortly published and edited the group's first newspaper, *Die Grossdeutsche Jugend*. By the end of the year, the Plauen branch had 150 members and there were around 600 altogether in the Vogtland. Branches had also been set up in other parts of Saxony, for example in Leipzig (50 members), Dresden (100 members), Zwickau and Chemnitz. In December 1924, there was a total of 56 branches in Saxony, representing 2,500 members, and organised in *Gaue* (provinces) and *Bezirke* (districts) within the *Landesverband* (state unit). The aims of the *Grossdeutsche Jugendbewegung* were similar to those of the earlier *Jugendbund der* NSDAP; it adopted the *Führerprinzip*, swore allegiance to Hitler, and acknowledged the *"völkisch* idea." The group's uniform was also virtually the same.[35]

In the series of transient amalgamations that characterised the extreme right-wing movement in Germany between 1923 and 1925, the *Grossdeutsche Jugendbewegung* in Saxony, now more or less independent of Lenk's section in Bavaria, joined forces with youths attached to General Erich Friedrich Wilhelm Ludendorff's radical *völkisch Tannenbergbund* at the end of 1924 to form the *Frontjugend*.[36] This became the youth association of Captain Ernst Röhm's broad, national socialist-oriented, paramilitary *Frontbann* organisation.

The situation was bound to change, however, following Hitler's release from prison. The Führer found his movement in disarray and its leadership dispersed. Moreover, the republic had achieved a new economic and political stability: inflation was under control, the Ruhr and the first zone of the demilitarised Rhineland evacuated, the burdens of reparations eased by the Dawes Plan, and Stresemann's policy of reconciliation with the Allies had given Germany a new self-esteem, which was consolidated by the Locarno Pact and admission to the League of Nations. This favourable trend for the republic had been confirmed at the Reichstag elections held two weeks before Hitler was freed. The SPD, champions of the republic, had attracted a massive 8 million votes and obtained 131 seats, while the National Socialists, in league with some *völkisch* groups in the National Socialist German Freedom Movement, had won only 14 seats. Undaunted, and delighted in a way that absence had merely emphasised his importance to the movement, Hitler refounded the NSDAP at an emotional rally in Munich on 27 February 1925.

Gruber's *Frontjugend,* anticipating Hitler's post-1925 policy of isolating the NSDAP from the *völkisch* movement, immediately severed connections with the *Tannenbergbund* to follow the Führer, and re-adopted the name *Grossdeutsche Jugendbewegung* (GDJB).[37] Although pronational socialist, Gruber's group was still organisationally independent of the NSDAP. Indeed, Gruber's early independence obviously influenced his later efforts to keep the Hitler Youth free from party control as much as possible. During the course of 1925, the GDJB spread outside Saxony to Mecklenburg, Franconia, the Rhineland, and Rheinpfalz. In view of this expansion, Gruber called a meeting of Saxon leaders in Plauen in October in order to give more unity to the leadership and to clarify the aims of the organisation.[38] It was a procedure to be adopted on many other occasions by Gruber in the Hitler Youth.

Despite the success of the GDJB in Saxony, it had made no impression in Bavaria, and for this reason was distrusted in some high party quarters. Hitler shared this suspicion, and this is the main factor in explaining why official recognition was not extended to Gruber's organisation by the NSDAP. Had Gruber been working as successfully in Bavaria as in Saxony, the NSDAP would almost certainly have acknowledged the GDJB as the party's own youth group sometime in 1925. But Hitler preferred, now as later, to deal with people whom he knew and who were based in Munich. With the delicate task of recontruction to accomplish, the Führer was determined to give the NSDAP as much cohesion as possible. In any case, the wayward northern wing of the movement did not encourage him to delegate authority outside of his own immediate surroundings. It was not altogether surprising, therefore, that Hitler issued a laconic decree on 6 May entrusting Edmund Heines, caretaker leader of the *Schilljugend* in Germany, and an NSDAP and SA leader based in Munich, with all affairs relating to the national socialist youth movement.[39]

This was the beginning of Hitler's attempt to reactivate the party's youth movement on a unified basis. It was not an impetuous or ill-considered manoeuvre, for during his incarceration Hitler had spent at least part of his time meditating on the future role of German youth, and the fruits of his cogitations were included in *Mein Kampf*. He wrote that "if we do not lift our youth out of the morass of its present surroundings, it will be submerged in it," and he lamented "the slow prostitution of our future, for the latter lies in the coming generation."[40] Hitler deprecated the alleged moral degradation of the Weimar Republic and its detrimental effects on the mental and physical development of German youth. He advocated the application of proper remedial action before it was too late. Yet Hitler was convinced that the regeneration of Germany could only be achieved by the efforts of youth:

> Above all, we turn to the powerful host of our German youth.
> They grow up in an era of great change and . . . the inertia and
> indifference of their fathers . . . will force them to fight. German

youth will one day be either the builder of a new, national state or it will, as the last witness, experience the complete collapse, the end of the bourgeois world.[41]

Meantime, it was Hitler's intention to incorporate all existing national socialist groups, including Gruber's GDJB, in the *Schilljugend*, whose founder and leader was the former well-known *Freikorps* commander and homosexual friend of Röhm, *Oberleutnant* Gerhard Rossbach.[42] Gruber predictably rejected this proposal in a letter to Hitler on 25 May 1925, declaring that his group was superior to the *Schilljugend* and a worthier contender for official recognition from the NSDAP. Writing to Rossbach on 16 July, Gruber made it clear that at the very most he was interested in only a loose confederation with the *Schilljugend* in which most of his independence would be respected. Rossbach contemptuously rejected Gruber's conditions on 26 July.[43]

Because of the unwillingness of both sides to compromise, a great deal of time was spent in discussing the terms under which the incorporation of other youth groups in the *Schilljugend* should take place. The deadlock was broken only when Rossbach, allowed to return from exile in Austria by a political amnesty, had an unsuccessful interview with Hitler in February 1926 in Munich. Rossbach refused to allow his group to be formally integrated in a political party and Hitler, adhering to his principle of moulding a tightly welded movement over which he had unquestioned authority, lost interest in the project.[44]

It was an interview that changed the course and decided the future development of the national socialist youth movement. The way was now clear for the GDJB to emerge as the officially recognised youth group of the NSDAP. Even in the interlude of indecision from May 1925 to February 1926, the *Schilljugend* had not been accorded this status by Hitler. The Führer was now more favourably disposed towards Gruber, who had manifested his eagerness to work for national socialism. During the first half of 1926, it was apparent that the GDJB was already cooperating closely with the NSDAP and that it was in fact the youth auxiliary of the party in all but name.[45] There was also a more pressing organisational reason: having eliminated the threat from the north German radicals in early 1926, Hitler wanted to achieve unity and symmetry in the NSDAP as quickly as possible (see chap. 4). The youth question was one of the loose ends and it was Hitler's desire to settle the matter that made it possible for a final deliberation on the future form of the national socialist youth movement to be made at the forthcoming NSDAP *Reichsparteitag* in Weimar.

Notes: Chapter 1

1. There was a socialist youth movement founded in 1904 that was ideologically sympathetic to but organisationally independent of the Social Democratic party. The war split the movement and a fresh start had to be made in 1918. Other parties also had youth groups, but connections between them were so weakened during the war that new foundations had to be laid in 1918.

2. W. Z. Laqueur, *Young Germany: A History of the German Youth* Movement (London, 1962), p. 15. *Wandervogel* literally means "wandering bird." Although numerically powerful, the existent youth organisations of the period, such as the confessional, sports, trades, and various political and nationalist groups, could not validly claim detachment from, or independence, of adult control. Their total strength in 1914 was about 2 million (H. Siemering, *Die Deutschen Jugendpflegeverbände* [Berlin, 1918]).

3. Laqueur, *Young Germany*, p. 7.

4. The first serious split, led by Siegfried Copalle, occurred in 1904, causing Fischer to establish a new organisation called the *Altwandervogel* the same year. Fischer soon lost control to Wilhelm Jansen, but he himself resigned shortly afterwards to set up his own association, the *Jungwandervogel*. In 1905, the *Bund Deutscher Wanderer* was founded in Hamburg by Knud Ahlborn and Ferdinand Goebel, and by the end of that year there were already no fewer than seventy-eight distinguishable sects within the youth movement, each one defiantly egotistical and particularistic; confusingly, many groups retained the name *Wandervogel* (H. Becker, *German Youth. Bond or Free* [London, 1946], p. 92).

5. G. L. Mosse, *The Crisis of German Ideology* (New York, 1964), p. 10. The most important attempt to create solidarity and unity among the different groupings was made at a special convention of the youth movement on the Hohe Meissner, a mountain near Kassel, on 11 October 1913. The projected grand alliance was not achieved by the 3,000 delegates. Though each group retained its own name and personality, they nearly all agreed to merge into a loose confederation entitled the *Freideutsche Jugend*. The speakers at the meeting vigorously attacked contemporary society, and under the influence of Gustav Wyneken, they issued the Meissner Confession, which asserted the determination of the youth movement to go its own way (Becker, *German Youth*, pp. 99–100).

6. Mosse, *Crisis of German Ideology*, p. 184.

7. See H. Blüher, *Wandervogel, Geschichte einer Jugendbewegung* (Berlin, 1912).

8. K. O. Paetel, "Die Deutsche Jugendbewegung als politisches Phänomen," *Politische Studien* 86 (July 1957): 2.

9. The only reference to youth in the programme was made in Point 21, but this was no more than a rather vague pronouncement on the obligations of the state to the youth of the nation:

    > The state must see to raising the standard of health in the nation by . . . increasing physical efficiency through obligatory gymnastics and sports laid down by law, and by extensive support of clubs engaged in the physical development of the young.

    See G. Feder, *Das Programm der NSDAP und seine weltanschaulichen Grundgedanken* (Munich, 1932).

10. A. G. Whiteside, "The Nature and Origins of National Socialism," *Journal of Central European Affairs* 17 (1957): 48–73.

11. BA:Akte NS 26/333; BA:Akte NS 26/336.

12. BA:Akte NS 26/333; BA:Akte NS 26/362.

13. The SA *(Sturmabteilung)* was informally created in the summer of 1920 and officially founded on 3 August 1921 as a gymnastics and sports division within the party. From 5 October 1921, it became known as the SA. Johann Ulrich Klintsch, a former comrade of *Freikorps* leader Captain Ehrhardt, was appointed the first commander of the SA. In 1923, he was replaced by Hermann Goering.

14. BA:Akte NS 26/336; BA:Akte NS 26/362; BA:Akte NS 26/333.

15. BA:Akte NS 26/333; BA:Akte NS 26/331.

16. Until it was dissolved with the NSDAP and SA in November 1923, the *Jugendbund* was financially dependent on the party. Indeed, the small monthly allowance it received was the most important piece of evidence used by the Bavarian authorities to include it in the *Verbot* since this proved that the *Jugendbund* was part of the NSDAP (Bay. HSA:ASA:Akte NS/1805).

17. BA:Akte NS 26/336.

18. BA:Akte NS 26/333. On the tenth anniversary of this rally in 1932, Hitler issued a special badge of honour for the youths who had taken part (BA:Akte NS 26/336).

19. BA:Akte NS 26/336; BA:Akte NS 26/333. On 15 July 1923, Munich police broke up an NSDAP rally and confiscated the *Jugendbund* flag; it was kept by the police until 15 March 1933 when it was returned to the Hitler Youth (Reichsjugendführung der NSDAP, *HJ im Dienst* [Berlin, 1940], p. 7).

20. BA:Akte NS 26/333. In 1923, a National Socialist German Workers' Youth (NSDAJ) was set up in Vienna by Walter Gattermayer, but it counted as a *Landesverband* of Lenk's group. A pro-Nazi group in the Sudetenland under the command of Eugen Weese was also attached to the *Jugendbund* as a *Landesverband*.

21. BA:Akte NS 26/333.

22. BA:Akte NS 26/336. The rally was held to celebrate the Prussian victory over Emperor Napoleon III at Sedan in September 1870.

23. BA:Akte NS 26/336; BA:Akte NS 26/333.

24. Bay. HSA:ASA:Akte NS/1538. For his alleged treachery, von Kahr was brutally murdered during the Röhm Purge in June 1934. On the same date [1923], the right-wing nationalist organisations, *Bund Oberland* and *Reichskriegsflagge*, were also banned.

25. The parties included the *Deutschvölkische Freiheitspartei*; Gregor Strasser's *Nationalsozialistische Freiheitspartei*; and the *Grossdeutsche Volksgemeinschaft* of Alfred Rosenberg, Julius Streicher, and Anton Drexler. The groups included the *Kyffhäuserbund, Wandersportverein Vogtland, Schlageter-Jugend, Bund Deutschvölkischer Jugend*, and others.

26. Bay. HSA:ASA:Akte NS/1805; BA:Akte NS 26/333; BA:Akte NS 26/336.

27. FSGNS:NSDAP/239; BA:Akte NS 26/336; BA:Akte NS 26/332.

28. BA:Akte NS 26/332.

29. Ibid.

30. Ibid.

31. Ibid.

32. Ibid.

33. BA:Sammlung Schumacher:Gruppe VIII. No. 239. The eight youths consisted of two schoolboys, a student, a shopkeeper's apprentice, a labourer, a locksmith, a cutter, and one who was unemployed.

34. BDC:K. Gruber file; BA:Akte NS 26/333; BA:Sammlung Schumacher: Gruppe VIII. No. 239.

35. BA:Sammlung Schumacher:Gruppe VIII. No. 239; FSGNS:NSDAP/239; SAB:4.14b-II-E-3-a-13 Vol. 1/1925; SAB:4/65 781/146. Vol. I; BA:Akte NS 26/332.

36. BA:Akte NS 26/332. Hitler specifically forbade dual membership in the NSDAP and the Tannenberg Association at the end of 1925 (D. Orlow, *The History of the Nazi Party 1919–1933* [Pittsburgh, 1969], p. 68).

37. K. O. Paetel, *Handbuch der deutschen Jugendbewegung* (Flarchheim, 1930), pp. 17–18.

38. SAB:II 137/CVIII HJ; BA:Sammlung Schumacher:Gruppe VIII. No. 239.

39. VB:13 May 1925.

40. A. Hitler, *Mein Kampf* (Reynal and Hitchcock, New York, 1939), p. 348.

41. Ibid., p. 611.

42. The *Schilljugend* was founded in Salzburg in February 1924.

43. BA:Akte NS 26/335.

44. G. Rossbach, *Meine Weg durch die Zeit* (Weilberg, 1950), pp. 87–88.

45. BA:Akte NS 26/332; BA:Akte NS 26/335.

Chapter 2

The Hitler Youth, 1926–29

In 1925 Hitler was obliged to start afresh. During his imprisonment he reflected on the consequences of the ill-fated putsch, and the lessons he observed were of decisive importance for the future history of national socialism. He renounced the idea of staging an armed coup against the republic and resolved instead to win power by using legal tactics within the prescribed constitutional framework of the state. This never amounted to much more than a pseudo-legality: though adhering to the strict definition of the law, Hitler and his national socialists violated its spirit with impunity time and time again. But Hitler maintained his "legal" course throughout the *Kampfzeit*, reaffirmed it at the famous *Reichswehr* trial in 1930, and even came to power in 1933 by a pseudo-legal procedure, not by a violent seizure of power. The adoption of these new tactics meant that the movement had to enter the field of parliamentary politics and electoral battles in a more determined fashion than in 1924. Thus after 1925 the NSDAP was transformed from a revolutionary elitist party to an "evolutionary" mass movement of national proportions with totalitarian aims.

Hitler was politically sagacious enough to realise that an aspirant totalitarian party in the twentieth century had to possess as a precondition of success a fundamentally powerful organisational basis under dictatorial control with mass propaganda capability. The quiet years of the republic were therefore employed by Hitler to construct and develop these two aspects of the movement. Without the preparatory work in the two interdependent disciplines of organisation and propaganda in the mid-1920s, the NSDAP would never have been able to achieve its meteoric rise between 1930 and 1933.

But it was not only the NSDAP that was to play a role. As part of his plans to make national socialism a mass movement, and following an established pattern of Weimar politics in which specialised affiliates within a party directed appeals to specific groups of the community, Hitler decided to branch out into as many sectors of German society as possible. It was as a result of this policy that the Hitler Youth was set up to attract German youth to the swastika. The foundation of the Hitler Youth was not an isolated event, but rather a chapter of a series. Also in this pattern were the establishment of the SS in 1925, the reorganisation of the SA in 1926, and the creation within the next few years of the *Nationalsozialistische Deutscher Studentenbund* (NSDStB; National Socialist German Students' Association), the *Deutscher Frauenorden Rotes Hakenkreuz* (German Womens' Order Red Swastika), the *NS-Lehrerbund* (NS Teachers' Association), the *Bund NS Deutscher Juristen* (Association of NS German Lawyers), the *NS-Schülerbund* (NS Schoolboys' Association), and others. These affiliated organisations arose in consequence of Hitler's change of political tactics and were designed to embrace as many followers as possible so that ultimately the *Führer* and national socialism could legally triumph in Germany.

The Foundation of the Hitler Youth

The dispute in national socialist circles regarding the future organisation of the party's youth group was finally ended at the NSDAP *Reichsparteitag* in Weimar on 3 and 4 July 1926, which was held in an effort to rejuvenate and publicise the national socialist movement as it struggled to find a new foundation. Weimar was chosen as the venue because Thuringia was one of the few states in which Hitler was still allowed to speak in public. In addition, since it was the city where the National Assembly had accepted a new democratic constitution for Germany in 1919, the 7,000 NSDAP members present could spectacularly reaffirm their repudiation of the republic and its system of values.[1] The youth question was one of the most important on the agenda. The intention was to gather together all leaders of the various pronational socialist youth groups in the Reich, so that with guidance from the party they could devise a formula to give united leadership within one organisation. The GDJB leader, Kurt Gruber, was officially invited to attend.[2]

On Sunday, 4 July, a special convention of youth leaders and party members was held in the *Bühnenzimmer* of the Armbrust Inn on the theme, "Educational Questions and Youth Organisations." Among the speakers were Julius Streicher, NSDAP leader in Nuremberg, and Bernhard Rust, NSDAP *Gauleiter* of Hannover and later minister of education in the Third Reich. The outcome was an agreement to establish as the official youth organisation of the NSDAP the *Hitler-Jugend. Bund deutscher Arbeiterjugend* (Hitler Youth. Association of German Workers' Youth), a name suggested by Streicher.[3] Kurt Gruber was appointed its *Reichsführer* and advisor for youth affairs on the NSDAP *Reichsleitung*. Hitler's official recognition of these decisions was conveyed to Gruber in a letter from Rudolf Hess on 27 July 1926.[4]

Though the initiative for a solution of the youth problem had come from Hitler, the Weimar meeting was a triumph for Gruber's determination that his group alone should be recognised above all other contenders. In essence, the decisions merely involved changing the name *Grossdeutsche Jugendbewegung* to *Hitler-Jugend. Bund deutscher Arbeiterjugend,* for the former was the principal component of the new organisation.[5] Various national socialist groups that had arisen independently of the NSDAP between 1925 and 1926, as in the Rhineland, Rheinpfalz, and eastern Germany, now merged into the *Hitler-Jugend* (HJ). It was rather significant that the fulcrum of the national socialist youth movement should be in Saxony, for the NSDAP remained for some years a predominantly Bavarian and north German phenomenon, but the HJ was at least until the early 1930s a mainly Saxon affair, with headquarters in Plauen. The later development of the HJ clearly demonstrated the importance of the distance of its headquarters from the centre of the national socialist movement.

The Development of the Hitler Youth

Gruber's immediate task was to construct the central organisational framework of the HJ, and in this he could at least attempt to emulate Hitler's corresponding endeavours in the NSDAP. In 1925, Hitler's aim of forging a strongly disciplined party was based on the erection of an effective central leadership in Munich. Following his victorious confrontation with the northern faction of the party in 1926, by 1927 he had asserted his full control of an already powerful authoritarian apparatus. Hitler's power was very far-reaching and the party was clearly his political instrument to a much larger extent than the Italian Fascist party was Mussolini's during the early years. Hitler was the focal point, the ultimate and omniscient arbiter, the unifier of the conglomerate ideological and sociological elements which constituted the movement. He maintained his authority by manipulating a delicate system of checks and balances; applying the principle of divide and rule, the charismatic Führer emerged as the sole symbol of loyalty and the basic source of stability in national socialism.

The NSDAP organisation was fashioned in such a way that it could at a later date replace the institutional foundation of the state. The party developed, therefore, as Hitler had decreed it should in *Mein Kampf,* as a microscopic state apparatus. In 1926, the NSDAP *Reichsleitung* was set up, incorporating offices for every field of party activity, while in the provinces, the party was organised in *Gaue* and *Ortsgruppen.* Military discipline and hierarchical gradation gave cohesion to the whole structure. Bearing Hitler's example in mind, Gruber established in Plauen the HJ *Reichsführung,* which was organised as follows:[6]

HJ Reichsführung

DIVISION *(ABTEILUNG)*		LEADER *(ABTEILUNGSLEITER)*
(1)	Secretarial Affairs and Treasury	Otto Schindler
(2)	Youth Organisation and Education	Erich Kunz[1]
(3)	Youth Welfare	Adolf Einert
(4)	Racial Questions	Dieter Johs, Herbert Schönfeld, Max Undeutsch
(5)	Film Service	Hans Kluge
(6)	Youth Trade Unions and Social Politics	Willy Künnemann
(7)	Propaganda	Dieter Johs
(8)	Art and Culture	Herbert Schönfeld
(9)	Young Boys' Section *(Jungmannschaften)*	Gerhard Stöckel
(10)	Girls' Section	Helene Kunold, Anna Bauer
(11)	Sports	Hans Gruber[2]
(12)	Press	Max Pilz
(13)	Travel and Excursions	Heinrich Bennecke
(14)	Military sports *(Wehrsport)*	Unknown

1. Kunz was appointed deputy *Reichsführer* in August 1926 (SAB: 4/65 781/146).
2. Younger brother of Kurt Gruber.

It is important to appreciate that both the structure of the *Reichsführung* and the personnel involved changed frequently throughout the pre-1933 period. Significantly, all *Reichsführung* members in 1926 were from Plauen, with the exception of Künnemann of Zwickau. The creation of a Film Service Division at this early stage is surprising because the HJ did not make its first film until 1932, and even the NSDAP did not have a film unit until late 1928.[7]

The HJ was organised into *Gaue, Bezirke* and *Ortsgruppen*, the latter being further divided into *Wanderabteilungen* for the sixteen-eighteen year olds, *Jungmannschaften* for the fourteen-sixteen year olds, and *Knabenmannschaften* for the ten-fourteen year olds. Additionally, each *Wanderabteilung* was sectioned into *Gruppen, Scharen*, and *Abteilungen*. The personnel in charge of these various divisions were: *Gauführer*, commanding a *Gau* and responsible only to the *Reichsführer; Bezirksführer*, commanding a *Bezirk* and, according to the leadership principle, answerable to his immediate superior, the *Gauführer;* and *Ortsgruppenführer*, under the authority of the *Bezirksführer*, directing all HJ units within his branch or local area. The HJ's uniform corresponded to that of the SA, except for the armband; this sartorial similarity was indicative of a more comprehensive organisational connection between the HJ and SA.[8]

Once the organisational basis had been arranged, the first indication of what kind of relationship the HJ would have with the movement came on 1 November 1926 when the HJ was made responsible to the SA Supreme Command by decree of the NSDAP *Reichsleitung,* and Gruber, as *Reichsführer,* was made personally answerable to the SA Supreme Commander, Captain Franz Felix von Pfeffer (von Salomon). In fact, on his appointment as SA leader, von Pfeffer, hitherto NSDAP *Gauleiter* and SA leader of *Gau* Ruhr, insisted that Hitler place the HJ under his jurisdiction.[9] The decision seemed to signify that the HJ was to be merely the youth division of the SA.

As part of his reorganisation programme after 1925, Hitler decided that the SA should become, as it had been in 1920-21, a party political instrument, dedicated to disseminating the national socialist *Weltanschauung* and to acting as the strong-arm force of the movement. He rejected Röhm's strategy that the SA should revert to the paramilitary status which it had held in 1922-23. Hitler believed that the era of paramilitary formations was over, and that in any case, a military group would be incompatible with his new tactics of legality. When Röhm refused to incorporate his *Frontbann* in the NSDAP under Hitler's leadership, preferring it to be an independent unit within the movement under his control, he resigned from the party in 1925.

Hitler was determined that the NSDAP alone should become the spearhead of the German radical right, and he required a closely knit organisation for this purpose. Not only was the SA to be politicised and integrated into the movement under Hitler's undisputed authority, but all alliances, however tenuous, with *völkisch* and paramilitary groups were to be repudiated. As it happened, these groups underwent a crisis in the mid-1920s, during which they also discarded putsch plans in favour of more concentrated political activity, and the NSDAP and SA, especially in northern Germany, attracted many former *völkisch* and paramilitary group members. This is a crucial factor in explaining the substantial increase in party membership during a phase of political quiescence in which the NSDAP did not win any new voters.

Moreover, Hitler's resolution never again to oppose the *Reichswehr* was a relevant factor in his new policy for the SA. After 1925, he sought to win the army over to his plans and convince it that its best interests lay in supporting the NSDAP, for Hitler was aware that he could come to power only with the army's toleration. An important problem in the reorientation of the SA on a legal, political course, which was not finally settled until June 1934, was how to retain the extremist elements who gave the party its élan. This problem was reflected in the permanent state of latent tension between the NSDAP and SA, a tension which turned to rebellion when it seemed that the path of legality was not likely to succeed. Hitler's solution lay in the development of a political style whose dominant feature was feverish propaganda activity combined with physical terror towards political adversaries. Although the SA became a political force, it nonetheless took on the appearance of a paramilitary organisation before 1933 because its main activity was concerned with the battle for the streets. On the other hand, the SA's unconditional subordination to the party in political affairs provoked conflict, basically over the question of what constituted "political" affairs and what did not. According to the regulations establishing the SA, the supreme SA leader was responsible to the NSDAP leadership in political matters but had autonomous powers regarding military aspects. But this was an imprecise definition and as the SA developed an esprit de corps of its own which separated it psychologically from the NSDAP, the controversy continued. From 1926 on, NSDAP and SA leaders at a local level often disagreed over the competence of the political leadership in SA affairs and with its expansion, the SA became more independent minded.

Because of the similarities in uniform and organisation between the two groups, the HJ has been dismissed by some writers as a junior branch of the SA *(Jung-SA)*.[10] While this is a gross exaggeration, there can be no denying that at this early stage the HJ did inherit much of its style from the senior organisation but it did not resemble a paramilitary association on the whole. The HJ's main activity in the 1920s lay in propaganda and publicity work for the movement, and it did not acquire a truly combative nature until the early 1930s. Nevertheless, the link was to have important repercussions for the political orientation of the HJ. Meantime, the NSDAP, making no effort to hide the fact that the HJ was a party youth affiliate, sought to clarify its organisational relationship with Gruber's group.

At the first national congress of the HJ in Weimar on 5 December 1926, which was attended by fifty-five youth leaders and chaired by von Pfeffer, directives governing relations between the HJ and NSDAP were promulgated. These defined very closely the position of the HJ and the degree of control that the party should exert.[11] All members of the HJ who had reached the age of eighteen years were obliged to become NSDAP members, while dismissal from the party was to automatically result in expulsion from the HJ, and vice versa. The appointment of HJ leaders from *Ortsgruppenführer* upwards was to be ratified by a written declaration of consent from the local NSDAP leader. Thus the NSDAP intended to control the HJ from its grass roots. The HJ was required to have the permission of the local NSDAP leadership before it could appear in public, especially appearances involving propaganda for the movement. If the party wished to boost the attendance at its local meetings, it had authority to instruct the neighbouring HJ unit to turn up in full complement. In the event of disputes arising between the NSDAP and the HJ, both parties could appeal to their next highest offices for assistance, though in practice, of course, the NSDAP could usually bring its greater influence to bear on a situation like this. An HJ leader would never find himself taking on responsibilities of NSDAP leadership, for he was strictly forbidden to act simultaneously as a leader in either the SA or NSDAP. At the proposed quarterly meetings of the HJ *Gau* leaders (which in fact did not take place according to a regular schedule), the equivalent-ranking NSDAP leaders were to be at least invited, so that they might observe, but not dictate, the proceedings. In general terms, the NSDAP was to provide the HJ with advice and assistance, and above all, to give its protection against "Red Terror."[12]

The definitive tone of these directives, which formed the theoretical basis for HJ-NSDAP relations until 1929, appears to leave no doubt that the NSDAP meant to control the HJ as tightly as possible. They were similar in principle and scope to those given out at approximately the same time to regulate the relationship between the party and the SA. Hitler was obviously determined to have every important party auxiliary heavily subjected to and dependent on the NSDAP. The decrees for the HJ showed Hitler's determination to firmly tie the HJ to the NSDAP from the beginning, thus obviating the possibility of future deviationism, as had happened in the pre-1923 SA. The HJ was to be a political agent of the party. Some writers have blandly accepted the practical authenticity of this theoretical relationship and have concluded that the HJ, being compelled to follow the whims of the party, had little freedom to shape its own development.[13] There is little doubt that after 1933 when the NSDAP in effect became the state that the HJ did form a mere unit of a vast apparatus over which the NSDAP had ultimate control.[14] But was this necessarily the case prior to 1933? Was the HJ as rigidly directed from above as has been suggested? In fact, there seems to have been considerable discrepancy between what was meant to happen in theory and what actually did happen in practice, not only in the SA, but also in the HJ.

Despite the apparent assertiveness of the 1926 directives, there was much confusion and uncertainty in the NSDAP and SA circles regarding the role of the HJ. Many doubted the value of having a youth organisation at all because they believed that if the tough political fight was to be won, it would surely be through the efforts of adults and not under-eighteen year olds. There was even considerable opposition on the part of many SA and NSDAP leaders. Local party branches actually prohibited the establishment of an HJ formation in their area, or forbade NSDAP members from associating with the HJ in any way. Others regarded the HJ as a group competing with the SA and NSDAP for recruits, thus diluting the strength of the movement, and believed that the HJ leadership was constructing a worthless administrative body which made the whole movement overorganised.[15] In 1929, Gregor Strasser complained that the NSDAP was suffering from excessive organisation, and in 1930 Hitler himself warned that the party organisation was threatening to become an end in itself.[16] These conflicting attitudes towards the HJ meant that in practice the influence of the SA and NSDAP was not felt as powerfully as the directives would appear to indicate, for many of the leaders were simply at a loss as to how to approach the HJ. In due course, indecision engendered apathy and the friction between the SA and NSDAP tended to prolong that apathy.

The HJ headquarters was in Plauen, 150 miles from the centre of the NSDAP in Munich, until 1931, and only then did the NSDAP leadership begin to exert more decisive influence on the HJ; the previous geographical separation of their respective focal points resulted in only loose organisational bonds between the NSDAP and the HJ. In consequence, the HJ was permitted a far greater degree of initiative for independent action than directives superficially intimate.

Kurt Gruber was a dedicated national socialist, but at the same time he had certain political views of a more idiosyncratic kind, especially his social revolutionary theories. Though unquestionably loyal to Hitler, Gruber had a personality that demanded outlets for individualistic expression and he was ambitious to an extent for the HJ. Due to its inherent vagueness, national socialist philosophy of the pre-1933 variety had more flexibility and room for different interpretations than the form that developed in the Third Reich, so that persons like Gruber could conceive ideas and act upon them. His influence was important in the 1926–29 period in allowing the HJ to develop not as a mere adjunct of a rigidly controlled organisational system, but as a youth movement with a large amount of independence. Gruber was not the type to be kept in tight harness, and he tended to bitterly resent interference from external sources. He was proud of his achievement in building up the *Grossdeutsche Jugendbewegung*, and the idea that the HJ was somehow his property remained with him. Furthermore, the fact that the HJ was able to develop a special ideological ethos of its own within the national socialist movement clearly shows the slackness of the NSDAP's and SA's authority over it (see chap. 3).

The organisational machinery of the NSDAP whereby orders, decrees and directives were carried out was efficiently developed in the 1920s, unlike that of the HJ (see chap. 6). It is difficult to imagine that every directive in the HJ's rather primitive organisational system was executed exactly as it was designed. The HJ machinery remained ineffective until 1931 when the first major reforms were applied; until then the HJ incontrovertibly did not possess the administrative wherewithal to put directives into effect, even if ordered to do so by the NSDAP or SA. In addition, the very fact that fresh regulations had to be issued at regular intervals even after 1930 is evidence that the earlier ones did not work satisfactorily.

Finally, evidence of the NSDAP's lack of real authority over the HJ is also furnished by the financial arrangements existing between the two groups before 1929. The 1926 directives for HJ-NSDAP relations stipulated that the HJ leadership should gradually try to stand on its own feet financially, but that the party would lend some assistance in the meantime.[17] This was not, however, a specific commitment, and could not be in view of the NSDAP's financial difficulties during the 1920s. The party relied for most of its income on membership subscriptions, revenue from the sale of party newspapers, entrance fees to meetings, and donations from wealthy sympathisers. In the latter respect, Göring's return from exile in Sweden in late 1927 proved of inestimable value to Hitler, for it was the former flying ace who cultivated contacts with rich members of the social establishment and persuaded some to contribute to party funds. During the 1920s, however, heavy industry, suspicious of the radical left-wing element of the NSDAP and its ambivalent standpoint on capitalism, tended to evince disinterest. On the other hand, Hitler could afford to live well on the royalties from *Mein Kampf*. In view of this situation, Gruber was more or less left to his own devices to make ends meet, yet these invariably proved inadequate. Membership dues in the HJ were 50 pfennig per month before 1929; the *Gau* leadership normally sent 10 percent of its monthly income to the *Reichsleitung*, retaining entry fees and revenue from propaganda sales for its own use; the independent *Gaue* were required to send 30 percent of their monthly budget.[18] In reply to HJ pleas for money, the NSDAP treasury chief, Franz Xaver Schwarz, could only offer sympathy or at most a temporary loan of meagre proportions.[19]

Apart from the financial embarrassment of the party, there was also a vital political reason why the NSDAP did not try to lend more assistance to the impecunious HJ: until the early 1930s, when the HJ was brought under the control of von Schirach, the NSDAP leadership was wary of the HJ's social revolutionary radicalism (there were extremist manifestations in 1927), and was not, therefore, disposed to lending much help (see chap. 4). The general conclusion to be drawn is that any attempt by the NSDAP and SA to dictate policy or to interfere unduly in the affairs of the HJ would have led to HJ demands that they also assume full responsibility for its financial affairs. Since the NSDAP and SA were patently disinclined to adopt this latter course, it is reasonable to suggest that the HJ remained comparatively independent of them.

The general indifference, let alone active hostility, towards the HJ in wide circles of the SA and NSDAP virtually ensured that at least until the early 1930s the HJ would be allowed to remain on its own a great deal. There were too many other important tasks occupying the attention of the SA and NSDAP, including the destruction of the Weimar Republic. Measured against these objectives, control of the HJ did little to arouse the excitement of the elders of the movement. The establishment of the HJ passed off almost unnoticed in the NSDAP and SA and no great expectations were entertained for it. In the process of constructing the movement in the 1920s, the emphasis was on the NSDAP and SA; the HJ was present, but usually ignored. The presence of directives gave an air of orderliness, but those between the HJ and NSDAP and SA represented little more than a paper relationship which did not correspond to the facts of the pre-1929 situation. Referring to the position of the HJ in Bavaria, a police report of 23 July 1927 dryly remarked: "Insofar as can be observed, there is hitherto no special enthusiasm in national socialist circles for the youth organisation."[20] There is no reason to believe that this mood differed in any other part of Germany at this time, except possibly Saxony, or that it changed dramatically within the next few years.

It would, therefore, be erroneous to say that the HJ "spread like wildfire,"[21] for it began to develop only gradually outside Plauen and the Vogtland in Saxony. Before the end of 1926, branches had been founded in Osnabrück by Georg Schmied, in Hannover by Anton Bressel, in Bremen by Johann Röpke, in Brunswick by Georg Kedsig, in Halle by Ferdinand Hengst, in Franconia by Rudolf Gugel, in Sarstedt by Georg Salzer, in Hoheneggeben by Otto Ohlendorf, and in Berlin, Munich, Barsum, and Wiesbaden.[22] But the large majority of the eighty branches recorded by the end of this year were in Saxony. The HJ's membership, approximately 300 in July 1926, was unlikely to have exceeded 700 by the end of the year.[23]

Gruber's enthusiasm was undeniable, but he was confronted by many basic problems which did not have a ready solution, principally the shortage of adequate finance and the lack of trained leaders who could be relied upon to build up the organisation in the Reich. He had no one of the administrative calibre of Philip Bouhler, NSDAP secretary, or party treasurer Schwarz, both of whom gave invaluable assistance to Hitler in the difficult period after 1925. Initially, many HJ *Gaue* existed only on paper, and did not even have a *Gauführer*; in May 1927, for example, Gruber indicated that leaders were needed for no fewer than fourteen *Gaue*, including East Prussia, Schleswig-Holstein, Lüneburg-Stade, Hannover-South, Hesse-Nassau-South, and Halle-Merseburg.[24] By the end of 1927, there were about twenty *Gaue*, compared with twenty-five in the NSDAP (see Appendix III).

Another vital problem facing Gruber was how to advertise the HJ with his limited financial and press facilities. The national socialists had quickly realised that public demonstrations were comparatively inexpensive to organise and that they could be highly effective. This technique was later developed and exploited with particular success by NSDAP *Gauleiter* Joseph Goebbels in Berlin, and Gruber also decided to introduce it into the HJ. On May Day 1927, the HJ together with some SA and SS units staged a rally in Plauen to counter the traditional communist and socialist processions. The highlight of the year, however, was undoubtedly the participation of 300 HJ youths under Gruber on 19–20 August in the NSDAP *Reichsparteitag* in Nuremberg, which was already one of the leading national socialist centres.[25] Named the "Meeting of Awakening", this was the first massive demonstration of national socialist strength as a political power, and it was thus considered the first really important party rally of the post-1923 era.[26] A special meeting of the HJ in the *Kolosseum* on 20 August indicated that Gruber's youngsters now had an assured place in the organisational structure of the NSDAP. At this meeting, Hitler paid tribute to the sacrificial spirit of his young followers who had travelled from all parts of Germany to be present.[27]

At the end of a year of steady, if unspectacular growth, the NSDAP *Reichsleitung* tried to strengthen the bonds between the HJ and SA by decreeing that every HJ youth should join the SA on attaining his eighteenth birthday.[28] This would have had serious implications for the HJ organisational structure had not Hitler amended the ruling on 9 November 1928, when he ordered that the best HJ personnel could remain in the HJ even after the age of eighteen years if they so wished.[29] It was an important concession by Hitler, for it allowed the HJ to gradually build up a leadership corps, and thus to solve one of the most intractable problems besetting the group. At the same time, the arrangement resulted in an even further slackening of organisational links between the HJ and SA.

One indication of the HJ's gradual expansion was that in the early part of 1928 the *Reichsführung* moved into larger business premises in Plauen. In 1928 there was also a continuation of the policy of holding public demonstrations. On 7 and 8 April, 600 HJ youths from Saxony, Thuringia, and Upper Franconia marched at Bad Steben, and on 18 November, Gruber organised a *Reichsappell,* in which HJ units marched and held outdoor meetings at precisely the same time all over Germany.[30] The primary purpose of this exercise, the first of its kind, was to make the youths feel themselves to be soldiers of a mass, powerful, and invincible movement, but it was also the HJ's way of compensating for the absence of an NSDAP party rally in 1928.[31] The increasing economic and political consolidation of the republic was reflected in the failure of the extreme right in the Reichstag elections of 20 May 1928. Although the NSDAP obtained only 12 seats, a loss from its 1924 level, and the DNVP fell dramatically from 103 to 73 seats, even so the combined antidemocratic vote, including the KPD, at this ostensible zenith of republican development, was 27 percent. Despite relative economic prosperity, a large minority still remained alienated from the state and there was still an inherent weakness in the parliamentary and party system. With the onset of the economic crisis in 1929, this dissident minority, already vocal in depressed agricultural areas, would expand rapidly and substantially.

In view of the DNVP's setback, a right-wing coalition was no longer possible and the base of the bourgeois middle was so diminished as to give little chance to a bourgeois minority cabinet. The SPD was therefore constrained because of its success to renounce its role as an opposition party, which it did reluctantly. The party chairman, Hermann Müller, headed the new Grand Coalition government which had a safe majority in the Reichstag, a distinction denied its successors after 1930.

The NSDAP's poor showing in the elections belied the progress it had made since 1925. The movement branched out from Bavaria into northern and middle Germany especially, and by 1928 party membership had risen from 27,000 to 108,000. This was accomplished despite a severe lack of finances and the deprivation of Hitler's oratorical services, for the ban on his speaking in public was not completely raised until 1928. For a short time after 1925, the party's main activity was centered in northern Germany, but by 1928 Bavaria once again became the focal point. Furthermore, during this lean period, Hitler assembled around him the *Alte Kämpfer* (Old Fighters), from whose ranks a large part of the national socialist leadership of the Third Reich was drawn. The election results also concealed one significant fact anticipatory of the later growth of the NSDAP, namely, the party's comparative breakthrough in some agrarian districts of Schleswig-Holstein, Upper Franconia, and Lower Saxony, where depression had already reached a crisis point. It was axiomatic from the electoral results that the NSDAP's strategy of appealing to the working classes in urban centres was fundamentally unsuccessful because there the left-wing parties were too deeply rooted. Henceforth, NSDAP propaganda was reoriented towards the middle classes and peasantry.

HJ activities in 1928 were brought to a climax by a national congress of leaders on 28–31 December in the *Nonnenturm*, Plauen. Delegates from all the HJ *Gaue* except the Rhineland and East Prussia attended.[32] After Gruber had been given a vote of confidence, the meeting went on to discuss all aspects of the organisation's work, including its relations with the national socialist movement and with other German youth groups.[33] In addition, new divisions were created in the *Reichsführung*: a News Service "to break the Jewish monopoly of news" under Fritz Krämer; a new Sports Office; a Cultural Office; a Peasant Youth Office *(Landjugendamt)* under Erich Jahn; and most notably, a Border Land Office *(Grenzlandamt)* under Rudolf Schmidt.[34] These organisational changes in the HJ undoubtedly followed from corresponding major changes in the NSDAP effected by the new organisation leader, Gregor Strasser, as the party adjusted to its new political tactics.

In accordance with plans made at the meeting for the expansion of the HJ press, the monthly *Die Junge Front,* designed mainly for the leadership corps, and the fortnightly *Deutsche Jugendnachrichten* (DJN) appeared in March 1929.[35] Both now supplemented the established monthly newspaper, *Hitler-Jugend-Zeitung* (a compulsory purchase for every member), which by the end of 1928 claimed a readership of some 15,000.[36] These additional publications enabled a much wider public to learn of Gruber's unique tour of Germany *(Deutschlandreise)* in March-April 1929, during which he spoke at thirty-two meetings.[37] All things considered, the episode was a successful propaganda tour de force for the HJ, while it also accentuated its growing independent spirit. Probably more aware than anyone else of the gap between theory and practice in its relations with the HJ, the NSDAP reexamined the situation and decided to try to reshape this relationship in more concrete terms when it was reorganised in 1928. Accordingly, while the basic formula of the 1926 directives was retained, new statutes were promulgated on 23 April 1929 for the HJ-NSDAP and HJ-SA.[38]

These statutes implicitly recognised that the HJ had made considerable progress as an independent entity since 1926. Clearly, the NSDAP leadership was slowly coming round to taking an active interest in the HJ. For example, the *Hitler-Jugend-Zeitung* was now to be acknowledged as a party political organ, and every party leader was to make it compulsory reading in his area of control. The NSDAP press was to publish official statements of the HJ *Reichsleitung* and to remit articles on youth to an HJ censor in the *Reichsleitung*. It was agreed that at all future NSDAP party rallies there should always be a place for a special Hitler Youth meeting, and this practice, introduced at the party rally a few months later, was continued throughout the 1930s. To aid its propaganda work, the HJ was to be provided with speakers and officials by the party. Another noteworthy concession was that NSDAP leaders were expressly forbidden to reach agreements with other youth groups without the knowledge of the HJ *Reichsleitung,* or to become leaders in youth groups which were rivals of the HJ. This part of the statutes principally had in mind the youth associations of the *völkisch*-nationalist bloc, and foreshadowed the negotiations with them at the 1929 party rally (see chap. 5).

In the organisational sphere, it was reaffirmed that the appointments of HJ leaders were to be ratified by the corresponding NSDAP leaders, and as before, expulsion from one organisation meant immediate expulsion from the other, but the proposed sphere of practical cooperation between the HJ and party was mapped out more precisely. Both groups were generally to help each other whenever possible at every level, but particularly where their respective *Reichsleitungen* were concerned. HJ leaders were to participate in party meetings "whenever relevant" and NSDAP leaders were now required to give a copy of all work plans, decrees, and circulars to the corresponding HJ leader. The HJ leadership was obliged, however, to carry out the directives of the NSDAP where they affected the HJ. Moreover, HJ leaders were to submit monthly and quarterly reports to equivalent-ranking NSDAP leaders.[39]

At the same time, the HJ-SA relationship was redefined; on occasions when the HJ marched with the SA, the SA leadership had power of authority over the participating HJ formations, and higher-ranking SA leaders had supervisory rights over all public appearances of the HJ.[40] Importantly, the HJ was no longer duty bound to attend SA meetings and SA leaders were not allowed to intercept orders of HJ leaders. Furthermore, the recent practice was confirmed which allowed those eighteen year olds who were required as leaders to remain in the HJ without transferring to the SA on 9 November each year. Finally, SA expellees were not to be allowed to join the HJ and vice versa. Nonetheless, the role of both the HJ and SA within the movement was still fundamentally analogous in important respects: both remained basically political propaganda organisations. By 1929, both had the outward appearance of political armies, the SA more so because of its larger membership and more violent style. But there was a striking paradox here, for von Pfeffer wanted to construct the SA on elitist lines and restrict its membership to approximately 100,000, while the HJ always aspired to a mass organisation. The more the better; numbers meant strength, reasoned the HJ. In the long term, the SA and HJ saw themselves playing a more grandiose role in the movement, not only helping to create the conditions leading to the Third Reich, but becoming dominant influences in that Reich.

The outstanding feature of both sets of directives was the new esteem shown for the HJ and the tacit admission that it had to be accorded a position of some importance within the movement. The HJ was no longer to be regarded, even in theory, as a mere youth auxiliary of dubious value. The NSDAP gave its recognition in public for the first time that the HJ was a distinct entity with a life and soul, and indeed, this substantiates the argument that the HJ had been able to go its own way free of NSDAP and SA control since 1926. There is no evidence to suggest that these directives brought any vital change or that there was any weakening of the factors which had militated against the theoretical arrangements being applied in practice during 1926-29. The HJ and Gruber were more independent minded than ever before and better prepared to maintain their organisational integrity. The 1929 directives were obviously more generous to the HJ than those of 1926 and if anything, illustrated an even further decrease in control by the NSDAP and SA. Also, the HJ's organisational machinery had not improved by 1929; what could not be effectively applied in 1926-29 was unlikely to have a better chance of success in 1929-31 because the HJ's independence from the jurisdiction of the party and SA continued until the reform of the HJ in April 1931.

Baldur von Schirach, a keen student of the HJ in the years prior to his appointment as *Reichsjugendführer* in 1931, remarked on the SA's attitude at this time. He states that despite the 1929 statutes, Gruber's position was not definitely fixed vis-à-vis the SA: "He was more or less responsible to the Supreme SA leader . . . Captain von Pfeffer . . . who had too much work to do with the SA to be able to really concern himself intensively with the youth."[41]

This was indeed characteristic of von Pfeffer's outlook and that of the SA leadership in general from 1926 to 1931, for they had too much to do concerning their own organisation to be decisive in controlling the HJ. Von Pfeffer was a friend of Gruber and helped him vanquish his enemies at the 1929 party rally (see chap. 5); he had confidence in Gruber's leadership and was content to allow him to exercise his initiative. The *Reichsführer* did exactly that.

During the last year of the decade, the HJ displayed a more overt air of self-consciousness as it acquired a more perceptible individual identity. Not only did the HJ march less frequently in public with the NSDAP and SA and attend their meetings more intermittently, but it also paid more attention to conventional youth activities, though political work continued to predominate.[42] Gruber later spoke of this development:

> At this time (i.e. 1929) . . . young people worked and succeeded in giving the Hitler Youth its own characteristics. The results of this indefatigable, tough work shortly began to show; . . . The youths went their own way . . . exactly as they pleased.[43]

This trend was confirmed by two events in the second half of the year. Although the HJ had been publicly announced as an association with its own legal identity on 13 December 1928, this status was not legally validated until 31 May 1929 when it was inserted as the *Hitler-Jugend-Bewegung, e.V* in the Associations' Register.[44] The NSDAP had acquired a legal personality as early as 1920 when it was registered as the *Nationalsozialistischer Deutscher Arbeiterverein, e.V.*[45] The HJ was still a part of the national socialist movement, of course, but this gesture did nevertheless reinforce the attitudes conveyed in the 1929 HJ-NSDAP directives.

Furthermore, the unprecedented degree of self-confidence shown by Gruber and 2,000 of his HJ at the NSDAP rally in Nuremberg on 1–4 August was symptomatic of a larger growth of independence. Gruber regarded this "Party Meeting of Composure," which was attended by 60,000 people, as the perfect occasion to demonstrate the strength and discipline of his group.[46] Every HJ *Gau* was represented, the strongest contingents coming from Saxony, Berlin-Brandenburg, and South Hannover-Brunswick. Five youths from Hannover marched all the way to Nuremberg, a precursor of the famous "Adolf-Hitler-March" in 1937 when thousands of youths from every corner of the Reich walked to the same city as a token of loyalty to the Führer. Headed by the *Reichsschar* of Plauen, Gruber proudly led his HJ past Hitler in the market square, and in appreciation the Führer threw flowers from his reviewing stand at the marching columns.[47] He also dedicated the first HJ banner which depicted a black sword (nationalism) and a hammer (socialism) against a red background.[48] It was a satisfactory ending to the year.

In conclusion, the Hitler Youth, like the national socialist movement as a whole, enjoyed only modest expansion with limited resources during the period from 1926 to 1929. In relative terms, the HJ's progress was even unimpressive in comparison with other major organisations of national socialism. Although the number of HJ branches rose from 80 in 1926 to approximately 450 in 1929, and membership from 700 to 13,000, this did not remotely approach the membership of the NSDAP after the first four years of its existence, 1919–23, nor did it compare favourably with the growth of both the NSDAP and SA between 1925 and 1929.[49] It can be said that the HJ was larger than any *völkisch* youth group (see chap. 5) and that it had achieved a certain indeterminate status among the youth associations of the traditional nationalist right (despite the fact that many of these were numerically superior to the HJ), but measured against the more comprehensive spectrum of the German youth movement, which in 1927 had 4,338,850 youths organised in the *Reichsausschuss der deutschen Jugendverbände,* its impact had been inconsequential.[50]

The fundamental explanation for the slow development of the HJ during these years is simply that the relative political stability and economic well-being of the republic between 1924 and 1929 severely reduced the attractions of right-wing political radicalism for most Germans. The calm of this era did not by any means eradicate the political passions that had been engendered on both the extreme right and left before 1924, and indeed the KPD had gained slightly in voting strength between the 1924 and 1928 Reichstag elections, but in general, strong feelings were temporarily hidden. Like the NSDAP, the HJ was not furnished with the kind of turbulent atmosphere which radical movements of the right normally need if they are to prosper.

But there were also internal factors at work which hindered the HJ. The absence of financial support that was experienced by the whole movement and the difficulty of the HJ in finding sufficient competent leaders have already been noted. The HJ also had serious organisational problems to overcome and this took time. As became clear in the early 1930s, its organisational structure did not have the strength of the NSDAP's structure. To a considerable extent, this was Gruber's fault, for notwithstanding his energy as *Reichsführer,* he did not succeed in imposing his personality and authority on the organisation as Hitler did in the NSDAP or von Pfeffer in the SA. Provincial leaders had too much autonomy and too little central direction or discipline, which were necessary for cohesive unity.

Von Schirach had rather acerbic observations to make of the HJ in 1929. For example, writing on 5 January 1929 to his friend Werner Lass, leader of the *völkisch*-nationalist *Freischar Schill* youth group, he complained that the HJ was a "badly led and poorly disciplined organisation" which led "a miserable existence . . . between the military and youth movements."[51] More recently he wrote: "Many units led their own lives like the *Wandervogel* or Boy Scouts . . . and were commanded by people who had no idea of youth leadership."[52]

Instructions and orders were sent out throughout Germany without the *Reichsleitung* having the means of enforcing them. There were even groups antagonistic to one another, revealing a clash of personalities among HJ leaders.[53] Moreover, Gruber did not devote enough time to spreading the HJ outside Saxony; the HJ's character was Saxon just as before 1923 the NSDAP's had been Bavarian, so that the HJ in 1929 lacked the appearance of a national movement.

The inevitable concomitant of the HJ's substantial independence was minimal organisational and financial support from either the NSDAP or SA. Apart from the intrinsic indifference of these two groups towards the youth association for most of the early period, this situation may also be explained by Hitler's ambivalent attitude towards the HJ, whose leftist inclinations were at variance with the NSDAP's right-wing political course after 1928. Hence the observation of a contemporary is assuredly misleading in stating that despite its weakness in numbers and organisation the HJ was noted for its "fanatical and unconditional devotion to party doctrine."[54] There is no denying the fanaticism nor the unbounded enthusiasm of the HJ for the cause of national socialism, and it was this vitality that promised to make it a more important body in the 1930s, but the HJ's interpretation of what this philosophy meant revealed a significant unorthodoxy. The ideology of the HJ must, therefore, be analysed in order to understand what kind of a movement it was before 1933.

Notes: Chapter 2

1. SAB: 4/65 1734/293. Of the 7,000 present, 200 were youths.

2. BA:Akte NS 26/335.

3. BA:Akte NS 26/389; BA:Akte NS 26/335. Previously Dr. Hans Severus Ziegler, then deputy NSDAP *Gauleiter* of Thuringia, had given the name *Hitler-Jugend* to the Gera branch of the GDJB on 25 April 1926. But this name was not adopted elsewhere by the GDJB until Weimar (W. F. Hymmen, "10 Jahre Hitler-Jugend," in *Die Junge Kamaradschaft,* ed. E. Fischer [Berlin, 1935], p. 13). Streicher was also responsible for suggesting the name "Brown House" for the NSDAP headquarters in Munich in 1931, and for suggesting Nuremberg as the venue for later party rallies.

4. BA:Akte NS 26/335.

5. BA:Sammlung Schumacher:Gruppe VIII. No. 239.

6. Bay. HSA:ASA:Akte NS/1541.

7. Bay. HSA:ASA:Akte NS/1542.

8. Bay. HSA:ASA:Akte NS/1541; Bay. HSA:ASA:Akte MINN/71799.

9. BA:Akte NS 26/360. Though his full name was "Pfeffer von Salomon," he was known as "von Pfeffer" and signed himself as such. In the letter of 27 July 1926 from Hess to Gruber, Hess hinted that the HJ would be closely associated with the SA (BA:Akte NS 26/335).

10. For example, H. C. Brandenburg in *Die Geschichte der HJ* (Cologne, 1968).

11. Bay. HSA:ASA:Akte NS/1542; SAB:4/65 781/146.

12. *Wille und Macht. Führerorgan der NS-Jugend,* Sept. 1937.

13. See Brandenburg, *Die HJ.*

14. The Law for the Securing of Unity of Party and State, December 1933.

15. Bay. HSA:ASA:Akte NS/1544.

16. K. Heiden, *A History of National Socialism* (London, 1934), p. 111.

17. Bay. HSA:ASA:Akte NS/1542.

18. SAB:4/65 781/146. The amount of dues was determined from that date onwards by general meetings of the *Hitler-Jugend-Bewegung, e. V.*

19. BA:Akte NS 26/372.

20. SAB:4/65 1734/293.

21. As stated in H. Becker, *German Youth. Bond or Free* (London, 1946), p. 147.

22. SAB:4/65 781/146; BDC:F. Hengst file; BA:Akte NS 26/333. Although it is not certain, Ohlendorf may have been the same Otto Ohlendorf who was executed as a war criminal in 1951 in Landsberg Prison. He was commander of the notorious SS-*Einsatzkommando* Group D 1941–42 which was responsible for the murder of 90,000 Jews and Communists in Russia (See W. L. Shirer, *The Rise and Fall of the Third Reich* [London, 1960], pp. 953, 958–60).

23. SAB:4/65 781/146; Bay. HSA:ASA:Akte MINN/71799.

24. Bay. HSA:ASA:Akte NS/1541.

25. Ibid. Contingents from Austria and the Sudetenland were also present (SAB:4/65 1734/293).

26. H. T. Burden, *The Nuremberg Party Rallies 1923–39* (London, 1967), p. 38.

27. BA:Akte NS 26/390; *Wille und Macht,* Sept. 1937.

28. SAB:II 137 Bremen CVIII HJ.

29. BA:Sammlung Schumacher:Gruppe VIII. No. 239.

30. Ibid.; SAB:4/65 781/146; Hymmen, "10 Jahre HJ," p. 14.

31. Mainly because of pressing financial and organisational reasons.

32. BA:Sammlung Schumacher:Gruppe VIII. No. 239; Bay. HSA:ASA:Akte NS/1542.

33. SAB:4/65 1735/293. In June 1928, Martin Jordan, Reich propaganda leader, was appointed deputy *Reichsführer* (SAB:4/65 781/146).

34. SAB:4/65 781/146; BA:Akte NS 26/370. The main concern of the *Grenzlandamt,* which was based in Plauen and had only a few subsidiary offices in border areas, was to establish and maintain contact with *Volksdeutsche* communities outside Germany, especially with those in Hungary, Romania, Poland, and Czechoslovakia. The office tried to develop an interest in these separated Germans among HJ members through meetings and discussions, and occasional excursions were arranged to eastern Europe. The *Grenzlandamt* remained of negligible importance, however, though it did mark the birth of the HJ's foreign activities which began to flourish after 1933.

35. BA:Sammlung Schumacher:Gruppe VIII. No. 239. The DJN lasted only until 1931, reappearing in 1932 as the *Nationalsozialistische Jugendpressedienst* under the editorship of Willi Körber; after 1933, it was published as the *Reichsjugend-Pressedienst* (Hymmen, "10 Jahre HJ," p. 16).

36. SAB:4/65 781/146; Bay. HSA:ASA:Akte NS/1541. At least one subscription to the *Völkischer Beobachter* was required of all local NSDAP units.

37. BA:Sammlung Schumacher:Gruppe VIII. No. 239.

38. Ibid.

39. Ibid.

40. Bay. HSA:ASA:Akte NS/1541.

41. B. v. Schirach, *Die Hitler-Jugend. Idee und Gestalt* (Leipzig, 1934), p. 21.

42. Bay. HSA:ASA:Akte NS/1541.

43. *Nationalsozialistische Monatshefte*, Jan. 1930.

44. FSGNS:HA/NSDAP/239; Bay. HSA:ASA:Akte NS/1541.

45. D. Orlow, *The History of the Nazi Party 1919–1933* (Pittsburgh, 1969), p. 23.

46. Bay. HSA:ASA:Akte NS/1541; BA:Akte NS 26/372; Burden, *Nuremberg Party Rallies*, p. 47. Estimates of the HJ representation at the rally vary from 1,300 to 3,500, but a consensus of available archival material indicates 2,000 as the most likely figure.

47. H. Bolm, *Hitler-Jugend in einem Jahrzehnt* (Brunswick, 1938), pp. 76–80; BA:Sammlung Schumacher:Gruppe VIII. No. 239. In *Die Geschichte der HJ*, p. 37, H. C. Brandenburg writes that there was sharp criticism of the HJ from a group of visiting Sudeten Germans. Brandenburg has exaggerated this episode out of all proportion and has distorted the facts. The evidence (BA:Akte NS 26/372) indicates that the Sudeten German, Felix Ringhut of Karlsbad, who made the complaint to Border Land Office Leader Rudolf Schmidt, praised the HJ for its polished turnout, but criticised the *Reichsschar*, the Plauen group which headed the march past Hitler. Ringhut considered the slovenly performance of the *Reichsschar* incompatible with the high standard achieved by other HJ contingents.

48. Reichsjugendführung der NSDAP, *HJ im Dienst* (Berlin, 1940), p. 9.

49. Bay. HSA:ASA:Akte NS/1541; BA:Sammlung Schumacher:Gruppe VIII. No. 239. A report in the latter file gives the HJ membership on 1 January 1931 as 13,806. Making allowances for departures and new recruits, it is most unlikely that at the end of 1929 the membership exceeded 13,000. However, when the HJ applied (unsuccessfully) for membership in the *Reichsausschuss der deutschen Jugendverbände* in December 1929, it gave its membership as 23,000. This was obviously a fabrication (BA:ZSg 3/1477). For the later growth in HJ membership see chap. 8.

50. K. O. Paetel, *Die Jugend in der Entscheidung 1913–33–45* (Bad Godesberg, 1963), p. 63. This means "National Committee of German Youth Associations."

51. BA:Akte NS 26/354.

52. B. v. Schirach, *Ich Glaubte an Hitler* (Hamburg, 1967), p. 102.

53. Bay. HSA:ASA:Akte NS/1544.

54. K. O. Paetel, "Die Heutige Struktur der Nationalen Jugend," *Das Junge Deutschland* 6 (June 1929).

Chapter 3

Ideology and Sociology before 1933

Anyone who seeks to understand the nature of the HJ's development during the tempestuous years of struggle before 1933 must ask what its motivating ideas, ideals, and spirit were. One must also identify and examine the conditions which stimulated these beliefs, and study the social backgrounds of German youth who were particularly attracted by them. An additional justification for such an enquiry is that in the few postwar studies made of the HJ the ideological and sociological aspects of its evolution have been either neglected entirely or dealt with in a most superficial fashion.[1] There has been instead an almost unanimous dismissal of the HJ as a mere "party association," or "fighting and propaganda troop" with the clear insinuation that it had no unique ideological ethos.[2] This view would maintain that the NSDAP, and indeed the SA, always decreed more or less what the HJ should think. This argument fails, however, to take account of at least two important points.

Firstly, it has been shown that prior to 1931 the HJ was not as tightly bound organisationally to either the NSDAP or SA as has been generally supposed. The precise directives that were issued between 1926 and 1933 to govern the relationship between the HJ and the senior branches of the movement might indicate that the HJ was shackled by the dictates of the party and the SA. But the evidence is that these directives were rarely applied in practice as comprehensively or as accurately as they were meant to be in theory; the HJ was compelled to regulate its activities only to a limited degree and at certain times, notably 1931–32 (see chap. 6). For much of the pre-1933 period, the HJ retained a certain area for manoeuvre independent of the NSDAP and SA and consequently was allowed to develop specific ideological traits recognisable by their manner and sincerity as exclusive to the HJ. These special ideological features were above all the HJ's expressions of socialism and nationalism. Not only did these reveal an HJ deviation from conventional national socialist doctrine, but they also helped to give the HJ characteristics which differentiated it from contemporary youth organisations in Germany.

Secondly, in the now general vituperation against the HJ as a mere party affiliate, it has been conveniently forgotten that the HJ was after all a youth group whose rank and file were aged from fourteen to eighteen years. It is difficult to believe that this association of youths was content to submissively accept exactly the same political notions as their elders in the movement without any differences whatsoever, at a time when there was no efficient apparatus for political indoctrination in that movement. It is doubtful that the HJ was so spineless that it had nothing to say and contribute of its own accord. For a youth organisation whose vitality earned a great deal of respect from even its most vehement adversaries in the Weimar Republic, this is an improbable state of affairs.

Because of the extraordinary elasticity of national socialism's philosophy and its susceptibility to varied interpretation (the Strasser brothers furnish the best-known examples of nonconformity in the NSDAP), aspects of national socialist teaching were taken up and accentuated more in some of the movement's organisations than in others, for example, the emphasis placed by the SS on Nordic racialism. It should not be inconceivable that the HJ, while loyal to national socialism, should also wish to stress particular ideological elements in the same way as the SS did. The thesis which denies the HJ an ideological ethos obviously assumes that it was incapable of forming one. This was not so, for the HJ did value some doctrinal assertions of national socialism more than it did others.

Historians differ in their interpretation of the ideological origins and character of national socialism. Marxist writers adduce a socio-economic analysis, arguing that the NSDAP was not a social or political revolutionary movement but rather the expression of a crisis of capitalism. A second school of thought places national socialism in an exclusively German context, perceiving it as the macabre apotheosis of a long tradition of nationalism, imperialism, authoritarianism, and anti-Semitism in German life. Finally, some historians feel that national socialism was a specific outgrowth of a disturbed twentieth-century Europe. This point of view tends to shift the blame for national socialism away from Germany exclusively and towards Europe as a whole, stating that Hitler could have been any country's misfortune and that it happened to be Germany's due to certain historical events, mainly the defeat of 1918 and the wild inflation of the 1920s and early 1930s.

The most satisfactory explanation would appear to lie in a synthesis of the last two theories which, while stressing the role of national socialism in a general perspective of European historical development, shows that it was the culmination of Germany's intellectual and political course since the French Revolution. In the Weimar Republic, national socialism was only a part, albeit the most important, of a disparate movement of the right which shared the common attributes of a powerful nationalism, anticommunism, anti-Semitism, hatred for parliamentary democracy, and a yearning to replace the republic with a Führer-led authoritarian state.[3] It is as a section of this wider intellectual phenomenon, therefore, that the ideological attitudes of the HJ are to be comprehended.

To appreciate the ideological motivation of the HJ, it is essential to recognise that it was, in the words of *Reichsführer* Gruber, "the youth of revolt,"[4] imbued with an inveterate abhorrence for the republic as the embodiment of all that was wrong with Germany. As such, the HJ emerged, especially in the last few years of Weimar democracy, as one of the most dynamic manifestations among German youth of the despair and hopelessness experienced by a steadily increasing proportion of the younger generation.[5] The independent youth periodical *Der Zwiespruch* described this feeling at the beginning of 1931:

> German youth lives full of concern for the future. It sees this future dark and gloomy, both for itself and the Fatherland. In general, youth sees no chance of developing a better future out of the insecure life led by itself and the broadest classes in these confused days.[6]

Among the host of youth leagues in this period, no group, with the single exception of the communists, could match the HJ's record for consistently violent denunciations of the republic, or emulate its incessant prognostications of the advent of a new state. In many respects, the HJ somewhat vainly considered itself the apostle of enlightenment for German youth. This reflects a reaction, partly responsible for the development of the HJ itself, against the manifold inadequacies of the German youth movement to cater to the rapidly changing and even traumatic moods of the nation, especially during the crucial

1930–33 period. Too large a percentage of the groups became engrossed in sterile academic debate to offer a clear solution to the problems affecting youth, which obviously reduced their capacity to attract support. Something new and exciting was wanted by the activist section of German youth and the HJ at least gave the impression from 1931–32 onwards, when it was better organised, of having the ability to achieve concrete results.

Moreover, few organisations could offer the aggressively pseudo-heroic idealism and none the passionate nationalism of the HJ. In the HJ, the youths were encouraged to regard themselves as young soldiers fighting against overwhelming odds for the attainment of their aims, and it was this irrepressible exhortation to fight that earned the HJ a reputation for unlimited activism. Other right-wing nationalist associations were afflicted by the widespread feeling of lethargy and had become inert and conservative. Hence, among a score of nationalist youth organisations, the HJ successfully made itself synonomous with the nationalist cause through an unmercifully proclaimed devotion to the German *Volk* and fatherland.[7] Just as the NSDAP gained immeasurably from the deficiencies of the democratic order and the political parties, the HJ benefited from the debilitated structure of the youth movement.

There were numerous facets of life in the republic repulsive to youth. The scale of materialistic values failed to satisfy the submerged idealism of those desperately seeking outlets for a self-sacrificial feeling. The republic was too passive, too prosaic for youthful exuberance, while national socialism, with its compulsion for discipline, obedience, and dedication to a nationalist objective, cynically manipulated this psychosis of dejection for its own political advantage. It held out tangible aims to fill the vacuum felt by so many, especially among youth. National socialism offered a fresh beginning, bright prospects and rewards for service during the *Kampfzeit*. The NSDAP, portraying the movement as one of youth and for youth, judiciously sensed the latent tensions between the generations in German society, played the young and new against the old and decayed with consummate skill, and denigrated the "system" as the vile creation of a declining, older generation.[8] The proposed alternative was the destruction of the republic by the dynamism of national socialism and its replacement by the Third Reich of Adolf Hitler. The goal of the HJ was to rouse youth and to direct their resentments against the state. In any case, the republic's system of parliamentary democracy had never been wholly acceptable to large sectors of youth, nor had the republic ever made a concentrated attempt to enlist more support for its authority from the younger generation. The NSDAP and HJ, aware of the maxim,

"Who has youth, has the future," took good care to emphasise in their petitions that "Who has the future, has youth."

Nonetheless, this approach has to be regarded in due perspective, for if national socialism had any valid pretensions to being a movement of youth, it must be with particular reference to the twenty- to thirty-year-old age group from which the NSDAP drew substantial support. Of course, fascist movements with their stress on activism also carried a profound attraction for youth in other European countries. Furthermore, despite the air of self-importance frequently displayed by the HJ, it is necessary to note that at no time prior to 1933 did the HJ attain appreciable numerical strength or achieve much political importance (see chap. 8).

The HJ was, therefore, a revolutionary organisation, animated by a bitter distaste for republican life and by an enthusiastic yearning for a better future in a national socialist state. The HJ fully subscribed to the basic political attitudes of the antidemocratic right wing, which did so much to pave the way for the victorious ascent of national socialism, and, in common with the NSDAP, the HJ espoused a ubiquitous totalitarianism.

There is one principle which deserves fundamental consideration because the manner in which it was interpreted in the HJ, as opposed to the national socialist movement in general and the German youth movement, revealed a distinctive HJ ideological ethos. The HJ added something different to go along with its nationalism, a genuine social revolutionary impetus based in the HJ's rooted commitment to a German-styled socialism. This distinguished the HJ's nationalism from that of other right-wing youth associations, and, more importantly, from the NSDAP's nationalism because Hitler, even before the party changed course in 1928, was never seriously influenced by socialistic ideals. Although the HJ's nationalism included the racist and imperialistic elements which dominated the NSDAP's nationalistic appeal, it had also a social revolutionary component which no other unit of the national socialist movement possessed.

Socialism

The full title of the HJ, *Hitler-Jugend. Bund deutscher Arbeiterjugend* (Hitler Youth. Association of German Workers' Youth), is of the utmost significance in understanding its approach to the concept and practice of socialism. It resulted in the HJ rejecting the class consciousness of the republic and its preponderantly bourgeois standards, because the HJ believed this divided the nation into sectional class interests, which consequently created other divisions. The ultimate development was an irreparable weakening of society and a lowering of Germany's status as a world power. Because the republic was universally identified as a bourgeois institution, the HJ was consciously antibourgeois and overtly proletarian in character and style before 1933, advocating the foundation of a *Volksgemeinschaft* (national community), the axis of what National Socialists liked to call "German socialism."

This view of socialism was indubitably simplistic and even utopian. On numerous occasions, the HJ cited "socialism" and confessed its reverence for this creed, but no spokesman, including Gruber and von Schirach, ever produced a comprehensive, definitive statement about what the HJ actually meant by "socialism." The following extract illustrates the vexatious imprecision of the HJ's attitude:

> The Hitler Youth exists as a young proletarian organisation
> at the flashpoint of the political struggle. This organisation, as
> the school of socialism, forms its aims and tasks from its inner
> socialist pulse alone. . . .

No intimation is given of what "inner socialist pulse" means. A further example is: "The Hitler Youth marches as the association of nationally unifying socialism. . . ."[9] "Nationally unifying socialism" is an unintelligible reference in this context.

The lack of elucidation is most unsatisfactory but not totally unexpected in view of the HJ's (and NSDAP's) intrinsically antiintellectual tenor and the resultant lamentable absence of philosophical profundity in its literature. The HJ did not in any case try to conceal its patent dislike of programmatic statements of a detailed nature:

> Our programme is simple: we want to make Germany free.
> We are always asked about our programme. The others have the
> programmes! Germany will not be set free by programmes, but
> by men and will-power![10]

It should be borne in mind, however, that at no time did an NSDAP official make a fully detailed pronouncement on the national socialist *Weltanschauung*, perhaps by design, or because this was an impossible undertaking anyway. In similar vein, the party's supposed early adherence to socialism was never properly explained, even by the likes of Gregor Strasser, Goebbels, Karl Kaufmann and others associated with the so-called Nazi left. What was a socialist according to the NSDAP? A typically bombastic remark Hitler made in June 1922 is not at all helpful:

> Whoever is prepared to make the national cause his own
> to such an extent that he knows no higher ideal than the welfare
> of his nation; whoever in addition has understood our great na-
> tional anthem, *Deutschland, Deutschland über alles,* to mean that
> nothing in the wide world surpasses in his eyes this Germany,
> people and land, land and people, that man is a socialist.[11]

One can only attempt to glean from a multitude of equally esoteric HJ affirmations what its interpretation of socialism amounted to. From the verbiage it emerges that it was based largely on a series of negatives: the HJ renounced both communism and capitalism, opposed everything that was redolent of traditionalism or conservatism, and aimed to do away with class divisions and personal selfishness. More positively, the HJ proffered in the *Volksgemeinschaft* what in essence was an extension of its nationalism—"German socialism"—which represented social justice and egalitarianism in the broadest sense for all classes, and the abolition of all distinctions founded on privilege, whether of class, rank, or occupation. The basic determinant of status would be German nationality, and thereafter the degree of achievement and service to the nation *(Leistungsprinzip).* This line of thought may be easily disregarded as nothing but wishful thinking and idealistic fantasy. But then the HJ was a movement of youths, and youths are often idealistic and prone to indulgence in fantasies.

Gunther Orsoleck, who left his HJ leader's post in Berlin in 1927 (see chap. 4), said some years later when a member of the SPD that the HJ pursued a "primitive socialism."[12] The evidence indicates this judgement to be substantially true, but the intensity of the HJ's "social-ist" beliefs should not be underrated simply because of the intellectual shallowness of those beliefs. After all, the most fanatical members in any organisation, particularly of an extremist persuasion, are not always those who think most.

HJ propaganda expounded these "socialist" ideas as a means of competing against socialist and communist youth groups for the alle-giance of working-class youths. Despite the relative failure of this approach, and the fact that the HJ attracted large numbers of recruits only after 1931 when it began to appeal to middle-class youth, the HJ believed every word it preached on this topic. It considered it a sacred duty to save working-class youth from Marxism, which denoted internationalism instead of nationalism and class warfare instead of the community of all classes. Indeed, the HJ claimed, although without much justification, that prior to 1933 it had achieved a *Volksgemein-schaft* in miniature, in which every boy was on the same footing from the beginning regardless of his background. Leading HJ personnel were eloquent, if not entirely lucid, on this point: von Schirach later wrote what he believed this concept meant in the HJ:

> All work serves the one great ideal, before which differences of occupation, background, and possessions are eliminated. One stands next to one another in this youth with equal rights and equal duties. There is no special Hitler Youth for the poor or the rich, no Hitler Youth for the grammar schoolboy or girl, or for the young worker. There is also no special Catholic or Protestant Hitler Youth. Everyone who is of German blood belongs to our group. Before the flag of youth, everyone is the same.[13]

He also affirmed that the equality at which the HJ aimed was conveyed outwardly by its symbols:

> The son of the millionaire does not dress differently from the son of the unemployed worker. Both wear the attire of the community of comrades ... the brown shirt of the HJ. The uniform of the HJ is the expression of an attitude that does not ask after class or occupation, but only after duty and achievement. ... The symbol of the classless community of our youth is the flag of the HJ. ... In it has been shaped the socialist will of the new generation.[14]

Although similar thoughts were discussed in other national socialist formations, in no other were they apportioned more pious observance than in the HJ, and this peculiarly German-oriented socialism constituted an integral component of the HJ's *Kampfzeit* credo. National socialist anticapitalist and socialist slogans such as *Freiheit und Brot!* (Freedom and bread!), *Durch Sozialismus zur Nation!* (Through socialism to the nation!),[15] and *Gemeinutz geht vor Eigennutz!* (The common good before oneself!) were vital to HJ aspirations for the future socialist composition of German society. The HJ's unshakeable fidelity to the economic theses of the NSDAP's political programme supplied the innate substance of the HJ's pre-1933 social revolutionary animus. Social revolution on an egalitarian framework remained a constant objective of the HJ. As Gruber said in Plauen in December 1928:

> The Hitler Youth is the new youth movement composed of social revolutionary people of a German kind ... who are chained to the destiny of the nation ... in order to emancipate the state and economy from the bonds of capitalist, anti-national powers. Thereafter, the new socialist peoples' state *(Volksstaat)* of Adolf Hitler will follow.[16]

On many occasions before 1933, the HJ's nationalism and anticapitalism coalesced to prescribe its activities. One such occasion occurred in March 1930 when the HJ participated along with other youth organisations in nationwide demonstrations against the Young Plan, which had been accepted by the Reichstag and President Paul von Hindenburg as a final settlement of the intractable reparations question.[17] Although the plan was less severe than the earlier Dawes Plan, it was inevitably attacked by the German right in the form of a "Front of National Unity" sponsored by the NSDAP, DNVP, *Stahlhelm,* and Pan-German League. The front gained in momentum once the disastrous repercussions of the Wall Street crash in late October 1929 were felt by the German economy.

The NSDAP's new political course after 1928 created the opportunity for cooperation with the conservative nationalists, and the resultant national committee was able to force a referendum on its "Law Against the Enslavement of the German People" in December 1929. The anti-Young Plan campaign provided Hitler for the first time with a national audience via the vast press and publishing complex of Alfred Hugenberg, the DNVP leader since 1928, and allowed him to become an established and respectable politician of the right. It also drew the NSDAP out of the political isolation in which it had been languishing since 1923. One immediate benefit to the party was financial support from heavy industry, whose fears of national socialist radicalism were largely dispelled by Hitler's alliance with Hugenberg. This linkup was in fact symptomatic of a general rightward trend in German politics from 1928 onwards.

In rapidly deteriorating economic circumstances, more and more Germans came to regard the Young Plan as yet another attempt by the victorious powers of World War I to crush the Fatherland. The younger generation, outraged by the implication that it had to bear the consequences of its parents' alleged guilt, was especially furious in its opposition. The HJ, like the NSDAP, believed that Germany and German youth would be economically enslaved to Jewish-controlled finance capitalism for decades. At the same time, the HJ was specifically protesting against what it was convinced to be the intolerably high degree of international control exercised over the German economy, particularly by foreign banks. It is significant, therefore, that Gruber made Robert Gadewoltz, *Gauführer* of Berlin-Brandenburg, responsible for the arrangements relating to the HJ's involvement in this action, for Berlin-Brandenburg was a notoriously "socialist" branch of the HJ and Gadewoltz a leader celebrated for his leftist views.[18]

Throughout the campaign, the HJ relegated its nationalist fervour to second place behind its anticapitalist platform, in lucid contrast to the hysterical, almost exclusively nationalist stance adopted by the NSDAP.[19] In other words, in 1930 the HJ had not yet conformed to the NSDAP's post-1928 political reorientation. This argument is substantiated by a typical example of the HJ's propaganda content during this agitation:

Young workers!! Cast off the bondage of international world capitalism! Rise up against the dictate of slavery from Dawes to Young! Must we go under as the paid slaves of a capitalist clique? Working Germany! Young manual and intellectual workers of Germany awake, break off your chains![20]

It is inconceivable that the NSDAP, seeking middle-class votes by 1930, would have dared make such a blatant appeal to the working classes as the HJ did (except in the larger industrial areas, where this approach was maintained in reduced form after 1928). The political consequences of this dichotomy were to unfold within the HJ in due course.

HJ units marched in selected towns and cities behind black flags signifying slavery and ignominy in what was probably the largest display of solidarity between prodemocratic and right-wing youth organisations in the Weimar Republic.[21] While these groups were essentially activated by their patriotism in varying degrees of intensity, only the HJ agitated on a primarily anticapitalist basis. No one was more indefatigable in pursuing this line of policy than Kurt Gruber.

During his tenure of office as *Reichsführer,* Gruber was instrumental in infusing the HJ with his own social revolutionary ideals, and his influence determined one of the outstanding characteristics of the HJ before 1933. Because the HJ was permitted a magnanimous amount of freedom from NSDAP and SA tutelage, and because national socialist doctrine was so flexible, Gruber was given ample scope for his ideas. His home environment in heavily industrialised Saxony, which had large communist strongholds, often produced national socialists who, in addition to their nationalism, cherished notions of a new socialist order of society. Martin Mutschmann, the well-known NSDAP *Gauleiter* of Saxony (1925–45), exemplified this genre in his early party career. Saxony remained the focal point of the HJ's development until its headquarters were transferred to Munich; therefore, during the crucial first five years of its existence, the HJ was very much the child of men like Gruber who put their trust in "German socialism." As the most recent addition to the national socialist movement, this group consequently tended to be more fanatical in the prosecution of its avowed faith. Furthermore, the people Gruber gathered around him to staff the HJ *Reichsführung* were for the most part drawn from what was usually alluded to as "Red" Saxony, and they invariably shared their leader's social revolutionary vista.

On the other hand, if the HJ had been stationed in Munich from the beginning, the more conservative and procapitalist nature of national socialism in Bavaria would have counteracted the HJ's social revolutionary tendencies, so that the character of the HJ during the

Kampfzeit would have been totally different. Although after 1931 von Schirach did all in his power to diminish the HJ's socialism, when the move to Munich did come in May 1931, it was too late to effect any immediate or thoroughgoing alteration in the HJ's personality. Until the *Machtergreifung*, the HJ was still the most alertly "socialist" branch of the movement. There were areas, of course, where this feature was more marked than others. These were mainly located in large urban conurbations and extensive industrial growth belts which had normally a long history of socialist traditions, such as Saxony, the industrialised Ruhr and Rhineland, Westphalia, the Saarland, and cities like Berlin, Hamburg and Leipzig. Conversely, in areas like Schleswig-Holstein, Rheinpfalz, Hesse, and Pomerania, the HJ's socialism was somewhat tempered.

Insofar as historical generalisations are possible, the HJ can therefore be said to have had a distinct social revolutionary element. Indeed, in the more militant socialist regions, the extremist fringe of the HJ social revolutionaries, frustrated by what they considered to be reactionary moderation of the socialist aims of the movement by the NSDAP and HJ leadership, actually seceded several times from the HJ before 1933 (see chap. 4). These insurrectionary episodes were part of the general phenomenon of radical left-wing ideological and political dissension within the whole national socialist movement.

Nevertheless, there is an important qualification to be made at this point regarding the attitudes towards socialism held by the top HJ leadership after 1931, when Gruber was no longer *Reichsführer*. In this connection, the views of von Schirach must be subjected to careful scrutiny, despite his many public statements on socialism. There are several relevant factors to be taken into consideration. First and foremost, von Schirach's social background was an obvious embarrassment, if not an insuperable impediment, to any aspirant socialist (see Biography of HJ Leadership). Born of an upper bourgeois-aristocratic family in southwest Berlin on 9 May 1907, Baldur Benedikt von Schirach was educated at an exclusive private school in Bad Berka, Thuringia, and at the *Realgymnasium*, Weimar, where he took his *Abitur*. He then attended the University of Munich where for a short time he studied history, Germanics, and history of art. His father was a Prussian army officer and after the war, manager of the Court Theatre in Weimar. Von Schirach grew up, therefore, in an intellectually and culturally stimulating home atmosphere, far removed from the vicious economic and social dislocation that afflicted Germany between 1918 and 1933.

Von Schirach initially gained prominence in National Socialist party politics as the successful leader of the NSDStB, which was founded by Wilhelm Tempel on 26 January 1926 in Leipzig. As

Reichsführer, Tempel sought to give the NSDStB a leftist direction which only incurred the disapprobation of Hitler and led to Tempel's dismissal in July 1928. Von Schirach succeeded him and immediately fashioned the NSDStB's appeal towards middle-class students, who constituted an overwhelming majority of the university student population. Thus brought into line with the NSDAP's post-1928 policies, the NSDStB under von Schirach went on to become the most important student association in German universities by 1931.[22] His policies as NSDStB leader singled out von Schirach as a loyal adherent of the Führer's right-wing programme.

It is also noticeable that following Gruber's departure from the HJ, the content of that group's propaganda, though not dramatically altered, underwent a change in emphasis.[23] Though socialistic themes still formed an important element of propaganda at the end of 1932, nationalist and chauvinistic themes became progressively dominant during that year, after von Schirach's appointment as *Reichsjugendführer.* Only at this time did the HJ's propaganda come close to the orientation adopted by the NSDAP in 1928. Von Schirach had actively tried from 1929 onwards to bring the HJ on to a bourgeois-oriented course like the party's. If von Schirach did have socialist leanings, these were extremely circumscribed, and transcended by his nationalism and anti-Semitism.[24] He was in no way sympathetic to Gruber's social revolutionary ideals and his public acknowledgement of socialism was expressive more of a propagandistic stratagem than personal conviction.

On the other hand, there is the example of Artur Axmann, leader of the Social Office in the *Reichsjugendführung* from 1933–40, and von Schirach's successor in 1940 as youth leader of the Greater German Reich. Axmann was undoubtedly attracted to the HJ before 1933 by its socialism, and in the Third Reich, he more than anyone else in the organisation personified the social revolutionary ethos of the *Kampfzeit.* Axmann's background provided the seedbed of his socialist views: born the eldest of five children in Hagen, Westphalia, on 18 February 1913, he was brought up in difficult circumstances in the tough working-class district of Beusselkietz in north Berlin.[25]

An important question is whether there were any ideological or intellectual forces, apart from national socialism, acting on the HJ's socialist ideology. In particular, it is important to know whether any writers of the republic's antidemocratic movement of the right, in which the National Socialists were joined by Conservative Nationalists, National Bolsheviks, *Völkisch* Nationalists, Revolutionary Nationalists, and Conservative Revolutionaries, exerted influence on the HJ as some did on other streams of the youth movement. For example, Moeller van den Bruck, the intellectual champion of the Conservative Revolutionaries, and Stefan George both had a powerful bearing on the thought of *Bündische* Youth. The Conservative Revolutionaries were concerned with the social question but were insufficiently radical or revolutionary to have had much impact on the HJ. Their vision of a Third Reich, the title of Moeller's magnum opus published in 1922, was ill-defined and did not correspond to the later Hitlerian Reich.

The Revolutionary Nationalists had more in common ideologically with national socialism; their nationalism derived from the war experiences *(Fronterlebnisse)* of 1914–18 and as a result, the military ethic conspicuously overshadowed their thinking. They also entertained ambitions of founding a nationalist *Volksgemeinschaft*, but this was to be chiefly activated by the military idea, and did not incorporate the HJ's political or revolutionary socialist objectives. The unbending antibourgeois and anticapitalist philosophy of Ernst Jünger and his circle was echoed in the HJ, but the Revolutionary Nationalists' ideals were more important in the youth movement from the late 1920s and at best only indirectly influenced the HJ.

National Bolshevism, representing an attempted marriage between the extreme nationalism of the NSDAP and the communism of the KPD, arose in the 1920s. Although remaining a negligible political force, National Bolshevism affected socialist pockets in the NSDAP, SA, and HJ (notably in some of the most radical social revolutionary circles in Berlin and Hamburg), but its progressively pro-Soviet, communistic proclivities were repudiated by the mass of HJ members.[26] The National Bolsheviks ultimately sought a proletarian, nationalist state, which to the HJ was no better than a bourgeois state like Weimar. The HJ deprecated the hegemony of any class and desired the equality of all classes within a *Volksgemeinschaft*.

The Conservative Nationalists were looked upon by National Socialists as the epitome of political reaction, which especially in HJ vocabulary was as obnoxious as Marxism. The Conservative Nationalist position was influenced by the precepts of the traditionalist pre-1914 society in Germany, embodying above all the monarchical principle and class privilege, and excluding anything connected with socialism. The absence of a radical nationalism and a revolutionary socialism meant, therefore, that there was little intellectual affinity between the Conservative Nationalists and the HJ, though they cooperated on a political level during periods of NSDAP-DNVP/Stahlhelm alliance. The *Völkisch* Nationalists were intrinsically national socialist, but because both camps shared virtually the same dubious origins of ideological inspiration, the former did not comprise a special body of influence on the HJ.

There was, therefore, no one particular source of thought within the German right from which the HJ's concept of socialism derived;

nor for that matter did any thinker or organisation in the past history of the youth movement influence the HJ in this respect. The HJ rather collated ideas from a number of sources, which enabled it to devise an almost idiosyncratic brand of socialism. As such, the HJ's socialism was a curious if somewhat undistinguished contribution to the intellectual ferment on the nationalist right prior to 1933, arising from a desire among a certain section of youth to discover a new ideological confession, an integrated combination of nationalism and socialism. On the other hand, the significance of the HJ's socialism in the outer world was inconsequential.

The socialistic ideal constituted an integral part of the HJ's ideological ethos, as observed, and unlike NSDAP propaganda and the generally insincere socialist statements of party leaders, the HJ was not simply content to voice its allegiance to socialism. The HJ's pragmatic approach to issues, which distinguished it from the hazy romanticism of the *Wandervogel* and the detached elitism of the *Bündische* Youth, demanded a more concrete stand to be adopted on matters which affected the daily life, not only of its own membership, but also of the wider segments of German youth which the HJ hoped one day to encompass. Thus, before 1933 the HJ proposed constructive policies of social, industrial, and economic reform which were aimed at ameliorating the ordinary life and living standards of working-class youth. In revealing this sensitive social conscience, the HJ showed itself to be not only in advance of the social welfare legislation of the Weimar Republic, but also further ahead on this topic than any other contemporary youth group, except some socialist organisations. The HJ's solicitude was notably discernible in connection with young factory workers and apprentices, which was not surprising in view of the large percentage of its membership supplied by this social group.

The anticapitalist denunciations that became more vocal in the HJ press as the economic crisis deteriorated in the early 1930s added vigour to the group's insistence on more equitable working and recreational conditions for proletarian youth. As early as 1930 when the economy was already tottering and the HJ was active against the Young Plan, the enactment of a National Youth Law *(Reichsjugendgesetz)* was called for by the HJ leadership. This was another example of the HJ's determination to continue its pro-working-class policy at a time when the NSDAP was courting the bourgeoisie. The law was designed to afford economic and social protection and security to the young working class so that "a powerful youth can create a new state out of the present decayed system. . . ."[27]

The HJ took further steps to complement and sustain this independent programme: it created in July 1930 a Trades School Cell Organisation of the Berlin Hitler Youth *(Berufsschulzellen-Organisa-*

tion der Berliner Hitler Jugend), and in January 1931 set up a Young Workers' School *(Jungarbeiterschule)* in Berlin.[28] Both of these had propaganda functions, but were also meant to help alleviate the distress of working-class youths in the capital. The more ambitious National Socialist Youth Factory Cell Organisation (NSJBO, *Nationalsozialistische Jugendbetriebszellen-Organisation)* was founded in September 1932 as a division of the NSDAP Factory Organisation, but failed to fulfil expectations.[29] Hence, most of the HJ's proposals in this sphere were not translated into legislative practise until after 1933 when Axmann's Social Office had some success.

In view of the HJ's socialist predilections which did so much to determine the style and character of the organisation before 1933, it would be interesting to ascertain the relationship between this ideological basis and the HJ's sociological composition. The most appropriate question to ask is from which part of the German social structure did HJ personnel originate, and furthermore, was one class more heavily represented than others? The social revolutionary outlook of the HJ furnishes the initial clue to these questions.

Sociology

It has been established beyond doubt in previous works on the rise of national socialism that the NSDAP gathered a great proportion of its support from that section of German society which had been most devastatingly crippled by the economic dislocations and financial vicissitudes of the early 1920s and the early 1930s, namely, the lower middle and middle classes and the peasantry. The economic lifeline of these bourgeois classes collapsed and their political reaction was perhaps in some ways inevitable. They nourished a bitter loathing and an acute contempt for democratic government. Their economic and social deprivations led them to assume an antiparliamentarian, antirepublican posture, and at the same time, led them into the current of right-wing political extremism, of which the supreme protagonist was, of course, the NSDAP. From 1928 onwards national socialist propaganda was openly structured to capture the votes of these disillusioned classes, and met with resounding success at the expense mainly of the other middle-class parties, except the Catholic Centre. The national socialist portrayal of a Third Reich in which the bourgeoisie were promised a restoration of their economic well-being and social prestige was irresistible.

It should be stressed that the NSDAP won only relatively small backing from either the working class or unemployed working class.

Their deeply ingrained class consciousness and dogged adherrence to the well-disciplined Social Democratic and communist organisations made the working classes largely impervious to the allures of national socialism, and they maintained their traditional voting patterns until 1933. Only to a limited extent, therefore, did the NSDAP achieve its goal of becoming a *Sammelpartei* of a new kind. The NSDAP was a mainly middle-class phenomenon and was not an omnipotent *Volksbewegung* (popular movement), as its propaganda delighted in making out.

There is a high probability that the sons of the proletarianised bourgeoisie constituted a substantial part of the HJ's membership before 1933. They would, furthermore, be the section most attracted by the social revolutionary standpoint of the HJ, just as their parents were in the ranks of the NSDAP and the SA. The sons of the small businessmen and shopkeepers ruined by the economic catastrophe found the HJ the only youth association that satisfied their nationalism simultaneously with their socialist perspectives. The HJ also had a large percentage of young workers, many of whose parents had been constrained by dint of economic circumstances to join the ranks of the proletariat. The HJ never tired of proclaiming that it was a movement of all classes. This is a perfectly valid contention; there were even aristocrats in the HJ, among them Baldur von Schirach and Adrian von Renteln, *Reichführer* of the HJ from 1931–32. Nonetheless, there is sufficient statistical evidence to indicate unequivocally that the personality of the *Kampfzeit* HJ was proletarian.

It has been calculated that in 1931–32, 69 percent of HJ members were composed of young workers and industrial apprentices; 10 percent were shopkeepers' assistants; 12 percent were schoolboys; and 9 percent either unemployed or belonging to miscellaneous occupations.[30] These figures were compiled by the HJ itself, but there is no reason to dispute them, for they do conform to the sociological pattern naturally expected of an antibourgeois and anticapitalist movement. But there is independent evidence which corroborates this picture. For example, in HJ *Gau* Munich-Upper Bavaria at the end of 1930, 51 percent of the members were trades and factory workers and apprentices, 14 percent were industrial apprentices, 16 percent were schoolboys, 11 percent were shopkeepers' assistants, 6 percent were agricultural workers, and 2 percent were in the unemployed-miscellaneous category.[31] Hence, 71 percent may be classed as manual workers, which corresponds to the salient feature of the 1931–32 figures. At the beginning of 1930, HJ *Gau* South Bavaria had a rather higher percentage of manual workers, 77 percent.[32] Of a reported influx of new members into the HJ in the first half of 1930, 69 percent were manual workers of various description, 10 percent were shopkeepers' assistants, 12 percent were schoolboys, and 9 percent unemployed or miscellaneous.[33] Once again, the predominant characteristic is the working-class content of the HJ. Finally, the Hamburg HJ showed the same trend in August 1930 when 69 percent were manual workers.[34]

This selection of occupational distribution in the HJ *Gaue* pinpoints a quite remarkable consistency in the percentage of manual workers involved. It is noticeable that even in Bavaria, a relatively nonindustrial province, it was working-class youths who joined the HJ, although because of the weaker emphasis on socialism it is possible that this development was significantly altered in favour of middle-class youths in other mainly agrarian regions, such as Schleswig-Holstein, Hesse, Hannover-Brunswick, East Hannover, Pomerania, and East Prussia. The situation in Hamburg was certainly indicative of HJ membership trends in heavily industrialised districts. The lowest documented percentage of manual workers was in *Gau* Rhineland in 1930 when the figure was 55 percent, while an unusually high percentage, 30 percent, was made up of schoolboys.[35] This obviously runs contrary to national trends and may be explained by the fact that in 1930 the HJ had made little progress in the Rhineland, and working-class youth there still allied themselves with left-wing organisations.[36] As the HJ gradually made inroads on this monopoly, however, the number of young workers in *Gau* Rhineland increased and drew closer in time to the national norm. Since there were virtually no educational scholarships available, very few workers could afford to allow their children to continue scholastic careers after the age of fourteen. Therefore the 12 percent of HJ schoolboy members was drawn almost entirely from the middle classes.

A further indication is given by the sociological background of the sixteen members of the national socialist youth movement who were killed or murdered before 1933 (see chap. 8). This astonishing casualty rate, which no other youth association sustained, was a result of the HJ's radical ebullience and total involvement in political strife. Eight of the sixteen youths were apprentices in working-class occupations, while two of them were manual labourers.[37] Three were schoolboys, though at least one, fifteen-year-old Herbert Norkus, who became the martyr-hero par excellence of the HJ, was of proletarian origin; like Axmann he was brought up in Berlin-Beusselkietz. The background of the other three youths is unknown. Eleven of the sixteen, or 69 percent, who were all rank and file members, may be accordingly classified as working class. Again the national average of working-class HJ youths is confirmed.

A striking difference is apparent, however, in the social makeup of the HJ leadership. Biographical details of 200 of the most significant HJ leaders of the pre-1933–34 era reveal that while the social classification of 80 leaders is unavailable, 107 were of middle-class origin and 13, or 6.5 percent, were from a proletarian background (see Biography of HJ Leadership). In other words, although the HJ's ordinary membership was predominantly working class during the *Kampfzeit* especially until 1931-32, when more middle-class youths were attracted by von Schirach's policy, the leadership was overwhelmingly bourgeois. Moreover, most of the working-class leaders had ceased by 1931 to hold high-ranking offices; only Axmann and the two Stegemann brothers in Berlin-Brandenburg retained top posts after 1931. The dismissal of Gruber as HJ *Reichsführer* in 1931 did not mark a dividing line between the predominance of either bourgeois or proletarian leadership, for since 1926 the HJ leadership had always been more middle than working class.

This state of affairs need not engender undue surprise. HJ leaders, who were naturally older than the rank and file membership, were also NSDAP members, and the vast majority of these came from the middle classes. Nevertheless, the HJ leadership was filled with nationalists who were also socialists, and inevitably HJ propaganda in stressing nationalism and socialism attracted most of all working-class youths with nationalist sentiments. The middle-class leaders accepted and promoted the social revolutionary ethos of the HJ (although von Schirach's position was doubtful), so that the HJ never lost its proletarian style before 1933. If the HJ had not been brought under more concentrated bourgeois leadership after 1931 by von Schirach, it is conceivable that in due course a growing number of ordinary working-class HJ members would have become leaders. This would have fundamentally changed the sociological character of the leadership and brought it more into line with that of the rank and file as it was until von Schirach arrived.

Since the sociological formation of the HJ leadership was similar to that of the NSDAP leadership and ordinary membership, the contrast to the rank and file makeup of the HJ for most of the pre-1933 era is revealed by the fact that workers constituted only 26.3 percent of the NSDAP membership in 1930, and only 32.5 percent in 1933.[38] Without even making allowances for the percentage of former middle-class elements forced into this category, these figures are well below the proletarian figure for the HJ. This dichotomy in the social background of members is obviously critical to an explanation of why the HJ was more social revolutionary in orientation than the NSDAP.

Like the party leadership as a whole, the HJ leaders were young and compared favourably with the average age of leaders in other sections of the German youth movement; of the 200 leaders, 138, or 69 percent, were born during the decade 1900-10, the years 1906-08 being the most popular, when 54, or 27 percent, were born. Only twenty-five leaders were born before 1900. A small number, nineteen or 9.9 percent, of them had a university education and only a further twelve are known to have completed the *Abitur*. Nonetheless, the three *Reichsführer* of the HJ before 1933, Gruber, Adrian von Renteln, and von Schirach, all attended university, though neither Gruber nor von Schirach took his degree. The NSDAP also showed a lack of well-educated personnel before 1933, reflecting the anti-intellectual bias of the movement.

A noticeable number of party leaders were born outside Germany: for example, Hitler in Austria, Rudolf Hess in Egypt, Walther Darré in Argentina, and Alfred Rosenberg in Russia. A comparable pattern is also discernible in the HJ leadership: von Renteln was born in Russia, and seven other top leaders were born in places as far apart as Lithuania, Poland, the Sudetenland, Bosnia, and Austria. Furthermore, von Schirach had strong American ties. Foreign-born leaders *(Volksdeutscher)* were, however, the exception in the HJ. Most of the party *Alte Kämpfer* had joined the NSDAP before 1930, while the evidence on the 200 HJ leaders indicates that the years 1928–31 were the heaviest for recruitment, and by the end of 1931, 98 or 48 percent had already joined the HJ. A large part of the NSDAP *Alte Kämpfer* came from a rural or small-town environment, but the HJ leadership was fairly evenly divided between a large town-city and small town-rural background.

Not until after Hitler's appointment as Reich chancellor and after the HJ had absorbed the other youth groups in Germany through the *Gleichschaltung* programme, was there a more significant influx of middle-class youths into the HJ from the *Bündische* Youth, the sports youth associations, and a whole galaxy of right-wing nationalist leagues. Only then did the HJ show a more diversified sociology. This may be illustrated by the following table for the occupational structure of the HJ membership in 1939:[39]

Occupational Structure of HJ Membership in 1939

	Category	Membership
1.	Workers	20.9%
2.	Shopkeepers' Trades	25.5%
3.	Schoolboys	16.4%
4.	Technical & Artisan Workers	8.7%
5.	Agricultural Workers	3.4%
6.	Students	5.9%
7.	Teachers	5.4%
8.	Unemployed	2.5%
9.	Miscellaneous	11.3%

The representation of working-class members fell from an average of 65–70 percent during the pre-1933 period to 24.3 percent (i.e., categories 1 and 5) in 1939. In specific terms, the change was brought about by an appreciable augmentation in the number of shopkeepers' employees, from an average of 10–12 percent before 1933 to over 25 percent in 1939, and in the number of schoolboys from around 12 percent to over 16 percent in the same period. More importantly, two classes which were hardly represented before 1933, students and teachers, constitute a relatively high 11.3 percent in 1939. The general conclusion, therefore, is that the HJ of the Third Reich had a more balanced class distribution than the pre-1933 HJ. After 1933 the HJ relinquished its proletarian image, the ordinary membership became more middle class, but the leadership remained, as before, mainly bourgeois.

Ideological Training

Only as the bitter political battles of the 1930s got under way did the HJ leadership devote any serious thought or time to schooling its members in the aims of the HJ and national socialism. The main reason for the early laxity was the widespread tendency of the leadership to assume that those who joined the group already possessed some understanding of why they chose the HJ in preference to another youth organisation, and that they were at least aware of the basic tenets of the HJ's philosophy. There was also a significant political factor involved in the new approach; because of the unrest in the national socialist movement in 1930–32, Hitler decided to intensify the political education of the SA, NSDAP, and HJ. Formalised political instruction of leaders would hopefully prevent further discontent and at the same time provide the various branches of the movement with the numbers of leaders they so badly lacked. In any case, the huge growth of national socialism after 1930 demanded more supervisory control of this kind. In June 1931, for example, an SA National Leaders' School was established, and in October of that year, every SA district unit *(Gruppe)* was ordered to set up a school for leadership training.[40]

These changes must be seen in a more general context of greater centralisation and tightening of control in the HJ (see chaps. 6 and 7). The first intimation of a new attitude came in a HJ *Reichsleitung* report in 1931 which informed the organisation that henceforth the Educational Division would issue so-called *Schulungsbriefe* (educational letters) every month to each HJ *Gau* in order to better acquaint members with the objectives and content of HJ ideology. The report envisaged the establishment of educational camps for ideological seminars and courses on public speaking, the development of the HJ and the national socialist movement, history, racial theory, and other related subjects.

Furthermore, the *Reichsleitung* stressed that "more value is to be placed on the acquisition of homes or rooms in which our youth can hold their *Heimabend*" (home evening). The *Heimabend,* a popular practice in the HJ, was a weekly discussion held by a local HJ group. Until the early 1930s, the debates on ideological matters which were sometimes held were the only source of formal instruction on the aims of the HJ available to the membership. Frequently, however, discussions in the *Heimabend* were reduced to a minimum, depending on the HJ *Gauführer* of a particular area, and the time used to plan the propaganda activities of the coming week. Every meeting was concluded on an active note in any case, for in September 1926 Gruber ordered that a battle song *(Kampflied)* be sung at the end of the proceedings. These evenings were often held in NSDAP or SA premises because the HJ did not usually have the financial resources to buy or rent its own accommodations. The 1931 report courageously denounced this reliance on the senior organisations as unsatisfactory because the smell of alcohol and tobacco in the party offices was having an adverse effect on the youths.[41]

It was normal for the HJ membership to be politically educated in an informal manner through the HJ's press and propaganda apparatus, and this remained the most consistent and important mode of instruction until 1933.[42] The HJ press differentiated itself from the press of other youth groups by its aggressive and polemical style, and its poor taste frequently drew considerable criticism from opponents. Like the NSDAP, the HJ presented its aims in a simplified form and commonly used eye-catching slogans. For the primary benefit of members, Gruber or some other high-ranking leader would occasionally write a long article expressing the HJ's ideas on a particular problem, but it is doubtful whether these normally prolix efforts were read by the average member.

The Young Workers' School set up by the HJ in Berlin in 1931 was the first response to the *Reichsleitung's* recommendations, for the school was partly designed to provide lectures on national socialism. In November 1931, Emil Klein, leader of *Gau* Munich-Upper Bavaria, founded a Hitler Youth Leadership School which aimed to provide well-informed leaders; the first course lasted from November 1931 to 31 March 1932. The leader of *Gau* Rheinpfalz, Karl Hofmann, established a similar school called the *Horstwesselburg* the same year, and in spring 1932 Hartmann Lauterbacher, then leader of *Gau* South Hannover-Brunswick, set up the first Reich Leadership School at Flechtorf, dedicating it to his hero, Albert Leo Schlageter. A second

Reich Leadership School was later created in Munich, but it was intended only for high-ranking leaders.[43]

The appearance of these schools showed a new awareness on the part of the HJ leadership of the value and necessity of systematic ideological training, but nonetheless these endeavours were relatively tentative and did not offer a complete solution to the problem. The inadequate *Heimabend,* the poor-quality HJ press, and the erratic improvisations of local leaders continued to guide the vast majority of members. Ideological instruction in the HJ prior to 1933 was badly organised and unmethodical in comparison with the expertise that was utilised in this sphere during the Third Reich. It would therefore be incorrect to speak of political indoctrination in the HJ simply because there was not the organisational machinery for this to be effected.

Conclusion

Because of the HJ's emphasis on socialism together with its radical social revolutionary dynamism, which formed a constituent of its nationalism, one may legitimately refer to a distinctive HJ ideological ethos during the *Kampfzeit.* This gave the proletarian-oriented HJ its own ideological importance within the national socialist movement. Its political commitment and the fanaticism with which it prosecuted that commitment furnished the HJ with unique features as a youth organisation. A spontaneous and constant dedication to the principles of nationalism and socialism were the very essence of the HJ's message. The Hitler youth was a political soldier of a nationalist type; socialism was his conviction, Adolf Hitler his idol, and Germany his passion. Hardness, discipline, activism, and toughness were demanded of him, though these qualities could too often degenerate respectively into ruthlessness, rigidity, boisterousness, and hooliganism.

There were undeniably also considerable elements of idealism in the HJ before 1933, just as there were in the NSDAP. That this was a totally naive and misguided idealism is easily seen today, but before he became Reich chancellor no one could really judge how far Hitler would implement the ideas expressed in *Mein Kampf.* Before 1933, people joined the national socialist movement with a wide variety of motives, some of which were honestly based. Many did not believe that the nefarious aspects would be put into practice; others, while repudiating the negative side, were attracted by what they considered to be the positive side of the NSDAP.[44] Thus, many believed in good faith that national socialism had the necessary potential to solve the manifold problems which beset Germany at that unhappy time. Only during the Third Reich did national socialism reveal all its crudities and inhumane distortions, and a second world war was required to terminate its criminal course.

This applied especially to those who were too young to know better; youths joined the HJ, not because they were the roughest and toughest elements of young Germany, though the group did certainly attract its share of the milieu, but because they believed that the HJ more than any other contemporary youth association offered prospects of helping to create a better Germany. The conditions which formed the background for their beliefs—economic distress on a calamitous scale, political turbulence, governmental incompetence, and social flux—must be taken into account. The HJ represented a revolutionary organisation which rejected these conditions in the hope of achieving something better.

But while the idealistic motivation of the rank and file membership may be partially excused on these grounds, the motives of the HJ leadership and of the national socialist leadership in general allow for no such consideration. They were old enough to know what they were doing, as von Schirach admitted at Nuremberg in one of his more candid moments, and for them there can be nothing but the sharpest censure.[45] In view of the HJ's poverty before 1933, it must be conceded that its leadership was not activated by the hope of immediate material reward. The same may also be said of Hitler, yet this does not render him any the less odious. He had a voracious political ambition, a thinly disguised opportunism, and an enormous lust for power; and similar reasons, albeit on a somewhat lesser scale, undoubtedly played a large part in the outlook of the HJ leadership. In this respect, therefore, the idealism of the ordinary Hitler youth was exploited by his own superiors.

How far was the HJ itself exploited, if at all, by the NSDAP? This first of all raises the larger moral question regarding the legitimacy of involving youth in the tense politics of the Weimar period, and the NSDAP, but also other political parties which had youth affiliates, must be condemned for this practice. In the case of the NSDAP, the condemnation must necessarily be greater because of the unparalleled turpitude of the ideology which youths in the HJ served. The NSDAP founded the HJ to help it win more support and in this sense, therefore, the HJ became the tool of the party. Nevertheless, the HJ enjoyed relative independence from the NSDAP for long spells before 1933, and those ideological characteristics which gave the HJ its uncommon character were taken up and developed on its own initiative. Nor was the idealism of the ordinary membership forced on the HJ by the NSDAP. Moreover, the HJ did fulfil a certain need of a section of the German youth. Thus, though the HJ was used by the NSDAP on a long-term basis for its political ends, these qualifications must be taken into consideration.

Notes: Chapter 3

1. A. Klönne's *Hitlerjugend: Die Jugend und Ihre Organisation im Dritten Reich* (Hannover, 1956); W. Klose's *Generation im Gleichschritt* (Gütersloh, 1964); and H. C. Brandenburg's *Die Geschichte der HJ* (Cologne, 1968), all lack a serious analysis of the HJ's pre-1933 ideology.

2. The description used by U. Schmidt in "Die Jugendbewegung und Ihre Nachwirkungen in die Hitler-Jugend" (Unpublished manuscript, Hochschule Bielefeld, 1960), p. 26.

3. See K. Sontheimer, *Antidemokratisches Denken in der Weimarer Republik* (Munich, 1962).

4. SAB:4/65 781/146.

5. In 1932–33, the number of suicides among German youth rose considerably, and the growing rate of juvenile delinquency was a clear indication of the dissatisfaction felt by youth with life in the republic.

6. *Der Zwiespruch,* 25 January 1931.

7. An extract from an HJ song of the *Kampfzeit* composed by Werner Altendorf, leader of the HJ in Silesia, illustrates this spirit, if somewhat crudely:

   > We bear hunger and pain,
   > Which do not hinder our step,
   > We carry in our thumping hearts, Faith in Germany!
   > We carry in our thumping hearts, Faith in Germany!
   > Here our body, here our life,
   > Everything to give in sacrifice for Germany,
   > Freedom and Honour the only reward!

   (Blut und Ehre: Liederbuch der Hitler-Jugend, [Berlin, 1933]).

8. The age composition of the NSDAP before 1933 contained a higher proportion of people under forty years than any other party. The respective differences in age between the NSDAP and SPD memberships, for example, is most striking (See S. Neumann, *Die Deutschen Parteien* [Berlin, 1932], p. 134).

9. BA:Sammlung Schumacher:Gruppe VIII. No. 239.

10. *Die Junge Front. Führerblatt der Hitler-Jugend 2* (Easter 1929).

11. K. Heiden, *A History of National Socialism* (London, 1934), p. 331.

12. R. Kühnl, *Die Nationalsozialistische Linke, 1925–30* (Meisenheim, 1966), p. 200.

13. B. v. Schirach, *Revolution der Erziehung* (Munich, 1938), p. 45.

14. B. v. Schirach, *Die Hitler-Jugend: Idee und Gestalt* (Leipzig, 1934), pp. 77–78.

15. V. Schirach coined this slogan in 1932.

16. Bay. HSA:ASA:Akte NS/1541.

17. Ibid.

18. SAK:Abteilung 403:16754; BA:Akte NS 26/362.

19. Bay. HSA:ASA:Akte NS/1541.

20. Ibid.

21. At a rally in Brunswick on 16 March, the HJ expressed its protest along with the *Bund deutscher Pfadfinder*, one of the Free *Bündische* groups, the *völkisch* groups *Wehrwolf* and *Adler und Falken*, and the military-nationalist *Jungstahlhelm*, *Bismarckjugend*, and *Kyffhäuserjugend* (H. Bolm, *Hitlerjugend in einem Jahrzehnt* [Brunswick, 1938], p. 106). In Bremen, a resistance bloc was specially formed in which the HJ was joined by the Free *Bündische Deutscher Pfadfinderbund* and *Jungnationaler Bund*, *Wehrwolf*, *Adler und Falken*, *Bismarckjugend*, *Jungstahlhelm* and *Scharnhorstbund* (SAB:4/65 781/146 and Bay. HSA:ASA:Akte NS/1541). The *Jungstahlhelm*, *Geusen*, and *Adler und Falken* also marched with the HJ in Hamburg (*Hansiche Warte*, 22 March 1930). Finally, at a rally in Berlin, a letter of protest to von Hindenburg was signed by the HJ, the *Deutsche Akademische Gildenschaft*, *Deutsche Pfadfinderbund*, and *Jungnationale Bund* of the Free *Bündische* (SAK:Abt. 403:16754), the *völkisch Freischar Schill*, *Eidgenossen*, *Adler und Falken*, and *Wehrwolf* (Bay. HSA:ASA:Akte NS/1541), and the *Jungstahlhelm* and *Kyffhäuserjugend* (SAK:Abt. 403:16754). Inevitably, there were several incidents with the police, and in Munich on 22 March, the rally was actually forbidden to take place (Bay. HSA:ASA:Akte NS/1824).

22. See H. P. Bleuel and E. Klinnert, *Deutsche Studenten auf dem Weg im Dritten Reich* (Gütersloh, 1967).

23. Bay. HSA:ASA:Akte NS/1541.

24. Hence his statement at his trial in Nuremberg in 1946 that he was initially attracted to national socialism by socialism must be viewed with suspicion (Inter. Mil. Trib. Nuremberg, vol. XIV, p. 369).

25. Orientalischen Cigarreten-Compagnie, pub., *Männer im Dritten Reich* (Bremen, 1934), p. 28.

26. Bay. HSA:ASA:Akte NS/1541–44.

27. BA:Sammlung Schumacher:Gruppe VIII. No. 239. The law embodied what the HJ considered to be the most important reforms at stake. Eighteen points were enunciated, including medical supervision for all young workers under twenty years of age; a forty-hour week, Sundays free and three weeks' paid holiday per annum; the establishment of rest houses in the countryside and mountains to allow urban working youth to enjoy a more salubrious climate during weekends and holidays; the prohibition of child labour; adequate protection and safety devices for factory youth; the fixation and fair control of wages; the non-

employment of youth in dangerous jobs; and the creation of an apprentices' law with provisions enabling an apprentice who had completed his training to remain in the employment of his master and not, therefore, to be dismissed to the ranks of the unemployed when his training ended.

28. Bay. HSA:ASA:Akte NS/1541.

29. Reichsjugendführung der NSDAP, *HJ im Dienst* (Berlin, 1940), p. 10.

30. G. Kaufmann, *Das kommende Deutschland* (Berlin, 1940), p. 19. The author acknowledges that these clear-cut percentages and those which follow in the analysis do oversimplify a rather more complex sociological situation. Given the degree of economic and social mobility in Germany 1930–33, there was often no distinct division between the lower strata of German society. Hence, terms like "proletarian," "bourgeois," etc., may be used in a loose sense in some cases here. But we feel justified in employing both the percentages and class designations because they do indicate unmistakable general trends in the HJ membership.

31. Bay. HSA:ASA:Akte NS/1555.

32. BA:ZSg 3/2849.

33. Bay. HSA:ASA:Akte NS/1541.

34. *Hansiche Warte*, Sept. 1930. Twenty-four percent were factory workers; 17 percent agricultural workers; 21 percent manual labourers, 7 percent miners, 12 percent schoolboys; 10 percent shopworkers; and the remainder either unemployed or of indeterminate status.

35. SAK:Abt. 403:16754.

36. SAB:4/65 781/146.

37. BA:Akte NS 26/369.

38. W. Hofer, ed., *Der Nationalsozialismus: Dokumente, 1933–45* (Frankfurt, 1957), p. 23.

39. Kaufmann, *Das kommende,* p. 45.

40. A. Werner, "SA: 'Wehrverband,' 'Parteitruppe,' oder 'Revolutions-armee'? Studien zur Geschichte der SA und der NSDAP 1920–33," (Ph.D. diss., University of Erlangen, 1964).

41. Bay. HSA:ASA:Akte NS/1555; SAB:4/65 781/146; BA:Akte NS 26/339.

42. The principal press organs of the HJ were established in the late 1920s, and the production of literature by individual *Gaue* was expressly forbidden in September 1929 because it might give rise to internecine squabbling and upset the unity of the organisation (SAB:4/65 781/146). The example of the NSDAP, in which there were often several competing newspapers in one *Gau,* probably gave a salutary lesson. When the ban was later relaxed in the HJ, the Berlin branch was the first to produce its own official newspaper in early 1931, *Der Junge Sturmtruppe,* under the editorship of Joachim Walter (Bay. HSA:ASA:Akte NS/1555). On 10 December 1931, Walter was named in charge of the entire HJ press and in January 1932 took over the leadership of the new *NS-Jugend-Verlag,* of which Gotthard Ammerlahn became chief editor (BA:Akte NS 26/356/366). In January 1932 the *Hitler-Jugend-Zeitung* was retitled

Der Junge Nationalsozialist, which continued to be the main organ of the HJ while *Der Junge Sturmtruppe* was the recognised battle organ *(Kampfzeitung)* (BA:Akte NS 26/366). During his period of leadership (1931–32), von Renteln added the monthly *Die Deutsche Zukunft,* and the fortnightly *Das Jungvolk* for the junior section of the HJ, the *Deutsches Jungvolk* (BA:Sammlung Schumacher:Gruppe VIII. No. 239). On 1 January 1933, the *NS-Jugend-Verlag* was renamed *Deutsche Jugend-Verlag* (BA:Akte NS 26/337).

43. Bay. HSA:ASA:Akte NS/1541; SAB:4/65 1736/294; Bay. HSA:ASA:Akte NS/1776; BA:Sammlung Schumacher:Gruppe VIII. No. 239; Bay. HSA:ASA:Akte NS/1849. Schlageter was executed by the French occupation forces in 1923 for organising resistance to them in the Ruhr. He was regarded as a supreme patriot by many Germans, but especially by the National Socialists who elevated him to second place behind Horst Wessel in their pantheon of heroes.

44. See M. Broszat, *Der Nationalsozialismus* (Hannover, 1960).

45. Inter. Mil. Trib. Nuremberg, vols. V-XXIII.

Chapter 4

Ideological Dissension, 1926–33

       Contrary to the impression created by its propaganda before 1933, the HJ did not in fact present a wholly united front. Firstly, there were notable left-wing groups which occasioned a substantial degree of unrest at various times and ultimately seceded from the main organisational body during the *Kampfzeit*. This element of left-wing protest, of which the extreme social revolutionaries were the most important part, constituted the principal source of dissension within the HJ.

       Propaganda or mere silence also did much to conceal disturbance in HJ ranks which was not generated by ideological disagreement, but by the inevitable clashes which occur in the ordinary day-to-day administration of an expanding organisation. There was even disquiet felt in an increasing number of quarters about Gruber's leadership and this was to explode into the open at the end of 1931 (see chap. 6). The inside atmosphere of the HJ was strained in certain areas, and characteristic of this inner tension was not only the prolific turnover in leadership personnel (see chap. 6 and 7), but more significantly, the number of expulsions, dismissals, and reprimands that took place in the top echelons of the HJ prior to the *Machtergreifung*.

There were also, of course, tense relationships and altercations in the NSDAP, but whereas Gruber, as HJ leader until 1931, was often directly attacked by adversaries, Hitler's charisma was so swiftly and powerfully asserted over the movement after 1925 that only rarely was revolt oriented against him personally. Divergent groups invariably took great pains to pledge their loyalty to the Führer while making it clear that they merely sought to win Hitler over to their way of thinking. Consequently, factionalism in the NSDAP, in contradistinction to ideologically based socialist and communist movements, never carried a fundamental or enduring threat to the cohesion of the party. The NSDAP and Hitler's authority withstood all dissentient cliques, which simply disappeared after a brief and ineffective moment of activity. Charismatic leadership, represented by the god-like and mythical person of Hitler, the centrist symbol of all loyalist sentiment, gave the NSDAP a special immunity to discord. In left-wing parties, secessionists were a more serious factor because they invoked ideological argumentation as the source of their legitimacy; this constantly endangered the unity of parties which had no single leader whose lofty eminence was sufficient to forestall damaging splits.

The most noteworthy cases of upset in the HJ which do not appear to have been politically motivated involved high-ranking leaders. The following were dismissed from their posts for sheer incompetency: Ferdinand Hengst, a former Gauführer of Halle-Merseburg and then Reich sports leader in the Reichsleitung, in November 1929; Gauführer Helmut Quitzerau of East Prussia in 1930; Eberhard Müller, Gauführer of South Hannover-Brunswick in March 1930; Karl Heinz Bürger, leader of Gau Mecklenburg-Lübeck in early 1931; Gauführer Josef von Stebut of Hesse and Gauführer Fritz Steinert of Hesse-Nassau in June 1931; and Paul Otto, leader of Gau Württemberg in October 1931.[1] Curt Brieger was dismissed as Bundesführer (national leader) of the Deutsches Jungvolk on 5 February 1932 and as many other expellees were to do he took the path of vengeance against his erstwhile comrades.[2] Brieger became involved with the Jung-Ostara youth group, whose primary object was to harass the HJ as much as possible.[3] Brieger relished this task and incessantly attacked the HJ through the columns of the group's newspaper, Sig-Run, of which he was editor. Although HJ members were warned to beware of the activities of Jung-Ostara, it never developed as a danger. Finally, Heinz Schladitz, Gauführer of North West Saxony, received a severe reprimand instead of an expulsion order from Uschla (Untersuchungs-und Schlichtungsausschuss, Investigation and Settlement Committee) after he had alleged in November 1930 that a colleague, Herbert Peter, had been denigrating the work of Gruber and other leaders, thus causing some restlessness in the HJ.[4] Uschla considered the complaint unfounded and sternly warned Schladitz on 25 January 1931 not to bother it in future with "bagatelle," insinuating that the next time he would be dismissed.[5]

Apart from the personal shortcomings of those concerned, the atmosphere enveloping the course of the HJ before 1933 was laden with a nervous tension that was most unconducive to stability. This factor must be taken into account when assessing the background to these episodes of strife. The HJ was feeling its way and continually eliminating elements which failed to make good, especially at leadership level, where more effort and discipline were required. All in all, the HJ of the *Kampfzeit* was a tough school where even temporary failings were not readily tolerated.

The radical social revolutionaries of the HJ attracted most of the attention directed towards the disunity within the ranks before 1933. This stratum was favourably disposed more to the socialistic parts of the national socialist *Weltanschauung* than the nationalism, or they at least desired a more equitable synthesis of these two major components than was offered in either the HJ or NSDAP. The social revolutionaries were committed to the realisation of the economic aspects of the NSDAP programme, and believed wholeheartedly in the socialist catchwords of the movement. The HJ was the most prominent unit of national socialism dedicated to the principles of social and economic equality and it had followers who were determined to fight for them, even if this meant rebellion.

This left-wing influence was initially manifested in the NSDAP, however, centering around Gregor Strasser, that group's leading "socialist." During Hitler's imprisonment, Strasser, whose socialism was formulated by his war experiences at the front and a vague adherence to the ideas expressed in Oswald Spengler's *Preussentum und Sozialismus* (1919), had built up a powerful, radical, proletarian wing of the party in north Germany. In September 1925, a Working Association of the North West German *Gauleiter* of the NSDAP was formed at his instigation; its purpose was to coordinate organisation and propaganda, but also to promote socialism, and as such, constituted a challenge to the Munich group for control of the party, but not to Hitler himself.[6] The move threatened to divide the NSDAP into north German social revolutionaries and south German "pragmatists."

Josef Goebbels, at this time executive secretary of NSDAP *Gau* Ruhr, was a loyal Strasserite and edited the association's organ, *NS-Briefe*. It was Goebbels who suggested at a meeting of pro-Strasser *Gauleiters* in Hannover on 24 January 1926 that "the petty bourgeois Adolf Hitler" be expelled from the party.[7] The meeting was summoned to mobilise the northern wing of the NSDAP behind the socialist and communist-inspired campaign to have the estates and wealth of the deposed royal families expropriated by the republic, and also to introduce a new anticapitalist economic programme in place of the "reactionary" party programme of 1920. Hitler opposed the first proposal because he stood to lose the financial support which some former princes had given the NSDAP, and the latter proposal mainly because it might allow Strasser, the only figure comparable to himself in the movement, to exercise more and more influence. Only Robert Ley, NSDAP *Gauleiter* of Rhineland-South and later leader of the German Labour Front *(Deutsches Arbeitsfront),* and Gottfried Feder upheld Hitler's case at the meeting, which was tantamount to an open revolt of the NSDAP's socialists.[8]

Hitler, however, reasserted his authority at a counter-meeting in Bamberg (Bavaria) on 14 February 1926, at which the party's left wing was underrepresented. The meeting did much to persuade Goebbels that the future lay with Hitler, and he was finally won over during a visit to Munich in April 1926. Hitler increased the organisational centralisation of the NSDAP and the socialists' morale was destroyed, for the time being at any rate. The Strasser programme was abandoned, and for the next few years Hitler succeeded in maintaining the external unity of the NSDAP, though Otto Strasser continued to feel discontented and was to provoke a crisis in 1930.

The socialist and extreme social revolutionary elements proclaimed their existence in the HJ, and gave warning of further trouble to come in the 1930s. Berlin, a stronghold of left-wing opinion, first revealed this tendency in the HJ barely a few days after the foundation of the group in July 1926. A *Nationalsozialistische Deutsche Arbeiterjugend* (NSDAJ, National Socialist German Workers' Youth) with marked leftist propensities was set up that month, and obviously offered an immediate challenge to the HJ in the city. The background to the advent of the NSDAJ was the radical agitation of the north German wing of the NSDAP, and the bitter disillusionment with which the failure of the Strasser initiative had been received by many of the party's socialist-inclined members, of whom there were a few in Berlin. On 16 July, the *Völkischer Beobachter* warned NSDAP and HJ members not to join the breakaway youth association.[9] The threat was soon overcome but not entirely eradicated, chiefly because at this early stage the HJ's organisational machinery was unequal to the task. Therefore the problem occurred again in a more widespread form the following year.

The *Gaue* of Berlin-Brandenburg, Hamburg, Hannover-Brunswick, Anhalt-Saxony and the Ruhr detached themselves from the HJ and organised in the *Bund deutscher Arbeiterjugend* (League of German Workers' Youth, BDAJ). In Hannover-Brunswick, twenty to twenty-five former HJ members formed a BDAJ group in June 1927, and in Hamburg, Arnold Peters founded a branch. The *Sturmjugend* became the BDAJ's newspaper, and Gunther Orsoleck, hitherto HJ *Gauführer* of Berlin-Brandenburg, emerged as its *Bundesführer*.[10]

A declaration issued by the NSDAP *Reichsleitung* on 14 December 1927 informed all party *Gauleiters* that the only official party youth organisation was the HJ, and that the BDAJ, which had been accorded recognition by three NSDAP *Gaue,* was an enemy.[11] It would have considerably tarnished the party's image during this delicate period of reconstruction if the HJ's very existence, so soon after it had been established, had appeared to be threatened by a rebellious group. The NSDAP was understandably loath to have its internecine conflicts publicly advertised. Although the BDAJ, which may be regarded as the final effort of those northern elements sympathetic to Strasser and his leftist associates, stunted the growth of the HJ in the secessionist regions for a short period, it stagnated and never materialised into the serious menace it once promised. The BDAJ's appearance was nonetheless an indication of what lay ahead for the HJ from its more radically leftist membership, particularly in northern Germany, Berlin, and the heavily industrialised areas of the Ruhr-Rhineland, where anticapitalist, antibourgeois, and prosocialist ideas were strongest. Like many other disenchanted HJ leaders, Orsoleck went into active opposition; he later joined the *Reichsbanner* in 1930 and wrote anti-HJ/NSDAP articles for the SPD press.[12]

The NSDAP's left wing was quiet until the 1929 party rally, when a programme entitled, "Suggestions for the Revision of the Programme of the National Socialist German Workers' Party (NSDAP)," which had nineteen clauses and was signed "Social Revolutionary Left of the NSDAP," was distributed.[13] This was the overture to the Otto Strasser episode.

The background was Hitler's change of political tactics in 1928 and the belief of the party's left wing that socialism had consequently been betrayed. The Hitler-Hugenberg alliance, the financial support from heavy industry, and the onset of the economic depression with its concomitant widespread social despair only served to strengthen the socialists' conviction that the NSDAP was taking the wrong course and brought the voice of dissent within the movement actively to the surface. The National Bolshevik-inclined circle around the *Kampfverlag* had disseminated the socialist gospel in north and middle Germany, and following the disagreement with Hitler over support for a strike in Saxony in April 1930, Strasser led the revolt. Despite attempts by Hitler to pacify him, especially during an interview in Berlin's Hotel Sanssouci in May, there was no reconciliation.[14]

On 4 July 1930, Strasser publicly announced the crisis in an article in his *Der Nationalsozialist;* banner headlines screamed, "The Socialists leave the NSDAP." It represented the protest of the national socialist left. Among the twenty-five signatories to the proclamation were former HJ *Gauführer* Richard Schapke; a member of the HJ *Gauleitung* of Württemberg, Karl Baumann; and the one-time HJ *Gauführer* of East Prussia, Rolf Becker.[15] But there were no important NSDAP names attached. Gregor Strasser renounced solidarity with his brother in favour of loyalty to the Führer, at least for the present, while none of the NSDAP leaders who had attended the Hannover meeting in 1926 lent their support: Karl Kaufmann, *Gauleiter* of Hamburg; Bernhard Rust, *Gauleiter* of Hannover; Friedrich Hildebrandt, *Gauleiter* of Mecklenburg; Erich Koch, *Gauleiter* of East Prussia; and Graf Ernst zu Reventlow all remained distant from Strasser, and so did Kurt Gruber.[16]

On 8 July, Strasser created the Militant Society of Revolutionary National Socialists *(Kampfgemeinschaft Revolutionärer Nationalsozialisten,* KGRNS), which purported to stand for all anticapitalist socialist forces in the NSDAP, and was the precursor of the "Black Front." The KGRNS published the "Fourteen Theses of the German Revolution" outlining its policy, adopted the hammer and sword as its insignia (significantly, as the HJ had done since its foundation), and used the salutation, *Heil Deutschland!*[17] The crisis, which was not too surprising in view of the heterogeneous composition of the national socialist movement, had an immediate and direct impact on the social revolutionaries of the HJ in the form of individual defections, expulsions, and organisational disruptions.

Two of the most notable defectors to the Strasser circle in July 1930 were Karl Baumann and Artur Grosse, who was a former member of the HJ *Reichsleitung* and *Gau* education leader of Berlin-Brandenburg-Ostmark.[18] Both were eloquent about their reasons for deserting Hitler. Baumann declared: "The adhesion of numerous reactionary and capitalist-oriented personalities to the party, the alliance with Hugenberg, . . . indicate the openly anti-socialist and unrevolutionary character of the NSDAP."[19] Grosse published a statement attacking Hitler for having misled so many faithful colleagues, and above all, denouncing him for having betrayed German socialism:

> With complete seriousness and deep bitterness, we youths have experienced how German socialism, which is born first of all in the soul of a proletarian, has gone through an endless course of blood, iron, hunger, and slavery . . . to the slogans of unscrupulous demagogues as a means to an end of wild petty bourgeois types and revolutionary mercenaries.[20]

Apart from these voluntary withdrawals, the HJ took offensive action against certain individuals, especially in the leadership corps, who were known or suspected radical left-wingers. Just as Hitler instituted a purge of the NSDAP, the HJ also expelled a series of its leading members for political reasons. This was initially illustrated by the expulsion on 29 July 1930 of Alfred Bach, editor of the *Hitler-Jugend-Zeitung* and chief of the *Jungfront Verlag*, for "opposing the aims of the movement."[21] This referred to the fact that under Bach's direction, the HJZ had continued, as it had done since 1926, to pursue a decisive socialist line; in view of the shock the Strasser crisis gave the whole movement, those who controlled the propaganda system were even more liable to disciplinary measures.

Another expellee in August 1930 was Karl Kroll, a press officer in the *Reichsleitung* and leader of district Greater Plauen, who had allegedly quarreled repeatedly with his superiors. It is true that Kroll was sharply critical of Gruber's leadership, and he subsequently conducted a smear campaign against him from the pages of the left-wing press, accusing the *Reichsführer* of all kinds of faults and misdemeanours. But Kroll's later activities indicate fundamental political reasons for his dismissal. He organised the leftist *Jung-Ruhrvolk* youth group in Essen in conscious opposition to the HJ and succeeded in causing much trouble there for the HJ, including attempts to persuade high-ranking leaders to defect. In 1931, Kroll became involved with an extremist social revolutionary youth group and joined the Black Front.[22]

Even more consequential were the efforts of dissident leftists to establish rival organisations to the HJ. In the summer of 1930, Richard Schapke, aided by Grosse, founded a youth group within the KGRNS called the *Nationalsozialistische Arbeiter-und Bauernjugend* (NSABJ, National Socialist Workers' and Peasants' Youth), which was radically social revolutionary. The focal point of this group appeared in Western Germany, in *Gau* Westmark which embraced Westphalia and the Rhineland.[23] Karl Heinz David was named *Gauführer* of Berlin-Brandenburg. The NSABJ's aim was "to secure the inner and outer freedom and independence of the German people," "to bring about the realisation of German socialism," and to work for the enactment of youth legislation in industry, education, and the economy. This would appear to reflect an admirable degree of idealism, but a police report of June 1931 spoke the more mundane truth that the NSABJ activities consisted of giving theatre performances, singing, and excursions into the provinces to distribute propaganda material.[24] The NSABJ *Reichsführung* was headed by Schapke, who subsequently became editor of *Der Nationalsozialist* and emerged as one of the most important ideologues of the Black Front.[25]

Grosse also helped establish along with former HJ leaders Orsoleck and Rolf Becker the national revolutionary *Gruppe Sozialrevo-*

lutionärer Nationalisten (Group of Social Revolutionary Nationalists, GSRN) in 1930. The GSRN was nationalist but social revolutionary in the sense that it wanted a socialist reformation of the economy and it was passionately antinazi. Although it remained very small, with only 200 members and 2,000 readers of its literature, it has been (dubiously) claimed that the GSRN had one-third of the Berlin HJ under its influence by the end of 1932.[26]

Apart from its relative strength in West Germany, the left-wing exodus from national socialism in 1930 did not have a significant effect on the HJ in other parts of the Reich. A police report of 15 August 1930 stated that "only a few individual members have left the HJ for the NSABJ." No defections for the period 1930–32 were reported in Munich or in Bavaria as a whole. The Stuttgart police reported on 7 September 1930 that "the groups of the revolutionary national socialists around Otto Strasser have sought unsuccessfully to gain a foothold in the Württemberg HJ." A further report from Stuttgart on 14 October 1930 stated that ". . . the secession has hitherto made no impact. . . ." The situation in Württemberg remained well under control and Oskar Riegraf, deputy *Gauführer* there, was active in keeping the HJ in line. The Berlin police announced on 1 December 1930 that "the rupture of the KGRNS has exerted no influence on the shape of this HJ *Gau*," that is, Berlin-Brandenburg-Ostmark. A further report of 1 June 1931 affirmed that the NSABJ "has made no progress" in Berlin, having only twenty-five members, all organised in one branch, so that the report went on, "the development in Berlin has not moved from the initial position."[27] This was rather unexpected, taking into account the social revolutionary tendencies shown in the Berlin HJ in 1926 and 1927 and also Berlin's traditionally socialist political atmosphere.

In Schleswig-Holstein, a social revolutionary group was set up in October 1930 by Werner Hansen, a former leader in the Sports Section of the Flensburg HJ and a one-time leader of the *völkisch Grenzlandschutzbund Germania*. The group did not grow beyond twelve members, so the HJ in the province was hardly disturbed. The situation was more serious in Bremen, where in September 1931 Walter Burchhard, HJ *Gruppenführer* North; every member of *Gauleitung* Weser-Ems; the *Bezirksführer* of Bremen, Rolf Jaenisch; and the whole leadership of the Bremen city branch left the HJ. The reason was a clash of social revolutionaries and loyalists. Burchhard, who was very outspoken against Gruber's leadership, had close contact with Otto Strasser and was even suspected of having communist leanings.[28]

In July 1930, the NSDAP *Gauleiter* of Mecklenburg-Lübeck, Dr. Herbert Albrecht, declared that every national socialist organisation in his *Gau* "stands united behind Adolf Hitler. Only three Hitler youths, among them the HJ *Gauführer* . . . were expelled because of their lack of discipline."[29] Lothar Hilscher was the *Gauführer* concerned, having been leader of Mecklenburg-Lübeck from 1929 until his expulsion for leftist activities on 1 July 1930. He joined the Black Front and then the KPD, which made a lot of political capital from his association with the HJ.[30] The refractory HJ youths of this province were few in number, but they were articulate regarding their disillusionment. A proclamation issued by them in June 1930 read:

> We youths have followed the development of the Hitler Youth during the last months with full concern and gloomy foreboding, how in ever-increasing measure it developed into a party youth (group); . . . as long as the NSDAP and its leaders honestly sought to fight according to the twenty-five points of the national socialist programme . . . this situation was still bearable. Lately, however, the NSDAP has on "tactical grounds" taken courses which are in strict contrast to the national socialist *Weltanschauung*, and no longer afforded us youths the expectation that our revolutionary demands would ever be fulfilled. We declare that we will not participate in this continued betrayal of the twenty-five points of the national socialist revolution by the NSDAP, and from this very day, we leave the Hitler Youth. . . . We will now continue the fight as NSABJ . . . for the revolutionary realisation of the twenty-five points.[31]

The feelings expressed here illustrate the point that among a goodly percentage of social revolutionaries it was not the HJ as such with which they were in dispute, but rather the NSDAP and its deviation, as the radicals saw it, from the official party programme, above all from its social and economic objectives.

In addition to these outright secessions which clearly did not cause important problems for the HJ, a Roland Circle *(Roland-Kreis)* was formed in Bavaria in 1930 which believed that the HJ should take a more socialist direction, but preferred to work for this within the HJ itself. "It includes young socialist people who are in the Hitler Youth as leaders and junior leaders, and who have vowed to dedicate their whole strength for the attainment of the socialist idea." The Roland Circle was not thought of as a splinter group within the HJ, but rather as a body of left-wing protest which was nevertheless loyal to the basic principles of the organisation. On the other hand, it was opposed to the course being taken by Gruber. The *Reichsführer* was a sincere social revolutionary, but of a pronouncedly more conservative type than the angry young men of dissident and Roland Circle groups. The latter was determined that "the Hitler Youth must become, be and remain the organisation of the socialists for the workers and their rights." Although the names of the leaders implicated were not disclosed, a Munich police report singled out Emil Klein, *Gauführer* of Munich-Upper Bavaria, and two of his fellow Bavarian leaders, Oskar Neff and Max Dallinger, as probable Roland Circle members.[32]

Because it was a clandestine organisation, the actual extent of the Roland Circle's influence is difficult to ascertain, but its presence and activity provided the ideological and political scenery for the heated controversy that erupted in the Bavarian HJ in August 1932. Klein, now *Gebietsführer* of the Hochland region, was dismissed for having allegedly misappropriated 3,000 reichsmarks of HJ funds and for having a Jewish fiancée.[33] The episode, however, has all the hallmarks of a typical national socialist power struggle between two leaders with basically divergent ideological sympathies and personalities. Klein's successor was Kurt Haller von Hallerstein who as an aristocrat and a former NSS *(Nationalsozialisticher Schülerbund,* National Socialist Schoolboys' League) *Gauführer* of Württemberg did not share Klein's radical views.[34] Hallerstein wanted to free the HJ from party political influences and alter its functions to such an extent that its raison d'être would be dramatically changed. The HJ in Bavaria was torn asunder for a time by the rival factions; Klein and another left-wing Munich leader, Richard Etzel, organised an oppositional HJ group and a ferocious battle for control ensued. The outcome was a triumph for Klein's tenacity and strength of character rather than his socialist views: Hallerstein was removed from his post on 10 November 1932 and Klein reinstated in January 1933.[35]

Because the hard-core militant social revolutionaries in the HJ were vociferous, they earned a great amount of attention at the time which was totally disproportionate to their true strength. The Berlin police reported on 1 June 1931 that the NSABJ had a mere fifty members in the whole of Germany, intimating that the group had progressed hardly at all from the situation in July 1930 when it was described as existing "on paper only." Though the police probably underestimated the social revolutionary strength in the Ruhr-Rhineland area, it is nonetheless evident that the overwhelming mass of the 18,000 HJ members in mid-1931 remained loyal to Hitler.[36]

The Strasser crisis, however, was only the first, if the most important, to affect the unity of the HJ and NSDAP. The social revolutionary forces in the SA found their expression in a revolt in the spring of 1931 which had its genesis in the SA discontent of late 1930, mainly over the question of political tactics.[37] The activist elements of the SA leadership, including von Pfeffer, had never completely given up the putschist notions abandoned by Hitler after 1924. Dissatisfied with the NSDAP's apparent failure to become a major political force, they rebelled at a most inauspicious moment shortly before the Reichstag elections of September 1930. The growth of the SA from 1929–30 onwards as a mass movement amidst extensive unemployment posed a difficulty for the party's "legality" course, for it became impossible to contain the inherent revolutionary élan of many SA members. Furthermore, by 1930 the SA had come to regard itself as the strongest part of the movement and sought to assert that status. Considerable resentment against the NSDAP leadership culminated in the 1930 revolt which Hitler interpreted as an attempt by the SA to win more organisational independence at the expense of the NSDAP, and thus of himself. The result was the resignation of von Pfeffer on 29 August and a wave of ominous SA rumblings which the Führer quelled by force of his personality and charisma. On 2 September, Hitler assumed supreme command of the SA and persuaded his former associate, Ernst Röhm, who had spent some time in Bolivia as an army instructor, to take over as SA chief of staff in January 1931.

Walter Stennes, SA leader of east Germany based in Berlin, was not placated by the accommodation reached with Hitler. The NSDAP's legal path, even though boosted by the September elections, continued to anger activist SA groups, especially in eastern Germany, and social revolutionary radicals were repelled by the party's increasingly steadfast procapitalist direction.[38] Moreover, Röhm's reorganisation of the SA in early 1931, which deprived provincial SA leaders of much of their previous independence, was resented. The occasion for the Stennes insurrection was Hitler's refusal to forcefully resist a governmental emergency decree of 28 March 1931 designed to deescalate political rioting.[39] Stennes at first aligned with Strasser's KGRNS, and attracted a significant measure of support among the Berlin SA and other north and east German SA units.[40]

The initial SA unrest in late summer 1930 did not produce any overt insurrectionary activity in the Berlin HJ. The *Gauführer*, Robert Gadewoltz, made his position clear when he affirmed:

> The quarrels between the Berlin SA and the Berlin NSDAP do not interest the HJ. The Berlin HJ stands as a united group under my command! I do what I consider the proper thing according to the situation. The principle in every case is unswerving loyalty to Adolf Hitler and the NSDAP.[41]

But due to Gadewoltz's reputation as a radical social revolutionary in the HJ, the tense atmosphere pervading the whole movement in Berlin brought him increasingly under suspicion from the HJ leadership and in February 1931 he was dismissed. He was alleged to have been financially incompetent and extravagant, and to have bequeathed debts totalling 5,000 reichsmarks to his successor.[42] While there is no reason not to believe this, allegations of financial corruption were a well-established national socialist stratagem for getting rid of unwanted members. In Gadewoltz's case there is little doubt that his political attitudes primarily caused his downfall.

In April 1931, *Reichsführer* Gruber declared "with proud happiness" that "not one group of our Hitler Youth in the whole Reich was involved in the Stennes affair," and that "from the last Hitler youth to the *Reichsführer* himself, the Hitler Youth stands as a solid rock behind Adolf Hitler."[43] Gruber then travelled around Germany to determine the position more closely and on 30 June he reported that "the Stennes affair has hardly disturbed the HJ." The Berlin police corroborated this opinion when they estimated that altogether some 150 youths had left the HJ for the Stennes camp.[44] In the SA itself, the Stennes revolt had practically collapsed by the autumn of 1931.[45] Furthermore, the HJ was not affected by the storm caused by Lieutenant Richard Scheringer in 1931, which attracted only dissenting NSDAP, Strasser and *Reichswehr* people.[46] Rolf Becker, the former HJ leader who was earlier associated with Strasser and the GSRN, became a member of Scheringer's procommunist group.[47]

Isolated examples of disaffection among HJ members cropped up from time to time after the main revolutionary outbursts had taken place. One of the most serious was that of Wilhelm Kayser, who was expelled from the important post of *Gebietsführer* of the northwest region in April 1932. Kayser, a former *Reichsführer* of the radical *Kommunistische Arbeiterjugend* (see chap. 5), had been insubordinate to the HJ *Reichsführung*, but more interestingly, he had also disagreed over party policy with the area's NSDAP *Gauleiter*, Josef Grohé, and the local NSDAP Reichstag deputy, Schaller. Above all, Kayser had encountered strong opposition to his radically socialist and left-wing standpoint, which was decisive in causing his expulsion. Kayser alleged the HJ had betrayed its basic principles and "no longer embodied what we have long fought for." He held a public meeting in Cologne to voice his disappointment and succeeded in winning over a large number of HJ members to his side. Kayser subsequently joined the leftist *Schwarze Jungmannschaft,* and later set up the Revolutionary National Socialist Workers' Youth *(Revolutionäre Nationalsozialistische Arbeiterjugend).* His revolt stimulated a great deal of instability in the Rhineland HJ at this time; for example, the independent *Rheinische Zeitung* published a declaration by ten anonymous HJ leaders supporting Kayser against the "boss-controlled NSDAP," and calling on members to leave the HJ. Some time elapsed before Kayser's highly capable successor, Hartmann Lauterbacher, was able to bring the situation under control.[48]

A little earlier, in January 1932, friction appeared between the leftist-inclined HJ *Gauführer* of Baden, Felix Wankel, and the strictly orthodox NSDAP *Gauleiter* there, Robert Wagner. The situation stead-ily deteriorated until in October 1932 Wankel was expelled for alleg-edly leading the HJ against Hitler. Wankel's failure to heed the party line cost him his position. Following the example of previous HJ expellees, Wankel went into active opposition, and directed attacks on the HJ and NSDAP in the newspaper *Alemannische Grenzland-nachrichten;* he joined the SPD and continued his propaganda war from the SPD press.[49]

The last concerted social revolutionary attempt to create havoc in the HJ occurred at the end of 1932 when Heinz Gruber, a former member of the Berlin HJ, founded the radical *Schwarze Jungmann-schaft* (of which Kayser was the most notable recruit).[50] The establish-ment of this group was a repercussion of a crisis which rocked the NSDAP at this time, culminating in the resignation of Gregor Strasser from his party posts in early December. Strasser's move was a signal for another wave of defection from the remaining socialists in the movement. Gruber's organisation became closely connected with the Black Front and managed to entice a relatively high number of HJ youths in Berlin to its ranks.[51] Social revolutionaries also forsook the HJ in Königsberg; they founded the procommunist, revolutionary *Der Kampfbund* but it did not make much headway, even in East Prussia.[52]

As a result of these defections, the HJ made another careful appraisal of the reliability of its leadership, and consequently some well-known figures were abruptly expelled. This was particularly so in Berlin, where the loyalty of the whole HJ leadership and those recently associated with it was called seriously in question by this latest leftist explosion. Hence, Elmar Warning, a former *Gebietsführer* of Berlin-Brandenburg, was dismissed as HJ chief of staff in December, and Joachim Walter, HJ *Gauführer* of Berlin from February to No-vember 1931, lost his position as leader of the *NS-Jugend-Verlag* in January 1933. Among other radicals who are known to have fallen on account of their politics was Emil Georg Schäfer, press warden of the NS Youth Factory Cell Organisation (NSJBO), who was a Strasser agent. Indeed, the HJ leadership showed how preoccupied it was with left-wing activity when it warned all HJ members to beware of ap-proaches by the Black Front, a warning that was ironically repeated as late as November 1933.[53]

Taken in general perspective, the social revolutionary ructions in the HJ during the *Kampfzeit* were not serious and did not apprecia-bly hinder its development. The HJ retained its social revolutionary character first given to it by Kurt Gruber throughout the pre-1933 period, but these organisational breakaways represented the work of no more than a hard core of militant and fanatical leftist members of the HJ. The fundamentally important reason for the weakness and incohesion of the HJ's extreme left was that, with the exception of Bavaria, the HJ was more powerful in lightly industrialised parts of Germany where radical socialist and extreme social revolutionary ideas generally failed to make an impact. The nationalist ethic and a moderate social revolutionary ideology were the stringent rules in regions like Hesse-Nassau, Rheinpfalz, Hannover-Brunswick, East Prussia, and Pomerania.

Therefore the HJ extremists were confined on the whole to those areas where there was a tradition of left-wing radicalism which affected even those who joined the HJ and NSDAP. Severe economic distress in the early 1920s and 1930s greatly stimulated the acceptance of socialist and communist ideas in places such as Berlin, Ruhr-Rhineland, Westphalia and industrialised north and middle Germany, and it was here that the HJ faced opposition from its diehard left-wingers. Significantly, the HJ remained weakest in these districts, with the exception of Saxony and Thuringia, before 1933. The extremists consequently had only a limited audience to which they could appeal for support, and because of their failure to secure the necessary base for revolutionary action, their rebellion proved abortive. In the national socialist movement as a whole, the internal threat from the left lingered on until ideas of a social revolution were destroyed once and for all by Hitler's ruthless "Night of the Long Knives" on 30 June 1934.

Notes: Chapter 4

1. BDC:F. Hengst file; SAB:4/65 1685/282; BA:Akte NS 26/342; Bay. HSA:ASA:Akte NS/1555; BA:Akte NS 26/364.

2. BDC:C. Brieger file. The *Deutsche Jungmannschaft, Bund der Tatjugend* (German Junior Section, Association of Activist Youth) was founded in 1929 by the HJ as an independent youth group in theory, but in practice as a preparatory organisation for the younger adherents of the HJ (BA:Akte NS 26/372). Hence, the leadership of the new group was specially chosen by the HJ to give its members instruction in national socialist doctrine. The first *Bundesführer* was the Saxon HJ leader, Hans Schlupper, who was replaced by Franz Schnaedter at the end of 1929. The *Jungmannschaft* became principally centered in Saxony and Thuringia (BA:Akte NS 26/370), and following an alliance with some *völkisch* groups in Austria, it was renamed the *Deutsches Jungvolk, Bund der Tatjugend* on 18 August 1930 (H. Volz, *Daten der Geschichte der NSDAP* [Berlin, 1943], p. 133). Brieger became the new leader, but he was succeeded by Bun Geissler in June 1932 (Bay. HSA:ASA/MINN/71799). The DJ's membership remained small and was only 7,580 in March 1932 (SAB:4/65 781/146).

3. Bay. HSA:ASA:Akte NS/1849.

4. BA:Akte NS 26/372. This special organisation was originally founded in 1925, but when shown to be incapable of halting the northern radicals, it fell into disuse. Hitler reestablished it in 1926 as part of his efforts to increase the centralisation and also to tighten his personal authority in the NSDAP. Designed to supervise the discipline of the party membership, *Uschla* became in effect a party court with power to expel, fine, suspend, and reprimand errant members. Bruno Heinemann led *Uschla* 1926–28 and Major Walter Buch, an old friend of the Führer, took over when the party was reorganised in late 1928 (see VB:4 Sept. 1926).

5. BDC:H. Schladitz file.

6. G. Schildt, "Die Arbeitsgemeinschaft Nord-West," (Ph.D. diss., University of Freiburg, 1964).

7. K. O. Paetel, *Versuchung oder Chance?* (Berlin, 1965), p. 209.

8. A. Bullock, *Hitler: A Study in Tyranny* (London, 1962), p. 137.

9. Bay. HSA:ASA:Akte NS/1804.

10. H. Bolm, *Hitler-Jugend in einem Jahrzehnt* (Brunswick, 1938), p. 52–53; A. Krebs, *Tendenzen und Gestalten der NSDAP* (Stuttgart, 1959), pp. 50–51; BA:Sammlung Schumacher:Gruppe VIII. No. 239.

11. BA:Sammlung Schumacher:Gruppe VIII. No. 239.

12. R. Kühnl, *Die Nationalsozialistische Linke 1925–30* (Meisenheim, 1966), p. 200. The *Reichsbanner Schwarz-Rot-Gold* was established in 1924 as the paramilitary organisation of all republican forces in Germany, though in time it became in practice an organisation very much under the control of the SPD (see K. Rohe, *Das Reichsbanner Schwarz-Rot-Gold* [Düsseldorf, 1966]).

13. Paetel, *Versuchung*, p. 160.

14. Bullock, *Hitler*, p. 157. Following his victory over the North German socialists, Hitler consented to the establishment of the *Kampfverlag* in March 1926 as the propaganda centre of the NSDAP in northern Germany. The political orientation of the KV was intensely nationalist, anticapitalist, and pro-Russian, and by 1930 it was recognisably National Bolshevik and not National Socialist in outlook. The KV leadership, headed by Otto Strasser, refused to move to the right with Hitler after 1928, and in 1930 the Führer was compelled to dissolve the KV as part of his purge campaign against the party's socialists.

15. Kühnl, *Nationalsozialistiche Linke*, p. 252; LASH:Abt. 309:Regierung Schleswig:No. 22576.

16. Paetel, *Versuchung*, p. 211.

17. LASH:Abt. 309:Regierung Schleswig:No. 22576; BA:Sammlung Schumacher:Gruppe VIII. No. 239; Paetel, *Versuchung*, p. 211.

18. Bay. HSA:ASA:Akte NS/1508; BDC:A. Grosse file.

19. Bay. HSA:ASA:Akte NS/1508.

20. Kühnl, *Nationalsozialistiche Linke*, p. 376.

21. SAB:4/65 781/146; BDC:A. Bach file.

22. SAB:4/65 1682/281; Bay. HSA:ASA:Akte NS/1555; BDC:K. Kroll file. Kroll alleged, among other things, that Gruber would not speak at HJ meetings unless he received a full fee, that he was a heavy drinker, and a generally dishonest and unworthy character. Kroll even threatened in a letter to the HJ *Reichsleitung* on 17 November 1930 to come to Plauen and inflict serious bodily harm on Gruber. Kroll's vindictive character made him a considerable nuisance and the *Reichsleitung* at one time thought of taking him to court because of his incessant anti-Gruber campaign (Bay. HSA:ASA:Akte NS/1555).

23. LASH:Abt. 309:Regierung Schleswig:No. 22576. In September 1931, this *Gau* was organised in five groups: Essen, led by Oskar Bergien; Wesel, by Walter Straatmann; Dorsten, by Friedrich Brück; Düsseldorf, by Heinrich Klöpper, another HJ expellee (in July 1931); and Cologne, by Karl Naske.

24. Ibid.

25. BDC:R. Schapke file; Kühnl, *Nationalsozialistiche Linke*, p. 249; K. P. Tauber, *Beyond Eagle and Swastika: German Nationalism since 1945* (Middletown, Conn., 1967), p. 1030. Other members of the national leadership included Friedrich Kopp, Grosse, and Alfred Franke-Gricksch (SAB:4/65 1682/281).

26. Paetel, *Versuchung,* p. 159; O. E. Schüddekopf, *Linke Leute von Rechts* (Stuttgart, 1960), p. 335. In early 1932, Grosse became a member of the newly established *Deutsche Sozialistische Kampfbewegung* (German Socialist Fighting Movement), which attracted disgruntled NSDAP, KPD, and SPD members; it aimed at an anticapitalist economic order, and a pro-Russian foreign policy, but it did not obtain support from the HJ (Bay. HSA:ASA:Akte NS/1541).

27. SAB:4/65 1682/281; Bay. HSA:ASA:Akte NS/1834; SAB:4/65 1760/301; SAB:4/65 781/146; LASH:Abt. 309:Regierung Schleswig:No. 22576.

28. LASH:Abt. 309:Regierung Schleswig:No. 22576; SAB:II 137 CVIII. HJ Bremen; BDC:W. Burchard file.

29. BA:Sammlung Schumacher:Gruppe VII. No. 205.

30. BDC:L. Hilscher file.

31. BA:Sammlung Schumacher:Gruppe VII. No. 205.

32. Bay. HSA:ASA:Akte NS/1542; *Die Kommenden,* 8 August 1930.

33. Bay. HSA:ASA:Akte NS/1544; BDC:E. Klein file.

34. BA:Akte NS/364. The NSS was officially established on 17 November 1929 *(Das Deutsche Führerlexikon 1934–35* [Munich, 1934]) by Adrian von Renteln, who became *Reichsführer* (BDC:A. v. Renteln file). The NSS was organisationally independent of the HJ and appealed mainly to middle-class youths in secondary schools. Thus, tension soon existed between the bourgeois NSS and the proletarian HJ, though the HJ's attempts to incorporate the other group into its organisation were also a factor in this. There was a considerable interchange of leadership personnel between the HJ and the NSS, and it was not uncommon for high-ranking HJ leaders to hold a similar rank in the NSS simultaneously (Bay. HSA:ASA:Akte NS/1542). The NSS's strength lay mainly in north and middle Germany, and in March 1932 it had 16,623 members (Bay. HSA:ASA:Akte NS/1555). The NSS was disbanded in the summer of 1933.

35. Bay. HSA:ASA:Akte NS/1541; BDC:K. Haller v. Hallerstein file; BA:Akte NS 26/337.

36. LASH:Abt. 309:Regierung Schleswig:No. 22576; SAB:4/65 1682/281; BA:Sammlung Schumacher:Gruppe VIII. No. 239.

37. See A. Werner, "SA: 'Wehrverband,' 'Parteitruppe,' oder 'Revolutionsarmee'? Studien zur Geschichte der SA und der NSDAP 1920–33," (Ph.D. diss., University of Erlangen, 1964).

38. Schüddekopf, *Linke Leute von Rechts,* p. 322.

39. Bullock, *Hitler,* p. 168.

40. Schüddekopf, *Linke Leute von Rechts,* p. 321; Paetel, *Versuchung,* p. 221.

41. BA:Akte NS/26/362.

42. Ibid.; SAB:4/65 1686/283.

43. Bay. HSA:ASA:Akte NS/1544.

44. BA:Akte NS 26/339.

45. Schüddekopf, *Linke Leute von Rechts,* p. 322.

46. Paetel, *Versuchung,* p. 176. Scheringer was the central figure in the famous *Reichswehr* trial in Leipzig's *Reichsgericht,* 23 September–4 October 1930, along with two other officers, Leutnant Hans Ludin and Oberleutnant Hans Wendt. The episode showed how deeply national socialism had infiltrated the officer corps, and considerable public controversy was aroused. During his subsequent imprisonment in Gollnow Prison, Mecklenburg, Scheringer sensationally denounced Hitler for having betrayed the "revolution," and became a fanatical convert to communism, joining the KPD on 18 March 1931. Wendt joined the Black Front, and only Ludin remained loyal to Hitler (see Schüddekopf, *Linke Leute von Rechts,* p. 294; F. L. Carsten, *Reichswehr and Politics* [Oxford, 1966], p. 319; and W. L. Shirer, *The Rise and Fall of the Third Reich* [London, 1960], p. 141).

47. Schüddekopf, *Linke Leute von Rechts,* p. 294.

48. Bay. HSA:ASA:Akte NS/1544; Bay. HSA:ASA:Akte NS/1555; BDC: W. Kayser file; BA:Sammlung Schumacher:Gruppe VIII. No. 239.

49. BA:Akte NS 26/340; BDC:F. Wankel file; BA:Akte NS 26/339.

50. H. C. Brandenburg, *Die Geschichte der HJ* (Cologne, 1968), p. 83. Heinz Gruber was no relation to Kurt Gruber.

51. BA:ZSg 3/103.

52. Schüddekopf, *Linke Leute von Rechts,* p. 381.

53. BA:ZSg 3/103; BA:Akte NS 26/362; BDC:J. Walter file.

Chapter 5

The Hitler Youth and the Youth Movement in the Weimar Republic

The *Bündische* Youth

As related earlier, one of the most outstanding aspects of the post-1918 era in Germany was the development of the youth movement. Amidst the institutional chaos of that time, there followed a mushroom growth of every possible form of group: political, paramilitary, nationalist, democratic, *völkisch,* confessional, sports, and others. Included among these were organisations of the youth movement proper, from 1923 onwards known as the *Bündische* Youth.

The paramount feature of the *Bündische* Youth was its incohesiveness; within it were a variegated multitude of associations, each profoundly jealous of its own individualism and independence. Three main groupings, however, emerged in the period before 1933: the Free *Bündische,* whose affiliates were the most authentic heirs of the *Wandervogel;* the *völkisch*-nationalist; and the nationalist-military. Each of these types will be examined separately later, but the *Bündische* Youth movement as a whole can be usefully compared with the Hitler Youth to ascertain their differences in outlook and whether the *Bündische* Youth had any influence on the evolution and content of the HJ.

In the ideological sphere, it is clear that a substantial section, perhaps even a majority of the *Bündische* Youth, especially the *völkisch*-nationalist bloc, shared or appeared to share many of the important ideas which formed an integral part of national socialist ideology. There is one basic reason why these ideas became popular: the *Bündische* Youth was a revolutionary movement, at least in the sense that it rejected parliamentary democracy and the Weimar Republic, and in place of the latter, sought a new Reich. Extensive circles of *Bündische* Youth were anxious to achieve a new type of society which was to enshrine concepts such as *Volksgemeinschaft,* a "leader and followers," a "greater Germany," and the *Führerprinzip,* all of which were the same concepts venerated by the HJ and the entire national socialist movement. It would be erroneous to deduce, however, that the ideology of *Bündische* Youth was exactly analogous to national socialism, or that even its ultimate political direction was similar to that of the HJ and the NSDAP. Some qualification is necessary.

Unlike the HJ, the *Bündische* Youth never committed itself wholeheartedly to serious politics in the 1920s, and only began to evince an active interest from 1929–30 onwards as a result of the confusion into which the political order was thrown by the succession of crises in the early 1930s. From the very beginning, the HJ was devoted to one political doctrine and was resolved to help establish its complete mastery over Germany. Once the *Bündische* Youth decided to participate in politics, it was notoriously hesitant and refrained from giving full support to any one party or political programme. The *Bündische* leadership was apparently so overwhelmed by contemporary events that all capacity for initiative and forceful endeavour was drained out of it. This attitude was predictably repellent to the all-action HJ, which rarely missed an opportunity to scathingly attack the *Bündische* Youth's vacillation. In 1930, for example, HJ leader Franz Schnaedter remarked deprecatingly on the *Bündische* Youth's lack of "political action and will to fight."[1]

The one real effort of the *Bündische* Youth to take decisive political action came in July 1930 when several leading groups of the Free *Bündische* segment headed by the *Deutsche Freischar* helped to set up the German State Party (DSP).[2] The foremost concern of the new DSP was to stress that its loyalty was owed to the state alone and that it was not susceptible to the pressures of interest groups. This standpoint obviously appealed to some above-party *Bündische* groups; in addition, the *Jungnationaler Bund* supported the new Conservative Peoples' party (KVP).[3] But both parties failed dismally in the Reichstag elections a few months later, and this signified the end of any worthwhile political advance from the *Bündische* Youth, except for the unsuccessful support given to General Kurt von Schleicher's government in late 1932 by the *Deutsche Freischar* and a few other groups.

On the whole, therefore, the *Bündische* Youth played its politics from a safe distance during the critical final years of the republic. Its dilettantism may be partly explained by the lingering romanticism inherent in many sections of the *Bündische* Youth, which prevented them from tackling problems seriously and making hard-headed decisions, while the HJ's earnest and down-to-earth attitude demanded its active political involvement. The *Bündische* Youth was too fond of intellectual discourse for its own sake, which incapacitated it when definite decisions had to be taken. In consequence, the *Bündische* Youth, like the *Wandervogel* before 1914, never possessed a coherent political programme of reform; it wanted to change society, but proved incapable of offering a constructive alternative, or of supplying the impetus to execute any of its ideas.

Apparent similarities between aspects of *Bündische* and national socialist ideology do not automatically imply that both gave the same meaning or put the same interpretation on these ideas. Critics of the *Bündische* Youth who do not make allowance for differences in this respect contend that because some *Bündische* Youth theses also constituted part of national socialist doctrine, the former must bear some of the responsibility for the rise and final victory of the NSDAP in 1933. *Bündische* Youth apologists argue that these ideas were interpreted in a distinct manner in the *Bündische* Youth, and that ideological correlation with national socialism is sophistical and largely irrelevant.

The truth seems to be that the *Bündische* Youth did see these ideas differently; for example, the notion of a "new Reich" was certainly widely prevalent in *Bündische* circles, but these circles did not envisage or desire the Third Reich of national socialism. The *Bündische* concept of a new Reich was not clear, and represented only a vague longing for a future state which would replace the Weimar Republic. This vagueness was in harmony with the pseudo-romantic orientation of the *Bündische* Youth. Its concept of a *Volksgemeinschaft* was circumscribed by its sociological elitism, confined to a bourgeois community, and did not embrace the comprehensive nation as planned by the HJ. Likewise, though many *Bündische* groups incorporated the *Führerprinzip* in their organisation, this was never emphasised in such an authoritarian fashion as in the HJ. Anti-Semitism, though particularly rampant among the *volkisch*-nationalists, was never expressed in quite the virulent way employed by the HJ or NSDAP.

It is fair to say that the *Bündische* Youth did not wilfully pave the victory path of Hitler, though its ideas may have allowed its youths to reconcile themselves all the more readily to the Third Reich when it did emerge. Its rejection of the republic and the democratic system created a political vacuum which in the long run made *Bündische* Youth liable to national socialist infiltration, but since it did not actively promote national socialism, the responsibility of *Bündische* Youth can only be indirect and partial. To affirm otherwise would come close to putting *Bündische* Youth on an equal footing with the HJ, which would be indefensible. The HJ was a unique political youth organisation, and had no peer in the *Bündische* Youth.

The *Bündische* Youth repudiated the fanaticism of the HJ and national socialism and abhorred the HJ's renunciation of the elitist ethic in favour of a mass movement status. Though the HJ claimed to include the elite of German youth, it did not wish to produce a sociologically or numerically restricted elite. No less was the scorn shown by the *Bündische* Youth for the HJ's unreserved political commitment. Finally, the only *Bündische* groups which had any valid claim to an ideological rapport with the HJ were the *völkisch*-nationalists. The ideological resemblance between the *Bündische* Youth and the HJ was in fact more apparent than real. But the divergencies between both movements were not simply pertinent to this sphere.

The sociological composition of the *Bündische* Youth differed strikingly from that of the HJ. The former was almost totally a preserve of middle-class secondary schoolboys, thus perpetuating the pattern set by the *Wandervogel,* while on average only 12 per cent of HJ members came from this group (see chap. 3). The exclusiveness of the *Bündische* Youth was a constant source of irritation to the HJ, which accused the former of deliberately fostering divisions and class interests among German youth. Also, the HJ insisted that the *Volksgemeinschaft* should submerge the individual and his independence for the common good, whereas the *Bündische* Youth stressed the *Bund* (group) as the central experience of its followers.

Though nationalism was more pronounced in the *Bündische* Youth than in the *Wandervogel,* it was more moderate there than in the HJ. This was consistent in a way with the equanimity generally displayed by the *Bündische* Youth, in contrast to the dynamic temperament of the HJ. With the exception of the nationalist-military and *völkisch*-nationalist associations, the *Bündische* Youth did not countenance militarism, unlike the young soldiers of the HJ and their cult of the heroic.

To a certain extent, the HJ adopted some of the exterior paraphernalia of the *Bündische* Youth, as it did also from the *Wandervogel.* The national socialist movement began early to borrow practices and ideas from its rivals and opponents, using them on an enlarged scale for its own purposes and usually claiming the credit for thinking of them in the first place. Thus, the national socialists copied many of the agitational methods originally developed by the communists, including the use of mass demonstrations and physical violence, though the communists never organised anything in Germany to compare with the NSDAP Nuremberg rallies of the 1930s. Hitler himself frequently showed a willingness to learn from others what he believed would be helpful to his course.

Although the ideological content and sociological complexion of the *Wandervogel* and HJ revealed a profound dissimilarity, the HJ took over some external forms and symbols like *Wandervogel* songs and folk customs.[4] In its organisational structure, the HJ copied designations applied by the *Wandervogel*, for example, *Ortsgruppe* and *Gau*. In common with other groups, the HJ observed the use of the familiar *Du* form in verbal communication between the leadership and ordinary membership, which had been established as a tradition in the youth movement by the *Wandervogel*.[5]

Furthermore, the HJ uniform and insignia, excepting the more conspicuous national socialist characteristics like swastikas and flags, resembled those of many *Bündische* groups. Some of the names given to organisational units in the HJ were patently taken from the *Bündische* Youth, including the terms *Gruppe, Kamaradschaft, Schar, Bann,* and *Stamm*. The idea of having a girls' section in the HJ, the *Bund Deutscher Mädel* (BDM), and a junior boy's section, the *Deutsches Jungvolk* (DJ), had *Bündische* origins.[6]

The work forms of both movements showed elements in common. The HJ *Heimabend* was standard practice in the *Bündische* Youth, as were marches, camps, excursions, and field exercises. However, in the HJ, especially after 1933, these practices were used as a means for political instruction, or were generally endowed with a political connotation they did not have in the *Bündische* Youth, and were better organised and larger than in the *Bündische* Youth. Two specific ideas which were applied extensively by the HJ in the Third Reich were voluntary labour service *(Arbeitsdienst),* introduced in the youth movement by the *Deutsche Freischar* in 1931, and land service *(Landdienst),* begun by the *Artamanen* movement in 1924.[7]

After 1933 the similarities between the HJ and the *Bündische* Youth were even fewer. The HJ became a bastion of Hitler's state, fulfilling educational and political tasks among German youth; the *Bündische* Youth had been in revolt against the state before 1933, and some *Bündische* factions continued to work underground against the national socialist regime.[8] Although the *Bündische* Youth was an important educational agency prior to 1933, it never possessed the executive power or the scope of the post-1933 HJ. The *Bündische* Youth sought to influence the development of an individual's character; the HJ taught that the state was everything and the individual nothing.

Nor did the *Bündische* Youth compare with the huge, highly systemised organisation that the HJ eventually became. This meant, for example, that an individual had no free selection when he wanted to join a particular group within the HJ. He was simply told which group to join, unlike the unrestricted choice available in the *Bündische* Youth. Admittedly, however, liberty of choice was not feasible in an organisation as large as the post-1933 HJ; the result would have been organisational chaos. The post-1933 HJ leadership also lacked the spontaneous individualism of their counterparts in the *Bündische* Youth, having been trained methodically in leadership schools; hence, the HJ leader took on the appearance of an executive officer rather than of a youth leader in the traditionalist sense. Additionally, all HJ leaders were appointed from above, while the *Bündische* leader was always elected democratically by his group.

It was without doubt the ideological, political, and sociological differences between the *Bündische* Youth and the HJ, both before and after 1933, which made them irreconcilable enemies. This was also ineluctable because both were competitors in the same market for the support of German youth, especially after 1931 when the HJ steered itself more towards middle-class youth. Von Schirach expressed the anger and antipathy felt for the *Bündische* Youth by the HJ. He had no benign words for it as he had for the *Wandervogel,* and he regarded the *Bündische* Youth as a "pale imitation" of the latter. "What was right until 1 August 1914 was false after 9 November 1918," he remarked, and described the 1918–33 period of the youth movement in Germany as "a long, grey time."[9]

Von Shirach's judgement is obviously tendentious, of course, but it does serve to illustrate the gulf felt by the HJ to separate it from the *Bündische* Youth in general. Apart from adopting some externals, the HJ had indeed little in common with the *Bündische* Youth. Both groups had essentially conflicting ideas of the problems confronting the Weimar Republic and of the action required to solve these problems. More importantly, both had distinct ideas on what the intrinsic role of a youth association should be in dealing with the issues which affected it.

Free Bündische *Youth*

This grouping consisted mainly of boy scout organisations and groups which were descended from the pre-1914 *Wandervogel* and post-1918 *Freideutsche Jugend*.[10] Despite a membership of only 12,000 in 1930, the boy scouts remained a recognisable entity within the youth movement, but their internationalist, liberal outlook aroused the antagonism of the HJ, so that there was rarely a basis of cooperation between the two sides.[11] In 1930, the HJ singled out the *Deutscher Pfadfinderbund* for special consideration when it coarsely assailed that group's internationalism and affiliations with the British scout movement: "We publicly declare that this youth does not embody the Germany of the future. We intend to mount the sharpest attack against this slimy and dishonest betrayal of German youth."[12] Because of the boy scouts' numerical insignificance, the HJ did not harbour any real apprehension of them, and was content to deliver an occasional diatribe against their activities. After 1933, the HJ reaped the benefit of the scouts' work when it took over their excellent range of foreign contacts, including those in Britain.

The groups of the other section of the Free *Bündische* Youth represented approximately 30,000 members prior to 1933.[13] They thought of themselves as being the quintessence of *Bündische* Youth, and in view of the vast difference between the HJ and the *Bündische* Youth, it was to be expected that direct contact between them would be reduced to a bare minimum. Moreover, because these groups personified the ideals of the *Bündische* Youth, the HJ's offensive against them was especially vitriolic; in fact, the HJ came to regard them as the most dangerous enemies of German youth besides the communists. These groups reciprocated with a supercilious contempt which only incensed the HJ even more.

The most representative of these groups, the *Deutsche Freischar,* nonetheless, had a wary respect at times for the HJ which was shown as early as 1929. The *Deutsche Freischar* was concerned that its own lack of political decisiveness could be inimical to its interests, and it felt some rethinking was required, "otherwise, the Hitler Youth with its revolutionary political élan will win over our young idealistic activists."[14] Very few of this group's members, however, did join the HJ before 1933. Von Schirach, with tongue firmly in cheek, recently recorded his appreciation of the *Deutsche Freischar's* development of activities for youth: "Their excursions, camps, songs, and sport were perfect forms of youth culture."[15]

At the end of 1929, Erich Kulke, *Bundesführer* of the *Deutscher Wandervogel,* made a tentative move to establish contact with a view to eventual cooperation with the HJ. But the leader of the HJ Border Land Office, Rudolf Schmidt, rejected the proposal in his reply of 13 November 1929, alleging that Kulke's group had *Reichsbanner* men in its ranks.[16] There was only one occasion when the HJ and the Free *Bündische* groups forgot their differences to join together in concerted action, and that was for the anti-Young Plan campaign in early 1930. Almost immediately afterwards, relations returned to their cold normalcy. The HJ was first to resume the attack in April 1930 when it bitterly denounced the *Jungnationaler Bund* for making critical remarks about national socialism. The *Jungnationaler Bund* had also stated categorically: "We have no yearning for Hitler and we will take no oath on his banner. . . ."[17] The HJ at once ordered all connections to be severed with this group.[18] Though Free *Bündische* organisations were sometimes present thereafter at HJ meetings and discussion evenings, there was no further cooperation between them. Ideological attitudes were too deeply apart for either side to compromise, and the Free *Bündische* bloc offered stout resistance to the HJ's *Gleichschaltung* programme in 1933.

Völkisch-*Nationalist Youth*

Völkisch nationalism, which had first appeared in Germany in the late nineteenth century, was dedicated to the idea of the German *Volkstum* and the creation of a *völkisch* state. The movement was obsessed with racial hygiene and the fictitious purity of the German race; it was committed to racist nationalism and its corollary, anti-Semitism, and generally interpreted concepts such as *Führerstaat* and a Third Reich as the HJ and NSDAP did. As stated previously, the NSDAP had been primarily a *völkisch* organisation before 1923, and many leading national socialists had at one time belonged to a *völkisch* association like the *Deutschvölkischer Schutz-und Trutzbund,* but the party deliberately moved away from the *völkisch* front, though not from *völkisch* racialism, after 1925.[19] Ideologically, the *völkisch* movement was in essence national socialist, and its youth groups were closer to the HJ than any other branch of the whole youth movement.[20]

The *Adler und Falken* identified itself very early in the 1920s with national socialism, and on 12 October 1926 it was actually invited to merge with the recently formed HJ, but negotiations were unsuccessful. Its links with Hitler were not broken, however, and at a national meeting on 28 March 1929 in Bad Berka, Thuringia, a favourite rendezvous of *völkisch* groups, the leadership of *Adler und Falken* officially adopted the political ideology of national socialism.[21] The *Schilljugend,* which had seemed likely in 1925–26 to become the official youth organisation of the NSDAP (see chap. 1), thereafter stood more on the periphery of national socialism.

Of more significance was the *Bund der Artamanen,* whose association with the NSDAP was the most enduring of all these groups. The first *Artamanen* group was set up in Saxony in 1924 on the estate of Georg Oberdorfer in Limbach. Under the leadership of August Kenstler, its principal aim was to offer its services on east German estates so that the Polish labourers who worked there would be progressively reduced in numbers.[22]

The long-term political objective of the *Bund der Artamanen* was a greater Germany based on eastward expansion and the racialist precepts of *Blut und Boden* (blood and soil). Not surprisingly, therefore, many of its members in the 1920s were simultaneously in the NSDAP. These included Heinrich Himmler, leader of *Gau* Bavaria of the *Bund Artam* in 1929, later *Reichsführer* of the SS; Walther Darré, later *Reich* minister of agriculture; Alfred Rosenberg, Nazi philosopher and an editor of *Artam-Blätter,* organ of the *Bund Artam;* and Rudolf Hoess, later commandant of the Auschwitz concentration camp. Von Schirach became interested in this right-wing group in 1929 and was often invited to attend and speak at *Bund Artam* meetings.[23]

Another group with a clearly defined faith in national socialism was *Geusen*. In 1928 at a meeting in Weimar, Rosenberg and Goebbels tried without success to persuade it to join the HJ. *Geusen* refused on the grounds that it was an "educational society" while it categorised the HJ as a "combat organisation."[24] Its confidence in national socialism remained unshaken, however, and in December 1928 a *Geusen* leader declared: "The only flag which is acceptable for the common fight of youth against the ignominy of our time . . . is the red flag with the swastika!"[25] Early in 1929, *Geusen* described itself as the "strongest group" among the *völkisch*-nationalists in its support of Hitler and said furthermore: "We take this course because we know that the national socialist movement is the Germany of the future."[26]

Geusen often worked closely at a local level with the HJ, occasionally even forming an unofficial alliance, as in February 1929 when the Nordmark district of *Geusen* incorporated itself into the NSDAP and worked with the HJ. Recognition of its affinity with the NSDAP was forthcoming at the national convention of *Geusen* in Bad Berka in April 1929 when guest speaker Alfred Rosenberg, an important but shadowy figure in youth affairs at this time, referred to it as a "national socialist *Wandervogel* league."[27]

At a purely regional level, the activities of the *Grenzlandschutzbund Germania* indicate an intimate liaison with the HJ. In 1927, the group actually formed itself into an HJ branch, though it broke up shortly afterwards over tactics into an HJ and a reconstituted *Germania* organisation. The *Germania* leader, Wilhelm Lönnecker, declared in May 1929 that his group was national socialist and an HJ branch in all but name.[28]

The close association of all these groups with national socialism was particularly manifest in the later 1920s, to such an extent that plans were sketched for a unification of the *völkisch*-nationalists with the HJ into one youth organisation. This was the fundamental reason for the special convention at the 1929 NSDAP party rally which was attended by leaders Gruber (HJ), von Schirach (NSDStB), Alfred Pudelko *(Adler und Falken)*, Werner Lass *(Freischar Schill)*, Georg Anton *(Geusen)*, and Hugo Hoffmann *(Bund Artamanen)*. The aim of the convention in the *Kolosseum* on 3 August was to amalgamate all *völkisch* groups under the leadership of the HJ into a more *Bündische*-oriented national socialist youth movement.[29]

There were specific political considerations operating at this juncture which formed an indispensable background to the proposed *völkisch*-HJ alliance. Although the NSDAP had gained from the preparation achieved by the various *völkisch* and anti-Semitic groups in 1918–20, and the party had expanded in the 1920s mainly by absorbing members of the declining *völkisch* (and paramilitary) movement, Hitler had consciously separated the NSDAP from these groups after 1925. The Führer's attitude began to change after 1928, however, following his reappraisal of political strategy, which led to the NSDAP's increasing alignment with the conservative right in German politics. Seen in this context, the envisaged plan of bringing together the HJ and middle-class *völkisch* elements was a direct, consistent, and in many ways, logical consequence of the NSDAP's political reorientation.

At the same time, there were factors at work within the national socialist movement which made this alliance appear desirable. The HJ was still numerically very weak (13,000) and the linkup would appreciably improve this situation. But of greater importance, Hitler indubitably believed that as a result of the alliance the HJ would eventually be divested of its social revolutionary radicalism and would comply with the more conservative ideological character of the NSDAP.

His agent for the implementation of this policy was von Schirach who made his first overt attempt to put an end to the HJ's leftist propensities by promoting amalgamation with these groups, with whose leaders he had already established important contacts and exchanged ideas. Von Schirach, one of the foremost sponsors of the special convention, was contemptuous of the HJ, and the corollary of his scheme was an intention to force Gruber's resignation as *Reichsführer* and to replace him with his own nominee and associate, Werner Lass.[30] In this perspective, the meeting had something of the characteristics of a showdown, and was an exercise in organisational discipline and political conformism carried out by von Schirach, with the backing of Hitler, against Gruber and the "socialist" HJ. The convention developed, therefore, into a battle for supremacy between two rivals, Gruber and von Schirach, each personifying a different conception of how the HJ should develop.

Gruber rightly regarded this direct challenge as the most serious crisis yet in his office, and he spared no pain to win his case, going so far as to enlist the support of SA commander von Pfeffer, who was unhappy himself at this time with the political tactics being pursued by the NSDAP.[31] Gruber came out in unequivocal opposition to the projected union, and by insisting that all the groups were to be put unconditionally under his control in the HJ, he contributed significantly to the final collapse of negotiations. For their part, the *völkisch* groups intransigently refused to join anything other than a loosely knit confederation, and in any case, decided in the last analysis to retain their existence independent of any political party. This attitude was decisive. However willing Hitler and von Schirach were to compel Gruber to accept an accommodation, they could not legislate for the actions of the *völkisch* camp.

Only when the project had been irretrievably sabotaged by the *völkisch* side's obduracy did Hitler and the NSDAP feel they had to close ranks behind the man they had been prepared to dismiss, Gruber. Hitler made a pitiful attempt to try to save face by later publishing a declaration in the *Völkischer Beobachter* and Goebbel's paper, *Der Angriff*, confirming Gruber's leadership of the HJ as well as the HJ's status as the only official youth organisation of the NSDAP:

> In order to clarify the position of National Socialist youth, Adolf Hitler states unequivocally . . . that the only national socialist youth organisation with official party recognition is the Hitler Youth, and that recognition of another youth association is neither proposed nor in question. Thus, the numerous current rumours may be measured against this clear affirmation of the truth by Adolf Hitler. According to Adolf Hitler, national socialist youths belong in the Hitler Youth.[32]

Just as Gruber had forestalled Rossbach's *Schilljugend* in 1926, so his tenacity and resolve to stand firm had again proved useful in 1929.

Von Schirach had sustained a severe setback to his plans, but he wrote later that this failure determined him to follow a course of action which was of crucial importance to the HJ and these same groups after 1933:

> At that time [i.e., 1929], I already saw that an agreement with the *Bündische* leaders would never be possible and advocated the principle of HJ totalitarianism which in 1933 cost all these groups their existence.[33]

In other words, von Schirach claims that he decided on the *Gleichschaltung* of all German youth organisations in 1929. True to form, however, he fails to point out that the same totalitarian principle had been acknowledged by Gruber and the HJ from 1926 onwards. Von Schirach does not deserve the credit, however doubtful, of having conceived of this principle; in 1933 he brought to fruition an idea established and cherished by the HJ before his involvement with it. Moreover, von Schirach did his best, despite his bitter disappointment, to maintain friendly contact and establish an understanding with right-wing groups after the debacle of 1929; thus his subsequent actions contradict his statement.

The negative outcome of the 1929 negotiations, while augmenting the personal enmity between Gruber and von Schirach, also led initially to a violent verbal battle between the HJ and the *völkisch* associations which was conducted through their respective press and propaganda organs.[34] This is illustrated by exchanges between the HJ and *Freischar Schill* arising from confusion about the precise political status of the latter. On 21 September, 1929, *Der Angriff* stated that the group was not national socialist and warned national socialist-inclined youths not to join it. In October, the *Freischar Schill* retorted by describing itself as an "activist storm troop of young national socialists," working with the HJ and NSDAP "to prepare the revolution."[35] The position became clear when the Strasser crisis arose in the NSDAP in 1930, for under the direction of Werner Lass the *Freischar Schill* gravitated towards Strasser and indeed it even showed a liking for the more leftist ideas of the National Revolutionaries. By 1931, Lass had concluded that though the NSDAP was a necessary step towards "national regeneration," it was not the full answer to Germany's needs.[36] In the light of later events, therefore, the 1929 convention was vital with regard to relations between the *Freischar Schill* and the HJ and NSDAP. There was virtually no cooperation between them after 1930.

The *Freischar Schill* was an exception, however, for although the relationship between the HJ and the *völkisch* groups was undeniably strained for a time, both sides quickly resumed a degree of cooperation and a reasonably courteous dialogue, so that in fact there was no "irrevocable break" in 1929.[37] Indeed, in December 1929, barely four months after the breakdown of talks, von Schirach tried to arrange another HJ-*völkisch* meeting in Weimar, but it was postponed indefinitely "because of technical difficulties."[38]

Friendlier contacts were reestablished, as indicated by the joint action between the HJ and the *völkisch* groups during the anti-Young Plan campaign in March 1930. Later the same year, when Goebbels, Rosenberg, and Wilhelm Frick revitalised the *Kampfbund für deutsche Kultur* (Combat League for German Culture), which was founded in 1927, the HJ participated along with the *Bund Artamanen, Adler und Falken, Freischar Schill,* and *Geusen* in a meeting in Weimar.[39] Although this was a temporary experiment and the last large-scale display of solidarity between both sides before 1933, they did continue to work together locally at least to the end of 1931, but more infrequently thereafter. In Schleswig-Holstein the HJ's connections with the *Germania* continued uninterrupted and the two groups grew increasingly inseparable, but the *Geusen*-HJ relationship affords perhaps the best example of joint endeavour.[40]

Shortly after the 1929 meeting, the Danzig branch of the HJ, which had thirty youths led by Hans Buchholz, formed a Working Society of Völkisch Youth (*Arbeitsgemeinschaft der Völkischen Jugend*) with the Danzig *Geusen* and Wehrwolf associations.[41] Before the end of 1929, the HJ and *Geusen* in Berlin were cooperating; in January 1930 both urged their respective national leaderships to come together on an official basis; and their bonds in Berlin lasted until the end of 1931.[42] It would have been most difficult, even unnatural, for contact to have been completely severed, because many of the leading *Geusen* personnel and ordinary rank and file were NSDAP members, and the HJ and NSDAP press continued to regard the *Geusen* as belonging, albeit unofficially, to the broad national socialist youth movement.[43] A *Geusen* leader made the revealing comment: "Hitler Youth and *Geusen* are equal parts of the national socialist youth front. . . . We do not regard ourselves as competitors of the HJ, but as its complement."[44]

There is no doubt that of the *völkisch*-nationalist groups, the *Geusen* was nearest to the HJ and NSDAP. Thus, when the NSDAP *Reichsleitung* decreed on 17 May 1930 that party members were not permitted to belong to a youth organisation other than the HJ or NSS, an amendment was agreed upon on 2 October 1930 between Hitler and Gruber which specifically exempted the *Geusen* from the ruling.[45]

The problem of double membership also arose at this time for other national socialist organisations. A ban was imposed, for example, on NSDAP members being attached to the *Stahlhelm*.[46] This development was indicative of a more general tightening of control by the NSDAP *Reichsleitung* in Munich. The policy now followed by the HJ was of immediate relevance to Peter Berns, elected leader of *Geusen* in June 1930, for he was an NSDAP member as well as a former NSDStB leader. Berns was a good friend of von Schirach and their friendship was an important factor in keeping affable relations between the HJ and *Geusen*. In June 1930, von Schirach wrote to Berns that he was a friend of both the HJ and *Geusen*, and that the "youth movement and Hitler Youth cannot be divided."[47]

Both men communicated often on the subject of youth and held discussions. As a result of one such discussion, *Geusen* issued a statement on 12 November 1931 which seemed to auger well for its future position vis-à-vis the HJ: ". . . the relationship between the Hitler

Youth and *Geusen* has been determined in such a way as to facilitate close cooperation and friendly understanding between the two groups."[48]

Nonetheless, these sentiments of goodwill were not realised, for HJ-*Geusen* interchanges became noticeably less cordial in 1932. Neither side was prepared to concede too much ground to the other, and HJ suspicions were aroused when the Strasser circle began to make some headway on the *Geusen* periphery. In view of the political consequences of the Strasser crisis within the HJ, the HJ's coolness is understandable.

The evidence is clear that there was no conclusive split between the HJ and *völkisch* groups in 1929. Von Schirach, still concerned with the political task of bringing the HJ into closer union with middle-class youth, was mainly responsible for this development. It would be more accurate to say that by 1931 the *völkisch* bloc, while still retaining their belief in the national socialist *Weltanschauung*, had abandoned the idea of organisational affiliation with the HJ. This outcome was partly due to the continued uncompromising attitude of Gruber, who would not accept any dealings with these groups unless preceded by their unqualified surrender of independence. The *völkisch*-nationalists intensely disliked the aspirations of the HJ to become a mass *Volksjugend*, for this gravely offended their typically *Bündische* elitist conceptions. In addition, they also perceived a basic incompatibility between the political agitation of the HJ and their own educational aims.

A powerful awareness of their organisational independence, despite similar ideological tastes (if the HJ's social revolutionary outlook is discounted), finally decided the *völkisch* groups against combining with the HJ. But this stalemate was not brought about until both sides had tested one another's standpoint during the two years that followed their 1929 meeting. For these reasons, it can be said that the HJ did not benefit from the pioneer work of the *völkisch* youth groups as the NSDAP had done earlier from their elders.

Nationalist-Military Youth

A prominent section of middle-class youth who were repelled by the immoderation of the extreme right-wing groups in the republic were organised in conservative-nationalist and paramilitary nationalist associations.[49] Politically, these generally did not support the NSDAP, but the less radical parties of the right, particularly the DNVP.

Although one observer reported that the *Bismarckjugend*, "despite upholding the monarchical principle, appears to sympathise" with the HJ,[50] the HJ's ideological content was unacceptable to all but the more reactionary of the right-wing groups. The HJ was no less hostile because it looked upon the conservative nationalists as the living embodiment of political reaction.

From time to time, however, political circumstances might arise, such as an alliance between the NSDAP and a nationalist organisation, which constrained the HJ to establish temporary working arrangements with the other group's youth representatives. Thus at intervals between the anti-Young Plan campaign in 1929 and the formation of the Harzburg Front in 1931, the HJ joined forces with the *Jungstahlhelm*, *Kyffhäuserjugend*, and others. This alliance with "reaction" was naturally inconsistent with the social revolutionary momentum of the HJ, but political expediency obliged it to make a transient rapprochement with these groups. When Hitler indicated his withdrawal from alliances such as the abortive Harzburg Front in early 1932, the HJ was pleased to resume its usual policy of animosity against its former allies.

Left-Wing Youth

The ideological disparity between communism and national socialism resulted in bitter political battles between the KPD and NSDAP. This antagonism was carried over to the respective youth organisations of the two parties and throughout the *Kampfzeit* communist youth groups were a principal target of HJ attacks.[51]

Although both the NSDAP and KPD had a number of features in common, such as a powerful hierarchical structure, a deep aversion for the republic, mass propaganda techniques, fanaticism, and totalitarian aims, the political ideologies confronting each other were too radical in outlook to permit any basis of mutual understanding. National socialism and its organisations represented the extreme rightist political viewpoint, while communism represented the extreme left. There was no question of compromise, neither side expecting to give or to receive quarter. From the very beginning, Hitler had marked out communism (or "bolshevism," to use the usual national socialist term) as one of the implacable foes of the fatherland and national socialism, with the additional charge that Jewish intellectuals controlled and manipulated the communist movement for their own selfish ends. Hitler, of course, regarded every adversary of national socialism as either Jewish-led or Jewish-inspired so that aggression could thus be directed against a single, clear-cut scapegoat.

The KPD, which arose from the *Spartakusbund* at the beginning of 1919, was most active during the turbulent periods of the Weimar Republic, 1919–23 and 1929–33.[52] The party lamely submitted to the

Soviet-controlled Third International throughout the pre-1933 era, but especially under the leadership of Ernst Thaelmann from 1925 onwards. The KPD abandoned its unsuccessful revolutionary tactics in 1923, reorganised its structure after the highly centralised and oligarchically based Russian Communist party, and until 1928 pursued a parliamentary policy. The adoption of "ultraleftist" tactics from 1928 until 1934–35 was disastrous; the whole working-class movement in Germany was split as Hitler made his rapid ascent, thereby facilitating the national socialist *Machtergreifung*.

The very nature of both the HJ and the communist youth movement made it impossible for them not to clash repeatedly, for both had activist, assertive memberships and a percentage of fanatics. More ominously, both sides accepted violence as a natural political weapon to be used whether occasion demanded it or not. Furthermore, until at least the end of 1931, the HJ and its rivals were competing for support in the same section of German youth, the working class, and in the tense political atmosphere of the times, this competition inescapably bred bloody violence. The communists looked on the HJ as a parvenu invading their rightful sphere of influence, while in accordance with the HJ's proletarian image its main objective was, until its rightward turn, to "save" working-class youth from Marxism. Hence there was a stormy battle for supremacy between the two sides, especially in heavily industrialised areas. Since both were also consciously revolutionary in style but aiming at quite different kinds of revolution, their struggle assumed the distasteful characteristics of a civil war (see chap. 8).

Their propaganda machines were maintained at full pitch throughout the pre-1933 period. HJ propaganda was particularly vicious about the role of communist youth as the tool of Moscow, which was anathema to the ultranationalistic HJ. "A foreign policy troop of the Russian bolshevik state" was a typical HJ comment.[53] "Never again war!" was a favourite slogan of the German radical left in the Weimar Republic, and this professed antimilitarism was interpreted as defeatism and dishonourable cowardice by the soldierly HJ; even worse, pacifism was regarded as high treason. Gruber was notably disdainful of communist youth, saying, "The youth masses of the KJVD qualify . . . as cannon fodder for the Russian foreign legion in Germany, the KPD."[54]

Additionally, the Marxist concept of class warfare ran counter to the national socialist idea of a *Volksgemeinschaft* of all classes, and the HJ's strong belief in this hypothesis gave its fight against communist youth more impetus.

There was, therefore, rarely any question of cooperation between the two sides, nationally or locally. On occasion, one group would invite the other to a discussion evening where everyone would be allowed to speak on the platform, but more often than not a fracas would ensue.[55] Neither side was intellectually prone in any case, and recourse to the physical invariably proved too attractive to be resisted. It was a matter of course that in 1933 one of the first groups to be forcibly dissolved by the HJ was the communist youth.

The socialist youth organisations had a vast numerical superiority over both the HJ and communist youth, and like the SPD itself, they usually retained the loyalty of their members.[56] HJ propaganda made little or no discrimination between the two left-wing groups, both being castigated together as the mortal enemies of the HJ. The HJ stigmatised socialist youths as supporters of the "November criminals" and the "system"; its nausea for them was boundless. This was also the attitude endorsed by most socialist youths towards the HJ, and consequently in 1933 their organisations were summarily destroyed.

Confessional Youth

Catholic

The political attitudes of Catholic youth in the Weimar Republic, particularly towards the HJ and national socialism, were determined to a large extent by their intellectual and spiritual dependence on the church hierarchy and Catholic political organisations, notably the Centre party.[57] Because the Weimar Republic was accepted by the Catholic clergy and politicians, the latter having been one of the principal founders of the new state in 1918, Catholic youth were more impervious than most to the rising tide of rebellion against democratic government that was so prevalent in the youth movement as a whole. More to the point, Catholic youth found the attractions of national socialism less inviting than did the majority of German youth.

The clergy's hostile view towards national socialism on theological and political grounds was defined after the NSDAP electoral successes in 1929 and 1930. Catholic theologians proclaimed the innate disharmony between Christian doctrine and Hitler's *Weltanschauung*. In some parts of Germany, Catholics were even forbidden to join the NSDAP and its affiliated groups and those who defaulted were not allowed to participate in church ceremonies. Leading clerics delivered admonitions against the radicalism of national socialism and on the eve of the many elections held in Germany during 1930–33, the clergy often instructed their congregations from the pulpit to vote for the Centre party, or at least to vote against the NSDAP.[58]

It must be said, however, that Catholic clerical and lay opposition to Hitler was neither as universal nor as unanimous as Catholic apologists often contend. Hitler did receive support from Catholics before 1933, even in Catholic Bavaria, where nationalist, conservative, and antidemocratic concepts were powerfully entrenched. National socialism's rejection of liberalism and parliamentary democracy, its desire for a restoration of the authoritarian state, and its stand against communism was alluring to some sections of the Catholic community who had the courage to defy the bishops. The official and most authentic Catholic viewpoint was nevertheless expressed by the ecclesiastical and political leadership, both of which preached consistently against national socialism, and Catholic youth organisations followed the lines of policy enunciated by them.[59]

Referring to the national socialist and communist movements at the sixth national meeting of the *Katholischer Jungmännerverband* in Trier in 1931, Georg Wagner, a leading spokesman of this organisation, declared that no member of the group "who stands by the banner of Christ and by the young Catholic Peoples' Front can belong to these movements."[60] Statements of a similar nature were frequently made by Catholic youth officials, and numerous publications intimated their disavowal of the HJ and Hitler. There was much suspicion about the NSDAP's dubious approach to Christianity, for Point 24 of the party programme obscured rather than clarified this aspect of its policy. The blatant racism and radical nationalism of the national socialists also repelled Catholic youth.

It is edifying to note that the pre-1933 HJ was weakest in traditionally Catholic areas of Germany, for example, in Bavaria, the Rhineland, Saarland, and parts of Silesia, where Catholic organisations were already solidly established (see chap. 8). There were, of course, some Catholics in the early HJ; two of the most competent leaders of the *Kampfzeit*, Hartmann Lauterbacher and Emil Klein, were Catholics. So was Hans Baumann, author of the notorious HJ marching song, *"Heute gehört uns Deutschland, und Morgen die ganze Welt"* ("Today we own Germany, and tomorrow the whole world"), who joined the HJ from the Quickborn association in 1932.[61] Generally, however, Catholic membership of the HJ was small.

This did not deter the HJ press and propaganda systems from exhorting Catholic youth to defect. In the *Nationalsozialistische Jugendpressedienst* on 15 May 1932, HJ press chief Edgar Bissinger appealed for Catholic youth to break their connections with the Bavarian Peoples' party (BVP) and Centre party:

We have nothing against a Catholic youth association which concerns itself solely with religion. But we will fight against any association which uses religion as a facade for transparent political aims. Catholic youth, tear the pro-Centre and pacifist poison from your hearts. Join us in the freedom front of Adolf Hitler. Join the national socialist youth movement and in it make good what you have hitherto been guilty of by intensified activity. Then we will be able to say thanks to you also in payment for your struggle for a free and happy Germany.[62]

Such appeals usually proved futile. After 1933, the struggle between the national socialist regime and the Catholic church grew in intensity once the latter had perceived the insincerity of Hitler's promises regarding the safety and integrity of the Christian churches.[63]

Protestant

There was an important difference in the approach of the Protestant (Evangelical) church towards national socialism, reflected to a certain extent by the posture of organized Protestant youth who did not support the Weimar Republic as firmly as Catholic youth. The republic's materialism, antiauthoritarianism, atheistic communism, attacks on the church by the left-wing parties, and democracy itself produced a more thoroughgoing reaction of revulsion among Protestant youth. Consequently, some sections of the church's youth organisations became dangerously susceptible to national socialist ideology, if not always to the HJ.

Moreover, a group of Protestant clergy who found aspects of Hitler's teachings compelling exerted some influence on the minds of younger Protestants. These clerics welcomed the stated NSDAP objectives of annihilating the republic and its political system, establishing a powerful Reich under an authoritarian government, and defending Christianity, or more precisely, "positive Christianity." Thus, although officially averse to the NSDAP before 1933, the Protestant church was more circumspect and reserved in its opposition than the Catholic church. This body of support for national socialism was of significance, for the Protestant youth associations were strong and well-organised.[64]

One Protestant organisation in particular, the *Bund Deutscher Bibelkreise*, manifested pronational socialist tendencies and gave many "old fighters" to the NSDAP.[65] A contemporary onlooker wrote in 1930:

> Typical of the attitude of youth to national socialism is the
> honest statement of the *Bund Deutscher Bibelkreise* which says
> that . . . "70 percent of its youths regard national socialism with
> glowing sympathy because of a feeling that this movement must
> bring something new and great."[66]

The same observer recorded shortly afterwards that the Silesian branch
of the *Bibelkreise* was thoroughly national socialist, and this may also
have been the case in several other areas where it was active.[67] Another
writer went even further:

> . . . in 1931 it could be affirmed . . . that the young mens'
> association of the entire *Bündische* and Protestant youth . . . belong
> either to the NSDAP and its youth or combat organisations, or
> at least . . . they stand very near to them.[68]

This is an overstatement of the truth, but it does suggest the degree
to which contemporaries were sensitive to increasing national socialist
influence in the ranks of Protestant youth. But not all groups were
as openly or as comprehensively pronational socialist as the *Bibelkreise*. Moreover, there is no evidence that the HJ and Protestant
associations ever had direct dealings with one another.

HJ Recruitment from the Youth Movement

In the state of political instability which the Weimar Republic
experienced between 1930 and 1933, a transference of personnel from
one group to another was to be expected. This kind of situation was
to the advantage of an ascendant organisation like the HJ which, in
posing as something new and different, could attract those who felt
dissatisfied with the association of which they were members. There
is some indication that at least until 1931 the HJ recruited from a
varied range of contemporary youth groups, according to statements
made by officials of the youth movement and the HJ, and material
pertaining to the background of a cross section of leading members
of the HJ before 1933.

Demonstrating the diverse sources of HJ membership, among
those joining the Berlin branch during the first part of 1930 were youths
from the Free *Bündische Deutscher Pfadfinderbund, Grossdeutscher
Jugendbund,* and *Jungnationaler Bund;* the nationalist-military *Jungsturm, Fichtebund,* and *Kyffhäuserjugend;* the communist *Jungspartakusbund;* and the Protestant *Bund Deutscher Bibelkreise.* This
diversity was also the case in another part of Germany: a report made

in April 1930 by Wilhelm Kayser, secretary of the HJ in the Rhineland, states that the HJ in that region had drawn from the *Deutscher Pfadfind-erbund, Grossdeutscher Jugendbund, Jungnationaler Bund, Ring Deutscher Pfadfinder, Deutsche Pfadfinderschaft, Jungstahlhelm, Fichtebund, Werewolf, Kyffhäuserjugend, Jungspartakusbund, Roter Jungsturm* (communist), and the *Jungbanner* (socialist).[69]

Recruitment from the *Bündische* Youth and left-wing groups is conspicuous from these reports, though they do not say how many came from each group. Contemporary observations point to the same sources: "Youths joining the Hitler Youth originate from the Marxist and *Bündische* camps."[70] HJ statements tell a similar story: "Youths who not so long ago stood critically against us in the *Bündische* Youth are now with us."[71] HJ leader Franz Schnaedter wrote in 1931: "A whole series of perceptive young leaders from the *Bündische* and non-*Bündische* Youth recently . . . joined us."[72]

Occasionally, a group of a local nationalist organisation would go over en masse to the HJ, especially if the group's leader showed a marked preference for transferring his allegiance and was able to convince his charges that his decision was the correct one. In 1926, for example, the members of the first HJ branch in Osnabrück origi-nally came from the *Hindenburgbund*. In Munich, the nationalist *Blücherbund* went over to the HJ en bloc on 19 July 1928. Also, during the brief existence of the Harzburg Front, local units of the *Jung-stahlhelm* joined the HJ, like the band section of the Oldenburg branch which left in February 1932 to form the basis of the HJ propaganda service in that area.[73]

The HJ claimed to have attracted youths from both the communist and socialist youth organisations. There was a certain degree of per-sonnel interchange between the NSDAP and KPD on a local level, particularly in densely populated areas and large towns, but the HJ's success in competition with left-wing youth groups was slight, despite the exaggerated statements of its press.[74] It is clear that only when the HJ ceased directing its appeal primarily to working-class youth in 1931 did it show signs of important expansion (see chap. 8). Although the communists did not provide many members for the HJ, it is inter-esting to note that two former adherents of the *Kommunistischer Jugendverband Deutschlands* attained responsible positions of leader-ship in the pre-1933 HJ. Wolfgang Thiess became editor of the HJ newspaper *Der Sturmtrupp* in 1931, and Wilhelm Kayser, also once a communist youth leader, subsequently became an HJ *Gau* and *Ge-bietsführer*.[75]

A most revealing intimation of HJ recruitment sources and of the transfer of personnel from other youth associations to the HJ before 1933 is afforded by a study of the careers of people who were appointed to leadership posts. There is evidence that many of the most able and well-known leaders spent a period of time in another group before joining the HJ, even if they did not move directly from that organisation to the HJ. It is certain that the experience which they had acquired elsewhere was a valuable recommendation when appointments were being made by the HJ *Reichsleitung.*

Many people who formerly belonged to one of the *völkisch*-nationalist groups became prominent in the HJ. This was not unexpected in view of the narrow ideological differences between these groups and the HJ, their close working relationship from 1929–31, and the HJ's more bourgeois-oriented course after 1931. There were, furthermore, many former nationalist-military youth members in the senior HJ ranks. The HJ did not entice many youths from the Free *Bündische* organisations, but among those who did come over were three who attained top posts in the HJ.[76]

Between the end of 1931 and the beginning of 1933, the HJ was more successful in attracting youths from the right wing of the *Bündische* Youth, especially since the HJ gravitated to the right during that period. Before 1931 new members tended to come from more scattered sources, including Free *Bündische,* communist, socialist and Protestant organisations, but these were all on a comparatively small scale. On the other hand, the HJ found a substantial percentage of its pre-1933 membership among the millions of non-Catholic German youths who were not gathered in a youth group of any description, just as the NSDAP after 1929–30 found support among the "floating vote" of the right and new voters, i.e., the unorganised, unpolitical bourgeoisie of the pre-1930 era.

It is evident that with regard to ideology and organisation, the HJ was a unique phenomenon in the German youth movement; it was neither a continuation of the pre-1918 youth experience nor a component of the Weimar youth movement in a conventional sense. Instead, the HJ represented a complete break in the youth tradition of Germany, just as the NSDAP was a new kind of party; neither made a positive contribution to German political history. The HJ lacked the character of a genuine youth organisation, for it was always essentially a party political group. While the youth movement wanted ultimately to triumph over the party system, the HJ through the NSDAP desired to triumph over the youth movement. In the last resort, the HJ felt it had to prove its uniqueness by destroying the youth movement and its tradition, which the HJ deemed superfluous and irrelevant in the hard times of the 1930s. The youth movement nonetheless sowed the seeds of its own eventual destruction to a considerable degree, for its manifold deficiencies, which the crises of 1930–33 revealed in full, created a vacuum which the HJ was able to exploit for its own advantage even before 1933. The NSDAP benefited from the weaknesses of the democratic order and the political parties; likewise the HJ benefited from the debilitated structure of the German youth movement.

The evidence finally shows that there was increasing collaboration from 1929 onwards with middle-class groups and that von Schirach was the protagonist of this development against Gruber. In consequence, there was a greater influx of middle-class elements into the HJ. This had important repercussions in the organisation and administration of the HJ.

Notes: Chapter 5

1. BA:ZSg 3/1477.

2. W. Z. Laqueur, *Young Germany: A History of the German Youth Movement* (London, 1962), pp. 149–50.

3. F. Raabe, *Die Bündische Jugend* (Stuttgart, 1961), p. 10.

4. This was to compensate for the HJ's own rather poor musical literature in the *Kampfzeit*; the HJ usually inserted lyrics of a nationalist-political-military nature, although the first song book of the HJ, *Blut and Ehre,* published in 1933, contained some *Wandervogel* songs in the original version.

5. An interesting link between the HJ and *Wandervogel* was forged at the end of 1933 when the founder of the *Wandervogel,* Karl Fischer, accepted an honorary advisory post in the *Reichsjugendführung* (B. Schneider, *Daten zur Geschichte der Jugendbewegung* [Bad Godesberg, 1965], p. 120).

6. A girls' division had been created in the HJ *Reichsleitung* in 1926 (see chap. 2) and several unofficial girls' groups grew up in the Plauen area, but it was not until December 1928 that the HJ decided to establish a *Schwesternschaft* (SAB:4/65 781/146), which formed the basis for what in July 1930 became the BDM (H. Volz, *Daten der Geschichte der NSDAP* [Berlin, 1943], p. 133). In April 1931, a *Jungmädelgruppe* (JM) was set up as a junior branch of the BDM; neither made much headway before 1933. The BDM had 5,184 members in March 1932 and the JM a mere 750 (Bay. HSA:ASA:Akte NS/1555).

7. A. Klönne, *Hitlerjugend: Die Jugend und Ihre Organisation im Dritten Reich* (Hannover, 1956); British Foreign Office, *Germany, Basic Handbook* (London, 194?), pt. 2, chap. 14, p. 436.

8. A. Klönne, *Gegen den Strom* (Hannover, 1957).

9. B. v. Schirach, *Die Hitler-Jugend: Idee und Gestalt* (Leipzig, 1934), pp. 14–15.

10. The most important boy scout groups were: *Deutsche Pfadfinderbund, Deutsche Pfadfinderschaft, Deutsche Pfadfinderbund Westmark, Ring Deutscher Pfadfindergaue, e.V, Ringgemeinschaft Deutscher Pfadfinder, Ringgemeinschaft Freier Pfadfinder,* and *Neudeutscher Pfadfinderbund* (Günther Wolff-Verlag, *Die Deutschen Jugendbünde* [Plauen, 1931]). The foundation of the *Deutscher Pfadfinderbund* in 1911 marks the beginning of the German boy scout movement. Although generally modelled on the European pattern, the movement was particularly conscious of the British contribution to this field, and many exchanges were arranged between the two countries before and after World War I. The scouts initially enjoyed widespread popularity in Germany, and by 1914 they

numbered about 80,000 (Laqueur, *Young Germany*, pp. 73–74). But the movement disintegrated after 1918 and consequently the scouts never attained anything like the importance of their counterparts in Britain.

The *Freideutsche Jugend* groups included the *Deutsche Freischar*, the largest and most influential; *Bund der Wandervogel und Kronacher; Deutsche Akademische Gildenschaft; Freischar junger Nation e.V; Deutscher Wandervogel; Nerother Wandervogel;* and *Jungnationaler Bund* (G. Wolff-Verlag, *Jugendbünde*).

11. British Foreign Office, *Germany*, pt. 2, chap. 14, p. 434.

12. BA:ZSg 3/2849.

13. O.E. Schüddekopf, *Linke Leute von Rechts* (Stuttgart, 1960), p. 240.

14. *Deutsche Freischar* 3:II (1929), p. 182.

15. B. v. Schirach, *Ich Glaubte an Hitler* (Hamburg, 1967), p. 181.

16. BA:Akte NS 26/372.

17. BA:ZSg 3/2849.

18. SAK:Abt. 403:No. 16754.

19. See Uwe Lohalm, *Völkischer Radikalismus: Die Geschichte des Deutschvölkischen Schutz-und Trutzbundes 1919–1923* (Hamburg, 1970).

20. The best known were:

    (a) *Adler und Falken*, set up in Bad Salzbrunn by Wilhelm Kotzde in 1920; had 3,300 members organised in 302 local branches in 1932 (British Foreign Office, *Germany*, pt. 2, chap. 14, p. 434).

    (b) *Bund der Artamanen*, founded in 1924, with 1,800 members in 1930. A splinter group, the *Bund Artam*, was erected in 1929 (ibid).

    (c) *Bund Geusen*, established in 1919; in 1930, it had 1,150 members (H. Pross, *Jugend. Eros. Politik* [Munich, 1964], p. 476).

    (d) *Schilljugend*, set up by Gerhard Rossbach; in 1929 it had only 250 members (G. Ehrenthal, *Die Deutschen Jugendbünde* [Berlin, 1929], p. 50). In 1930 the group was renamed *Bund Ekkehard e. V.*

    (e) *Freischar Schill*, a breakaway group from the *Schilljugend*; founded in 1927 by Werner Lass. In 1932 there was a membership of 1,500 (ibid.).

    (f) *Deutsche Falkenschaft*, a secessionist group of *Adler und Falken* set up in 1929 by Kotzde (ibid.).

    (g) *Eidgenossen*, the adult section of the *Schilljugend*.

    (h) A miscellaneous collection of more locally based groups, including the *Grenzlandschutzbund Germania*, which was established in Schleswig-Holstein in 1920 (LASH:Oberpräsidium Schleswig:Abt. 301. No. 4556).

21. H. Bolm, *Hitlerjugend in einem Jahrzehnt* (Brunswick, 1938), p. 51; Schneider, *Daten zur Geschichte der Jugendbewegung*.

22. E. F. Bartelmäs, *Das Junge Reich* (Stuttgart, 1935), p. 135.

23. Raabe, *Bündische Jugend*, p. 77; Pross, *Jugend*, p. 357; R. Hoess, *Commandant of Auschwitz* (London, 1959); BA:Akte NS 26/1285.

24. F. W. Hymmen, "10 Jahre Hitler-Jugend" in *Der Junge Kamaradschaft*, ed. E. Fischer (Berlin, 1935), p. 29.

25. *Die Kommenden,* Dec. 1928.

26. *Die Kommenden,* 29 March 1929.

27. SAB:4/65 781/146; Bay. HSA:ASA:Akte NS/1542.

28. LASH:Oberpräsidium Schleswig:Abt. 301. No. 4556; BA:Akte NS 26/371.

29. Bay. HSA:ASA:Akte NS/1824; BA:Akte NS 26/391.

30. BA:Akte NS 26/354; SAB:4/65 781/146.

31. BA:Akte NS 26/372.

32. Ibid.

33. V. Schirach, *Hitler-Jugend,* p. 23.

34. J. Fischer, "Die Nationalsozialistiche Bewegung in die Jugend," *Das Junge Deutschland,* Aug. 1930.

35. BA:Akte NS 26/372; SAB: 4/65 781/146.

36. Bay. HSA:ASA:Akte NS/1819.

37. As suggested by H. C. Brandenburg in *Die Geschichte der HJ* (Cologne, 1968), p. 38.

38. BA:Akte NS 26/354.

39. Bolm, *Hitlerjugend,* p. 119.

40. LASH:Oberpräsidium Schleswig:Abt. 301. No. 4558.

41. BA:Akte NS 26/372.

42. Bay. HSA:ASA:Akte NS/1555.

43. BA:Akte NS 26/354.

44. *Die Kommenden,* 14 February 1930, p. 74.

45. BA:Akte NS 26/364.

46. See V. R. Berghahn, *Der Stahlhelm. Bund der Frontsoldaten 1919–1935* (Düsseldorf, 1966).

47. BA:Akte NS 26/354.

48. Bay. HSA:ASA:Akte NS/1555.

49. The total membership of the right-wing organisations was nearly 250,000 in 1930 (Schüddekopf, *Linke Leute von Rechts,* p. 240). The most important were:

    (a)   The *Jungstahlhelm,* youth group of the ex-soldiers' association, the *Stahlhelm,* with 100,000 members in 1930 (Pross, *Jugend,* p. 473).

    (b)   The *Kyffhäuserjugend,* the youth group of another veterans' league, the *Kyffhäuserverband der Kriegsvereine;* in 1930, 65,000 members (ibid.).

    (c)   The *Bismarckjugend.* Founded as the youth auxiliary of the DNVP, this group had a membership of 40,000 in 1930 (British Foreign Office, *Germany,* pt. 2, chap. 14, p. 436).

    (d)   The *Jungsturm Kolberg* was established in Kolberg in 1897. In 1930, there were 25,000 members (ibid.).

(e)   The *Hindenburgjugend*, the DVP youth group, with 12,000 members in 1930 (ibid.).

(f)   The *Scharnhorstjugend*, the junior branch of the *Jungstahlhelm*, had 5,000 members in 1930 (Pross, *Jugend*, p. 473).

50.   J. Fischer, *Das Junge Deutschland*, Feb. 1930, p. 55.

51.   The leading communist groups were:

(a)   *Kommunistischer Jugendverband Deutschlands* (KJVD), founded in 1919 and the largest communist youth organisation. In 1929 it had 25,000 members, and in 1932, 40,000.

(b)   *Jungspartakusbund*, established in 1924 as the children's organisation of the KPD; it had 25,000 members in 1930.

(c)   *Rote Jungfront*, the youth group of the extremist *Roter Frontkämpferbund* (banned in 1929); 25,000 membership in 1930.

(d)   *Kommunistische Arbeiterjugend*. Formed in Berlin in 1920 and the most radical communist youth association of all; only 500 members in 1929 (British Foreign Office, *Germany*, pt. 2, chap. 14, p. 436).

52.   See O. K. Flechtheim, *Die KPD in der Weimarer Republik* (Offenbach, 1948).

53.   *Die Junge Front* 2, 1930.

54.   BA:ZSg 3/3105.

55.   SAB:4/65 781/146.

56.   These included:

(a)   *Jungbanner*. Founded in 1924 as the youth organisation of the *Reichsbanner*, it had 220,000 members in 1930 and 495,000 members in the senior section (18–25 years) (Pross, *Jugend*, p. 474).

(b)   *Rote Falken* catered to 10–14-year-olds; 150,000 members in 1929 (British Foreign Office, *Germany*, pt. 2, chap. 14, p. 436).

(c)   *Sozialistische Arbeiterjugend*, the youth affiliate of the SPD; 56,000 members in 1933 (Pross, *Jugend*, p. 474).

57.   See J. S. Conway, *The Nazi Persecution of the Churches 1933–45* (London, 1968).

58.   H. Müller, *Katholische Kirche und Nationalsozialismus. Dokumente 1930–35* (Munich, 1963), p. 5.

59.   Catholic youth organisations represented in the *Reichsausschuss der deutschen Jugendverbände* had a membership of 1,300,000 in 1930 (BA:ZSg 3/2849). The leading Catholic youth groups were:

(a)   *Katholische Jugend Deutschlands*, a cover organisation for all Catholic groups set up in 1928 (Pross, *Jugend*, p. 471).

(b)   *Katholische Jungmännerverband;* 390,000 members in 1933 (G. Lewy, *The Catholic Church and Nazi Germany* [London, 1964], p. 4).

(c)   *Deutsche Jugendkraft;* led by Adalbert Probst (shot by Gestapo in 1934); membership of 250,000 in 1933 (ibid.).

(d)   *Katholischer Gesellenvereine;* 84,000 members in 1929 (British Foreign Office, *Germany*, pt. 2, chap. 14, p. 435).

(e)   *Reichsverband der deutschen Windthorstbünde*, established as the Centre Party youth organisation; 10,000 members in 1929 (ibid.).

(f)   *Zentralverband der katholischen Jungfrauenvereinigungen Deutschlands* (Young Women's Associations); 767,000 members in 1930 (Pross, *Jugend,* p. 471).

(g)   *Quickborn;* 5,900 members in 1929 (British Foreign Office, *Germany,* pt. 2, chap. 14, p. 435).

60.   Müller, *Katholische Kirche,* p. 6.

61.   H. Lauterbacher interview: Munich, 30 April 1969; BDC:E. Klein file; BDC:H. Baumann file.

62.   Bay. HSA:ASA:Akte NS/1849; BA:ZSg 3/1450.

63.   See L. D. Walker, *Hitler Youth and Catholic Youth 1933–1936* (Washington, 1971).

64.   At the end of 1929, Protestant youth groups in the *Reichsausschuss der deutschen Jugendverbände* (excluding [g] below) had 596,000 members (BA:ZSg 3/2849). The most influential were:

(a)   *Reichsverband der Evangelischen Jungmännerbünde Deutschlands;* founded in 1921 as an umbrella organisation for Protestant youth groups; by the beginning of 1933 there were 200,000 members. Not all Protestant groups were members (Wolff-Verlag, *Jugendbünde*).

(b)   *Jugendbünde für Entschiedenes Christentum;* created in 1896, it had 46,500 members in 1929 (British Foreign Office, *Germany,* pt. 2, chap. 14, p. 435).

(c)   *Christdeutsche Bund;* 23,000 members in 1933 when it amalgamated with the *Bund deutscher Jugendvereine* to form the *Bund Christdeutscher Jugend* (Wolff-Verlag, *Jugendbünde*).

(d)   *Christliche Pfadfinderschaft Deutschlands;* 21,000 members in 1933 (M. Priepke, *Die Evangelische Jugend im Dritten Reich 1933–36* [Frankfurt, 1960], p. 237.

(e)   *Bund Deutscher Bibelkreise;* 20,000 members in 1933 (ibid.).

(f)   *Arbeitsgemeinschaft der Christlichen Vereine Jünger Männer Deutschlands* (Christian Young Men's Society) (Wolff-Verlag, *Jugendbünde*).

(g)   *Bund evangelisch-lutherischer Jungfrauenvereine in Preussen, e.V.* (Young Women's Association); 932,000 members (Pross, *Jugend,* p. 470).

65.   Priepke, *Evangelische Jugend,* p. 11.

66.   J. Fischer, *Das Junge Deutschland,* Feb. 1930, p. 56.

67.   J. Fischer, *Das Junge Deutschland,* Aug. 1930.

68.   W. Kindt, "Bund oder Partei in der Jugendbewegung?" *Das Junge Deutschland,* Dec. 1932.

69.   J. Fischer, *Das Junge Deutschland,* Aug. 1930; SAK:Abt. 403:No. 16754.

70.   K. O. Paetel, *Handbuch der deutschen Jugendbewegung* (Flarchheim, 1930), p. 23.

71.   Ibid., p. 26.

72.   BA:ZSg 3/1477.

73.   SAB:4/65 1707/287; SAB:4/65 1735/293; BA:ZSg 3/1473.

74.   BA:Sammlung Schumacher:Gruppe VIII. No. 239.

75. Klönne, *Hitlerjugend*, p. 45; BDC:W. Kayser file.

76. Those who joined from the *völkisch* groups included: Alfons Baumgartner, Karl Heinz Bürger, Werner Haverbeck, Ferdinand Hengst, Hugo Kroll, Lühr Oldigs, Paul Otto, Heinz Schladitz, Hein Schlecht, Wilhelm Scholz, Joachim Walter, and Kurt Wegner. The former nationalist-military members included: Erwin Baumann, Gunter Blum, Kurt Haller von Hallerstein, Lühr Hogrefe, Heinz Hünger, Erich Jahn, Hartmann Lauterbacher, Alfred Loose, Carl Nabersberg, August Patabel, Baldur von Schirach, Walter Schmidt, Franz Schnaedter, Franz Woweries, and Wilhelm Zerrahn. Members from the Free *Bündische* groups included: Gotthard Ammerlahn, Walter Burchhard, and Ernst Haefke. See the Biography of HJ Leaders for details of their lives.

Chapter 6

Organisational Structure, 1930–31

As the new decade started, Germany was faced by the first stage of a prolonged governmental crisis that was at least as serious as the economic problem. The Müller administration, having revealed symptoms of instability in 1929, especially over finance, was finally shattered in March 1930 by the contending interests of the SPD and DVP (two of the coalition partners) over employment insurance policy. The disintegration of the last truly democratic parliamentary government of the republic indicated a congenital weakness in both the constitutional structure and the party system. The way was now open for a right-wing authoritarian approach; Hermann Bruening, parliamentary leader of the Centre party, headed a new-style presidential cabinet which lacked a Reichstag majority for its legislative programme and was therefore obliged from July 1930 onwards to rely on the emergency powers accorded President von Hindenburg by Article 48 of the constitution. In this respect, Bruening's cabinet marked the beginning of authoritarian government in Germany which culminated in the appointment of Adolf Hitler as Reich chancellor in 1933.

Bruening's precipitate dissolution of the Reichstag in July 1930 had fatal consequences; the elections of 14 September resulted in a prodigious rise in the strength of the antidemocratic extremist parties, particularly the NSDAP. The intensive electoral campaign pursued by the NSDAP vindicated the major organisational and propaganda changes that had taken place in the party since 1928. The HJ played a role in the campaign, with *Reichsführer* Gruber speaking at meetings all over Germany.[1]

The NSDAP surpassed the expectations of everyone in Germany, including its own leadership, by achieving a spectacular success, polling 6,409,600 votes and winning 107 seats. This meant that the NSDAP was propelled from the ninth and smallest party in the Reichstag in 1928 to the second largest behind the SPD. The result should perhaps not have occasioned so much surprise, for the NSDAP had already hinted at its potential by scoring well in state elections in Thuringia (December 1929) and Saxony (June 1930). In September 1930, the National Socialists attracted a substantial percentage of the previously nonvoting electorate who came forward to register their protest at the political and economic crisis; the younger generation of new voters also flocked heavily to the swastika, and for the first time in NSDAP history, the peasantry was a major source of strength. The severe depression which afflicted the agrarian areas of Germany from the late 1920s onwards radicalised the peasantry and pushed it into the NSDAP camp.[2] Having devoted special attention to the plight of agriculture since 1928, the NSDAP publicly affirmed its support for the peasantry in early 1930, and appointed Walther Darré leader of an agrarian division in the NSDAP *Reichsleitung* in order to coordinate the party's appeal.

The absence of effective governmental measures to combat the crisis, the incapacity of the existent peasant organisations to contain the radicalism of their members, the latent anti-Semitic and antidemocratic attitudes of the peasants, and the efficacy of national socialist *Blut und Boden* propaganda were the principal factors explaining why the NSDAP did so well in 1930 in agriculturally depressed areas like Schleswig-Holstein, Pomerania, East Prussia, Mecklenburg, Hannover, Hesse, and the Rheinpfalz.[3]

Above all, the NSDAP gained at the expense of the bourgeois parties, the DVP, DNVP, DSP, and other small middle-class groupings. The decline of German liberalism, already presaged in 1928, was accelerated by the poor showing of the DVP and DSP, and both continued to lose ground until 1933.[4] The DNVP was the most conspicuous sufferer, falling from 14.2 percent of the vote in 1928 to 7.0 percent in 1930. The intrinsic weakness of the DNVP stemmed from its own conglomerate nature, for it embraced many shades of right-wing opinion; tension was therefore inevitable and secession always possible.[5] Thus in 1920, the Free Conservative group left and in 1922 the Racists; the party was also split by the Dawes Plan in 1924 and by the Locarno Pact in 1926, but it was in reaction to DNVP leader Alfred Hugenberg's radicalism that the most crippling defections occurred in 1929–30, when some conservative nationalists and more moderate elements seceded.

Hugenberg's policy of alliance with Hitler also rebounded against him, for he forfeited the support of the remaining conservatives in the party who repudiated the NSDAP and failed to hold on to the radicals who were attracted by Hitler's extremism.

Because of these shifts in the voting structure, Bruening was unable to form a coalition with a parliamentary majority; negotiations to bring Hitler into a coalition failed because Hindenburg disliked the Führer's antics, while Hitler demanded too many concessions. The KPD, NSDAP, and DNVP were now ranged against Bruening, and Hindenburg was determined to keep the Social Democrats out of office at all costs. Bruening continued to rule by emergency decree, though in the interests of safeguarding the republic from the enemy on the right, the SPD decided to tolerate the government. The introduction of authoritarian government in Germany in 1930 was not unique, for elsewhere in Central and Eastern Europe in the 1930s democratic regimes frequently gave way to demands for an authoritarian attitude. The hour of the strong man had arrived.

Its elevation in political status forced the national socialist movement to reorient its functions to a considerable extent and a more far-reaching strategy of action was adopted. Although the HJ did not expand to a degree comparable with the NSDAP or SA, the increase from around 13,000 members at the beginning of 1930 to over 55,000 members by the end of 1932 did necessitate significant organisational changes (see chap. 8). There is no doubt that during the *Kampfzeit,* the HJ was constantly searching for a satisfactory organisational formula, which sometimes involved important changes within a few months of each other. The complexities of the often bewildering changes and prolific turnover in personnel in the central and provincial administrations were indicative not merely of natural growth but also in many ways of the whole character of the HJ itself in these years, groping in the dark for something better. In addition, political developments within the national socialist movement also contributed to this considerable degree of upheaval.

At the beginning of 1930, the HJ was organised in *Ortsgruppen, Bezirke,* and *Gaue,* at the top of which stood the *Reichsleitung.* This pattern was initially experimental when established in 1926, but was finally accepted in 1927 and confirmed at the leaders' meeting in Plauen at the end of 1928. The arrangement duplicated the NSDAP organisational model, as decreed in December 1926.[6] In practice, however, this did not always work out as it should have done during the 1920s, mainly because the administrative structure of the HJ had serious defects which made for inefficiency. Hence, on 22 May 1930, NSDAP organisation leader Gregor Strasser ordered that the HJ was to be organised in units "exactly parallel to the *Gaue* districts of the political party," and the same month Gruber endorsed this view.[7] As part of the changes introduced by Strasser on taking up his appointment in 1928, the boundaries of NSDAP *Gaue* had been redefined to correspond with those of the electoral districts, and in 1930 this also applied to HJ *Gaue*.

The HJ membership in 1930 fell into three groups which showed that changes had occurred since 1926:

(a) An elder section, over eighteen years old, who were obliged to be party members; most of this group, which was numerically the smallest, were leaders and referred to as the *Führerring* (Leaders' Circle).

(b) The so-called *Schar* youths *(Scharjungen)*, who were aged from sixteen to eighteen years, and who were organised in *Scharen;* each *Schar* had a maximum of twenty-four boys, who were subdivided again into three groups *(Gruppen)* of eight boys each. A police report of May 1930 described the *Scharen* as embracing "the really active members of the Hitler Youth."

(c) The younger members, aged fourteen to sixteen years, were gathered in *Jungmannschaften*.[8]

An indication of the relative size of these components is given in a police report of 16 April 1930 which states that 30 percent of HJ *Gaue* Rhineland members were between fourteen and sixteen years of age, and 54 percent between sixteen and eighteen years.[9] These figures are probably a fair reflection of the national situation at this time.

As controller of the *Reichsleitung,* the central administrative body of the HJ based in Plauen, the *Reichsführer* had an ultimate veto on appointments and dismissals (in consultation with the NSDAP and SA leadership), and he had to countersign orders given out by each separate division; those decrees which did not comply with this regulation could be changed at any time by him and even rescinded. The *Reichsführer* thus enjoyed, in theory at least, as powerful a status within the HJ *Reichsleitung* as Hitler did in the NSDAP leadership. As was the case in the early NSDAP especially, one of the most vital divisions of the *Reichsleitung* was the secretarial office *(Reichsgeschäftsführung)* which directed the internal transactions of the whole *Reichsleitung* as well as all matters pertaining to the HJ throughout Germany. Every HJ *Gau* had its own secretarial office which was responsible to the central office; this kept in touch with the *Gaue* through circulars, decrees, and directives, and in return, received reports regarding all aspects of HJ activity.[10] In early 1930, the composition of the *Reichsleitung* was as follows:

HJ Reichsleitung

	Division	Leader
1.	*Reichsführer*	Kurt Gruber
2.	*Reich* Secretary	Richard Wagner (appointed 1 April 1928)
3.	*Reich* Treasurer	Gerhard Stöckel (appointed in 1929)
4.	Sports	Ferdinand Hengst (appointed in 1929)
5.	*Jungmannschaften*	Ferdinand Schlupper (appointed in 1929)
6.	Youth Welfare	Unknown
7.	Propaganda & News Service	Franz Woweries (appointed in 1929); replaced by Franz Schnaedter in early 1930.
8.	Economic Office	Alfred Köhler. This office was abolished in November 1930.
12.	Peasant Youth	Erich Jahn (appointed in 1928)
13.	In 1929 there was an office for HJ-*Bündische* Youth relations led by Heinrich Reinhardt, but it was abolished shortly after the unsuccessful meeting between both organisations at the 1929 party rally.	

Sources: Bay. HSA:ASA:Akte NS/1541; BDC:R. Wagner file; SAB:4/65 1678/280; BA:Akte NS 26/372; SAB:4/65 781/146.

During the course of 1930, several important offices were added to the *Reichsleitung*, notably a separate organisation division, of which Franz Schnaedter was appointed leader in October 1930 and a *Schar* division under Theo Kienast. Personnel changes were also frequent.[11]

Unlike the strong, hierarchical NSDAP organisational structure built up by Hitler after 1925, which was reinforced by the changes of 1928, the power and authority of the HJ's *Reichsleitung* was particularly ineffective in the first years of the group's existence (see chap. 2). Beginning in 1930 the chaos of this situation was reduced somewhat as the HJ managed to instil a little more order into its administration and the NSDAP and SA gave more backing.[12] But despite the greater efforts towards centralisation in the HJ before 1933, which met with some degree of success under von Renteln and von Schirach, the ordinary HJ youths and even some leaders in remote regions continued to regard the *Reichsleitung* as something rather distant and invisible, whose presence and influence were never obvious. The most recognisable institution of authority was the local *Gauführer,* who normally had considerable scope to exercise his own initiative.

This was also the situation in the early NSDAP, but after 1925, though the party *Gauleiter's* role was still not absolutely clarified, his total subordination to Hitler was established.[13] From the beginning, Hitler appreciated that an efficient and dedicated work corps was essential for the smooth organisational development of the party and furthermore, that the *Gauleiter* would be a key figure. The 1928 party reorganisation brought an important new perspective to the position of the *Gauleiter,* for his increased involvement with the techniques of political electioneering made him a more tightly knit cog of a highly centralised apparatus.

A loyal elitist group of *Gauleiters* emerged at the top of the NSDAP administration, but due to the HJ's less exacting control from the centre and the absence of charismatic leadership, this did not happen to the same extent in the HJ under Gruber's leadership. Hence, much more came to depend on the HJ *Gau* leader's personality, enthusiasm, and energy, for this was the most crucial factor in determining how successfully the HJ would develop within a particular area. Every *Gau* leader continued, until late 1931 at least, to feel himself responsible for his own *Gau* without too much interference from the *Reichsleitung.* There was, therefore, no overbearing central authority; under Gruber, the *Reichsleitung* was primarily concerned with giving general guidelines, and was not mainly responsible for the growth of the HJ in the provinces. Consequently, the HJ *Gaue* leaders frequently came to look upon themselves as independent rulers, and though none constructed private empires within their *Gaue* as some NSDAP *Gauleiters* did (with Hitler's ultimate approval—for example, Goebbels in Berlin, Martin Mutschmann in Saxony and Erich Koch in East Prussia), the whole movement was deprived of coordination at a time when the HJ was struggling to assert itself on the national stage. In the NSDAP, the strategic position of the *Gauleiter* could be checked by the Führer; in the HJ things were quite different.

A *Gau* encompassed all HJ organisational units within a defined geographical district, over which the *Gau* leader had full jurisdiction. Although he worked independently within his sphere of command, the *Gauführer* implemented national decrees promulgated by the *Reichsleitung,* or decrees which were specially given out to his *Gau.* Moreover, he was supposed to forward, normally every quarter, a report to the *Reichsführer* giving details of all activities and events in his *Gau* during this period. He had usually to work under very trying conditions, including poor office accommodation, lack of trained assistants, and above all, vastly inadequate financial resources.[14]

The increase in the number of *Gaue* during 1930 reflected the gradual expansion of the HJ, and simultaneously added to the un-steadiness and state of change in the organisation. Some new *Gaue* were created, while others were reconstructed from existing ones; a number of *Gaue* still existed only in theory. Due to the lack of satis-factory documentary evidence, it is impossible to state exactly how many were functional, but there were probably about thirty at the beginning of 1930, and thirty-five by the end of the year, when the party had the same amount.[15] In October 1930, the *Gaue* were grouped under *Oberführungen* (higher leaderships) which were mapped out to correspond to the similar SA spheres of administration, and designed to facilitate organisational procedure in the provinces. In view of the innate defects of the organisation, however, this objective was not realised even to a limited degree until the reforms of April and October 1931. Seven HJ *Oberführer* were appointed to supervise the new ar-rangements, while a small number of *Gaue* were made directly respon-sible to the *Reichsführer*.[16]

Within each *Gau* was grouped normally from two to five *Bezirke*, in which the *Bezirksführer* had a certain independence but was in essence the executive of the *Gauführer*'s orders in his area and had no direct control of finances.[17] As the activities of NSDAP *Gaue* rose, the *Gauleiter* increasingly delegated responsibility to the *Kreisleiter* who became the link man between the *Gau* leadership and the local branches, and a parallel development may be traced between the HJ *Gauführer* and *Bezirksführer*. The local branch leader (*Ortsgruppen-führer*) had a more important position in the HJ than his lowly status might suggest, for it was he who had the task of establishing the HJ where there was none before. He had to solve the initial prob-lems of organisation, which could be the most intractable of all. He had to break fresh ground with virtually no support, and was in fact the spearhead of the HJ offensive in the provinces. Only if his work was successful could the HJ think in terms of *Bezirke* and *Gaue*.

In order to establish a new local unit, the leader of a neighbouring town or village would call a public meeting at which the aims of the HJ and national socialism would be explained and at the end those younger people present would be invited to join the HJ, forming the nucleus of a new branch. Alternatively, a local branch would be organised by a group of like-minded friends, or even by some unem-ployed youths attracted by the promises of national socialism. NSDAP and SA members were often urged by the HJ to send their sons into the organisation, or to allow them to set up a new branch. HJ members themselves were encouraged to bring along nonmember friends to meetings in the hope that they would be recruited.[18] As local branches expanded they were normally divided into groups comprising seven youths and a leader, and into *Scharen* made up of three groups and a leader.[19] HJ propaganda actions through towns and villages, often on fast banner-bedecked lorries in the style of the NSDAP, marches, parades, and noisy demonstrations were also favourite devices employed to attract new membership. The strongest HJ *Gaue* tended to be the most active, such as South Hannover-Brunswick, Saxony, Thuringia, Schleswig-Holstein, and Mecklenburg, while weak HJ areas like the industrial Rhineland, Berlin, Brandenburg, Oberpfalz, Hamburg, and Lower Franconia lacked enthusiasm.[20]

It must be emphasised, however, that the HJ never displayed the astonishing degree of adroitness in its propaganda appeal that the NSDAP did. The HJ tried, usually without much success, to imitate techniques of the party, such as mobilising resources to concentrate on one specific target at a time, but devoid of adequate funds, the HJ was largely unable to improvise and experiment with new and exciting mass media aids such as the NSDAP had. Due to a lack of money, the foundation of new local branches was made difficult.[21]

Until 1931 when greater uniformity was imposed by von Schirach, the character of HJ local branches revealed more diversity than in the NSDAP or SA. Fundamentally this was an indication of the weakness of a *Reichsleitung* unable to stamp the whole organisation with a united personality, but at the same time, the situation underlined the ability of the *Gauführer* to shape his province as he wanted. The nonexistence of a wholesale indoctrination apparatus in the pre-1933 HJ was also an important factor (see chap. 3). Hence, there were groups which were wholly proletarian in character, militantly social revolutionary in outlook, and found in large urban industrial areas; groups which were more nationalist, located in nonindustrial or lightly industrialised districts, in rural parts and in the smaller towns and villages; groups that had a definitely military personality more in keeping with the style of the SA (all HJ units were noted for their toughness and in the ranks there was no room for those who were unwilling to fight and even risk their lives, but units which copied the SA to the exclusion of every other consideration were in a minority and did not reflect the general tenor of the HJ); and finally, groups of younger members that indulged more often in the routine of a conventional youth organisation, therefore similar in some respects to the *Bündische* Youth, but this type was rare in the HJ.

Although the HJ welcomed recruits at all times, there were certain standards of entry to be met. HJ statutes before 1933 emphasised several important conditions before a youth could be allowed to join. For example, according to regulations issued in May 1929, it was specifically stated that only those of German nationality and of "pure Aryan stock" who were under eighteen years of age and who paid the entrance fee of 30 pfennig (subsequently raised to 50 pfennig) could become members. Local branch leaders had the right to refuse admission and they were under no obligation to say why. When admitted, each new member received a membership card; if he later left the HJ he was supposed to put his reasons in writing and return his card, but his membership dues had to be fully paid beforehand. It was also understood, of course, that all new members accepted the doctrine of national socialism and acknowledged Adolf Hitler's leadership. These same standards were reiterated in a decree of 1 January 1932, with the additional provision that all potential members had to be physically healthy.[22]

The maintenance of discipline was obviously a basic consideration for the HJ, but while the NSDAP had *Uschla* from 1926, there was no highly organised formal disciplinary machinery in the HJ before 1933, and nothing to compare with the HJ Patrol Service *(Streifendienst)* which developed after 1934. It was essentially the political fight that separated the loyal from the disloyal and the strong from the weak, so that those who became disinterested or disillusioned were permitted to withdraw. This informality was particularly true of the period from 1926 until May 1929, when the HJ became a legal association (see chap. 2).

By German law, every association had to adopt bylaws and in those for the HJ, paragraph 5 enunciated for the first time rules for the organisation of HJ discipline.[23] Members were now to be dismissed if they were found guilty of making defamatory statements, of working against the interests of the HJ, or of committing moral offences which brought ignominy or scandal to the group. Furthermore, members ran the risk of dismissal if they caused repeated disputes or quarrels; if, despite warning, they fell three months in arrears with their dues; or if they lost interest in the HJ. It was therefore a fairly strict code of discipline which was introduced in 1929; because of the HJ's expansion, however limited, the laxity of earlier years could not be allowed to continue if the organisation was to retain any semblance of integrity.

The decisions for the expulsion of members were the responsibility of the chairman of the local branch, the area *Gau* leader, the *Reichsführer* in his capacity as chairman of the HJ Association, and finally a members' meeting of the local branch concerned, which would vote in democratic fashion on the case pending.[24] Every expellee received a letter signed by the person or persons responsible for the decision with the reasons stated; it was possible to appeal to a higher-ranking HJ leader within eight days of the expulsion order to ask for a reexamination of the case. The decision of the *Reichsführer,* however, was final and irrevocable. When an entire local branch committed offences warranting expulsion, the *Reichsführer* was empowered to dissolve it en bloc and to confiscate its assets for the *Reichsleitung.*

After having been expelled, a former member was usually put on an unofficial "Black List," which virtually prohibited him from rejoining the HJ at any time in the future.[25] To provide additional authority for the execution of these disciplinary arrangements, an experimental *Uschla* was established on 15 June 1931 in the HJ. Led by Willi Stein-decker, this office had functions similar to those of the party *Uschla*, but Gruber was slightly embarrassed by its presence and his successor, von Renteln, firmly denied its existence on 26 February 1932, reaffirming that the local leader and ultimately the *Reichsführer* decided on all matters of discipline.[26]

The regulations of 1929 remained operative without modification until 7 March 1932 when von Renteln indicated significant changes. The grounds which warranted expulsion were widened so that members who now refused to obey a lawfully given order were immediately dismissed. Also, to those authorised to expel were added the local *Bezirksführer, Gefolgschaftsführer, Gebietsführer,* and vice-chairman of the HJ association.[27] But at the same time, the democratic procedure whereby a local members' meeting could vote on an expulsion issue was abolished, a development which must be seen in a wider context of progressive centralisation.

In a confidential letter of 15 January 1931, Gruber thanked his colleagues for the work of the past year which, he said, made the HJ organisation "stronger than ever before."[28] However, the HJ had in reality done comparatively little in 1930 to ensure a stable and efficient structure. The manifold changes in personnel and the creation of new *Gaue* resulted merely in a degree of uncertainty in the administrative framework which the HJ would have to remedy quickly if it were to withstand the strains and tensions of the 1930s. The year 1930 had brought only a marginal improvement on the organisational slackness of the 1920s, so that the necessity for more constructive and comprehensive solutions weighed heavily.

Germany's grave economic condition intensified in 1931. The registered number of unemployed assumed gigantic proportions, and no relief was afforded by Bruening's ill-conceived deflationary economic and financial policies.[29] The financial crisis reached a new peak in July 1931 when, following the failure of the *Kreditanstalt,* Austria's greatest banking institution, the *Darmstädter-und National Bank* collapsed. In these circumstances, President Herbert Hoover's issue of a one-year moratorium on reparations payments was doubly welcome to the tottering German economy, but it acted only as a temporary alleviation. Instead of joining together despite long-established differences, the democratic parties made the deadly mistake of failing to be aware of the political and constitutional dangers of the situation;

there was no rallying together in a common endeavour to defend democracy. The government fared no better abroad and suffered a profound humiliation in September 1931 when France vetoed the proposed Austro-German Customs Union. In October 1931, under pressure from Hindenburg, Bruening built a cabinet free of party connections, thus clearing the way for a purely presidential cabinet of experts. The legitimacy of the government now rested solely on the emergency powers of the president. Parliamentary activity further decreased and as the Reichstag vacated power in the state, a vacuum was created in which various interest groups battled for supremacy.[30]

The domestic and foreign scene in 1931 continued, therefore, to play into the hands of the antidemocratic forces, especially on the right. The impressive electoral success of the NSDAP in Oldenburg (May), Hamburg (September), and Hesse (November) was complemented by the increase in NSDAP party membership to 450,000 during the year. Moreover, DNVP leader Hugenberg's continued hostility to the republic led to an ephemeral revival of the National Opposition alliance with the NSDAP and other right-wing organisations in the Harzburg Front in late 1931. This was foreshadowed the previous February when the NSDAP and DNVP (and KPD) walked out of the Reichstag in protest against the government. Hugenberg expected to win over Hitler as his "drummer" and through him exert a decisive influence on national politics, while the Führer agreed to participate only after slowly overcoming a reluctance to ally once again with "bourgeois reactionaries." As if to reassert his independence of the Harzburg meeting on 11 October, Hitler arranged his own national socialist demonstration in Brunswick a few days later when 100,000 SA and SS men, accompanied by 3,800 Hitler youths, showed the power of the movement.[31] Despite his increasing popularity, Hitler was nonetheless no nearer the chancellorship, and Hindenburg's aversion to him was strengthened during their abortive interview on 10 October.

General Kurt von Schleicher, the conservative-minded and extremely able political affairs expert of the army who exercised considerable influence on von Hindenburg, played a decisive role in political events from that time forward. He gave Bruening his confidence until the spring of 1931, but as the economic crisis deepened and opposition to the unpopular chancellor increased, Schleicher's attitude began to change. He realised that Bruening was not fulfilling the purpose for which he had been appointed, namely, to rally the moderate elements of the right and thus to take the steam out of the extremists. Schleicher now began to think in terms of bringing Hitler into a coalition government where he could be "tamed."[32] The general's greatest fear was that the struggle between the government and NSDAP would eventually explode into civil war in which the *Reichswehr* would become unavoidably involved. Schleicher was determined to prevent any implication of this kind.

An organisational development of significance to the whole national socialist movement was the opening on 1 January 1931 of its new central headquarters, the Brown House, in Munich's Briennerstrasse. This was an indication of the huge expansion of the NSDAP's organisational and bureaucratic structure which necessitated a move to more spacious premises, and the event also reflected the NSDAP's continued search for respectability among the German bourgeoisie; hence the Brown House was looked upon as a political status symbol. More importantly perhaps, the fact that the NSDAP could afford to purchase this large mansion stressed the recent improvement in the party's pecuniary situation.

Following Hitler's alliance with Hugenberg in 1929 and the NSDAP's orientation towards a bourgeois, antisocialist course, but especially following the Reichstag elections in 1930, the large amount of public interest generated in the national socialist movement resulted in substantial financial backing by a number of Bavarian and Rhineland coal and steel magnates. They were anxious to bolster the NSDAP against the rising threat of left-wing radicalism. Moreover, Hitler's promises of destroying the Versailles Treaty, introducing an enlarged rearmament programme, lifting trade restrictions, and stopping reparations payments sounded good to many industrialists, and a minority were prepared at this stage to actively support him. Fritz Thyssen, head of the Vereinigte Stahlwerke complex and Emil Kirdorf, the Ruhr coal baron, made particularly generous contributions. Others included Cologne banker Baron Kurt von Schröder, at whose home the famous Hitler-Papen meeting took place in January 1933, Georg von Schnitzler of I.G. Farben, and the piano manufacturer Carl Bechstein, an early admirer of the Führer. At the same time, big business still lent support to other parties like the DVP and DNVP. In central Germany, large firms such as Siemens and AEG remained aloof while Krupp, whose later involvement with the national socialists personified the collaboration of industry, gave nothing until after 1933. On balance, however, the NSDAP now had unprecedented sources of funds.

Nonetheless, very little of this money was passed on to the HJ. Gruber complained in 1930 that the HJ *Reichsleitung* had no money, and von Schirach also stated that "the greatest worry of the year of struggle 1930–31 was the shortage of money."[33] In January 1931, Gruber stressed again that the poverty of the organisation was a serious handicap to its expansion. He promised to try to rectify the situation by asking the NSDAP *Gau* leaderships to help the corresponding HJ *Gaue*.

The only financial support given by the party at this time was a paltry average of 100 reichsmarks per month to the HJ *Reichsleitung,* while NSDAP and SA local branches gave virtually nothing. A report of 9 May 1931 refers to the "unfavourable" financial state of affairs in HJ *Gaue* Berlin, Brandenburg, and Ostmark, but the same could also have been said of many other *Gaue.* Rudolf Schmidt complained in May 1931 that his work with the Border Land Office was continually hampered by inadequate finance, and that he even had to meet expenses out of his own pocket.[34]

This neglect of the HJ by the NSDAP and SA even when they were in a position to lend assistance substantiates the hypothesis that organisational links between them were insecure at least until 1931. Minor financial concessions were a reduction in the entrance fee to NSDAP meetings for HJ members who produced their HJ membership card and who were wearing civilian dress, and a payment of a smaller monthly membership fee to the NSDAP for those HJ youths who were also party members. Because of the extraordinary pressure to make every mark count, the most overworked leaders in the HJ *Reichsleitung* were surely treasurer August Schröder and his predecessor, Gerhard Stöckel.[35]

The contributions of individual *Gaue* to the *Reichsleitung* between 1 January 1931 and the end of June 1931 shows the kind of revenue at the HJ's disposal (see Appendix VI). The largest amounts were sent by Saxony, Thuringia, Pomerania, Breslau and Württemberg, in that order, but most donations were pathetically small, notably that from Berlin. These *Gaue* had a hard struggle to remain solvent, though the Berlin HJ was in more serious trouble than most; by January 1932 it had accumulated debts of 1,413.50 reichsmarks. The inept financial administration of *Gauführer* Robert Gadewoltz between 1928 and 1931 was a primary cause (see chap. 4), but the fact that the HJ membership in Berlin was drawn from the poorer classes who had little extra money to spend on anything was also an important factor.

From these meagre funds, a certain proportion had to be laid aside for the salaries of *Reichsleitung* members, although the provincial leaders did not receive a regular income from the HJ. Occasionally, they would be given a small subsidy, depending on the needs of their *Gau.* This position was likened to that in the NSDAP where only a few *Gauleiters* were paid a salary. The monthly salaries of the principal members of the *Reichsleitung* before and after 16 March 1931, when an increment was paid, were particularly exiguous; Gruber, for example, received 108 reichsmarks before and only 400 reichsmarks afterwards.[36] Others received payments before 16 March ranging from 65 to 330 reichsmarks, with Reich secretary Richard Wagner receiving the latter amount. Besides Gruber, Wagner continued to be given the largest amount, 330 reichsmarks, after 16 March, followed by organisation leader Franz Schnaedter, with 220 (see Appendix VII).

The smallness of these salaries suggests that the HJ leaders had supplementary sources of income. Those who were unable to find a civilian job would for a time draw an unemployment allowance from the state. Gruber collected fees for public lectures, personal appearances, and newspaper articles, but a lucrative source was his ownership of the *Jungfront-Verlag* in Plauen, which published all HJ propaganda and press material until the end of 1931. *Reichsleitung* salaries amounted between 1 January 1931 and 16 March 1931 to 3,182.50 reichsmarks and to 6,860 reichsmarks between 16 March and the end of June 1931, a total of 10,042.50 reichsmarks.[37] The total funds available to the *Reichsleitung* from the *Gaue* during this six-month period amounted to 11,282.85 reichsmarks, so that even with the addition of money from other sources, very little remained for the general running of the central administration. It is not surprising that in November 1931 the *Reichsleitung* had a debt of 2,808.25 reichsmarks.[38] This figure might well have been more substantial had not the NSDAP taken a renewed interest in the HJ in April 1931.

Despite the party's acquisition of the Brown House, the HJ continued for the time being to be centred in Plauen, though in addition to important personnel changes in the central leadership in the first quarter of 1931, alterations were made in the *Reichsleitung*'s structure as part of Gruber's attempt to infuse badly needed order into the organisation.[39] Notwithstanding some slight improvement, these efforts were insufficient to allow the HJ to adapt to the new conditions of the 1930s. The organisation still retained the legacy of the ineffective structure of the 1920s, and it was an awareness of the need to bring the organisation more into line with the requirements of the national socialist movement that partly prompted the first major reform of the HJ in the spring of 1931.

More specifically, the measures undertaken were a consequence of Röhm's reorganisation of the SA. The latent tension between the NSDAP and SA burst into the open under the strain of the economic crisis in 1930 over the question of political tactics.[40] Röhm was appointed SA chief of staff because Hitler believed him to be the only man capable of enforcing discipline in the SA and making it accept subordination to the party leadership. Röhm had not changed his basic ideas about the SA since 1925, however, still thinking of an above-party association of combat leagues dedicated to an authoritarian state, so that from the viewpoint of the NSDAP his appointment was merely a temporary solution to the refractory SA problem. In the meantime, because of the vast increase in the SA membership after 1930, Röhm determined to refashion it to enable it to expand to mass proportions, and the same principle was to be extended to the HJ. The SA had been reshaped along strong, centralised, hierarchical lines and the leadership had been purged, and this served as a model for the HJ.

Moreover, both the NSDAP and SA now appreciated, as they grew more aware of the youth organisation, how little control they actually possessed over it; hence, the HJ was to be brought into firm harness for the first time in its history. On the other hand, although these organisational considerations were obviously crucial, of greater significance was the political motivation behind the reform. Hitler was seriously worried about the threat the social revolutionary extremists in the SA and HJ posed to the unity and cohesion of national socialism, especially following the recent Stennes affair. In this context, therefore, the HJ reforms constituted part of the Führer's drive in April 1931 to more fully integrate every important ancillary organisation into the movement.

The decree issued by Hitler on 27 April, which was to take formal effect from 1 May, involved not only a reorganisation of the HJ, but also affected the relationship between the HJ and SA.[41] The HJ was no longer made responsible to the Youth Office of the NSDAP; as an "integrated organisation," it was made subordinate to the SA Supreme Command and Gruber was made directly answerable to the SA chief of staff, though he was also appointed to Röhm's staff as an advisor on youth questions.[42] In other words, the HJ was once again subject to SA control as it had been from 1926 to 1930, but effective measures were now taken to ensure that this jurisdiction would be in fact wielded by the SA.

To facilitate this, and to increase coordination between both formations, the HJ provincial organisational structure was refashioned according to that of the SA; hence the existing Oberführungen were dismantled and replaced by ten Gruppen and two independent Gaue. The HJ Gruppen, in each of which were organised a number of Gaue, were Ostland, East, North, Northwest, West, Southwest, South, Middle, Silesia, and Austria; Berlin and Munich were the independent Gaue. The HJ leaders of these twelve units were made responsible to the corresponding SA leaders in each area; HJ leaders below the rank of Gauführer were not, however, answerable to corresponding SA ranks, but "in the interests of the movement" they were advised to work together whenever occasion demanded.[43] The SA had authority over the vital positions of command in the HJ, and a firm grip, therefore, on the hub of the organisation. The extent of SA control was also precisely calculated; it was to supervise HJ participation in marches and demonstrations as well as all its other public appearances. The SA had the right to protest against the appointment of personnel to the posts of HJ *Gruppenführer* and HJ *Gauführer* of Berlin and Munich. The HJ leaders in those cities were to be youth advisors to the SA *Gruppen* and *Gau* leaderships, respectively, to ensure cooperation between the two organisations at the highest level; they continued also to be youth advisors to the corresponding NSDAP leadership, a point emphasised by an HJ memorandum of 20 July 1931 to dispel any ambiguity about this matter.[44]

The ten *Gruppenführer* constituted the new aristocracy of the HJ leadership. It was the task of each *Gruppenführer* to oversee the work of all *Gaue* grouped within his area, and he alone bore responsibility for the development of his region. Nonetheless, his powers were carefully defined.[45] The *Gruppenführer* was not allowed to appoint or dismiss a *Gau* leader, nor was he to give advice in this matter. If he considered that a change in *Gau* leadership was necessary, he had to contact the *Reichsleitung* and state his reasons in a written report. If his report was accepted, the *Reichsführer* would commission the *Gruppenführer* to recommend in consultation with the regional NSDAP office a new *Gauführer*; the nominee, however, could only be finally appointed by the *Reichsleitung*. This procedure was indicative therefore of a greater degree of systemisation in the HJ's bureaucratic machinery. When a dispute arose in a *Gau* which made action on the part of the *Gruppenführer* appear necessary, he had the right to intervene as he saw fit on receiving a written order or telegram of instruction from the *Reichsleitung*. The special occasions on which a *Gruppenführer* could issue written orders in addition to circulars were when he was given explicit permission from the *Reichsführer* to do so, and when a mass demonstration involving more than one *Gau* was being prepared within his area of command. Under no circumstances was a *Gruppenführer* permitted to modify or contradict orders given out by the *Reichsleitung*. To assist in his work, the *Gruppenführer* had normally only one adjutant, but he could call on specialists as needed, and could also set up an advisory committee of selected *Gau* leaders. A vital task for the *Gruppenführer* was to select the correct personnel for posts in his area.

More immediately, the *Gruppenführer* had to apply the principles of reorganisation contained in the new reforms, including changes at a lower level. Hence, the smallest unit within the *Schar*, the *Gruppe*, was to be renamed *Kamaradschaft*, while the strength of individual formations was remoulded as follows: *Kamaradschaft* (comprising seven youths); *Schar* (with from four to six *Kamaradschaften*, representing not more than fifty youths); *Gefolgschaft* (composed of three *Scharen*); *Ortsgruppe* (made up of between two to four *Gefolgschaften*); *Bezirk* (controlling all local branches within a defined area); *Gau* (consisting of *Bezirke*); *Gruppe*, the top unit of the HJ structure.[46]

The HJ *Reichsleitung* remained largely unaltered in April, retaining the composition of four divisions *(Abteilungen)* which had been established in February. Indeed, the changes made at the centre in February had paved the way for the more comprehensive reforms a few months later.[47] As part of the overall rationalisation programme it was decided to centralise the despatch of orders and directives from the *Reichsleitung* to the higher HJ leaders throughout Germany. For this purpose, a small periodical called *Kommando-Brücke* was issued monthly from 20 July 1931.[48]

This wholesale reorganisation had two results. Firstly, as an exercise in strengthening and rationalising the HJ administrative structure, it had only limited success because the consequent improvement was relative in comparison with the laxity that had existed until 1931. In such a situation, any change was bound to be for the good. But the HJ report of June 1931 which expressed satisfaction with the outcome—"the organisation is so built today that it is sufficient for any demands made on it"—was to prove wildly overoptimistic within a few months.[49] Secondly, the HJ was undeniably brought under the effective control of the SA in crucial areas, so that the youth group did become a more integrated unit of the national socialist movement as Hitler had planned.

Moreover, these bonds were cemented by the new financial relationship between the HJ and NSDAP, a development consistent with the more stringent control now wielded from above. Beginning in June 1931, the NSDAP *Reichsleitung* assumed responsibility for the entire expenditure of the HJ central leadership, while in return it received 400 reichsmarks monthly from the HJ as a nominal reimbursement payment. The principle and practice was established that the HJ was to be for the first time financially dependent on the party. In addition, the ten HJ *Gruppenführer* were each given 30 reichsmarks monthly from the NSDAP, and HJ *Gauführer,* in their capacity as youth advisors to the party leadership of their area, were also entitled to a small monthly stipend. Both HJ *Gruppen* and *Gau* leaders could earn more if they were also appointed official party speakers.[50]

The SA had by no means a stranglehold on the HJ, for there were spheres of activity where it still had some initiative to act, especially in the lower echelons. Gruber exaggerated the position when he stated that "the Hitler Youth continues to be a fully independent organisation";[51] the HJ enjoyed no more than a limited freedom. Unlike previous directives, it is certain that those of April 1931 were fully implemented; they were lucidly defined, and the organisational machinery of the SA and to a lesser extent the HJ were better equipped to make sure that they were given practical application. Furthermore, the decision to transfer the headquarters of the HJ from Plauen to

Munich, next to the NSDAP and SA central administrations, as of 1 May 1931 meant that the HJ would no longer be able to evade regulations since they were issued almost literally from next door.[52] The time had come when the HJ had at last to toe the line.

This move was the first outward sign since 1929 that the NSDAP leadership was dissatisfied with Gruber's leadership of the HJ. Many party chiefs in Munich had been uneasy for some time about the HJ being administered from Plauen, and they felt that it would serve the best interests of the whole movement if the HJ was sited where it could be more readily observed by the party. Gruber would not have as much freedom as hitherto, and he would henceforth have to pay more attention to the views of the NSDAP. In addition to the political reasons intimated above, the move was also prompted by a genuine desire to give the HJ organisation more coherence. The party believed that this could be best done from Munich which, after all, was the "capital of the movement" (Hauptstadt der Bewegung). [53] Nonetheless, the transfer came as a shock to Gruber and he regarded it as a rebuff. In a letter to Major Walter Buch on 18 May 1931 one of Gruber's colleagues, Rudolf Schmidt, wrote that the Reichsführer "did not go willingly" to Munich.[54] Gruber must also have realised that there was now a question mark over his future as HJ leader, for he was now to all intents and purposes on trial before the NSDAP hierarchy. This situation largely explains the feverish activity of the HJ in the early autumn of 1931.

The HJ's resentment at the deepening economic and political crises in Germany triggered off a nationwide propaganda offensive at the beginning of April under the slogan, "The SPD is anti-youth,"[55] but this was only a prelude to the HJ campaign in September. Gruber intimated his intention to stage the "September action," as he termed it, on 20 July;[56] it was of crucial significance to his position as Reichsführer, for he was fully alive to the fact that unless he augmented the growth rate of the organisation very quickly, he would lose his office. For Gruber, therefore, the campaign was his final effort to convince Hitler of his capacity to lead the HJ, and the elaborate preparations he undertook reflected his desperation to do well. The action, also given urgency by the many embarrassments of the Bruening cabinet that autumn, was designed "to further weaken the Marxist youth front, to embrace the masses of confessional and unorganised youth within the sphere of national socialism, and to win every boy and girl of our party comrades for our organisation."[57] The battle cry adopted was, "No town, no hamlet, no village without the Hitler Youth!" and it was aimed to boost the membership to 50,000. Throughout that month, every Gau with the exception of Berlin (which was experiencing one of its periodic fits of lethargy) was immersed in a plethora of propaganda.[58]

The activity was concluded by a "National Hitler Youth Rally" which was staged in every *Gau* at the same time in all parts of Germany, and at which a specially written manifesto by Gruber entitled, "Manifesto of the Young Generation," was read out. The rallies lasted from 26 to 27 September and were conducted on the same lines as the HJ's *Reichsappell* in November 1928 (see chap. 2).[59] The manifesto stated:

> We, the youth of Germany, we, the coming generation, we, the youths of work and action, raise the right hand of awakening Germany as a pledge of German youth in the year of dishonour, ignominy, and enslavement of our nation, 1931. We, the children of the war . . . lower our flags and silently pray for our fathers and brothers who died for the freedom of German soil in the field of honour. [At this point, the flags were to be lowered and one minute's silent meditation observed.] We, who are of German blood and German race, struggle on! . . . Despite prohibition, terror, and wickedness, the youth of Germany will follow in the fellowship of Adolf Hitler. Despite everything! We will stay loyal to the flag! We are resolved to have our legitimate patrimony! We demand! End the payment of tribute! Down with the war guilt lie! Win back our stolen land! Freedom for the awakening nation! Social equality for all honestly industrious German workers of the mind and body, according to the meaning of Adolf Hitler! Create a government which has the full trust of the German people and German youth! Down with the wickedness of . . . the parties! Down with antinational and Jewish influences in the state, in German economic life, and in the culture of our nation! As the young guard of nationalism, we want to be the torchbearer of the German idea. Under the swastika . . . we want to fight and win space, bread and work for the nation! Youth, come here! Adolf Hitler leads the way! Raise up the banners! [To be followed by the first verse of the *Horst Wessellied*.][60]

Two aspects of the manifesto are particularly noteworthy. In comparison with most other statements issued by Gruber on the aims and tactics of the HJ, this declaration stands out because it emphasises not the socialistic but the nationalistic virtues of the HJ. The terms "Germany" and "German" are used twelve times, while there is not one single mention of "socialism" or "socialist." The themes harped upon are those pertaining to German national interests and honour, the termination of reparations, the recovery of the lost territories in the east, and the denunciation of the war guilt clause of the Versailles

Treaty. With the addition of an anti-Semitic reference, the manifesto becomes fundamentally analogous to the typical NSDAP declaration. To deliver a plea almost totally divested of socialist terminology was indeed most unusual for Gruber. But an explanation becomes apparent when the second interesting feature is examined, namely, the unashamed panegyric of Hitler, who is cited three times. It is obvious that by stressing the HJ's nationalism and his personal loyalty to Hitler, Gruber was endeavouring to convince his increasingly critical Führer of his own and the HJ's political trustworthiness in the national socialist movement. The tone and substance of this declaration were contrived to help save Gruber's position as *Reichsführer*.

Although the HJ claimed to have doubled its membership, its actual strength of 26,198 on 1 October 1931 fell well short of the planned 50,000 members.[61] In a long-term perspective, the "September action" nevertheless deserves much credit for the considerable increase in HJ membership by the end of 1931. Gruber's cardinal error was that once he had awakened to the party's displeasure at the way the HJ was developing, he became overambitious for himself and the HJ when it was too late. To set the impossible target of 50,000 members was suicidal, for anything that fell short of this figure would be easily interpreted as failure by his numerous critics. As events were soon to prove, this is exactly what happened.

Disenchantment with Gruber's leadership of the HJ had increased to the point where his dismissal was a strong probability. Instead, it was announced on 29 October 1931 that Hitler had accepted Gruber's resignation.[62] The news was sudden but not unexpected. Gruber had been a competent enough commander in the early days of the HJ, but it was apparent more and more from 1930 onwards that he did not possess the requisite ability to transform the HJ into a strong national movement of sizable dimensions. He had taken the HJ as far as his limited abilities would allow him, and had shown himself incapable of realising the more demanding schemes held for the group by many of his colleagues.

But this was not all. There had been rumours, accusations, and dark whispers concerning Gruber for some years. Von Schirach's doubts about him increased after their confrontation in 1929 (see chap. 5); Karl Kroll was a bitter enemy (see chap. 4); and Rudolf Schmidt maintained the momentum of dissatisfaction in 1931. There is an illuminating series of correspondence between Schmidt and NSDAP authorities.[63] Schmidt complained on 18 March 1931 that his work in the Border Land Office was being constantly hampered by Gruber's indifferent and unsympathetic attitude. Schmidt threatened to resign in March 1931 over this state of affairs, but Gruber persuaded him to stay on, promising him more assistance for his work in future. Schmidt's discontent quickly flared up again, however, and by May 1931 he had emerged as an outspoken critic of Gruber's leadership. He took the extreme step of writing to *Uschla* to demand that Buch hold an investigation; Schmidt added that there was much unrest throughout the HJ leadership and rank and file over Gruber and warned that a lot of tension was being created "which will lead to an unpleasant explosion" if matters were not swiftly rectified. Herbert Peter, Reich propaganda leader and an HJ *Gruppenführer,* alleged that Gruber was a drunkard and embezzler. An enquiry was begun shortly afterwards by Manfred von Fuchs of the Supreme SA Command, and the results of this may have had some bearing on the events surrounding Gruber's departure.[64]

The HJ press did not dwell on the episode; indeed its silence was ominous. The opposition press, for example, the *Münchener Post* of 26 November 1931, asserted that Hitler had been forced to dismiss Gruber, and went on to say that for a long time there had been many serious complaints against him from HJ and NSDAP circles, and that he led "a very dissolute life," was a heavy drinker (as both Kroll and Peter had alleged), and was altogether unfit to lead the HJ.[65] The NSDAP threw a blanket of secrecy over the affair, which only served to deepen the mystery. The official version of what happened was given by von Schirach in 1933:

> His nervous condition was such that he was simply no longer physically capable of continuing work, [and his resignation] was necessary because Kurt Gruber, especially during the last months of his leadership, was unable to devote all his powers to his duties.[66]

The view that ill health caused Gruber's "resignation" is, however, unsatisfactory. The comments made by von Renteln about the HJ organisation under Gruber reveal at least one fundamental reason why the NSDAP intervened in October to insist, not suggest, that Gruber resign. Von Renteln found the organisation in disarray. The compulsory reports made by the *Gaue* to the *Reichsleitung* were totally inadequate, and for October 1931 only one *Gau* had submitted an acceptable report and was up to date with the payment of dues. Gruber himself was not unaware of this slackness; in an order of 10 January 1931, he complained about unpunctual reports from the *Gaue.*[67] But it is obvious from von Renteln's observations that Gruber did not secure any improvement. It was even impossible to have a definite membership analysis because of the chaos. Von Renteln remarked:

The result was that on the one hand the organisation existed only on paper, and on the other, this and that had not been put into practice; a necessary strengthening was therefore prevented, which finally meant that individual *Gaue* worked without coordination and on their own resources. . . .[68]

Von Renteln did not spare any criticism of the manner in which the *Reichsleitung* functioned under Gruber, and he decided that the whole machinery had to be overhauled on a new basis quickly and thoroughly.[69] He spoke also of heavy financial debts contracted by inefficient management, and on 15 April 1932 referred to the "loose fashion" in which Gruber handled the HJ.[70]

There are, therefore, several important reasons why Gruber was forced to resign: firstly, he did not find favour with either Hitler or the NSDAP *Reichsleitung* once they were able to observe him closely in Munich. Both became progressively critical of his leadership of the HJ and by October had quite enough of him. There is little doubt that Hitler ordered Gruber's removal.[71] The HJ organisation, though tightened by the reforms of April 1931, was still imperfect. A great deal of slovenliness remained along with slack administration in vital areas, especially in the *Reichsleitung*. A more resourceful leader would have applied remedies; Gruber did not do so, and must bear the responsibility for this situation.

His careless approach was partly due to his somewhat easygoing Saxon manner, which was ill-suited to coping successfully with the HJ's limited expansion after 1930 and the more exacting burden of organisation, planning, and direction. Gruber's horizons were extremely restricted, and he was uncomfortable when the HJ headquarters were transferred to Munich. He was out of his depth there and at a loss as how to deal with the different working environment. In short, he simply did not have the qualities of a good *Reichsführer*. Moreover, Gruber had serious problems of character and personality. He was not physically strong, and had a complex about his diminutive stature, so that it was difficult for him to appear as a symbol of inspiration to his youths.[72] He had neither the appearance nor the strength of character to compel respect, and possessed no charisma to evoke enthusiasm; his authority reposed solely on the mandate he received from Hitler. Finally, too many varied sources expressed the opinion that Gruber drank excessively for it to be anything other than the truth.

Secondly, there were political implications which stand out clearly when the development of the national socialist movement in this period is examined. The common denominator of the disquiet in the movement in 1930–32 was the disillusionment of radical socialist elements with the respective leaderships of their formations, but above all with the right-wing policy of the NSDAP (see chap. 4). This dissent did nothing to convince Hitler to change his antisocialist, procapitalist course, which after all had brought him such gratifying success in September 1930. Instead, the Führer was determined to exorcise the movement of those people, particularly ones holding responsible posts, whose left-wing radicalism appeared likely to endanger his advance.

One precaution was to introduce more formal political education in the movement, including the HJ (see chap. 3). There was also the transfer of HJ headquarters to Munich. Another was to purge the NSDAP, SA and HJ of left-wing leaders. Hitler himself took over as commander of the SA, while he felt he could trust Röhm as his SA chief of staff. In the HJ, important leaders like Karl Kroll in Essen, Wilhelm Kayser in the Rhineland, Walter Burchhard in Bremen, Lothar Hilscher in Mecklenburg-Lübeck, Robert Gadewoltz in Berlin, Felix Wankel in Baden, and others were expelled during 1930–32 for social revolutionary activity (see chap. 4). It is also certain that Gruber was dismissed because of his social revolutionary outlook, despite the fact that he had manifested conspicuous loyalty to Hitler throughout his HJ career and had not been involved in any of the leftist secessions. Gruber was only one of a number of suspected left-wing leaders who were excluded from the organisation between September and December 1931. HJ *Gau* leaders Heinz Morisse in Hamburg, Hugo Maass in Düsseldorf, Heinz Mondelt in Essen, August Heymann in Danzig, August Patabel in East Prussia, Wilhelm Kaebisch in Silesia, and Walter Burchhard in Bremen all fell.[73] Hitler no doubt decided that in order to avoid any further leftist insurrections in the HJ, it was expedient to replace the social revolutionary Gruber with someone of a more orthodox national socialist stamp.

Gruber's successor as *Reichsführer,* von Renteln, was of aristocratic birth, held no strong views on socialism, and since 1929 had been leader of the middle-class NSS. Furthermore, by late 1931 most working-class leaders had been expelled and replaced by persons with a middle-class background (see chap. 3). The high-born von Schirach was appointed *Reichsjugendführer,* and he introduced many of his student friends into the HJ leadership, such as Werner Altendorf, Werner Haverbeck, Heinz John, Willi Körber, Heinrich Lüer, Carl Nabersberg, and Georg Usadel, who were all middle class and noted more for their nationalism than socialism (see Biography of HJ Leadership). The same characteristics applied to other *Gau* leaders who came into prominence in 1931 or after, like Gunter Blum in Bavaria, Lühr Hogrefe in Weser-Ems, Jacob Karbach in Koblenz-Trier, Werner Kuhnt in Silesia, Max Linsmeyer in Danzig, Hugo Mülbert-Schäfer in Essen,

Walter Schmidt in Württemberg, and Herbert von Schmieden in Hesse-Nassau.

Gruber's departure did not signify, however, the abrupt change-over of the HJ from a proletarian to a bourgeois organisation. As pointed out in chapter 3, the HJ leadership was largely middle class from 1926 on and its ordinary membership remained mainly working class until 1933. Although the HJ did not lose its social revolutionary character before 1933, the post-1931 leadership was not as socialistic as the earlier leaders and the HJ began to emphasise its nationalism more than its socialism. The HJ's socialists fell because Hitler was no longer prepared to tolerate their political views. He wanted reliable people around him who would attenuate the HJ's leftist leanings. Gruber was made the scapegoat of the HJ revolts of 1930–31, and was dismissed as part of Hitler's overall policy of pushing socialists out of the movement. Gruber's fate could have been worse. Although no longer in the HJ, he continued until his death in 1943 to hold office in the NSDAP and SA in Saxony, while other political persona non grata like Otto Strasser and Walter Stennes were expelled altogether and Gregor Strasser and Ernst Röhn were shot.

Notes: Chapter 6

1. BA:Akte NS 26/361. In *Gau* South Hannover-Brunswick, for example, *Gau* leader Lauterbacher organised fifteen rallies, nineteen publicity meetings, three "Freedom Days," sixteen marches, and numerous parents' evenings in August alone. In September, he organised seventy meetings of various kinds, three mass demonstrations, and a propaganda excursion through Lower Saxony in fast lorries (H. Bolm, *Hitlerjugend in einem Jahrzehnt* [Brunswick, 1938], p. 123).

2. See R. Heberle, *Landbevölkerung und Nationalsozialismus* (Stuttgart, 1963).

3. See G. Stoltenberg, *Politische Strömungen im Schleswig-Holsteinischen Landvolk, 1918–1933* (Düsseldorf, 1962); J. Noakes, *The Nazi Party in Lower Saxony 1921–33* (Oxford, 1971); E. Schön, "Die NSDAP in Hessen," (Ph.D. diss., University of Mannheim, 1970).

4. See E. Matthias and R. Morsey, eds., *Das Ende der Parteien 1933* (Düsseldorf, 1963).

5. See L. Hertzmann, *DNVP: Right-Wing Opposition in the Weimar Republic* (Lincoln, Nebr., 1963).

6. SAK:Abt. 403:No. 16754; SAB:4/65 781/146; SAB:4/65 1678/280; Bay. HSA:ASA:Akte NS/1541.

7. Bay. HSA:ASA:Akte NS/1849; Bay. HSA:ASA:Akte NS/1544.

8. BA:Sammlung Schumacher:Gruppe VIII. No. 239; LASH:Oberpräsidium Schleswig:Abt. 301. No. 4558; SAK:Abt. 403:No. 16754.

9. SAK:Abt. 403:No. 16754.

10. Ibid.

11. BA:Akte NS 26/361. Schnaedter was replaced as leader of the Propaganda and News Service by Karl Kroll. Schnaedter, who held various leading posts within an unusually short period in 1930, was named chief editor of the *Jungfront-Verlag*, but he was succeeded in May 1930 by Alfred Bach (SAB:4/65 781/146).

12. Bay. HSA:ASA:Akte NS/1544.

13. See P. Hüttenberger, *Die Gauleiter* (Stuttgart, 1969).

14. Bay. HSA:ASA:Akte NS/1542; SAK:Abt. 403:No. 16754; BA:Akte NS 26/339.

15. Bay. HSA:ASA:Akte NS/1541; also see Appendix IV.

16. SAK:Abt. 403:No. 16754. The seven *Oberführer* were: Robert Gadewoltz as *Oberführer* East (Bay. HSA:ASA:Akte NS/1542); Theo Kienast as

Oberführer Middle, Franz Schnaedter as *Oberführer* South West, Wilhelm Kayser as *Oberführer* West, Wilhelm Barth as *Oberführer* South East (SAB:4/65 781/146); Walter Burchhard as *Oberführer* North-North West, and Karl Heinz Bürger as *Oberführer* North (SAK:Abt. 403:No. 16754).

17. SAK:Abt 403:No. 16754.

18. BA:Akte NS 26/361.

19. Bay. HSA:ASA:Akte NS/1555.

20. BA:Akte NS 26/339.

21. BA:Akte NS 26/361.

22. SAB:4/65 781/146; Bay. HSA:ASA:Akte NS/1541; BA:Akte NS 26/339.

23. Bay. HSA:ASA:Akte NS/1541.

24. Ibid.

25. BDC, as indicated to the author by an examination of several hundred personal files.

26. BA:Akte NS 26/342; Bay. HSA:ASA:Akte NS/1849.

27. W. Tetzlaff, *Das Disziplinarsrecht der Hitler-Jugend* (Berlin, 1944), p. 13. These were new grades introduced in April 1931.

28. Bay. HSA:ASA:Akte NS/1849. See also Appendix V for details of the HJ *Reichsleitung.*

29. See W. Conze, "Bruenings Politik unter dem Druck der Grossen Krise," *Historische Zeitschrift* 199 (1964):529–50.

30. See K. D. Bracher, *Die Auflösung der Weimarer Republik* (Stuttgart, 1957).

31. Bay. HSA:ASA:Akte NS/1540. *Gau* South Hannover-Brunswick had by far the largest representation with 1,000 youths, while Berlin sent only 100 and Hamburg 50 (BA:Akte NS 26/342). This was the largest gathering of Hitler youths since the 1929 NSDAP party rally, and in a letter of warm congratulations to those concerned on 22 October, SA Chief of Staff Röhm specifically acknowledged the contribution of the HJ to the demonstration (FSGNS:Dokumente 102:NA/NSDAP/306).

32. T. Vogelsang, "Zur Politik Schleichers gegenüber der NSDAP," *Vierteljahrshefte für Zeitgeschichte,* Jan. 1958.

33. BA:Akte NS 26/361; B. v. Schirach, *Die Hitler-Jugend: Idee und Gestalt* (Leipzig, 1934), p. 28.

34. Bay. HSA:ASA:Akte NS/1849; BA:Akte NS 26/372; Bay. HSA:ASA:Akte NS/1544; SAB:4/65 781/146; BA:Akte NS 26/370.

35. BA:Sammlung Schumacher:Gruppe VIII. No. 239; FSGNS:Hann 80/II/770; BA:Akte NS 26/370; SAB:4/65 1678/280.

36. Bay. HSA:ASA:Akte NS/1555.

37. Ibid.

38. BA:Sammlung Schumacher:Gruppe VIII:No. 239.

39. A report of 1 February indicated that *Gauführer* of Munich-Upper Bavaria, Emil Klein, had been named *Oberführer* South, and Richard Nöthlichs, adjutant to Gruber, had been appointed *Oberführer* South West, thus replacing Franz Schnaedter (SAB:4/65 781/146). By the end of February, the *Reichsleitung* had been remodelled into four principal divisions *(Abteilungen): Abteilung* I was subdivided into seven sections to deal with specific areas of administration including organisation, education, press, propaganda, etc.; *Abteilung* 2 was devoted to business and treasury affairs; *Abteilung* 3 and 4 dealt with the Border Land Office and the *Jungfront-Verlag* respectively (BA:Akte NS 26/370; see also Appendix V).

40. See A. Werner, "SA: 'Wehrverband,' 'Parteitruppe,' oder 'Revolutions-armee'? Studien zur Geschichte der SA und der NSDAP 1920–33," (Ph.D. diss., University of Erlangen, 1964).

41. Bay. HSA:ASA:Akte NS/1541.

42. SAB:4/65 1686/283; BA:Akte NS 26/370. A youth committee of the NSDAP, of which Gruber was a member, had been created on 27 October 1927 to direct in a general manner all aspects of youth activity in the national socialist movement (Bay. HSA:ASA:Akte NS/1542). Under the chairmanship of von Pfeffer, however, the committee never wielded any executive power, and it remained a passive body of little importance which did nothing to enforce NSDAP control over the HJ. On 11 June 1930 Major Buch took over the leadership of what had since 1928 been called the Youth Office of the NSDAP (Bay. HSA:ASA:Akte NS/1542). In the short period between von Pfeffer's retirement in September 1930 and the issuance of the SA/HJ directives in April 1931, the HJ was formally subordinate to Buch as chairman of this body whose composi-tion in June 1930 was: Buch (chairman); Hans Schemm (chairman of the NS Teachers' League); Gruber *(Reichsführer);* Adrian von Renteln (NSS *Reichsführer);* Baldur von Schirach (NSDStB *Reichsführer);* von Holzschuher (adjutant to Buch); and Hans Dietrich (NSDAP deputy in the Bavarian *Landtag* with responsibility for youth affairs) (Bay. HSA:ASA:Akte NS/1542). The pattern of only loose control of the HJ nevertheless remained undisturbed. Buch was principally occupied with *Uschla* matters and played the role of a general supervisor rather than an innovator in HJ affairs.

43. BA:Akte NS 26/364; SAB:4/65 1686/283; BA:Akte NS 26/361; Bay. HSA:ASA:Akte NS/1541.

44. SAB:4/65 1686/283; BA:Akte NS 26/361; BA:Akte NS 26/364.

45. BA:Akte NS 26/364.

46. Bay. HSA:ASA:Akte NS/1541; SAK:Abt. 403:No. 16755.

47. The most notable personnel changes were the replacement of Georg Kenzler as *Reichsscharführer* by Willi Steindecker (BA:Akte NS 26/339), and the appointment to the NSDAP *Reichsleitung, Hilfkasse* Division (Aid Fund), of the HJ *Gauführer* of Thuringia, Albert Bormann, who was the brother of Martin Bormann, leader at this time of the NSDAP *Hilfkasse* (Bay. HSA:ASA:Akte NS/1541; see also BDC:A. Bormann file). In June 1931, it was also announced that Rudolf Schmidt had resigned his post (SAB:4/65 1685/282), and that the Border Land Office would

now be led by Hans Brüss (BA:Akte NS 26/370). On 15 June, an independent Personnel Office was set up in the *Reichsleitung* under Reich Secretary Richard Wagner (BA:Akte NS 26/342); hitherto, the Personnel Office had formed part of the Secretarial Division (BA:Akte NS 26/370).

48. BA:Akte NS 26/364; SAB:4/65 1687/283.

49. Bay. HSA:ASA:Akte NS/1555.

50. Ibid.; BA:Akte NS 26/361.

51. BA:Akte NS 26/370.

52. BA:Akte NS 26/361.

53. The transfer had been anticipated in official quarters for some time. A Berlin police report said the transfer would take place at the end of June 1930 (Bay. HSA:ASA:Akte NS/1541); the same police indicated on 15 August 1930 that the move had been postponed until September 1930 (SAB:4/65 1682/281). This evidence would seem to suggest that a member of the NSDAP *Reichsleitung,* or at least someone with access to the secret plans of the party, had tipped off the authorities in advance, for there is no doubt that neither Gruber nor the HJ knew anything until the last minute.

54. BA:Akte NS 26/370.

55. BA:Akte NS 26/361.

56. BA:Akte NS 26/342.

57. Ibid.

58. SAB:4/65 781/146; SAB:4/65 1686/283; BA:Akte NS 26/342.

59. SAB:4/65 781/146; BA:Akte NS 26/342.

60. BA:Akte NS 26/342.

61. SAK:Abt. 403:No. 16755; BA:Sammlung Schumacher:Gruppe VIII. No. 239.

62. Bay. HSA:ASA:Akte NS/1544.

63. BA:Akte NS 26/370.

64. Ibid.; SAB:4/65 1686/283. I did not find archival material indicating the outcome of the investigation, but it is likely that evidence was found to discredit Gruber and that this influenced the events of October 1931.

65. Bay. HSA:ASA:Akte NS/1544.

66. V. Schirach, *Die Hitler-Jugend,* p. 23.

67. BA:Sammlung Schumacher:Gruppe VIII. No. 239; Bay. HSA:ASA:Akte NS/1849.

68. BA:Sammlung Schumacher:Gruppe VIII. No. 239.

69. Ibid.

70. Bay. HSA:ASA:Akte NS/1555.

71. In an interview with the author in Munich on 24 April 1969, Hartmann Lauterbacher, one of Gruber's *Gau* leaders in 1931, confirmed that the

NSDAP *Reichsleitung* had become very dissatisfied with Gruber by this time.

72. Lauterbacher interview, Munich, 24 April 1969.

73. BA:Akte NS 26/337; Bay. HSA:ASA:Akte NS/1849; BDC:W. Burchhard file.

Chapter 7

A New Era under New Leadership

On 30 October, the day after Gruber's dismissal, it was announced that Baldur von Schirach, the highly successful and ambitious leader of the NSDStB, had been appointed *Reichsjugendführer der* NSDAP, chief of all national socialist youth organizations.[1] On joining the NSDAP in 1925, von Schirach could hardly have realised that within a short period he would become the leading figure of the national socialist youth movement, as well as the youngest member of the top national socialist hierarchy. Von Schirach soon became a fanatical admirer and close personal friend of Hitler, who in turn came to regard him as his protégé. Von Schirach now began to personify the HJ's reverence for the Führer, for even during the *Kampfzeit* the HJ manifested an almost pseudoreligious adoration for Hitler, placing unreserved faith in his putative infallibility. The overwhelming majority of HJ youths subscribed to the Führer myth, and felt honoured and privileged to belong to an organisation which bore the name of this messianic figure, whom they were convinced would lead the way for the resurrection of the fatherland. Von Schirach expressed these feelings in many of his poems which indubitably flattered Hitler's enormous vanity.[2] Hitler did not entirely reciprocate these fulsome sentiments, because his interest in the HJ before 1933 was generally intermittent, and he was not actively involved until he feared its political radicalism. As a supreme political realist who recognised that the future lay with the younger generation but that the immediate struggle for power was all-important, Hitler devoted his energies to developing the NSDAP and SA.[3]

Meantime, Hitler had at last found a person whom he could fully trust, and whom he believed was the ideal man to build up the HJ into a powerful national concern. Von Schirach was a capable, hard-working organiser, but was often naively idealistic and romantically nationalistic. He lacked maturity, always giving the impression of being an overgrown scout leader. That essential toughness found in other national socialist leaders, which von Schirach constantly demanded of the HJ, formed no part of his own personality. He could at times be evasive and dishonest, and consequently bred distrust in many quarters. Although devoid of the cynicism of people like Goebbels and Göring, von Schirach nonetheless shared the unbounding egotism common to the national socialist elite. He remained a frustrated intellectual throughout his career, as the mediocre quality of his songs and poems confirm, and he tended to be a cultural and artistic dilettante. Furthermore, von Schirach's rather inconsistent ability as a public speaker, and his pedestrian, unoriginal mind made him one of the less colourful personages of the Führer's entourage. His appointment as *Reichsjugendführer* was without doubt one of the most important events in the history of the HJ; an association commenced that was to stretch through the Third Reich and end before the dock at Nuremberg.[4]

While von Schirach was the grand overseer of national socialist youth, thirty-four-year-old Dr. Adrian Theodor von Renteln was the new *Reichsführer* of the HJ. Born on 14 September 1897 in Hotsi, Russia, of an old Westphalian aristocratic family who had emigrated to the Baltic in the 15th century, von Renteln came to Germany during World War I. He studied national economy and jurisprudence at the universities of Berlin and Rostock, taking his doctorate in 1924. From 1924 to 1929, he travelled extensively in Europe as a free-lance journalist, and joined the NSDAP in 1929.[5] Von Renteln was subordinate to von Schirach, though he exercised considerable influence as leader of both the HJ and NSS. It would be inaccurate to describe von Renteln as von Schirach's chief executive for the HJ, therefore, although the HJ *Reichsleitung* was supervised by a newly created administrative organ, the *Reichsjugendführung*. The objective of the *Reichsjugendführung*, as a more centralised body, was to give unity to the whole national socialist youth movement, to prevent rivalries from developing, and to coordinate all activities towards the same goals. This was only one aspect of a tendency towards greater centralisation; the relationship between the HJ and SA and the financial ties between the HJ and NSDAP were further consolidated at this time.[6]

Reichsjugendführer von Schirach was given the rank of SA *Gruppenführer* and made directly answerable to the SA chief of staff. Von Schirach's task was to keep Röhm informed of every organisational question concerning youth, but particularly those questions which also involved the SA.[7] On 5 November 1931, Röhm gave out instructions containing practical details of new arrangements between the HJ and SA. He stated: "I place the greatest importance on the fact that the work and relations between the SA and the youth leagues will now be even closer than hitherto."[8]

Röhm was anxious to extend SA control from the position of April 1931 so the scope of SA authority in all HJ service matters was considerably enlarged beyond the arrangements of that time. In cases of disagreement between the HJ *Gau* leader and the SA *Gausturm* leader, the matter was remitted for arbitration to the *Reichsjugendführer*. But if the SA *Gausturm* leader objected to a measure agreed to by the HJ *Gau* leader and *Reichsjugendführer*, the SA chief of staff could intercede.[9] Therefore the *Reichsjugendführer* could not effectively impose a decision on a higher SA leader, despite his rank of SA *Gruppenführer*. The final word lay with the SA and hence von Schirach's rank in it was devoid of any substantive functional significance. By November 1931, the HJ was in fact a unit of the SA and had lost much of its residual authenticity as a youth group. Organisational bonds between both formations were applied as theoretically designed, for Röhm was not the type of person to have his rightful authority over the HJ countermanded or loosely enforced. Because von Schirach was a member of his staff, Röhm could easily observe his actions, and had the *Reichsjugendführer* been incompetent the SA chief of staff would have assuredly intervened to bring his authority to bear. At the same time, von Renteln, determined to improve the HJ's efficiency, regarded it as his duty to scrupulously fulfil the HJ's obligations to the SA.

There is evidence that this integrated relationship prospered without too much friction. The HJ leader of the Hochland (Bavaria) region, Emil Klein, an earlier critic of the NSDAP's and SA's neglect of the HJ, expressed his delight on 11 November 1931 at the cooperation now being promoted by the NSDAP *Gauleiter* of Upper Bavaria, Adolf Wagner.[10] Also, connections between the Berlin HJ and the party and SA, led by Goebbels and Graf Helldorf respectively, were reported to be "very good."[11] The SA certainly used its interventionist prerogative as never before in HJ affairs, notably in the appointments of high-ranking HJ leaders. The SA selected personnel whom it thought could be relied upon to strengthen relations with the HJ. On 9 January 1932, for instance, Victor Lutze, SA *Gruppenführer* North and later successor to Röhm, requested in a letter to von Renteln that one of his former SA leaders, Albert Wallwey, who at this point was an HJ *Gauschar* leader in the Ruhr, be appointed *Gau* leader. Lutze described Wallwey as "a good leader, an impeccable person, and an old National Socialist . . . who has done and sacrified much for the movement." Wallwey was subsequently appointed an HJ *Gebietsführer* (one rank higher than *Gau* leader).[12]

In harmony with the HJ's stricter subordination to the SA was the increased financial dependence of the youth organisation on the NSDAP as a result of simultaneous reforms in November 1931. This meant that the financial position of the HJ was further improved because it was no longer bound to pay any reimbursements to the NSDAP, and in addition received a monthly grant of 1,000 reichsmarks plus expenses; total payments from the party amounted to 1,920 reichsmarks in December 1931 and to 1,795 reichsmarks in January 1932.[13] This turn of events may be explained partly by the substantial sums of money big business was giving to the NSDAP to an increasing degree, especially after Hitler's talk to the Industry Club in Düsseldorf on 27 January 1932. More pointedly, however, as a result of the sweeping personnel changes of October-November 1931, the HJ was no longer politically suspect to Hitler. There was, therefore, a distinct correlation between political reliability and financial assistance from the party. Between 1926 and 1931 when the HJ was led by the social revolutionary Gruber and showing radical leftist propensities, it was poverty-stricken. The new financial aid and the effectiveness of the organisational programme initiated by von Renteln reduced the debt of the HJ *Reichsleitung* from 2,808.25 reichsmarks at the end of October 1931 to 432.25 reichsmarks by the beginning of 1932. The first few months of 1932 even showed a slight surplus which was also due to the extra revenue accruing from the higher membership fees introduced at the end of 1931.[14]

The position in the provincial *Gaue* was correspondingly ameliorated, but finance still continued to be a headache for most of them, because the funds given by the NSDAP were mainly reserved for the HJ *Reichsleitung*. On 8 December 1931, the NSDAP *Gauleiter* of Ostmark, Wilhelm Kube, informed von Renteln of the debts owed by HJ Ostmark, which was led by Hartmut Stegemann. Kube was obliged to give the HJ 100 reichsmarks monthly to keep it going.[15] Other HJ leaders sought more enterprising means of bolstering their finances. *Gauführer* Lauterbacher of South Hannover-Brunswick conceived the idea in December 1931 of a lottery, which enjoyed modest success for a few months.[16] Others appealed to the *Reichsleitung* for help and received sums of between 10 and 80 reichsmarks per month, but this practice was neither systematised nor applicable to every provincial leader. Among recipients of small payments were noted leaders like Werner Altendorf, Emil Klein, Gerhard Stöckel, Gunter Blum, Lothar Lange, and Gunter Stegemann, while HJ *Reichsleitung* members were still paid a small salary after November 1931.[17] Taken as a whole, the period from November 1931 to April 1932 was perhaps the most solvent of the *Kampfzeit* for the HJ.

Once these organisational and financial relations with the SA and NSDAP had been clarified, von Schirach and von Renteln set about reorganising the HJ. For this purpose, a national leaders' meeting was convened in Munich on 15 November which was also attended by Hitler, Buch and Röhm. Important decisions were taken "to enable the struggle to be continued on the widest basis and with the most intensive power." The changes took effect from 23 November.[18] The *Reichsleitung* was divided into two principal parts, the Reich organisation leadership and the Reich education leadership; the final structure was as follows:[19]

HJ Reichsleitung

REICH ORGANISATION LEADERSHIP I	REICH EDUCATION LEADERSHIP II

Secretarial Division (I/1)
  This division included:
    Reich *Schar* Office
    Reich Organisation Office
    Jungvolk Office
    HJ *Uschla* Office
    Reich Personnel Office
    BDM Office
  Treasury Affairs Division (I/2)
	The divisions in this section were:
	Education and Defence Sports
	  (Wehrsport) (II/1)
	Propaganda (II/2)
	Press (II/3)
	Foreign Office (II/4)
	Publishing (NS-Jugendverlag
	  established 1 January 1932) (II/5)

The major appointments to the above posts were completed before the end of 1931.[20] Key figures were obviously Reich organisation leader Carl Nabersberg and Reich education leader Joachim Walter who, as *Gauführer* of Berlin in 1931, had earned the respect of von Renteln. The *Reichsführer* wrote of Walter that he had "many good and proper ideas regarding youth leadership," and that "he would also be . . . a good representative of the *Reichsleitung*."[21] Walter was ably supported by twenty-three-year-old law student Nabersberg, who was a friend of von Schirach and a former NSDStB and NSS leader.[22] Nabersberg's appetite for hard work and expertise in organisational affairs made him indispensable to von Schirach in the arduous years ahead.

The provincial organisational structure was also refashioned with the ten *Gruppen* and two independent *Gaue* being replaced by twelve *Gebiete,* each of which contained a number of *Gaue.*[23] The inner structure of the HJ was also slightly altered: the designation *Ortsgruppe* for a local branch was dropped so that the vertical gradation from the bottom upwards was now *Kamaradschaft, Schar, Gefolgschaft, Bezirk, Gau,* and *Gebiet.*[24] The chain of command in order of importance was now Hitler, Röhm, von Schirach, and von Renteln.

This overhauling and streamlining of the organisation was basically motivated by the aim of compensating for Gruber's careless administration of a growing movement and also of rendering the HJ more politically sound in the eyes of Hitler. The reforms of April 1931 had not brought about the comprehensive improvement that circumstances warranted. The new measures were designed to give the HJ a much-needed structural strength and stability which would enable it to expand into the powerful national group von Schirach passionately desired. The provincial setup seemed satisfactory and von Schirach was cautious in the appointments of personnel there. The provinces could be expected to function smoothly and decisively only if the central body itself was equal to its tasks and capable of giving energetic leadership. Hence, the *Reichsleitung* was rearranged on more rational lines and had two competent assistants in Nabersberg and Walter, whose spheres of influence were prudently divided so as to avoid the clash of personalities that had been one of the worst features of the Gruber era. With an experienced and shrewd *Reichsführer* in von Renteln to take advantage of the reforms, which had brought such dependable men as Altendorf, Lange, Klein, Blum, and Theo Kosiek to the forefront, it was with some confidence that the new HJ entered what was to be the final and decisive year of the Weimar Republic, 1932. During 1931 the HJ began to change its orientation, making itself in consequence more attractive to middle-class youth.

At the beginning of 1932, the NSDAP represented the largest and most powerful political party in modern German history. During this year the political atmosphere was charged with an electric tension as public disorder increased dramatically, and as Hitler strove to attain full power in the state against the perilously weakening forces of democracy. For the HJ, the issues at stake were no less important, and concentrated efforts were made to further strengthen its organisation in preparation for *Der Tag,* the day of reckoning.

Von Renteln demanded higher standards of administration and adopted a much stricter policy about the punctual execution of orders; he delivered frequent admonitions to his top leadership about this as, for example, on 15 April:

I allow there to be no doubt that I will carry out the leadership of the HJ in the strictest manner, and I also require this from the *Gebietsführer, Gauführer,* and lower-ranking HJ leaders. I believe that strong organisation alone will enable the young German generation to successfully raise the German people from the abyss in which it stands today. Not only is every order of the HJ *Reichsleitung* to be immediately carried out, but also each one of its decrees, whether for organisation, the sale of newspapers, or whatever, is to be implemented in all cases in the most scrupulous manner. I have taken over the office of HJ *Reichsführer* with the intention of making the HJ an exemplary organisation. . . . ' Elements who do not fit the part are to be automatically dismissed.[25]

This latter resolve led to a number of personnel changes in the central and *Gebiet* leadership during the early part of 1932.[26] As part of the centralisation drive, the last independent office of the *Reichsleitung* which still existed outside Munich, the Foreign Office *(Auslandsamt),* which operated from Plauen under Hans Brüss, was dissolved in March 1932. A few days later, on 8 March, Nabersberg also took over the new *Gebiet Ausland* of the HJ. Von Renteln succeeded in getting things moving fairly smoothly, though his claim that the unwieldiness of the apparatus had been eliminated by January 1932 was certainly an exaggeration. Nor was it likely that by the same date every HJ *Gau* was reporting on time or meeting all financial commitments, as he also alleged. He simply did not have sufficient time to accomplish all this by January. On the other hand, von Renteln managed to increase the HJ membership from 28,743 on 1 November 1931 to 43,334 by 1 March 1932.[27] He had the ability to impress on his leaders that their work was not merely for the abstract benefit of the movement, but that they personally stood to gain in the long term if national socialism came to power. Additionally, von Renteln boosted the morale of the whole movement a good deal.

The political efforts of the HJ were put to the test once again during the Reich presidential elections on 13 March and 10 April 1932. Chancellor Bruening had earlier tried to secure an agreement with the party leaders in the Reichstag which would provide the two-thirds majority necessary to prolong the presidential term of office without reelection. Bruening held negotiations with Hitler in January but the latter refused to accept the chancellor's proposals. Hitler then offered to make von Hindenburg the joint candidate of the NSDAP and DNVP if the field marshal would consent to dismiss Bruening, form a right-wing national government, and hold new elections for the Reichstag and the Prussian Diet.[28] The newly elected Reichstag, in which Hitler was confident of a majority for the far right, would then proceed to extend von Hindenburg's term of office. This plan was rejected by the president, however, and after much tortuous deliberation, the Führer decided to oppose him in an electoral contest.

The March campaign was the first of five major elections in Germany in less than nine months; it was fought with particular bitterness and poignant recrimination on all sides. The National Socialists had a propaganda feast, and true to their penchant for disregarding the conventional, they made effective use for the first time in a German election of films, gramophone records, and even aeroplanes. Hitler, who was hurriedly made a German citizen shortly beforehand by the DNVP-NSDAP-controlled Brunswick state legislature, made a determined attempt to topple von Hindenburg.[29] On the eve of 13 March, Hitler issued a special proclamation thanking the HJ for its support in making the national socialist movement the largest in Germany, and calling for its unstinted assistance in the present campaign. In return, von Renteln assured Hitler that "the Hitler Youth stands immediately in service" for his candidature, and in a provocative declaration he demanded that the "sea of tears, world of hunger, despair and need in Germany" be ended once and for all by voting for Adolf Hitler.[30] In the hectic but unsuccessful campaign which ensued, the HJ at least played its part by beating the NSDAP drum as loudly as possible. Von Hindenburg received 49.6 percent of the total vote, less than the required absolute majority, thus requiring a second election.[31]

Before the second presidential election took place on 10 April, a highly important HJ meeting in Brunswick on 27 and 28 March aroused confusion and controversy, mainly because the Reich Ministry of the Interior erroneously believed the meeting would contravene the peace decree (Bürgerfrieden) issued by von Hindenburg for Easter. But it was a leaders' conference behind closed doors and not a mass political rally, so no infringement was committed by the HJ. When finally allowed to go on, the meeting formulated a battle plan for the months ahead and discussed the future development of the HJ. A series of speeches were given on different facets of HJ work by Nabersberg on organisation, Edgar Bissinger on the press, and Walter on education, but the main report came from von Renteln on the growth of the HJ under his command.[32] Von Renteln was a little too optimistic, for there was still some petty bickering, apathy, and carelessness at a provincial and local level, which he was admittedly powerless to eradicate unless given more time. A Munich police report of April shows that by and large the HJ was not yet a totally united organisation. There were examples of gross inefficiency, and in Gau Rheinpfalz, Gau leader Karl Hofmann was forced to dissolve groups in Kaiserslautern, Grimstadt, Frankenstein, Ludwigshafen, Marnheim and others because of corruption, and to expel a large number of leaders for incompetence. Meanwhile, the meeting was concluded by the consecration of 22 HJ *Gau* flags, the last such ceremony of the *Kampfzeit*, and three *Sieg Heils!* for the Führer who had sent a message of good wishes to the delegates.[33]

The Brunswick conference was soon followed, however, by the severest test to date of the whole national socialist movement. On 13 April 1932, only three days after von Hindenburg was reelected president, General Wilhelm Groener, Reich minister of the interior, issued an "Emergency Decree of the Reich President for the Security of State Authority," prohibiting the SA, SS, HJ, and other national socialist formations.[34] There was some uncertainty at first whether the HJ was actually included in the *Verbot* because it was not specifically mentioned in paragraph I of the decree which listed the groups to be banned.[35] Groener therefore promulgated a directive on 15 April clarifying the position to the ministers of the interior throughout Germany:

> Regarding enquiries of the Hitler Youth: since the Hitler Youth, according to the service regulations for the SA of the NSDAP, pages 47 and 48, was incorporated into the general organisation of the SA, even if responsibility to the SA Command was regulated only in the higher posts and in isolated ways, it legally comes under the prohibition of the emergency decree. The NSDAP is not thereby forbidden, however, from later creating like the other parties a nonmilitary youth organisation on a new basis."[36]

Bruening's government, which had been under pressure from many sources to act, issued the ban in an attempt to end the violent street fighting and to prevent the breakdown of law and order in the republic. The *Verbot* implicitly shouldered the major responsibility for this chaos on the national socialist associations, for none of the paramilitary groups of the KPD or SPD, which also, of course, participated in the brawling, were affected. There were widespread fears of an impending SA insurrection, the plans of which were allegedly contained in the controversial Boxheim document, and the government sought to take preventive action.

More decisively, however, Groener's decision was influenced to a considerable extent by pressure brought to bear on him by leaders of the SPD, and especially by Carl Severing, minister of the interior in Prussia.[37] They threatened that unless the SA was dissolved, they would not support von Hindenburg in the second presidential election. The ministers of all the larger German states also endorsed this demand. At the beginning of April, Groener had concluded that it would not be feasible to try to suppress the whole national socialist movement by force—he preferred to include the NSDAP in state governments—but the SA could be eliminated.

Political expediency dictated his next move. In view of the government's dependence on SPD toleration and Groener's wish to avoid action against the SA by individual states, he informed the ministers of the interior on 5 April that he shortly intended to propose to the president that the SA and SS be dissolved. On 8 April, Groener told army and navy chiefs of his plan and they assured him of their support. The timing of the dissolution, and indeed the dissolution itself was, therefore, a payment to the left for its electoral backing on 10 April. Two days after the election, SPD ministers Otto Braun and Severing again demanded the SA's dissolution, threatening that otherwise the states would act independently. This line of argument was compelling. On the same day von Hindenburg, feeling more confident after his victory of dealing a direct blow at Hitler, signed the emergency decree. In addition, the *Verbot* was meant to split the SA and HJ. Groener sought to destroy the latter's organisational basis and eventually incorporate its members along with other youth groups of the nationalist right into one comprehensive youth association under *Reichswehr* control.[38]

Both von Renteln and von Schirach immediately sent telegrams of protest to the government to try to convince it that the HJ was organisationally independent of the SA. It was a dishonest and rather hypocritical endeavour, for as both leaders knew very well, the HJ had been subordinated to the SA by the statutes of 27 April and 31 October 1931 and von Schirach himself had been made directly responsible to the SA chief of staff on the latter date. Von Renteln further argued on the juristic technicality that because the HJ had been a registered association since 1929 it was legally independent.[39] Their pleas were, however, deservedly rejected.

Although this was the first national ban to be applied to the HJ, a comparable situation had arisen before on a local and provincial level. The first HJ branch in the Rhineland was established in Cologne in May 1927 under the leadership of Wilhelm Kayser, but in August of that year it was banned along with the SA and SS in that area by the police.[40] In Berlin, the police also disbanded the NSDAP and its affiliates, including the HJ, on 5 May 1927, although shortly beforehand *Gauführer* Orsoleck had led his Berlin youths out of the HJ altogether (see chap. 4).[41] During the period of the ban, which was not revoked until April 1928, the *Bund Nationale Pfadfinder* was founded as a cover organisation of the HJ, and when the new *Gau* Berlin-Brandenburg was set up in May 1928, it formed the first branch of the HJ.[42] The first provincial prohibition of the new decade was issued by the *Oberpräsident* of Hannover and former Reich Minister of Defence Gustav Noske on 16 January 1930, banning secondary and trades schoolboys from joining the HJ or any other national socialist youth organisation. Noske acted, in his own words, "in order to protect the law and order of school life."[43] Hamburg school authorities took the same course in 1930, and similar prohibitions had been in operation in Württemberg since 1921 and in Bavaria since 1924.[44]

The conflict between the HJ and the police in Bavaria over the issue of schoolboy political activity was prolonged and bitter. The Munich police warned HJ *Gau* South Bavaria on 11 September 1930 that they would be watching its involvement in the Reichstag elections three days later for violations of the law. Although the ban was occasionally disobeyed, and the Bavarian Ministry of Education saw fit to issue stricter instructions in February 1932, it did effectively discourage a goodly number of schoolboys from joining the HJ. Hence, a report of 18 February 1932 stated that only 21 of an estimated 300 youths of HJ Munich were schoolboys.[45] The police often attended NSDAP and HJ meetings, noting the names of schoolboys present and then referring the matter either to the appropriate headmaster or to the juvenile courts. Expulsions from school or fines were frequently the outcome for some, and HJ leaders suspected of contravening the law, such as Emil Klein and Richard Etzel in March 1932, were brought before the courts and fined.[46]

Consequently, it was common in Bavaria for HJ groups to disguise themselves as nonpolitical organisations to ward off unwelcome police scrutiny. In 1929 the *Christliche Freischar, Gruppe Grauer Bär* was set up; in 1931, the *Schwarzer Panther;* and in 1932, the *Heimatfreunde e.V,* the *Wanderbund Weiss-Blau,* and the *Freischar Florian Geyer.*[47] The animosity with which many state authorities regarded connections between their school children and national socialist youth groups was unrelenting until 4 October 1932, when the Prussian Ministry for Education raised its prohibition on schoolboy political action.[48]

The use of cover names or organisations was the customary means employed by the HJ to evade provincial bans and thus to be able to press on with its work in safety from police intercession. There are examples of this technique in most parts of Germany before 1933. The Breslau HJ was forbidden for a period in 1931 and in order to reach the SA rally in Brunswick in October of that year, the youths travelled by bus disguised as a *Wandervogel* group, hiding their HJ uniforms and flags in boxes concealed under their seats.[49] In May 1931, HJ Bremen informed the *Reichsleitung* that it had founded a sports group, the *Hanseatischer Jugendbund,* so that the HJ in Bremen could make use of civic amenities which were denied their members. In Franconia, HJ groups camouflaged themselves for a period beginning in early 1931 as the *Fränkische Jungenschaft,* and in *Gau* Rheinpfalz, *Gauführer* Hofmann established a *Vereinigung zur Erhaltung der Burg Spangenberg* (Association for the Obtaining of Spangenberg Castle) in April 1931 with the aim of acquiring use of the ruined castle for the HJ.[50] Hofmann explained to the *Reichsleitung* that this cover was necessary because if the authorities had known that it was the HJ which wanted to use the castle, the application would have been rejected.

In the Saarland, there were periods in the 1920s when the national socialist movement was prohibited by the League of Nations authorities who administered the region by provision of the Treaty of Versailles. The HJ was banned there in 1928, but at once a *Deutsche Arbeiterjugend des Saarlandes* was created under the leadership of Fritz Lorenz to continue activities underground. Although it had no outward link with the HJ in Germany, Lorenz's group was confidentially responsible to the HJ *Reichsleitung.*[51] Finally, as a result of the national *Verbot* of April 1932, the HJ in Berlin persuaded all nationalist youth leagues in the city to join in one large association called the *Deutsche Jugendring,* which was merely designed by the HJ to shield its work for the duration of the ban.[52]

The HJ had therefore considerable experience with the techniques of evasive action, and immediately made use of its knowledge in response to Groener's *Verbot,* which allowed the NSDAP to establish another youth group provided it was nonmilitary. Thus, the *Nationalsozialistische Jugendbewegung, Deutsche Arbeiterjugend* (NSJB, National Socialist Youth Movement, German Workers' Youth) which was founded was legally permissible, though thereafter national socialist propaganda deliberately created an atmosphere of mortal danger based on the NSJB's fictitious illegality in order to engender greater enthusiasm among its youth.[53] Consequently, von Schirach's oft-quoted description of the *Verbotzeit* is nonsense:

> It was a great time. . . . We were never so fortunate as then, because we lived in constant danger. We went through the Ruhr district with pistols in our coat pockets while stones were thrown at us. We quivered at every sound together, and we had to endure house searches and arrests.[54]

Nonetheless, this masterful subterfuge, of which von Schirach was undoubtedly the designer, produced the desired result, for the NSJB thrived on its spurious persecution. The membership was more united and loyal than ever before and new recruits surged forward. From 25 April to 31 May, the NSJB staged a nationwide propaganda offensive under the slogan, "The system is against youth!"[55] and the group's spirit of defiance is well illustrated by the appeal put out by *Gebietsführer* Klein on 1 May:

> Young Comrades! He who believes that the national socialist movement can be destroyed by emergency decrees must be fundamentally mistaken. We have two brownshirts, one in the wardrobe which can be taken from us, the other which we carry in our hearts, and no one in this world will succeed in tearing this brownshirt from our hearts because it represents an ardent love of our *Volk* and fatherland![56]

The organisational disruption occasioned by the ban was minimal and insignificant. The administrative structure itself remained largely intact and was incorporated as the basis of the NSJB, which in essence represented a change in only the external appearance of the HJ. The HJ discarded its brown uniform for what von Schirach described as an "unbelievable robber's outfit," consisting of a white shirt (which the SA had been wearing in Prussia since the uniform ban of 1930), blue sailor's cap, and a mountaineer's waistcoat or civilian coat. The NSJB also issued new membership cards, the first 10,000 of which were prepared by 25 April, and the HJ insignia was temporarily abandoned. The precaution was even taken of storing away all notepaper, stamps, flags, armbands, and pennants which bore the name "Hitler Youth." As a means of ensuring the NSJB's external uniformity a Material Office within the *Reichsleitung* was created on 25 April under Hermann Heinrich.[57] These changes were not an idle exercise, for during April the police raided HJ offices throughout Germany and even the homes of many leaders in the hope of finding incriminating material that would perhaps justify a permanent ban on the HJ. Rarely was anything of an objectionable nature discovered, although one particular article of value which the police did find was the HJ Personnel Index, which had copious details about every member.[58]

In a wider sense, the *Verbot* had critical repercussions on the power relationship within the national socialist movement, for it tended to reverse the process by which the HJ was becoming progressively subordinated to the NSDAP and SA. At first, Hitler feared that the HJ might suffer incalculable damage if it was included in the ban, and had decided to dissolve its organisational connections with the SA, thus making it a completely independent unit.[59] The decision was not taken quickly enough and the HJ was prohibited. But the Führer was not to be deterred from carrying out his new plan for the HJ, and on 13 May 1932 he appointed von Schirach an *Amtsleiter* in the NSDAP *Reichsleitung*. This marked a vitally important change in the sphere of command because it meant that as *Reichsjugendführer,* von

Schirach was no longer on the staff of the SA supreme leadership, and hence no longer responsible to Röhm, but directly to Hitler himself. The SA ceased to have any organisational control, in theory or in practice, over the HJ (NSJB), and von Schirach's powers were vastly augmented.[60]

There was another telling reason for this transformation. Hitler was genuinely worried about the potential detrimental effects of Röhm's moral depravity on the HJ. In April 1932, Hitler informed von Schirach that compromising letters written by Röhm to a homosexual friend in Berlin had been intercepted by the SPD. The national socialist leader was deeply troubled by this sordid episode, if only for political reasons, and he resolved that although Röhm was the best man to handle the SA and relations with the *Reichswehr*, ". . . he will be allowed to have nothing more to do with youth. We would soon lose the confidence of parents."[61]

It is clear that the *Verbot* was a most fortunate occurrence from von Schirach's point of view, for it presented him with the opportunity of bringing to fruition plans which he had been nurturing since at least 1929. It became apparent at the 1929 NSDAP party rally that von Schirach wanted to oust Gruber from his position as HJ *Reichsführer* because of von Schirach's double objective of acquiring the leadership of the HJ and bringing the group into line with the NSDAP's more right-wing, middle-class direction. The first crucial advance came when Gruber was dismissed in October 1931 and von Schirach was appointed *Reichsjugendführer*. Having achieved this, his next aim was to divest the HJ of SA authority. Apart from seeking an increase in his own power over the HJ, von Schirach must have been unhappy that his desire to curb the HJ's socialism could be checked by the SA, which contained many social revolutionaries, of whom Röhm was one. Von Schirach's objective of breaking the HJ's links with the SA had, therefore, a political as well as an organisational motive. In 1932 he could use the occasion of the *Verbot* to argue that Röhm's homosexuality and the SA's revolutionary dynamic posed a grave danger to the future prospects of the HJ, and Hitler, accepting this reasoning, agreed to free the HJ entirely from SA tutelage.[62] The Führer thus vindicated in part the motto he himself had coined at an NSDAP meeting on 2 May 1931, *Jugend soll durch Jugend geführt werden* (youth must be led by youth), which became a dominant theme of national socialist propaganda.[63] At the same time, the HJ was not the complete master of its own destiny, for in the last resort its leadership was answerable to Hitler.

The last act in the drama affecting the HJ in the summer of 1932 came on 15 June, when von Renteln announced his resignation as *Reichsführer* of the HJ and NSS. There was an official statement to the effect that he was to devote all his time to his other position as advisor for economic and political affairs in the NSDAP *Reichsleitung.* It is certain, however, that this latest crisis in the top HJ leadership was engineered behind the scenes by von Schirach as the finishing touch to his overall plan of gaining absolute jurisdiction over the HJ. There were to be no more intermediaries. This was confirmed by Hitler's announcement on 16 June abolishing the office of *Reichsführer,* thus leaving von Schirach, as *Reichsjugendführer,* in exclusive control of the HJ.[64]

The ruthlessness of von Schirach's power politics becomes even more starkly manifest when one considers that von Renteln's record as leader of the HJ in no way justified what was in fact his dismissal. A better educated, more experienced, and more diligent man than Gruber, von Renteln had succeeded in raising the HJ from the stagnation in which it had wallowed since 1930, and had applied his energy and intelligence to the problems facing the group, particularly concerning organisation, in a timely and reasonably efficacious manner. Von Renteln also had the ability to command authority and he had none of the unpleasant habits that afflicted Gruber. Above all, von Renteln could think in national terms for the HJ, which alone made him a more competent *Reichsführer* than his predecessor. Apart from this affair, the other personnel changes in the HJ before the *Verbot* was lifted by the von Papen government on 17 June reinforced von Schirach's power base because the new appointees were either former NSDStB colleagues or his close friends.[65]

General Groener was vigorously attacked by right-wing circles for having issued the *Verbot,* and he further antagonised these elements by his adamant refusal to prohibit the *Reichsbanner* as well as the national socialist organisations. Groener's policy shook von Hindenburg's confidence in him and when the former unimpressively defended his actions in the Reichstag on 10 April, a cabinet crisis developed. General von Schleicher, who had originally approved of the *Verbot,* quickly changed his mind when he realised that it did not accord with his political plans or his aims to preserve the interests of the *Reichswehr.* He consequently emerged as the leading figure in a campaign of political intrigue, not only against Groener, who was forced to resign on 12 May, but also against Chancellor Bruening, who stood loyally by his minister during the crisis. Von Schleicher believed that the critical parliamentary situation could not continue indefinitely and he thought that the largely friendless, extraparliamentary Bruening government would have to go.

His basic concern was to find a solution by forming a right-wing coalition government with NSDAP participation, so that simultaneously Hitler would be controlled and the national socialist threat to democracy eliminated. Moreover, he hoped to depoliticise the SA and incorporate it in a national defence organisation under army auspices. The architect of the *Verbot,* the *Verbot* itself, and the chancellor stood in his way, and von Schleicher resolved to bring about the downfall of the Bruening cabinet.[66] Developments played into von Schleicher's hands and President von Hindenburg finally decided to dismiss Bruening on 30 May. The president found von Schleicher's nominee for the chancellorship, fifty-three-year-old Franz von Papen, personally and politically acceptable. In the absence of Reichstag support, von Papen's conservative government, which assumed office on 1 June, relied on the president and *Reichswehr.* In a larger historical context, the fall of Bruening marked the constitutional end of the Weimar Republic.[67]

One of the most urgent tasks of the new government was to come to terms with the National Socialists. Von Schleicher, who was given responsibility for the Ministry of Defence, but was the real power behind the government, lost no time in opening negotiations with Hitler. The Führer understandably placed heavy emphasis on a revocation of the *Verbot.* At the end of May, the NSDAP faction in the Prussian *Landtag* led by Wilhelm Kube demanded that the ban on the HJ at least be lifted, and an NSJB memorandum of 10 June expressed confidence that the ban would be raised "within the next few days."[68] In the political deal which followed, Hitler was promised that the *Verbot* would be lifted for all national socialist organisations, and that the Reichstag would be dissolved and new elections held. In return, he agreed to tolerate the von Papen administration until the elections, after which, he was assured, a place would be found for National Socialists in a new cabinet. As it transpired, however, von Schleicher's plan to bring Hitler into a coalition gravely underestimated the conditions Hitler would demand and also von Hindenburg's aversion to him.

Whatever the justification for the prohibition of the SA and SS, the government's decision to include the HJ in the measure was unwise and rash. The ban not only did nothing to impede the progress of the HJ (see chap. 8), but also helped to advertise it on a scale which not even the HJ's own propaganda machine could achieve. Had Groener decided that the HJ did not constitute a threat to the state in the same way as the SA and SS did, and therefore left it undisturbed, it is most unlikely that the organisation would have enjoyed the success it did during the last six months of 1932. In this respect the ban achieved the exact opposite of what it was intended to do. Furthermore, once the *Verbot* was instituted, the government lacked the necessary vigilance and determination to make it effective. The government's policy revealed a fundamental inconsistency, for when it became apparent that the NSJB was merely the HJ under guise, and hence in flagrant defiance of the *Verbot,* the government did virtually nothing to assert its authority.[69] As a result, the HJ was permitted to make the government appear foolish and indecisive. When the ban was revoked, the NSJB at once resumed the name "Hitler Youth," and heartened by von Schirach's proclamation on 18 June that "with today's rebirth of the Hitler Youth, the last chapter of the national socialist struggle for power begins," activities surged ahead with vigour.[70]

The changes in the higher reaches of the HJ leadership were only a segment of the important reorganisation that occurred in the national socialist movement following its successful overcoming of the *Verbot*. The principal reforms pertained to the party; in July the NSDAP *Reichsleitung* was replaced by a Reich Organisation Leadership *(Reichsorganisationsleitung)*, led by Gregor Strasser and modelled on a revitalised version of the inspectorate system that was originally established in 1931.[71] The NSDAP provincial administration *(Gauleitungen)* lost some of its independent powers and was subordinated more to the centre. Because of the massive expansion of the NSDAP in 1932, these initiatives were meant to further secure the central authority and prepare the party for the takeover of power *(Machtübernahme)* which Hitler hoped would happen shortly. The HJ also reorganised in some measure. Now that von Schirach was undisputed leader of national socialist youth, he abolished the *Reichsleitung* and reformulated the *Reichsjugendführung* as the central mechanism of the HJ.[72] Other national socialist youth groups still had representatives on it, but with the addition of a remoulded HJ staff leadership, the *Reichsjugendführung* was henceforth decisively oriented towards the HJ as the most important youth association of the movement. Its composition on 20 July was as follows:

HJ Reichsjugendführung

	Office	Leader
1.	*Reichsjugendführer* (RJF)	Baldur von Schirach
2.	Adjutant to RJF	Heinz John
3.	Deputy of RJF	Karl Georg Schäfer
4.	Trades Schools	Heinz Otto
5.	Press and Propaganda	Willi Körber
6.	Press Advisor	Albert Urmes
7.	Culture and Education[1]	Werner Haverbeck
8.	Culture and Education Advisor	Heinz Leuchter
9.	*Gebietsführer* in Staff of RJF	Carl Nabersberg
10.	Leader of NSDSt.B.	Gerhard Rühle
11.	Adjutant to NSDSt.B Leader	Willi Kappl
12.	Leader of *Deutsches Jungvolk*	Carl Nabersberg (appointed 5 May 1932)
13.	Leader of BDM	Elizabeth Grieff-Walden
14.	HJ Staff Leader	Elmar Warning (appointed 16 June 1932)

The composition of the HJ Staff Leadership which formed an integral part of the *Reichsjugendführung* was:

Office	Leader
1. Staff Leader	Elmar Warning
2. Treasury Warden	August Schröder
3. Material Office	Franz Schnaedter
4. Social Advisor	Fritz Krause
5. NSS Advisor	Friedrich Krüger
6. NS Youth Factory	Artur Axmann (appointed 1 May
Organisation Advisor	1932) and Heinz Otto
7. Assistant Staff Leader	Heinrich Emsters
8. Index Advisor	Christian Keller

Sources: BA:Sammlung Schumacher:Part II. No. 389; BA:Akte NS 26/337; Bay. HSA:ASA/MINN/71799.

1.   When this was dissolved in December 1932, Körber took over the direction of NS youth educational work as part of the Press and Propaganda Division (BA:ZSg 3/103).

The designations of two HJ organisational units were changed: on 26 June, the *Gau* became known as a *Bann,* and hence *Gauführer* was now *Bannführer;* also, *Bezirk* was replaced by *Unterbann* and *Bezirksführer* by *Unterbannführer.* All other units remained unaltered. The provincial structure underwent some change, although the framework laid down in November 1931 was retained. Eleven *Gebiete* and seven independent *Banne* replaced the formula of twelve *Gebiete;* the geographical regions which the *Gebiete* embraced were slightly amended so that *Gebiete* North, West, East, Greater Berlin, Southwest, and Middle ceded territory to existing *Gebiete* and to five newly created *Gebiete,* namely, Nordmark, North Sea, Hesse-Nassau-North, Berlin-Brandenburg, and Ostsee.[73] A number of new *Banne* were founded, including Bremen, Hesse-Nassau-South, and a second one in Pomerania.

Perhaps the most remarkable aspect of this reorganisation is the light it throws on the astonishing turnover in HJ personnel before 1933, for of the eleven incumbent *Gebiet* leaders in November 1931 only three, Altendorf of Silesia, Klein of Hochland, and Blum of Mittelland, were still holding the same posts in June 1932. Moreover, of the forty-four *Gau* leaders in November 1931 only sixteen held equivalent positions *(Bannführer)* in June.[74] Taken as a whole, the changes after the *Verbot* confirmed recent trends, notably under von Schirach's influence, towards greater centralisation and rationalisation in the HJ, though not yet to the degree he ultimately aimed at.

The immediate post-*Verbot* period was characterised by the endeavours of von Papen's "cabinet of barons" to assert its authority, but it merely succeeded in expediting Germany's swing towards more authoritarian government. Von Papen argued that the Altona riot of 17 July had clearly revealed the sorely troubled Prussian coalition government's incapacity to maintain law and order, and acting on this pretext, he deposed it without opposition on 20 July and appointed himself Reich commissioner for Prussia.[75]

The chancellor's real objective, however, was to break his political isolation before the impending Reichstag elections—parliament having been dissolved on 4 June in fulfilment of a promise to Hitler—by a power action. On 31 July this policy was shown to be completely futile when the NSDAP won 13,745,000 votes and 230 seats, and replaced the SPD as the strongest party in the Reichstag. The KPD also increased its share of the vote, and together the two totalitarian parties were now in a position to prevent the formation of any majority democratic government. Von Papen still had to depend on the backing of von Hindenburg and the army, and on dissolutions of parliament. He tried to escape from his impasse by offering Hitler the vice-chancellorship and the Prussian Ministry of the Interior, but the Führer demanded full power and von Hindenburg was not yet disposed to give it to him. In addition, negotiations for an NSDAP-Centre party coalition, the only one feasible following the elections, produced no definite conclusion. In order to cling to office, von Papen was forced to dismiss the Reichstag once again on 12 September and call new elections in November.

It was against the background of the NSDAP's political triumph and the HJ's glee at having come through the *Verbot* unscathed that the *Reichsjugendtag der* NSDAP was held in Potsdam on 1 and 2 October.[76] There were definite reasons why von Schirach conceived the idea of staging this event, the largest in the history of the pre-1933 German youth movement. The *Reichsjugendtag* was to be the HJ's positive answer to the raising of the *Verbot*, for von Schirach wanted to demonstrate to the government and the German public how strong the organisation had remained. There was an excellent opportunity to score a huge propaganda success, and in the absence of an NSDAP party rally since 1929, the HJ felt the moment was opportune for a national celebration by way of compensation.

Von Schirach was also anxious to underline the value of the HJ to Hitler once and for all. The Führer was very sceptical of the need for a *Reichsjugendtag*, fearing that a failure would have severe consequences for his movement and thus play into the hands of opponents.[77] Despite misgivings until the last moment, however, Hitler was finally persuaded by von Schirach that the rally should proceed. Von Schirach himself had an acute personal stake to promote because he wanted to make himself known to the HJ. Although he had been

Reichsjugendführer since October 1931, he was still mainly connected in the popular mind with the NSDStB. More significantly, there was with good reason some distrust and suspicion of his aristocratic background in the proletarian-oriented HJ; hence he desired to prove to his youths that he was "one of them."[78]

Finally, there was a political factor in von Schirach's calculations, for despite the NSDAP victory in the July elections, it was widely feared in party circles that the movement had reached the zenith of its popularity and could only stand to lose in the next election. A successful national youth meeting, many thought, would be one way of forestalling a national socialist political recession. Potsdam was chosen to be the venue because the HJ leadership believed it epitomised more than any other German city the virtues with which they wanted the HJ to be associated: discipline, duty, patriotism, idealism, soldierliness, and socialism.[79]

Under the direction of Nabersberg, the preparations involved were on a gigantic scale and therefore brought the old problem of finances to the fore again. A great deal of expenditure was incurred in camouflaging the HJ during the *Verbot*, and an HJ memorandum of 26 June 1932 alluded to "the extraordinarily bad financial position" of the organisation.[80] Although the HJ became more financially dependent on the NSDAP in 1931–32, the latter's support was normally reserved for ordinary working expenses only, and did not extend to subsidies for special HJ activities. Thus, von Schirach complained that the party did not lend "a single pfennig" for the *Reichsjugendtag*, and since "our treasury had only 200 reichsmarks," the HJ had to rely for funds on the sale of its propaganda paraphernalia and the meeting fee of 1 reichsmark which each participant paid to cover the cost of meals and accommodation.[81]

Von Schirach should have been aware, however, that the finances of the NSDAP were in a parlous state in the autumn of 1932. The presidential and Reichstag elections that year made heavy demands on the party's resources, and there was another expensive campaign to be faced for the parliamentary elections in November. The support of heavy industry had been temporarily scared away because of recent national socialist collaboration with the Communists in the Reichstag. (They were again to join forces to stage a transport workers' strike in Berlin in early November.) Goebbels' diary is eloquent about the desperate situation at this time, and by the end of 1932 the NSDAP was financially bankrupt.[82] The whole movement would have had to drastically restrict its agitation in 1933 if big business had not come to the rescue through the offices of von Papen in January 1933. The HJ's position did not, therefore, perceptibly improve in the few months prior to the *Machtergreifung*, despite another rise in ordinary membership fees on 1 November from seventy-five pfennigs to one reichsmark per month. The HJ entered the Third Reich as an impecunious organisation, living on little more than the proverbial shoestring.[83]

A vast armada of national socialist youth descended on Potsdam; contemporary estimates of the numbers present varied, but a figure of around 80,000 would seem to be the most authentic. Among the audience were Hitler, Goebbels, Prince August Wilhelm, Berlin SA leader Graf Helldorf, and SS *Gruppenführer* Kurt Daluege. At the end of two days of speeches, marches, singing, and flag-waving, it was obvious that the *Reichsjugendtag* was a brilliant national socialist tour de force. Psychologically and politically, the timing of the rally could not have been more judicious from the national socialist point of view: it was an utter repudiation of those who had for so long scoffed at the HJ; it gave the entire movement a tremendous fillip; but above all, it intimated that a vociferous section of German youth was dedicated to Adolf Hitler and to a national socialist political victory.[84] Thus, the struggles of the *Kampfzeit,* on a national level at least, were brought to a climax in rather spectacular fashion for the HJ.

The success of the *Reichsjugendtag* was all the more valuable in bolstering party morale when the elections of 6 November provided the NSDAP with a severe setback which shattered the legend of its invincibility. Although the NSDAP remained the largest party in Germany, its loss of some 2 million votes and 34 seats caused opponents to euphorically forecast eventual disaster for the movement. The overall political current nonetheless continued to flow in the NSDAP's favour. The elections did not solve the government's problem of acquiring a secure basis, and when von Schleicher withdrew his support, von Papen was forced to resign. The general himself became chancellor on 2 December, but he too experienced difficulty in stabilising his administration while contending with von Papen's intrigues against him. Von Schleicher's plan of achieving a suitable platform for parliamentary government included winning over the "moderate" wing of the NSDAP. His bid to split the party resulted in overtures to Gregor Strasser. Although this was without success, Strasser's disapproval of Hitler's uncompromising political tactics, especially over the coalition issue, led to an internal crisis in the NSDAP when he resigned his official posts in early December. As on previous occasions, Hitler countered swiftly and effectively by instituting more organisational changes which further consolidated his authority over the party.

There were also consequences for the HJ. The expansion of the HJ in the second half of 1932 would have probably necessitated organisational changes, but the Strasser crisis now made this more imperative. The HJ staff leadership was abolished and the *Reichsjugendführung* expanded on 22 January 1933 to twelve divisions:

HJ Reichsjugendführung

Division	Offices
Abteilung I	Organisation; Reich Leadership Schools; Defence Politics; Equipment Office.
Abteilung II	Personnel Office; Law Enforcement; Foreign Affairs
Abteilung III	Social Office; Youth Welfare
Abteilung IV	Administration; Treasury; Index; Materials
Abteilung V	Press; Propaganda; Education; Publishing House
Abteilung VI	Social and Economic Education
Abteilung VII	Health
Abteilung VIII	NS Factory Organisation and Trades Schools
Abteilung IX	BDM
Abteilung X	*Deutsches Jungvolk*
Abteilung XI	NSS
Abteilung XII	NSDStB

Source: BA:Akte NS 26/337.

This represented in the first place an attempt at increasing the rationalisation and strengthening of the inner structure, but the continuing turnover in key personnel in both the central and provincial leaderships was a crippling handicap.[85] Further, the changes in leaders were undoubtedly aimed to a considerable extent at excluding suspected left-wing extremists from the organisation following Strasser's resignation (see chap. 4). Leaders who were appointed to high HJ posts at this time were all middle class (see Biography of HJ Leadership), so that the process of left-wing elimination begun in the HJ in 1930–31 was continued until 1932–33.

In terms of organisational and administrative development, the principles guiding the formulation of the HJ between 1930 and 1933 were essentially those employed by the NSDAP and SA, and reforms in the HJ were often the reflection of simultaneous and corresponding changes in the senior organisations. The common and ultimate objective was a powerful, centralised authority that would suffice to control the movement's expansion to mass proportions. The NSDAP achieved this aim, but the relative weakness of the HJ structure was conspicuous throughout the *Kampfzeit*.

In a hierarchical organisation most of the blame necessarily devolves to the *Reichsleitung* and to the man at the top, the *Reichsführer*. The first major reorganisation of April 1931, which had only limited effectiveness, was the prelude to further endeavours which did not halt with any degree of finality until the wholesale alterations devised for the enlarged HJ by von Schirach in July 1933.[86] The changes in the HJ leadership in October and November 1931 were framed to promote a leadership which would realise the potential of the HJ to be a powerful, national group after the stagnation of 1930–31 under Gruber, but there were also political motives present, as indicated. Though these reforms did provide the basic framework of the HJ organisation until after the *Machtergreifung*, and though there was an improvement on the measures of April 1931, they did not, however, give a fully satisfactory answer to the problem. Von Schirach knew this, and hence sought to tighten the structure more in June 1932 and January 1933.

Because of the rapidly changing situation in the political whirlpool that was the Weimar Republic from 1930 onwards, it may be argued that the HJ's failure to settle down to a firm organisational stability when all was in flux around it was unavoidable. The HJ was a growing association, having to frequently adapt and reorder its organisation to meet the fresh exigencies which such growth always entails. Yet the NSDAP and SA succeeded in surmounting these same obstacles, for they were also growing all the time. The HJ never cast off the character of organisational improvisation, and never mastered the difficulties of controlling a rising movement; constant change and experimentation with different patterns brought forth no conclusive solution.

Despite the political reasons for the appointments of von Schirach and von Renteln, they at least ensured that the HJ leadership would be more seriously preoccupied with organisational matters which Gruber had neglected. Efficiency was subsequently improved, largely due to the greater stress on centralisation made by both these leaders. Also, the changes of October-November 1931 inaugurated a period of more competent provincial leadership, which the reforms of 1932 reinforced. Men such as Altendorf, Lauterbacher, Usadel, Hogrefe, Klein, Karbach, and Richard Reckewerth provided a generally superior calibre of leadership. But the efficacy of the provincial leadership, like that of the central administration, was circumscribed by marked personnel fluctuation. The defects of its organisation partly explain, therefore, why the HJ did not enjoy the same magnitude of expansion before 1933 as the NSDAP and SA.

Notes: Chapter 7

1. Bay. HSA:ASA:Akte NS/1555.

2. An example of one such poem written before 1933 and simply entitled, "Hitler," was:

> In many thousands you follow behind me,
> And you are I, and I am you.
> I have experienced no thoughts which did
> not originate in your heart.
> And I form words, none of which
> are not in one with your will.
> Because I am you, and you are I
> and we all believe, Germany, in you!
>   (B. v. Schirach, *Die Fahne der Verfolgten* [Berlin 193?], p. 39.)

3. The attitude of other top-ranking national socialist leaders to the HJ before 1933 can at best be described as one of benevolent neutrality. Julius Streicher, NSDAP *Gauleiter* of Franconia, was active in HJ affairs at the very beginning (see chap. 2), but thereafter his interest was mainly passive, despite his close friendship with von Schirach. Alfred Rosenberg played a backstage role as an intermediary between the HJ and right-wing youth groups in the late 1920s (BA:Akte NS 26/372) and for a short time afterwards; although he contributed some articles on youth to the NSDAP and HJ press (BA:ZSg 3/2849), Rosenberg's interest in the HJ declined in the 1930s. Josef Goebbels sometimes addressed HJ meetings and published a few youth articles in *Der Angriff,* but the inherent cynicism of this man prevented him from having any enduring sympathy for the HJ. Others like Hess, Goering, Himmler, Darré, Frick, Rust, Amann, and Gregor Strasser were hardly involved at all. Apart from the fact that they were fully engaged in the political struggle, von Schirach made a valid point when on 7 October 1932 he talked of a "clique unsympathetic to youth" *(jugendfremde Clique)* around Hitler "who do not understand our struggle and who do not want to understand" (BA:Sammlung Schumacher:Gruppe VIII. No. 239). In effect von Schirach pinpointed a "generation gap" in the movement which helps explain the apathy of the NSDAP and SA towards the HJ during much of the pre-1933 period.

4. The full text of this vital decree which was dated Munich, 30 October 1931, and signed by Hitler, was as follows (Bay. HSA:ASA:Akte NS/1541):

   (1) Within the sphere of the Supreme SA Command a new office is to be created, *Reichsjugendführer* (RJF).
   (2) The *Reichsjugendführer* is directly responsible to the chief of staff. To be *Reichsjugendführer,* I appoint party comrade von Schirach.
   (3) The sphere of competence of the *Reichsjugendführer* extends to:

(a)   The National Socialist German Students' Association *(Reichsführer,* party comrade von Schirach).
(b)   The Hitler Youth (commissioned with the leadership, party comrade von Renteln).
(c)   The National Socialist Schoolboys' League *(Reichsführer,* party comrade von Renteln).

(4)   The *Reichsjugendführer* is to be the advisor for all three organisations named above, and he is to prepare every matter relating to youth in the staff of the supreme SA leader. He is to keep the chief of staff informed of all organisational questions pertaining to the youth organisations, and is to report in particular all matters which concern the SA. He is to hold the rank of *Gruppenführer,* and his service uniform will be decreed presently.
(5)   In questions of internal organisation, appointments to posts, and cooperative work with the SA, the *Reichsführer* of the Hitler Youth is to have the right of direct communication with the chief of staff. He is required to report about it in advance to the *Reichsjugendführer.*
(6)   The present *Reichsführer* of the Hitler Youth, Gruber, is to be appointed to the *Reichsleitung* of the NSDAP (Youth Committee). He is to join it at the special request of the supreme SA command in recognition of his service for the construction and expansion of the HJ.
(7)   The composition of the staffs of the RJF and Youth Leagues are to be submitted for approval beforehand by the *Reichsjugendführer* to the supreme SA command.

In practical terms, paragraph 6 is a typical example of Nazi euphemism; it was thought expedient to usher Gruber "upstairs" so as to save the HJ from the embarrassment of having its first *Reichsführer* publicly dismissed. Moreover, Gruber did not last long in the NSDAP *Reichsleitung,* being edged out the following year.

5.   BDC:A. v. Renteln file; *Das Deutsche Führerlexikon 1934–35* (Munich, 1934), p. 380; Orientalischen Cigaretten-Compagnie, pub., *Männer im Dritten Reich* (Bremen, 1934), p. 186.

6.   Bay. HSA:ASA:Akte NS/1555; Bay. HSA:ASA:Akte NS/1849.

7.   Bay. HSA:ASA:Akte NS/1555; Bay. HSA:ASA:Akte NS/1541.

8.   Bay. HSA:ASA:Akte NS/1541.

9.   SAB:4/65 782/147; Bay. HSA:ASA:Akte NS/1555.

10.   BA:Akte NS 26/352.

11.   BA:Akte NS 26/362.

12.   BA:Akte NS 26/340; BDC:A. Wallwey file.

13.   Bay. HSA:ASA:Akte NS/1555.

14.   Bay. HSA:ASA:Akte NS/1544; BA:Sammlung Schumacher:Gruppe VIII. No. 239; SAB: 4/65 1684/282. The fee payable by new members on entering the HJ was raised from 30 to 50 pfennig; 30 pfennig of this was to be sent to the *Reichsleitung,* 10 pfennigs to the appropriate *Gauleitung,* and 10 pfennigs was to be retained by the local group. The monthly dues payable by HJ leaders were increased to 1 reichsmark, but this was ordered to be reduced on 23 November 1931 to the amount paid by ordinary members (Bay HSA:ASA:Akte NS/1849). The monthly fees for

ordinary members was increased to 75 pfennigs, an extra 25 pfennig. Of this, the local group had to send 15 pfennig to the *Reichsleitung* and 30 pfennigs to the *Gauleitung* (SAB:4/65 1684/282). Finally, school-boys and apprentices were to pay 45 pfennigs per month, one-third of which was to be given to the *Reichsleitung* and one-third to the *Gauleitung* of the area (SAB:4/65 1684/282).

15. BA:Akte NS 26/340.

16. H. Bolm, *Hitler-Jugend in einem Jahrzehnt* (Brunswick, 1938), p. 168.

17. Bay HSA:ASA:Akte NS/1555; BA:Akte NS 26/339. During the period from December 1931 to February 1932, Joachim Walter (education) and Karl Nabersberg (organisation) each received 250 reichsmarks monthly; Franz Schnaedter (secretary) and Hein Schlecht (press) were given 220 reichsmarks apiece, while August Schröder (treasury) received 230 reichsmarks (Bay. HSA:ASA:Akte NS/1555).

18. BA:Akte NS 26/364; Bay. HSA:ASA:Akte NS/1541; Bay. HSA:ASA:Akte NS/1849.

19. Bay HSA:ASA:Akte NS/1849.

20. Karl Nabersberg as Reich organisation leader; Franz Schnaedter as Reich secretary; August Schröder as Reich treasurer (SAB:4/65 1688/283); Joachim Walter as Reich education leader; Wilhelm Barth as Reich propaganda leader; Hein Schlecht as Reich press chief; Hans Brüss as leader of the Foreign Office (LASH:Abt. 309:Regierung Schleswig:No. 22864); Curt Brieger as advisor on *Jungvolk* affairs (BDC:C. Brieger file); Willi Steindecker as chief of *Uschla* (BA:Akte NS 26/342); the *Schar*, personnel, and BDM offices were left vacant in the meantime.

21. Bay. HSA:ASA:Akte NS/1555.

22. *Das Deutsche Führerlexikon, 1934–35,* p. 342.

23. The twelve *Gebiete:* Ostland led by August Patabel, North by Lothar Lange, North West by Wilhelm Kayser, West by Gerhard Stöckel, Hochland by Emil Klein, Silesia by Werner Altendorf, East by Elmar Warning, Greater Berlin by Warning also, South West by Theo Kosiek, Mittelland by Gunter Blum, Middle by Herbert Peter, and Austria by Ludwig Erber (Bay. HSA:ASA:Akte NS/1849).

24. BA:Akte NS 26/337; BA:Akte NS 26/361.

25. Bay. HSA:ASA:Akte NS/1555.

26. On 2 January, Felix Wankel was appointed Reich organisation inspector of the HJ, and on 8 January Josef Fehr succeeded Brieger as advisor for *Jungvolk* affairs (BA:Akte NS 26/337). Karl Heinz Seidel was named adjutant to von Schirach on 1 February and on the same date, Fritz Krause became advisor for social affairs (Bay. HSA:ASA:Akte NS/1849) and Edgar Bissinger the new Reich press chief (BA:Akte NS 26/337). Christian Keller became advisor for the HJ Index Office on 15 February (BA:Akte NS 26/337), and on 20 March Thomas Freiherr von Fritsch was named Reich propaganda leader in succession to Barth (Bay. HSA:ASA:Akte NS/1776). In the *Gebiet* leadership, three changes were recorded: on 23 January, Fritz Albrecht replaced Stöckel as *Gebietsführer*

West, and on 9 February Albrecht Möller was appointed *Gebietsführer* East (BA:Akte NS 26/337). On 15 April, Wilhelm Kayser was expelled from the HJ (see chap. 4).

27. BA:Akte NS 26/370; see also BDC:H. Brüss file; BA:Sammlung Schumacher: Gruppe VIII. No. 239; Bay. HSA:ASA:Akte NS/1544; see also chap. 8.

28. A. Bullock, *Hitler, A Study in Tyranny* (London, 1962), p. 194.

29. Hitler formally renounced his Austrian citizenship on 7 April 1925, but his efforts to acquire German nationality after this date were rejected by the Bavarian state government. On 25 February 1932, it was announced that the National Socialist minister of the interior in the state of Brunswick, Dietrich Klagges, had appointed Hitler an attaché of the Brunswick legation in Berlin. Hitler thus automatically became a citizen of Brunswick and hence of Germany, and was now eligible to stand for the highest office in the state. For background in Brunswick see E. Roloff, *Braunschweig und der Staat von Weimar* (Brunswick, 1964).

30. Bay. HSA:ASA:Akte NS/1541; Bay. HSA:ASA:Akte NS/1849; *Hamburger Tageblatt,* 8 March 1932.

31. Bay. HSA:ASA:Akte NS/1849. The percentage results of the two presidential elections were:

	13 March	10 April
Hindenburg	49.6	53.0
Hitler	30.1	36.8
Duesterberg	6.8	—
Thaelmann	13.2	10.2

As a result of the election on 13 March, the Nationalists withdrew Duesterberg and appealed to their followers to vote for Hitler. On 10 April, von Hindenburg received 19,359,983 votes, Hitler 13,418,547, and Thaelmann 3,706,759.

32. BA:Akte NS 26/337; SAB:4/65 782/147; Bay. HSA:ASA:Akte NS/1541.

33. Bay. HSA:ASA:Akte NS/1776; SAB:4/65 782/147.

34. Bay. HSA:ASA:Akte NS/1776.

35. FSGNS:IA 1a 26 Vol. I.

36. Ibid.

37. F. L. Carsten, *Reichswehr and Politics* (Oxford, 1966), pp. 339–43.

38. Bay. HSA:ASA:Akte NS/1541.

39. Bay. HSA:ASA:Akte NS/1543; Bay. HSA:ASA:Akte NS/1557.

40. BA:Sammlung Schumacher:Gruppe VII. No. 203; Bay. HSA:ASA:Akte NS/1544.

41. See M. Broszat, "Die Anfänge der Berliner NSDAP 1926-27," *Vierteljahrshefte für Zeitgeschichte* 8 (1960):85–91.

42. BA:Sammlung Schumacher:Gruppe VII. No. 199A; BA:ZSg 3/1476.

43. Bay. HSA:ASA:Akte NS/1544.

44. *Hamburger Tageblatt,* 5 September 1932; Bay. HSA:ASA:Akte NS/1544; Bay. HSA:ASA:Akte NS/1555.

45. Bay. HSA:ASA:Akte NS/1541; SAB:4/65 781/146; Bay. HSA:ASA:Akte NS/1540.

46. Bay. HSA:ASA:Akte NS/1535; Bay. HSA:ASA:Akte NS/1544; BA:ZSg 3/1476.

47. Bay. HSA:ASA:Akte NS/1544.

48. *Hamburger Tageblatt,* 17 October 1932.

49. E. F. Bartelmäs, *Das Junge Reich* (Stuttgart, 1932), p. 31.

50. Bay. HSA:ASA:Akte NS/1544.

51. BA:Akte NS 26/371.

52. *Wille und Macht,* Sept. 1937.

53. Bay. HSA:ASA:Akte NS/1776.

54. B. v. Schirach, *Die Hitler-Jugend: Idee und Gestalt* (Leipzig, 1934), p. 26.

55. Bay. HSA:ASA:Akte NS/1555; BA:Akte NS 26/337.

56. BA:Akte NS 26/366.

57. V. Schirach, *Hitler-Jugend,* p. 25; BA:Akte NS 26/337; Bay. HSA:ASA:Akte NS/1544; Bay. HSA:ASA:Akte NS/1555.

58. Bay. HSA:ASA:Akte NS/1557; Bay. HSA:ASA:Akte NS/1556; Bay. HSA:ASA:Akte NS/1555.

59. Bay. HSA:ASA:Akte NS/1555.

60. Bay. HSA:ASA:Akte NS/1554. Von Schirach retained the rank of SA *Gruppenführer* until 1941, when he was promoted to *Obergruppenführer* (Inter. Mil. Trib. Nuremberg, vol. V, p. 284). The text of Hitler's decree of 13 May was:

   (1) Each and every National Socialist youth league is responsible to the *Reichsjugendführer* of the NSDAP, party comrade, Baldur von Schirach, who is answerable to me for National Socialist youth.
   (2) The *Reichsjugendführer* is to be an *Amtsleiter* (office leader) in the *Reichsleitung* of the NSDAP.
   (3) The *Reichsjugendführer* appoints and dismisses the *Gebiet* leaders of the National Socialist Youth Movement (NSJB), the provincial group leaders *(Gauverbandsführer)* of the National Socialist Schoolboys' League, and the district leaders *(Kreisleiter)* of the NSDStB, as well as the members and advisors of the national leaderships of the youth organisations. The proposed leaders of these offices are to be recommended by the permanent officers *(Bundesführer* NSJB, *Bundesführer* NSS, *Bundesführer* NSDStB) to the *Reichsjugendführer.* The right of appointment and dismissal of junior leaders in the youth leagues from *Gebiet* leaders, district leaders, and provincial group leaders upwards, lies with the permanent national leaders *(Bundesführer).*

61. V. Schirach, *Ich Glaubte an Hitler* (Hamburg, 1967), p. 133–34.

62. The accusation has frequently been made of widespread homosexuality in the HJ; indeed von Schirach was suspected by some of being a homosexual. There are known cases before and after 1933 of HJ leaders having been convicted of homosexual offences (see Biography of HJ Leadership) and they were usually expelled from the HJ on this account. Most youth organisations have at one time or another been confronted by this problem, but there is no reliable or conclusive evidence to show that homosexuality was particularly serious at any time in the HJ.

63. *Wille und Macht*, Aug. 1937; BA:Akte NS 26/336. In *Die Geschichte der HJ* (Cologne, 1968), H. C. Brandenburg states that this motto was first coined at an NSDAP leaders' meeting on 20 January 1929, but I have not found evidence to support this view. Brandenburg refers to the motto as "downright nonsense and a crude confidence trick" (p. 31), but he clearly failed to understand the organisational implications of von Schirach's appointment on 13 May.

64. Bay. HSA:ASA. MINN/71799; FSGNS:HA/NSDAP/239.

65. On 18 May, von Schirach appointed a number of new leaders to the *Reichsleitung*: Willi Körber as leader of the Press Division; Werner Haverbeck as leader of the Culture and Education Division; Heinz Otto as leader of the Trades School Division; Heinz Hugo John as leader of the Youth Statistics Office; and Karl Georg Schäfer as deputy of the *Reichsjugendführer* (BA:Akte NS 26/337).

66. See W. Conze, "Zum Sturz Bruenings," *Vierteljahrshefte für Zeitgeschichte* 1 (1953):261–88; and H. Muth, "Zum Sturz Bruenings," *Geschichte in Wissenschaft und Unterricht*, Dec. 1965.

67. See K. D. Bracher, *Die Auflösung der Weimarer Republik* (Stuttgart, 1957).

68. Bay. HSA:ASA:Akte NS/1544; BA:Akte NS 26/337.

69. By the end of May, the Bavarian police were satisfied that the NSJB was an illegal continuation of the HJ, and for this reason, they actually banned several scheduled NSJB meetings in Bavaria (Bay. HSA:ASA:Akte NS/1544).

70. Bay. HSA:ASA:Akte NS/1544; Bay. HSA:ASA:Akte NS/1541.

71. See D. Orlow, *The History of the Nazi Party 1919–1933* (Pittsburgh, 1969).

72. BA:Sammlung Schumacher:Part II. No. 389.

73. BA:Akte NS 26/337; BA:Sammlung Schumacher:Gruppe VIII. No. 239.

74. Lühr Hogrefe, Kurt Beier, Lorenz Loewer, Bernhard Kielmeyer, Jacob Karbach, Gunter Stegemann, Hartmut Stegemann (brother of Gunter), Karl Rentzel, Walter Schmidt, Karl Hofmann, Franz Lutz, Rudolf Gugel, Herbert Peter, Richard Reckewerth, Kurt Kräft, and Hans Kempfer (Austria).

75. See R. Morsey, "Zur Geschichte des 'Preussenschlags' am 20 Juli 1932," *Vierteljahrshefte für Zeitgeschichte* 9 (1961):430–39.

76. SAB:4/65 782/147.

77. V. Schirach, *Ich Glaubte an Hitler*, p. 153.

78. Lauterbacher interview, Munich, 24 April 1969.

79. BA:Akte NS 26/367.

80. Bay. HSA:ASA:Akte NS/1544; BA:Akte NS 26/337.

81. Inter. Mil. Trib. Nuremberg, vol. XIV, p. 373; V. Schirach, *Hitler-Jugend*, p. 29; BA:Akte NS 26/367.

82. See L. P. Lochner, ed., *The Goebbels Diaries* (London, 1949).

83. FSGNS:Verordnungsblatt der Obersten SA-Führung, 23 September 1932. The alternating periods of financial solvency and inadequacy were not stabilised until the HJ was taken under the wing of the national socialist state in 1933. The Law for the Securing of Unity of Party and State (Dec. 1933) declared that the HJ had no legal assets of its own; it was instead allowed access to state finances under the jurisdiction of the Reich treasury minister (BA:Sammlung Schumacher:Gruppe VIII. No. 239).

84. Bay. HSA:ASA:Akte NS/1544. The *Reichsjugendtag* was heavily criticised, perhaps inevitably, by the left-wing press. *Vorwärts*, the central organ of the SPD, reported on 5 October that "120 children lie in Potsdam hospitals as a result of the rally." Other left-wing papers spoke of "fully exhausted and half-starved children" being given inadequate accommodation and food; on 5 October, the *Berliner Volkszeitung* summed up the rally as a "crime against youth"(BA:Akte NS 26/367). There is little doubt, however, that most of these reports were exaggerated and amounted in some cases to gross distortions of the truth.
    To commemorate the occasion, the *Reichsjugendführung* issued the "Golden Hitler Youth Badge" on 23 June 1934. All youths who had been members of the HJ and other national socialist youth groups before the *Reichsjugendtag* and who had remained "loyal" were allowed to wear this badge, indicating that they were "Old Fighters" of the movement (G. Kaufmann, *Das kommende Deutschland* [Berlin, 1940], p. 45).

85. On 1 January 1933, Walter Kaul was appointed in place of Warning, and he also succeeded Karl Georg Schäfer as the *Reichsjugendführer's* deputy (BA:Akte NS 26/337). On the same date, Fritz Krüger resigned his post in the *Reichsjugendführung* (Social Affairs) (BA:ZSg 3/103). In January 1933, there were also no fewer than eight vital changes in the top provincial leadership (BA:Akte NS 26/337). On 1 January, the leader of *Bann* Cologne-Aachen, Rolf Jaenisch, was transferred to the staff of *Gebiet* Nordmark; on 11 January, Paul Morenga became *Bannführer* of *Bann* Schleswig-Holstein, Lühr Oldigs *Bannführer* of *Bann* West Holstein, and Bun Geissler *Bannführer* of *Bann* East Holstein; on 14 January, Rudolf Gugel was appointed *Gebietsführer* of *Gebiet* Franconia; on 18 January, Walter Unger became *Bannführer* of *Bann* Mecklenburg; on 19 January, Gunter Blum, leader of *Gebiet* Mittelland, was transferred to the leadership of *Bann* Thuringia, and Emil Klein replaced Kurt Haller von Hallerstein as leader of *Gebiet* Hochland.

86. See Reichsjugendführung der NSDAP, *Aufbau, Gliederung, und Anschriften der Hitler-Jugend* (Berlin, 1934), p. 12 ff.

Chapter 8

Hitler Youth Development, 1931-33

HJ Membership

The membership figures for the HJ before 1933 have been the subject of much disagreement and uncertainty. Statistics compiled by the HJ and NSDAP have been suspected of being dishonestly based and therefore dismissed as unreliable, while postwar writers have allegedly been without enough material to make accurate estimates.[1] But one important point has been overlooked, which is that the figures compiled by HJ leaders throughout Germany were frequently drawn up in the strictest confidence and with a genuine desire to ascertain the real position. Furthermore, in many cases, the HJ figures are lower than those usually given by outside observers, so that their authenticity is virtually certain. Nonetheless, discretion in reviewing information from every source is highly necessary.

By the end of 1930 the HJ allegedly had 18,000 members organised in 900 local branches, 5,000 more members than the previous year (see chap. 2).[2] This figure is certainly overblown, and no one was more aware of this than the HJ itself. In a secret HJ report, the figure given for 1 January 1931 is 13,806, which indicates that the organisation made little headway at all in 1930, and confirms the view that the HJ was stagnating under Gruber's leadership.[3] Gruber tried to deceive his own leaders on this question by claiming large increases in membership in 1930 in order to improve his reputation. Writing to his principal colleagues on 15 January 1931, for example, Gruber stated that the HJ had grown to over 20,000.[4]

There was a decided improvement in 1931, though Gruber continued to claim a far greater number of new recruits than was actually the case. Thus, in the period from 1 January to 30 June 1931, it was stated that an average of 2,000 youths per month joined, and that 618 new local branches were founded. By 1 February 1931, the HJ membership had reputedly risen to 19,800 organised in 33 *Gaue,* and to over 21,000 by 9 May. But the situation as described in a confidential HJ report dated 1 February 1932 is more acceptable: on 1 April 1931, the membership was 15,373; on 1 July, 17,902; on 1 November, 28,743; and on 1 January 1932, 37,304.[5] The notable increase, 8,561, recorded between 1 November 1931 and 1 January 1932, was attributable to the better organisation and enthusiasm which von Schirach and von Renteln instilled into the HJ, and also to the more favourable political atmosphere from which the national socialist movement as a whole benefited from 1930–31 onwards.

The regional distribution of this membership between 1 January 1931 and 1 January 1932 shows that, in numerical terms, the HJ strongholds at the beginning of 1931 clearly lay in northern, middle, and eastern Germany; that is, in order of strength, Saxony, South Hannover-Brunswick, Thuringia, Berlin, Pomerania, Schleswig-Holstein, East Prussia, and Breslau (see Appendix VIII). It was weakest, on the other hand, in northwestern and western Germany, in Hesse, Essen, North Westphalia, Hamburg, and Düsseldorf, and also in the free city of Danzig and Lower Franconia.[6] By the end of 1931 the areas of HJ strength remained exactly the same, with the exception of Berlin, which dropped out from the list of main centres in the spring of 1931. The weakest areas were also unaltered at the end of 1931, but also included districts which were paradoxically bastions of the NSDAP and SA, namely, North Bavaria, Oberpfalz, Swabia, and North Franconia.

After 1925, the NSDAP was less Bavarian-conscious, and became more powerful in northern, middle, and eastern Germany, particularly in small town-rural areas and communities which were predominantly Protestant.[7] Development in Catholic western and southwestern Germany, in large industrial belts, and in metropolitan centres like Berlin, Hamburg, Leipzig, Düsseldorf, and Cologne, stagnated. The most militant NSDAP parts were Schleswig-Holstein, Hannover-Brunswick, middle Silesia, Mecklenburg, East Prussia, Pomerania, Saxony, and Thuringia. The regional development of the HJ often, but not always, closely resembled that of the party.

Bare numbers, however, can be misleading. Perhaps a more realistic method of assessing the regional strength of the HJ would be to measure the figures for 1931–32 against the population between the ages of fourteen and eighteen years (age limits for HJ membership) of the areas concerned.[8] Hence, in November 1931, the HJ was strongest in northern (except Hamburg) and eastern Germany, and weakest in parts of Catholic Bavaria, traditionally Catholic areas of northwest and west Germany, and Berlin, despite the capital having had one of the largest HJ groups on a numerical basis at the beginning of 1931. These results corroborate, therefore, the overall position intimated by the numerical analysis. Based on the same relative-to-population scale, the leading HJ *Gaue* in November 1931 were South Hannover-Brunswick, Mecklenburg-Lübeck, Schleswig-Holstein, East Hannover, and Ostmark; those bringing up the rear were Hesse-Darmstadt, Westphalia-South, and Koblenz-Trier.[9]

The progress in membership, which significantly coincided with the HJ's rightward course under von Schirach, continued in 1932. The figure of 37,304 for 1 January 1932 was increased to 40,129 on 1 February, and to 43,334 on 1 March. North, east, and middle Germany were confirmed as HJ focal points, with Schleswig-Holstein, South Hannover-Brunswick, Ostmark, and Pomerania the leading *Gaue,* and the Saar, Hamburg, Berlin, Cologne-Aachen, Düsseldorf, Westphalia-North, Lower Franconia, and Essen lagging behind.[10] Examples of the HJ's numerical strength and specific evolution in different parts of Germany are as follows: in north Germany at the end of 1932, Hamburg had 450 members, Bremen 500, and Schleswig-Holstein, the first province in which the NSDAP achieved an absolute majority in an election (July 1932) before 1933, 3,500.[11]

The HJ's substantial development in South Hannover-Brunswick was intimately connected with the work of Hartmann Lauterbacher. Despite the HJ's abortive beginning in this area (see chap. 4), branches were reestablished in May 1928 in Börssum by NSDAP *Bezirksleiter* Kurt Schmalz and in Hannover by Fritz Kirch and Eberhard Müller. It was not until Lauterbacher was appointed *Gauführer* in March 1930, however, that the HJ's potential began to be realised.[12] Lauterbacher's enthusiasm and organisational skills led to an intensification of the *Gau*'s propaganda activities and to a centralisation of the command structure.[13] The advent of a DNVP-NSDAP coalition government in Brunswick in 1930 helped the whole movement and Dietrich Klagges' appointment as interior minister there in September 1931 resulted in less interference from the authorities in the affairs of the NSDAP and HJ.[14] By January 1932, South Hannover-Brunswick had over 2,000 HJ organised in 165 local branches. When Lauterbacher was posted to Cologne in the spring of 1932, he had already ensured the firm foundation of the HJ, and in January 1933 the *Gau* had 4,000 members.[15]

In West Germany, the HJ, like the NSDAP, found it exceedingly difficult to strike deep roots in the Rhineland-Ruhr, due to the presence of the large Catholic population and the powerful left-wing organisations. Despite being one of the most densely populated regions of Germany, the Rhineland-Ruhr could boast only 1,735 HJ in January 1932. Westphalia was also weak with only 1,737 HJ in April 1932, and the Saar even worse with a meagre 98 in February 1932. The HJ fared rather better in the Rheinpfalz, and even more so in Hesse-Nassau where a long tradition of *völkisch* activity and anti-Semitism among the peasantry made the state one of the strongest in West Germany for national socialism. In middle Germany, Saxony was the best area in the whole Reich for the HJ with 3,888 members in April 1932, while Thuringia, where the NSDAP entered state government for the first time following the *Landtag* elections of late 1929, had 2,893. *Gau* Halle-Merseburg was also fairly strong, but Magdeburg-Anhalt was by far the least successful HJ area in middle Germany.[16]

Eastern Germany was notably pronational socialist and provided fertile ground for the HJ. Following the establishment of the first branch in Stettin in November 1927, the HJ made considerable progress in Pomerania, which by April 1932 had 1,994 members. The first HJ *Gau* in Silesia was created by Franz Metzke in June 1927 but not until Werner Altendorf became *Gauführer* in 1931 did the organisation prosper. What Altendorf did for Silesia, the firm hand of Georg Usadel did for East Prussia, which had a succession of unsatisfactory leaders before Usadel came in late 1931; thus by April 1932, East Prussia had 1,926 HJ, a figure that grew considerably before 1933. On the other hand, Danzig had only 600 HJ in January 1933.[17]

When the ban against the NSDAP in Berlin was lifted in 1928, HJ *Gau* Berlin-Brandenburg was reestablished under Werner Teichert, who was replaced later that year, however, by Robert Gadewoltz.[18] The HJ languished in Berlin for several years mainly because the socialist and communist organisations were already entrenched in the working-class areas of the city where the HJ sought to win recruits. At the beginning of 1930, *Gau* Berlin-Brandenburg-Ostmark, as it had become, had only 350 members, of whom 200 were in the greater Berlin area. At the end of the year, the *Gau* had 800 youths, 500 of them in Berlin. Only under new *Gauführer* Joachim Walter did the HJ gain some semblance of cohesion in 1931, though membership continued to be low, 600, at the end of that year. Elmar Warning took over as

Gebietsführer of Greater Berlin in late 1931, extensively reorganised, and increased the numbers to 1,300 by April 1932. On the eve of the *Machtergreifung*, the HJ was weakened by social revolutionary secessions (see chap. 4), so that of the capital's population of 63,012 youths between the ages of fourteen and eighteen, probably only 1,500 of them were organised in the HJ.[19]

The HJ in Berlin made more human sacrifices and showed more fanaticism and loyalty than almost any other HJ group in Germany, yet compared with the vastness of the city and its teeming population (over 4 million in 1933), it remained insignificant. The cosmopolitan atmosphere of Berlin, where a brilliant cultural life flourished in the 1920s, and its long history as a left-wing stronghold made it extremely difficult for the HJ to break through. Even the NSDAP never won more than 24 percent (July 1932) of the vote there in a major election.[20] The HJ was outflanked on the one side by the left-wing groups and on the other by the conservative-nationalist associations. Caught between these two powerful camps, the HJ never succeeded in effectively freeing itself from this impasse before 1933.

In southern Germany, the HJ performed reasonably well in Baden (2,318 members in April 1932) but failed to make much headway in traditionally liberal Württemberg. In Franconia, which apart from Saxony had the longest and most consistent history of national socialist youth activity, personified by the service of Rudolf Gugel, the HJ's development was unsuccessful. There were only 1,096 HJ in the whole of Franconia, an NSDAP stronghold, at the beginning of 1932, and Catholic Lower Franconia remained one of the poorest HJ areas until 1933.[21]

In Bavaria, the HJ's record was also uninspiring. It was not until two months after the foundation of the HJ that Max Kobes appealed in the *Völkischer Beobachter* of 27 August 1926 for a branch to be set up in Munich. Kobes had little else to do thereafter with the HJ, for in September 1926 the newly erected HJ *Landesleitung* Bavaria was led by Paul Neumann of Nuremberg, while Alfons Baumgartner was responsible for the Munich section when it was finally established in July 1927. A mere seven youths attended the inaugural meeting of HJ Munich in November 1927, by which time a geology student, Horst Raecke, was the leader. Development was painstakingly slow—there were only sixty HJ youths in Munich in March 1928—so that a sweeping reorganisation of the whole Bavarian HJ took place in May 1928. Emil Klein, who was to become the principal leader in Bavaria, now headed the new *Gau* South Bavaria, while Josef Erlmeier took over *Gau* Lower Bavaria-Oberpfalz.[22] Organisational and personnel changes were frequent before 1933, thus indicating the continued depression of the HJ in the state.

At the end of 1929, *Gau* South Bavaria had only 100 members, and not until Adolf Wagner was appointed NSDAP *Gauleiter* of Bavaria in November 1930 did the HJ begin to show some life. By February 1931, the *Gau* had 346 members organised in twenty-three branches, and following the transfer of the HJ headquarters to Munich, the police noted "extraordinarily lively activity" in what was now *Gau* Munich-Upper Bavaria. In January 1932, there was a total of 1,194 HJ in Bavaria, of whom 220 were in Munich. But 1932 was a turbulent year for the Bavarian HJ with numerous clashes with state and police authorities and violent internal quarrels (see chap. 4). In January 1933, there were certainly no more than 2,000 HJ in Bavaria, of whom perhaps 500 were based in Munich.[23]

There were several reasons why the HJ was relatively weak in the adopted home of the national socialist movement. Rather than benefiting from the strong position of the NSDAP, the HJ was considered an encumbrance by many party officials who were intent on devoting all available time and resources to building up the party. The 1924 state law prohibiting schoolboy political involvement had to be contended with and there was also the active opposition of the Catholic church. Finally, apart from Klein, there was no other leader of good calibre who could give assistance in solving the manifold problems besetting the organisation of such a large area as Bavaria.

A number of interesting facts and some curious paradoxes emerge from the HJ's regional development. The HJ was generally unsuccessful in heavily industrialised areas like the Rhineland, Ruhr, and Saar, and in large industrial cities. The basic explanation was that the socialist and communist groups were too strong there for the HJ. Yet the HJ was successful in Saxony and Thuringia, which were also important industrial provinces, so that other factors, including nationalism and good leadership, managed to overcome leftist influence. The HJ was invariably poorly supported in those parts of Germany which had a predominantly Catholic population, as in the Rhineland, Lower Silesia, the Saar, Lower Franconia, and Bavaria. The HJ showed considerable growth, however, in the largely Catholic state of Baden.

In those areas where its leadership was either mediocre or subject to frequent change, the HJ usually developed indifferently as, for example, in Hamburg, the Saar, Franconia, Berlin (to 1931), and initially in Halle-Merseburg and Hesse-Nassau. But there are exceptions to this trend. Thuringia had no less than seven *Gau* leaders from 1928 to 1933, yet it was one of the strongest HJ areas.[24] Similarly, East Prussia, which had five changes in leadership between 1928 and 1931, became an HJ stronghold. Capable leadership was not necessarily the prerequisite for success if local conditions were not entirely favourable. Hence, Klein in Munich, Kräft in Magdeburg-Anhalt, Jung in Bremen,

Sell in Osnabrück, and Walter and Warning in Berlin did not bring their respective areas to the fore of HJ development. As the case of Baden demonstrates, however, good leadership did on occasion defeat a hostile environment.

In those regions where the background was propitious to national socialism, where the NSDAP was already well organised, and the youth leadership talented, the HJ usually flourished, as in South Hannover-Brunswick and East Hannover. Despite having these recognised ingredients of success, Bremen and Magdeburg-Anhalt were nonetheless relative HJ failures. Finally, a strong tradition of nationalism in a particular region, especially if that region was rural and Protestant, was invariably a guarantee of HJ expansion. Nationalist, Protestant, and nonindustrial areas like Schleswig-Holstein, Mecklenburg-Lübeck, Pomerania, and East Prussia were enthusiastically responsive. Alternatively, in Bavaria and Franconia, both nationalist and rural (but largely Catholic in the case of the former and Lower Franconia), the HJ stagnated.

It must be concluded, therefore, that no generalisation as to why the HJ should have been powerful in some areas and weak in others can be entirely valid, for exceptions to every rule are to be found in its development. The factors behind the HJ's history in individual regions are much more complex, and each region must be examined independently in order to ascertain the whole truth of the matter.

The year 1932 was by far the best for the growth of HJ membership, especially the latter half; when the governmental *Verbot* was raised, the HJ had 48,000 members, an increase of slightly less than 5,000 over the 1 March 1932 position, and on the eve of the *Machtübernahme*, 55,365.[25] By the beginning of 1933, the HJ had emerged as a leading youth organisation per se, but measured against the many millions in the youth movement as a whole, the HJ accounted for less than 1 percent of affiliated youth, and was therefore not important. The same may be said, however, for most other individual youth groups when this criterion is employed. At the same time, the HJ's 55,365 was insignificant in comparison with the NSDAP and SA memberships, both of which stood at over 700,000 in 1933.

Violence and Strife

Violence in its many forms was a permanent feature of the last years of the *Kampfzeit* for the HJ. In the clash of political extremists of the right and left, street fighting, brawling, beatings, and murder reached an appalling scale, with the national socialists and communists the most notorious participants. The tense political climate in Germany from 1930 onwards revealed a prompt readiness to appeal to the emotions, and a consequent propensity to use force as a means of stressing political views. It is argued that German youth was especially prone to radicalisation because of the traumatic effects of a lost war and hard economic times, which bred bitterness and a savage, coarse outlook on life among the lower classes who were the most severely hit.[26] Both national socialist and communist youth embodied this aspect of the younger generation more than any other youth organisation, the one identifying the other as an enemy that had to be destroyed and annihilated. Hence, if *Juda Verrecke!* (Perish the Jews!) was the opprobrious cry often uttered by national socialists in the streets, no less frequent or objectionable were the *Nieder mit dem Nazischwein!* (Down with the Nazi swine!) and *Schlagt die Faschisten tot!* (Kill the Fascists!) shouts of the communists. In this explosive situation, with its constant elements of danger and adventure, every death merely served to enhance the prestige of the group concerned, and every murder was used to stimulate even more hatred and fanaticism against the enemy.[27]

Persecution from the authorities added to the excitement; martyrdom became a part of the aura of the movement, and gave it a feeling of spiritual brotherhood and camaraderie that was a perennial source of strength. This was particularly true of the national socialist movement, which before 1933 went a long way towards creating an exclusive, substitute society for its members that was detached from the mainstream of life in the republic. Members of the enclosed elite were actively encouraged to feel somehow different from and even superior to the masses of the ordinary, nonparty population. Struggle formed part of the everyday life of the HJ; if it was not the physical attacks of enemies, it was opposition from state and police officials, or even from parents who disliked their children being involved in political activity, especially on behalf of the national socialists, who earned an unenviable reputation for rowdyism.

Fifteen-year-old Herbert Norkus, who was murdered by a gang of communist youths in Berlin on 24 January 1932, became the hero of the HJ, the epitome of the struggles of the *Kampfzeit,* in the same way as the murdered Berlin SA leader, Horst Wessel, became the idol of the whole movement.[28] Altogether, fifteen youths and one girl of the national socialist youth movement proved that "the flag is more than death" (the main line of a popular post-1933 HJ marching song) before 1933.[29] Along with those killed after 1933, they were honoured as the *Unsterbliche Gefolgschaft der Hitler-Jugend* (the immortal following of the HJ).[30] Norkus was singled out for special emphasis because of the peculiar brutality of his murder and because until that date he was the youngest HJ youth to die. In addition, *Gauleiter* Goebbels fully exploited the propaganda value of every dead national socialist, but particularly of HJ youths. Given the circumstances of this case, and the fact that Berlin personified the intensity of Weimar politics, his manipulations were also certainly responsible in part for the elevation of Norkus to the status of the prototype Hitler youth, symbolising the sacrificial spirit of the HJ for the cause, Führer and fatherland.[31]

Six of the pre-1933 fatalities occurred in Berlin, an indication of the political temperature even among youths in the capital. The year 1932 was the worst for HJ casualties when six youths and one girl were victims; the most tragic month was October when two youths and one girl died. The sixteen dead HJ members were part of the total of 205 followers of Hitler who were killed from the putsch of 1923 to the *Machtergreifung* just over nine years later.[32] To emphasise the martial spirit of the times, some HJ units consciously styled themselves after World War I army regiments, for example, in *Gau* Pomerania in early 1932. The practice appears to have spread as the fighting became more vicious, for it was reported on 20 October 1932 that the HJ as a whole had been following the long-established SA and SS ritual of carrying on the tradition of former army units.[33]

In view of the daily physical combat of the HJ, the HJ *Reichsleitung* stressed as early as 1927 that an insurance scheme intended primarily for the SA also applied to HJ members. The SA insurance was set up in 1927 by the supreme command to protect its membership at a low premium and to give monetary compensation for injuries, unemployment, or even death sustained in the street fighting. Before this scheme was initiated, individual SA branches took out policies with private insurance companies, but this turned out to be highly expensive. The fierceness of the political battle in succeeding years underlined the necessity of having a comprehensive policy. At the beginning of 1929, the NSDAP began to show an interest at the suggestion of Gottfried Feder, and on 1 September 1930 it took over the SA scheme, renaming it *Hilfkasse der NSDAP (SA-Versicherung)* (Aid Fund of the NSDAP, SA-Insurance). Henceforth, all members of the movement were expected to use the insurance, which for HJ members cost 30 pfennigs per month.[34]

Despite repeated admonitions between 1927 and 1930, however, the vast majority of HJ youths did not take part in the scheme, for a report of 1 November 1930 indicated that only 2,787 members, less than 22 percent, were insured. The HJ *Reichsleitung* lowered the tariff on 1 June 1931 for under-fifteen-year-olds and DJ members to 20 pfennigs per month in an effort to encourage greater participation. The *Reichsleitung* frequently urged this, especially in 1932 because of "the rising terror of the enemy." But due to the widespread economic adversity, the marginal 20 percent of HJ youths insured in *Gau* Rhein-pfalz in April 1932 was probably the average for Germany in general. In heavily industrialised places, which suffered most of all from the depression, this average might conceivably have been lower. The picture is unlikely to have improved before 1933.[35]

Another aspect of the HJ members' indulgence in polemics, physical or otherwise, before 1933, was their brushes with the law. Though no different from the NSDAP and SA, whose followers were repeatedly brought before the courts to answer criminal charges, the HJ had the doubtful honour of being one of the few youth groups in the republic which was continuously at cross-purposes with the legal authorities. Its members were subject to arrest and imprisonment mainly for street fighting, assault, and for writing provocative newspaper articles. In 1928, Wilhelm Kayser received a six-month term of imprisonment for having attacked a crowd of Jews in Cologne, and in early 1930 he was again arrested for fighting *Bündische* Youth members.[36] In 1931, Gotthard Ammerlahn, who earned a considerable notoriety as a virulent columnist, was faced with a court appearance after writing a scathing attack on Stresemann.[37] The same year, Adrian von Renteln, then NSS leader, almost landed in court because he had organised the illegal distribution of national socialist propaganda in schools in Naumburg-Saale, but the charges were dropped for want of evidence.[38] Von Schirach himself was arrested on 3 July 1931 after he had made a speech at Cologne University in defiance of a ruling by the rector of the university. On 10 July, he was given a suspended three-month sentence and a fine of 50 reichsmarks by a Cologne court.[39] In December 1931, Oskar Riegraf, deputy leader of *Gau* Württemberg, was sent to prison for three months for having led an illegal demonstration against a *Reichsbanner* gathering.[40]

The HJ's battle with the law continued unabated in 1932, and there was hardly a week during the 1930–33 period especially in which the HJ was not involved somewhere in Germany with the police and governing authorities in one way or another.[41] The HJ was aware from an early date that it was an outsider, a pariah beyond the pale of respectability in the state. This situation was most obviously manifested in the republic's nonrecognition of the HJ as a youth welfare association. In practical terms, this resulted in the HJ being deprived of access to various civic facilities that were accorded most other youth associations, that is, the use of sports halls, youth hostels, swimming baths, state insurance schemes, and the right to reduced fares on the *Reichsbahn*.

The HJ's first application for state recognition was rejected in 1927, although several local units acting individually were successful.

In May 1927, for example, HJ Nuremberg was given the status of a welfare association by the district government of Middle Franconia. In 1929, HJ South Bavaria was the only *Gau* in the organisation to be allowed a 50 percent reduction on the *Reichsbahn*. This prompted Kurt Gruber to try again on behalf of the HJ in December 1929 to gain admittance to the *Reichsausschuss der deutschen Jugend-verbände*, which would have meant automatic recognition by the state.[42] But the application was refused because the HJ could not satisfy, or promise to satisfy, the second sentence of paragraph 4 of the committee's statutes:

> Before being accepted as a member, an association must be pre-pared to work together with other associations, and, without prej-udicing its fundamental attitude, to recognise the existing state and its organs.[43]

The HJ's declared totalitarian aim of incorporating all other youth groups within its organisation and its determined objective of destroy-ing the Weimar Republic inevitably doomed its somewhat ironical candidature to failure at the committee's meeting in Berlin on 11 December 1929. This setback did not deter provincial leaders from trying where Gruber had failed, but they too met with nothing but rebuffs.[44] In December 1931, von Renteln submitted yet another appli-cation to the national youth committee, and he even arranged a per-sonal interview on the matter with General Groener, but the application was dismissed on the same grounds as before.[45] The status quo re-mained until after the lifting of the *Verbot* in the summer of 1932, when the HJ's perseverence finally paid off. On 4 August 1932, the decree of 22 May 1930 whereby the Prussian state had excluded na-tional socialist and communist youth groups from its youth welfare scheme, was repealed in what was partly a conciliatory gesture towards the national socialists by von Papen, who had taken over full power in Prussia a fortnight earlier.[46] The HJ was now "accepted," and the way was open for its membership of the national youth committee. Towards this end, von Schirach had set up an official umbrella or-ganisation, the *Deutsches Jugendwerk e.V.*, on 11 July 1932, representing all national socialist youth groups.[47]

The *Deutsches Jugendwerk* was simply a social welfare body whereby the HJ and other national socialist youth groups sought access to the civic privileges hitherto denied them; it did not assume any of the administrative functions of the *Reichsjugendführung*, nor was it incorporated into the organisational structure proper of the HJ. The *Deutsches Jugendwerk* was officially received into the national youth committee on 6 October 1932, the latter being unable to refuse admission this time because the HJ had already been recognised by the state.[48] It was a contradictory situation for the HJ to be in, and the development was not applauded by wide party circles which believed that the movement should take care of its own youth affairs entirely, and have nothing to do with the "system." Von Schirach dismissed these complaints on 30 November 1932 when he stated that Hitler himself had agreed to the creation of the *Deutsches Jugendwerk* and what it implied.[49] From a practical viewpoint, it was a wise move, but was regarded by the extreme political idealists of the NSDAP as an unforgivable compromise with a system of government they had sworn to bury. After 1933 the *Deutsches Jugendwerk* was seen as something of an embarrassment by the HJ because it represented collaboration with democracy, and the body ceased to have any significance.

Having averted a serious party crisis in December 1932, as the new year dawned Hitler was in a position to take advantage of the deteriorating political situation. When Chancellor von Schleicher failed to secure the necessary support for his regime and requested a dissolution of the Reichstag and powers to govern in an extraparliamentary fashion, President von Hindenburg refused, thus causing the chancellor to resign on 28 January. Within the next few days, the fate of Germany was decided in a veritable web of intrigue woven by personalities involved in a deadly game of power.[50] Von Papen emerged as the key figure; aided by Undersecretary of State Otto Meissner and the president's son Oskar, he finally persuaded aged and semisenile von Hindenburg to appoint Adolf Hitler, the forty-three-year-old "Bohemian Corporal," chancellor of the Reich on 30 January 1933.[51]

The significance of this event for the subsequent history of Germany and the world at large was to be seen in due course in its full perspective, but for the HJ and the other national socialist organisations it meant a sudden but welcome end to their struggle for power. The objective of victory had at last been achieved, even though national socialists occupied only three of the eleven cabinet posts in the national government that was formed. That evening, HJ columns joined the vast SA and SS march from the Tiergarten through the Brandenburg Gate and on past the Führer, who stood triumphantly reviewing the parade from an open upper window of the Chancellory. In all parts of the fatherland, national socialist formations celebrated the inauguration of a new age in a frenzy of excitement and jubilation.

In assessing the role of the Hitler Youth in the overall victory of national socialism, it must be accorded one subordinate to that of the NSDAP and SA. Nonetheless, the HJ made a progressively expanding section of nationalist youth, and to a lesser extent, the masses of German youth, at least aware of Hitler's political gospel and its aims, and it was responsible for bringing an increasing number of younger elements into the movement. To provide new recruits for the NSDAP, SA, and SS was an important function, and without the HJ, the NSDAP could also have hardly sustained its image as a party of youth. The HJ's usefulness to the movement as a vehicle of propaganda must not be disregarded. Although its general activity was not directly decisive in the fight for national political supremacy that was being waged by the senior organisations, the HJ was by no means banished to the periphery of this struggle, as its high fatality rate bears unimpeachable witness.

Moreover, in finally convincing Hitler that the national socialist youth movement was an asset, the HJ ensured that German youth as a whole would enjoy a superior status in the Third Reich. Although one cannot legitimately speak of the HJ's "successful" development, since the group only began to grow in some proportion from late 1931 onwards as von Schirach directed its appeal more and more towards middle-class youth, it may be said that the degree of lavish attention devoted to youth after 1933 is partly explicable in terms of the HJ's efforts before that date. The HJ's organisation contained many imperfections, but the concepts of organisational control for the central and provincial administrations, especially the need for maximum centralisation, were worked out in embryo and applied later, albeit with rather more refinement. Taking this aspect into consideration, the HJ's early contributions are seen to have been valuable. Thus, while the HJ did not enjoy much importance before 1933, and formed only a small segment of national socialism, its worth during the early phase of the movement's history must also be measured in terms of the long-term consequences of its exertions. The foundations of the HJ's undoubted practical significance in Hitler's Reich were laid during the *Kampfzeit*.

To define the importance of the HJ purely in relation to its concrete achievements, however, would be a grave injustice, for only with reference to the organisation's ideology and sociology can it be properly understood. The HJ's leftist ideological radicalism, which was reflected in its predominantly proletarian sociological makeup, made it a uniquely interesting entity in the national socialist movement. The HJ staked a substantial claim to its own individual social revolutionary ethos under the leadership of Kurt Gruber, and its pertinacity in adhering to socialist ideas, no matter how vaguely conceived, meant that in time the group became a large thorn in Hitler's flesh and a danger to the kind of political appeal being put over by national socialism from 1928 onwards. Hitler's response, as in so many other difficult situations, was to ruthlessly assert his own position and authority and eliminate the source of the threat. The clash which the HJ's outlook promoted with Hitler and his henchman, von Schirach, in late 1931, shows that the Führer at least believed the HJ worth bothering about, if only in a negative and destructive sense. Despite having been underestimated at the beginning of its history by virtually everyone in the movement, including Hitler, the HJ was still able to make a mark in the early political history of national socialism.

Notes: Chapter 8

1. The issue has been confused somewhat, however, by the practice adopted by recent observers of HJ development of selecting membership statistics compiled by the HJ or NSDAP when it appears to suit their purposes; for example, H.C. Brandenburg's *Die Geschichte der HJ* (Cologne, 1968), p. 40.

2. F. W. Hymmen, "10 Jahre Hitler-Jugend," in *Die Junge Kamaradschaft*, ed. E. Fischer (Berlin, 1935). This is a national socialist estimate, but it has been accepted by A. Klönne, *Hitlerjugend. Die Jugend und Ihre Organisation im Dritten Reich* (Hannover, 1956), p. 10; and by Brandenburg, *Die Geschichte der HJ*, p. 40. The latter is especially inconsistent in his discussion of HJ membership; on page 58 he attacks W. Klose's *Generation im Gleichschritt* (Gütersloh, 1964) for naively accepting national socialist estimates, yet Brandenburg accepts them himself on occasions.

3. BA:Sammlung Schumacher:Gruppe VIII. No. 239.

4. Bay. HSA:ASA:Akte NS/1849.

5. BA:Akte NS 26/339; SAB:4/65 781/146; FSGNS:HA/NSDAP/239; BA:Sammlung Schumacher:Gruppe VIII. No. 239. The 10,841 increase between July and November can be largely attributed to the results of the "September Action" of the HJ—the results of which were not good enough to prevent Gruber from being dismissed.

6. BA:Sammlung Schumacher:Gruppe VIII. No. 239.

7. See A. Milatz, *Wähler und Wahlen in der Weimarer Republik* (Bonn, 1965).

8. See statistics in H. Siemering, *Deutschlands Jugend in Bevölkerung und Wirtschaft* (Berlin, 1937).

9. BA:Akte NS 26/337.

10. SAB:4/65 781/146; BA:Akte NS 26/337.

11. *Hamburger Tageblatt*, 28 September 1932; BA:Sammlung Schumacher:Gruppe VIII. No. 239; Bay. HSA:ASA:Akte NS/1555.

12. BDC:K. Schmalz file; H. Bolm, *Hitlerjugend in einem Jahrzehnt* (Brunswick, 1938), p. 54; BDC:W. Jacobs file; *Das Deutsche Führerlexikon 1934–35*, p. 271.

13. Bolm, *Hitlerjugend*, p. 110.

14. See E. Roloff, *Bürgertum und Nationalsozialismus 1930–33* (Hannover, 1961).

15. Bolm, *Hitlerjugend*, p. 171; *Das Deutsche Führerlexikon 1934-35*, p. 271; BA:Sammlung Schumacher:Gruppe VIII. No. 239.

16. BA:Sammlung Schumacher:Gruppe VIII. No. 239; Bay. HSA:ASA:Akte NS/1555; Bay. HSA:ASA:Akte NS/1776; Bay. HSA:ASA:Akte NS/1541.

17. BA:ZSg 3/1476; Bay. HSA:ASA:Akte NS/1555; BA:Akte NS 26/335; Bay. HSA:ASA:Akte NS/1541; BA:Sammlung Schumacher:Gruppe VIII. No. 239; SAB:4/65 1685/282; BA:Akte NS 26/337; BA:Akte NS 26/339; BA:ZSg 3/1450.

18. BA:ZSg 3/1476.

19. SAB:4/65 1680/281; SAB:4/65 781/146; BA:Akte NS 26/362; BA:Sammlung Schumacher:Gruppe VIII. No. 239; Bay. HSA:ASA:Akte NS/1555; Siemering, *Deutschlands Jugend*, p. 104. W. Z. Laqueur's *Young Germany: A History of the German Youth Movement* (London, 1962), p. 193; and W. Klose's *Generation im Gleichschritt*, p. 17, estimate the HJ membership in Berlin at this time as fewer than 1,000, but this surely fails to take into account the growth of the HJ in the city during 1932.

20. See Milatz, *Wähler und Wahlen.*

21. Bay. HSA:ASA:Akte NS/1555; BA:Akte NS 26/300; BA:Akte NS 26/364; BA:Sammlung Schumacher:Gruppe VIII. No. 239; BA:Akte NS 26/337.

22. SAB:4/65 1734/293; Bay. HSA:ASA:Akte NS/1542; SAB:4/65 781/146; Bay. HSA:ASA:Akte NS/1540; BA:Sammlung Schumacher:Gruppe VIII. No. 239.

23. BA:ZSg 3/2849; Bay. HSA:ASA:Akte NS/1555; BA:Sammlung Schumacher:Gruppe VIII. No. 239; Bay. HSA:ASA:Akte NS/1541; Bay. HSA:ASA:Akte NS/1544; Bay. HSA:ASA:Akte NS/1540.

24. SAB:4/65 781/146.

25. BA:Sammlung Schumacher:Gruppe VIII. No. 239; G. Kaufmann, *Das kommende Deutschland* (Berlin, 1940), p. 42; see also Appendix IX.

26. J. Fischer, "Entwicklungen und Wandlungen in den Jugendverbände im Jahre 1931," *Das Junge Deutschland*, Feb. 1932. For a psychoanalytic approach to the problem see P. Loewenberg, "The Psychohistorical Origins of the Nazi Youth Cohort," *American Historical Review* 76 (1971):1457–1502.

27. See H. J. Gamm, *Der Braune Kult* (Hamburg, 1962).

28. A. Littmann, *Herbert Norkus und die Hitlerjungen von Beusselkietz* (Berlin, 1934), p. 7; Bay. HSA:ASA:Akte NS/1541. The date of Norkus' death coincided with the birthday of Frederick the Great, born in 1712. National socialist propaganda later thought this was somehow significant. Wessel, the son of a Protestant clergyman and allegedly a pimp, was murdered by communists in February 1930. He was the author of the stirring *Horst Wessellied*, which soon became established as the official song of the national socialist movement, and after 1933 as the second national anthem of the Third Reich.

29. The sixteen killed before 1933 were (BA:Akte NS/26/369):

(1) Fritz Kröber, born in Durlach (Baden) on 24 April 1908, and killed on 26 April 1925.

(2) Hans Queitzsch, born in Chemnitz on 24 October 1910 and an apprentice locksmith. He died on 20 June 1927.

(3) Paul Thewellis, born in Aachen on 3 March 1905; a bakery apprentice, he died on 23 January 1931.

(4) Rudolf Schröter, born in Leipzig on 10 September 1913, a plumber's apprentice and shot dead on 12 February 1931.

(5) Gerhard Liebsch, born on 3 December 1913 in Berlin. An apprentice motor mechanic, he was killed on 26 May 1931, thus becoming the first HJ youth in Berlin to die.

(6) Hans Hoffmann, born on 13 December 1913 in Berlin and killed on 17 August 1931 while still at school.

(7) Johannes Mallon, born on 30 June 1914 in Rügen (Pomerania), he died on 3 September 1931.

(8) Gerhard Wittenberg, born on 5 June 1913 in Zarrentin (Mecklenburg) and a gardener's assistant. He died on 17 September 1931.

(9) Herbert Norkus, born in Berlin on 26 July 1916, he joined the HJ in 1931 (B. Ramlow, *Herbert Norkus? Hier!* [Berlin, 1933], p. 36).

(10) Georg Preiser, born in Berlin on 21 March 1913; a machine construction apprentice, he was killed on 7 February 1932.

(11) Herbert Howarde, born in Wuppertal in 1914, he died on 20 June 1932.

(12) Werner Gerhardt, born in Zeitz on 22 December 1912; a woodcutter's assistant, he died on 30 June 1932.

(13) Erich Niejahr, born on 14 January 1917 in Cologne and died on 5 October 1932. He was a labourer.

(14) Josef Grün, born in 1921, he died at age eleven in Vienna on 26 October 1932 as a member of the DJ. He was the first to die in the Austrian HJ.

(15) Erika Jordan, born on 10 January 1915 in Berlin. This BDM girl died on 28 October 1932.

(16) Walter Wagnitz, born on 23 July 1916 in Berlin-Wedding; a tailor's apprentice, he was killed on 1 January 1933.

30. Another ten members of the HJ and DJ were killed between 31 January 1933 and August 1934 (BA:Akte NS 26/369):

(1) Christian Grossmann on 26 February 1933 in Lindenfels.

(2) Otto Blöcker on 26 February 1933 in Hamburg.

(3) Josef Neumeier on 16 March 1933 in Munich.

(4) Peter Friess on 17 March 1933 in Darmstadt.

(5) Otto Schmelzer on 4 April 1933 in the Saar.

(6) Karl Thomas on 31 August 1933 in Austria.

(7) Gerhard Kaufmann in early 1934 in Berlin.

(8) Hans Leistentritt on 24 July 1934 in Schladming.

(9) Johann Ehrgartner on 27 July 1934 in Frauental.

(10) Franz Ebner in August 1934 in St. Gallen.

The number of communist youth deaths before 1933 is given as ten (see *Zur Geschichte der Arbeiterjugendbewegung in Deutschland, Ein Auswahl von Materialien und Dokumenten aus den Jahren 1904–46* [East Berlin, 1956], p. 380; and *Deutschlands Junge Garde, 50 Jahre Arbeiterjugend-Bewegung* [East Berlin, 1954]). Of the ten, nine were killed by police during the infamous communist rioting in Berlin in May 1929.

31. See Littmann, *Herbert Norkus*, p. 112. *Der Junge Sturmtrupp* of February 1932 announced Norkus' death with the banner headline: "The Youngest Martyr for Hitler's Idea!" (BA:ZSg 3/1473). Von Schirach decreed that 24 January should henceforth be a day of mourning for Norkus and the dead of the national socialist youth movement (Bay. HSA:ASA:Akte NS/1541). After 1933, the Reich Propaganda Ministry made a successful film, *Hitler-Jugend-Quex,* which depicted the life of Norkus as one of uncritical devotion to national socialism and the Führer.

32. BA:Sammlung Schumacher:Part II. No. 374. The pattern of the national socialist deaths was:

1923: 22 deaths, including the sixteen of the Hitler putsch.
1924: 5 deaths; the NSDAP was banned at this time.
1925: 3 deaths; the first year of the reconstituted NSDAP.
1926: 4 deaths; a quiet period of NSDAP organisational development.
1927: 5 deaths.
1928: 5 deaths; the NSDAP made a poor showing in the Reichstag elections.
1929: 10 deaths; the national socialist agitation began to have a wider impact.
1930: 17 deaths; the NSDAP emerged as an important national movement.
1931: 42 deaths; political extremism on the right and left reached new heights.
1932: 87 deaths; the worst year of violence in the republic coincided with its imminent collapse.
1933: 5 deaths (from 1–30 January).

It is clear that deaths rose in number as political animosities grew sharper from 1928–29 onwards. The worst month for violence was July 1932, when 24 died, and the blackest day for the national socialists, apart from 9 November 1923, was 17 July 1932, when six of their members were killed.

33. Bay. HSA:ASA:Akte NS/1555; Bay. HSA:ASA:Akte NS/1541.

34. Bay. HSA:ASA:Akte NS/1542; BA:Akte NS 26/383; BA:Akte NS 26/370.

35. Bay. HSA:ASA:Akte NS/1541; Bay. HSA:ASA:Akte NS/1870; BA:Akte NS 26/364; Bay. HSA:ASA:Akte NS/1849; Bay. HSA:ASA:Akte NS/1776. As an incentive, the *Reichsleitung* rather distastefully stated in February 1932 that Norkus had not been insured (Bay. HSA:ASA:Akte NS/1542). On 30 September 1933, von Schirach withdrew the HJ from the *Hilfkasse der* NSDAP and instead contracted a cheaper insurance agreement with a private company in Cologne (BA:ZSg 3/103).

36. BA:ZSg 3/1476; Bay. HSA:ASA:Akte NS/1544.

37. Bay. HSA:ASA:Akte NS/1541.

38. Bay. HSA:ASA:Akte NS/1555.

39. BA:Akte NS 26/1366B; BA:Akte NS 26/1264.

40. BA:ZSg 3/1473.

41. Bay. HSA:ASA:Akte NS/1544.

42. Ibid.; Bay. HSA:ASA:Akte NS/1555.

43. Hymmen, "10 Jahre Hitler-Jugend."

44. BA:ZSg 3/1477. For example, in July 1931 Emil Klein sought to set up a *Landesverband Bayern der Hitler-Jugend* (Bavarian Regional Association of the Hitler Youth) officially independent of the *Reichsverband* (National Association) of the HJ as a means of gaining recognition in Bavaria as a youth welfare body. But the move was rejected by the state authorities (Bay. HSA:GSA:MA/100425).

45. Bay. HSA:ASA:Akte NS/1544.

46. SAB:4/65 782/147; BA:Akte NS 26/339; Bay. HSA:ASA:Akte NS/1536.

47. BA:Akte NS 26/339; BA:Akte NS 26/333.

48. SAB:4/65 782/147.

49. Bay. HSA:ASA:Akte NS/1536.

50. See T. Eschenburg, "Die Rolle der Persönlichkeit in der Krise der Weimarer Republik," *Vierteljahrshefte für Zeitgeschichte* 9 (1961):1–29.

51. See E. Matthias, "Hindenburg zwischen den Fronten 1932," *Vierteljahrshefte für Zeitgeschichte* 8 (1960):175–84.

Epilogue

Adolf Hitler's assumption of power in 1933 signified the trium-
phant climax of the national opposition's fourteen-year-old campaign
of denunciation and violence against the Weimar Republic. The forces
of the counterrevolution were now restored to the centre of influence
in the state. In the course of 1933, the national socialist revolution
destroyed the remnants of the parliamentary constitutional system and
laid the foundations for a totalitarian dictatorship in Germany.[1] Hitler's
plan was to achieve the same unqualified mastery over the country
that he had enjoyed over the NSDAP since the early days of the
Kampfzeit.

It was axiomatic that a new era also began for the HJ, for it
was no longer simply the youth auxiliary of a political party, but in
practice was henceforth the youth organisation of the Third Reich.[2]
As a power factor in the state charged with the political education
of German youth, the HJ's long-term work now had to be in a sense
constructive, rather than destructive as it had been during the Weimar
era, and the HJ had also to branch out into every aspect of youth
life. The propagandistic agitation and activities of the pre-1933 period
were therefore discontinued to a considerable extent, at least in their
old form, and increasingly as time went on. The HJ's functions had
to be reoriented to allow it to cope with its new elevated status. It
was the HJ's concern to instruct youth in the spirit and ideals of
national socialism, and to inculcate the teaching that all endeavour
was to benefit not themselves, but the state.

Implicit in this role was the conviction that the HJ alone should control the destiny of German youth to the exclusion of the 400 large youth associations, plus scores of smaller ones, which existed in 1933.[3] In order to accomplish its oft-repeated totalitarian aspirations, the HJ initiated its own programme of *Gleichschaltung* (literally, coordination) in 1933 by which every other youth group without exception was to lose its independence and be incorporated into the HJ. This was the most important feature of the HJ's development in the first year of Hitler's rule. Compromise had long been rejected; the goal was totality.

Hitler set an example for the HJ; armed with the Decree for the Protection of the State and People of 28 February and the Enabling Law of 23 March (both of which formed the constitutional basis of the regime until 1945), he smashed all political opposition and forced most public institutions into submission. On 14 July 1933, the NSDAP was declared the only legal political party in Germany. Under von Schirach, who was appointed youth leader of the German Reich on 17 June 1933, the HJ also acted ruthlessly, and by early 1934 all groups, except those of Catholic youth which were still protected by the Nazi-Vatican Concordat of July 1933, had been "coordinated." By that date, membership of the HJ had reached half a million, or ten times its strength on the eve of the *Machtergreifung* (see Appendix IX). The reorganisation now necessary was put into effect in July 1933 when the HJ acquired for the first time a fully centralised, efficient administrative structure.[4]

A new type of youth movement was set up in Germany in 1933, totalitarian in attitude and fanatical in persuasion; with an all-embracing power the way was now clear for the HJ to stamp its personality and wield a ubiquitous influence over every conceivable facet of youth life. To carry out its responsibility as a decisive instrument for the ideological indoctrination of German youth, a sustained programme was meticulously formulated by the HJ. The HJ permeated all spheres of its activity with political dialectics, so that even innocuous pursuits like camping and hiking always had an ulterior political purpose, and physical fitness was viewed as preparation for service to Germany. The HJ leadership never made any secret of its objective of shaping dedicated young national socialists. Political education consisted of inculcating racial theories, notions of German supremacy, distorted history, details of the national socialist movement, and other points of the new *Weltanschauung*.

Encouraged by the example of Geobbels' ministry of propaganda, the HJ constructed a sophisticated press and propaganda network with its own newspapers, theatre productions, films, and radio shows, and gradually transferred its instruction from the political plane to the "higher" level of a dogmatic, quasi-mystical doctrine. Another of the special tasks of the HJ was to provide qualified personnel for the perpetuation of the Thousand Year Reich. Apart from the large number of leadership schools which sprang up to specifically train leaders for the HJ, a string of highly organised educational establishments were erected to fashion the future elite of the party, its formations, and the state: these included the Adolf Hitler Schools, the National Political Institutes of Education *(Napola)*, and the National Socialist Order Castles *(Ordensbürgen)*, all of which stood outside the ordinary school system. In these, the national socialists sought to extirpate the emphasis on individualism, which had been the hallmark of the liberal and progressive educational system of the Weimar Republic, and replace it with a system which would encompass and impregnate the whole being of a person with their ideas. Even the German school system was rapidly nazified and the HJ also laid claims to a substantial influence in this area. These and other "achievements" often caused Hitler to express pleasure at the work done by the HJ: in 1934 he enthused over the "glorious sight of this youth of ours,"[5] and in 1942 spoke warmly of the "success of the Hitler Youth movement."[6]

Despite the HJ's omnipresence in the life of German youth, membership theoretically remained voluntary until 1939. The considerable violence employed by the HJ against opponents in 1933–34 lends support to the argument that youths were under a certain compulsion to join, but nonetheless it must be conceded that many did undoubtedly join of their own volition. An important juridical change in the situation came in December 1936 when the Law for the Hitler Youth was promulgated. The law, which was partly a follow-up from the introduction of universal military conscription in March 1935, legally confirmed that the HJ was a state youth organisation *(Staatsjugend)*, and formally recognised it as an educational institution along with the school and parental home. Furthermore, von Schirach was no longer responsible to Bernhard Rust, Reich Minister of Education, as had been the case since May 1934, but directly to Hitler himself. More importantly, the law affirmed that the entire youth of Germany was to be organised in the HJ. Nevertheless, the directives necessary for the implementation of compulsory membership *(Jugenddienstpflicht)* were not issued until 25 March 1939.[7] The 1936 law, on the other hand, gave youths and their parents the impression that it was somehow disadvantageous to remain outside the HJ, and the voluntary principle was further compromised in 1937 when it was announced that in the future the only way to become an NSDAP member was to have served for at least four consecutive years in the HJ or its affiliated groups, the DJ and BDM.[8] For the best positions of employment, party membership was usually a practical necessity.

It may be fair to postulate that pressure of the type utilised by the HJ between 1933 and 1939 was required to enduce a sizable minority to join the group. Although there was a membership of about eight million in 1939, the HJ had to face the sober fact that four million boys and girls between the ages of ten and eighteen years refused to join it. Hence, the introduction of compulsory membership may be regarded as evidence that the HJ's spurious voluntary hypothesis was a failure. Notwithstanding this, the HJ had grown by 1939 to the largest youth organisation in the world, and in so doing, it was able to successfully execute its allotted task of making whole generations of youth think and act in monotonous uniformity.

World War II ushered in yet another phase in the HJ's history, for the conflict produced changes in its concept and practice, and also caused it to become more militarised. The HJ became a significant constituent of the home front, engaging in a multifarious variety of occupations to bolster the war effort and to help release valuable manpower for service in the armed forces. War work (Kriegseinsatz) replaced normal HJ activities to an increasing degree as the war dragged on.

The essentially military contribution of the HJ was also note-worthy, particularly during the last two years, when it assumed a combative spirit and approach reminiscent of the Kampfzeit. A large percentage of HJ leaders joined the forces, normally elite regiments of the Wehrmacht or crack Waffen-SS units, and many thousands of them were killed. Ordinary HJ members manned antiaircraft batteries, but during the concluding stages of the war, some of them were called up for active field service, and in 1943 the 12th SS panzer division Hitler-Jugend was established. The division was composed largely of seventeen- and eighteen-year-old HJ volunteers under SS officer supervision and it fought courageously in the Battle of Normandy in the summer of 1944.[9] In 1945, HJ members fought with distinction on the eastern front and then in the final battle of Berlin under the command of Artur Axmann.

That mere youths could be used in this manner in defence of a political creed already on the inexorable road to Götterdämmerung poignantly illustrates the moral and physical bankruptcy of the national socialist regime. The HJ manifested a tragic loyalty and faith in Führer, Volk, and fatherland to the very end, for the ideological programme administered by the HJ since 1933 ensured a supply of fighters for national socialism when all was long lost.

With the disintegration of the Third Reich in 1945, the HJ represented a bewildered and betrayed generation of German youth. The glorious future so often promised them by their leaders was now nothing more than a shallow, unattainable chimera. Hopelessness, misery, and abject despair were their unwanted companions in the harsh world of a destroyed nation in which they faced the painful prospect of having to rebuild their lives on uncertain foundations. The HJ, after a history lasting nearly two decades, was no more.

Notes: Epilogue

1. See K.D. Bracher, "Stufen totalitärer Gleichschaltung: Die Befestigung der NS Herrschaft 1933/34," *Vierteljahrshefte für Zeitgeschichte* 4 (1956):30–42.

2. The HJ was officially recognised as an organ of the state when von Schirach was named youth leader of the German Reich, but to all intents and purposes the HJ already possessed this status from the day of Hitler's appointment as chancellor.

3. BA:Sammlung Schumacher:Gruppe VIII. No. 239.

4. Reichsjugendführung der NSDAP, *Aufbau, Gliederung, und Anschriften der Hitler-Jugend* (Berlin, 1934), p. 12. Also see Appendix X.

5. N.H. Baynes, ed., *The Speeches of Adolf Hitler, 1922–39* (Oxford, 1942), vol. I, p. 530. Speech of 8 September 1934.

6. H.R. Trevor-Roper, ed., *Hitler's Table Talk* (London, 1953), p. 428. Remark of 12 April 1942.

7. Following the introduction of *Jugenddienstpflicht*, there was an attempt to divide the HJ into a *Stamm-Hitlerjugend* and an ordinary HJ. The *Stamm-HJ* was to be somewhat superior to the latter, but the experiment was discontinued in 1941 because it was administratively too confusing.

8. Ten–fourteen-year-old boys were organised in the DJ, ten–fourteen-year-old girls in the *Jungmädel,* fourteen–eighteen-year-old youths in the HJ proper, and fourteen–twenty-one-year-old girls in the BDM. In 1938, a special unit for girls aged seventeen–twenty-one years, "Faith and Beauty," was added to the BDM *(Das BDM-Werk Glaube und Schönheit).* Transfer from the DJ to the HJ took place every year on 20 April (Hitler's birthday), and from the HJ to the NSDAP on 9 November each year, the anniversary of the 1923 putsch.

9. Most of the higher officers were supplied by the 1st SS panzer division, *Leibstandarte* Adolf Hitler.

Bibliographical Note

The information in this section was provided in the main by primary sources, the most rewarding of which was the Berlin Document Center's extensive holdings of personnel files pertaining to former members of the national socialist movement. Useful also was miscellaneous material in the collection Hauptarchiv der NSDAP (NS 26) in the Bundesarchiv, Koblenz, particularly folders 332, 339, 360, 364, 366, and 397 (see the general Bibliography for precise descriptions); and the Bayerisches Hauptstaatsarchiv: Allgemeines Staatsarchiv in Munich, folders 1535, 1555, and 1776. In addition, the Bundesarchiv's Munziger Archiv and Zeitgeschichtliche Sammlung (numbers 3/1450 and 3/1477) yielded interesting facts.

From secondary sources, a number of studies published during the Nazi era are for once reasonably trustworthy, and include *Das Deutsche Führerlexikon 1934–35* (Munich, 1934); H. A. L. Degener, ed., *Wer Ists?* (Berlin, 1935); and Orientalischen Cigarreten-Compagnie, pub., *Männer im Dritten Reich* (Bremen, 1934). More care needs to be taken with *Adolf Hitler und seine Kämpfer* (Munich, 1933); and H. Volz, *Daten der Geschichte der NSDAP* (Berlin, 1943). Among more objective studies from non-Nazi sources are the helpful handbook published by the British Government, *Who's Who in Germany and Austria 1945* (London, 1945); and E. Stockhorst's *Fünftausend Köpfe* (Gütersloh, 1967). Of limited use were M. Schwarz, *Biographisches Handbuch der deutschen Reichstage* (Bonn, 1965); and the East German publication, *Braunbuch: Kriegs-und Naziverbrecher in der Bundesrepublik* (East Berlin, 1965). For isolated details on a few of the top

Hitler Youth leaders, consult H. R. Trevor-Roper, ed., *Hitler's Table Talk 1941–44* (London, 1953); and K. P. Tauber's tour de force, *Beyond Eagle and Swastika: German Nationalism since 1945* (Middletown, Conn., 1967).

Space does not permit the listing of the wide range of German and English newspapers which reported on HJ personnel, but readers are recommended to use the Wiener Library's excellent newspaper-clipping collection for reference. Of the Nazi periodicals, those most relevant for the HJ leadership are *Das Junge Deutschland, Amtliches Organ der Jugendführer des Deutschen Reiches*, and *Wille und Macht, Führerorgan der Nationalsozialistischen Jugend*.

There are no special works on any HJ leaders, though a number of books touch upon the career of Baldur von Schirach. The most reliable of these are J. Fest, *Das Gesicht des Dritten Reiches* (Stuttgart, 1963); Henrietta von Schirach, *The Price of Glory* (London, 1960); and G. M. Gilbert, *Nuremberg Diary* (New York, 1947). Von Schirach's memoirs, *Ich Glaubte an Hitler* (Hamburg, 1967), are, however, extremely disappointing. The evidence he gave at his Nuremberg trial may be found in International Military Tribunal, *Trial of the Major German War Criminals* (Nuremberg, 1947–49), volumes, I, II, V, IX, XIV, XIX, XXII, and XVIII.

Biography of HJ Leadership

This section provides details of the background and post-1933 careers of the Hitler Youth leaders who were active either in the *Kampfzeit* or the early years of the Third Reich. No one of the *Jugendbund der* NSDAP, except Adolf Lenk, has been included, nor has any figure of the *Grossdeutsche Jugendbewegung* except, of course, Kurt Gruber. It has not been possible to trace everyone, and there are a few notable omissions in the following list, but the large majority of important names are cited. It has proved difficult to discover information pertaining to the postwar activities of most of those mentioned. German as well as English and American newspapers and magazines have occasionally contained articles and news items on some of the more prominent personalities, but for the general mass of leaders there is at present no systematic procedure for obtaining personnel data. Where information is given only to 1945 or earlier, therefore, the absence of postwar material does not imply that the persons concerned are deceased.

1. ALBRECHT, Fritz
     Born on 25 December 1905 in Olivia (near Danzig), and an engineer by profession, Albrecht joined the NSDAP on 1 August 1929, membership number 142924, but was expelled on 1 July 1931 for failing

to pay membership dues. He did not rejoin the NSDAP until 1 May 1937, number 5900371, in Schleswig-Holstein. He was HJ *Gebietsführer* of *Gebiet* Ostland in 1931 and *Gebietsführer* of *Gebiet* West in 1932. He joined the SA on 14 March 1933, and on 1 March 1937, he became a member of the *Nationalsozialistischen Kraftkorps* (NSKK).

2.   ALTENDORF, Werner

He was born the son of a local government official on 24 November 1906 in Neuruppin, Silesia; he studied law at the universities of Jena, Berlin, and Breslau 1925–30, but did not complete his degree. He was an NSDStB member 1929–30, joined the NSDAP on 1 March 1930, membership number 203120, and the HJ on 1 December 1930.

He was *Gauführer* of Upper Silesia 1931, *Gruppenführer* of Silesia in 1931, and *Gebietsführer* of Silesia 1931–34. On 5 March 1933, he became a member of the Prussian *Landtag,* and on 12 November 1933, a member of the Reichstag from *Wahlkreis* Mecklenburg. In 1934, he was appointed leader of *Gebiet* Mecklenburg-Lübeck.

Altendorf was recognised as one of the leading poets of the HJ; he wrote many panegyrics of Hitler, and was the author of the song of the Silesian HJ, *Noch leis, durch Schlesien's Wälder,* and of the well-known HJ battle song, *Rollt nun die blutig roten Fahnen auf;* he also wrote several books, including *Jungvolk steh auf* (1930), and *Denn wir marschieren* (1932).

He held the HJ and NSDAP Golden Badges of Honour, the latter having been awarded in 1939. From 1939 to 1941, he was a member of the *Wehrmacht,* which he left badly wounded with the rank of lieutenant. On 20 April 1942, Altendorf was promoted HJ *Obergebietsführer* as leader of *Gebiet* Mecklenburg, and was awarded the War Service Cross the same year for his outstanding work for the HJ during the war. In 1943, he was attached to the *Reichsjugendführung* for a short time, then transferred to the NSDAP Reich Propaganda Office. He remained there until 9 October 1944, when he joined the NSDAP *Gauleitung* of Upper Silesia as a *Kreisleiter.* In 1945 he was interned in the American-contolled Dachau camp, but committed suicide by taking poison in December of that year.

3.   AMMERLAHN, Gotthard

Ammerlahn, born on 1 February 1907 in Berlin-Steglitz, was descended from an old Dutch peasant family which had come to Germany under the Great Elector's scheme to populate Mark Brandenburg. He attended *Gymnasium* in Steglitz from 1913 to 1918, and the Berlin *Realgymnasium* 1918–25, where he took his *Abitur.* His father was a schoolteacher. From 1925 to 1931, Ammerlahn studied history, geography, and geopolitics at the University of Berlin. A former *Bündische* Youth member, he joined the NSDAP on 1 June 1928, number 89720, after hearing Goebbels speak in Berlin's *Kriegsvereinhaus*. He joined the HJ in 1929, leading the Berlin-Brandenburg branch of the *Jungnationaler Bund* over to the HJ with him. Initially NSS *Gauführer* of Berlin-Brandenburg, he was a leading HJ writer, editor, and propagandist before 1933. In 1933, he was appointed HJ *Obergebietsführer* East. He held the NSDAP Golden Badge of Honour, and though apparently still an NSDAP member in 1939, he was no longer in the HJ. In the late 1960s, Ammerlahn was a leading writer on the extreme left-wing periodical, *Neues Politik*.

4.   APEL, Rudolf
     He was born in Berlin on 17 October 1912, and joined the NSDAP on 1 November 1930, number 341887, and the SA on 1 December 1931. He remained in the SA until May 1933. After joining the HJ on 1 August 1929, he held important press positions in HJ *Gau* South Bavaria 1930–31, and was press and propaganda leader of *Gebiet* Hochland for a period in 1932. He remained a leader in the HJ until 9 November 1937 when he became a member of the SS *Sicherheitsdienst* (Security Service), and he was still in the SS in 1940. He was a holder of the HJ Golden Badge of Honour.

5.   AXMANN, Artur
     He joined the HJ in Berlin in 1928 (see chapter 3). In September 1932, he became organisation leader of the NS-*Jugendbetriebszellen*-Organisation, and from 1933 until 1940 he headed the Social Office of the *Reichsjugendführung*. In November 1933, he was promoted from *Gebiets* to *Obergebietsführer*. On 16 November 1934, he was also named leader of *Gebiet* Berlin, and in May 1939, he was chairman of the committee for the establishment of the Youth Service Duty Law of 1939 (see Epilogue). On 7 August 1940, he succeeded von Schirach as *Reichsjugendführer der* NSDAP and youth leader of the Greater German Reich, and retained these posts until 1945.
     From 15 June until 4 December 1941, Axmann served on the Russian front, suffering the loss of his right arm, a feat which Hitler thought would enhance Axmann's prestige among European youth. In October 1941, he became a member of the Reichstag from *Wahlkreis* East Prussia. During the war, Axmann directed the activities of the HJ home front, and he inspired German youth with his own fanaticism, particularly in the closing stages (see Epilogue).

He belonged to the inner circle of national socialist leaders who stayed with Hitler in the Reich Chancellory bunker until the end in April 1945, for despite everything, Axmann remained one of the most loyal and devoted followers of the Führer. He personally inspected the dead bodies of Hitler and Eva Braun on 30 April 1945. On 1 May, he joined a small group which included Martin Bormann trying to break out of the Russian encirclement of Berlin, and ultimately succeeded in escaping with some HJ groups to a secret hideout in the Bavarian Alps. He remained there for six months before being captured.

After a period of internment and interrogation, Axmann was convicted by a Nuremberg court on 30 April 1949 of having been a major offender of the national socialist regime because of his unwholesome influence on German youth. He was sentenced to three and a half years' imprisonment, but this was waived because of his detention since 1945. He was heavily fined, and deprived of many civic and political rights for an indefinite period. He was found not guilty, however, of having committed war crimes.

Axmann subsequently became a leading figure in the postwar national socialist underground movement; he was a member from the beginning of the *Bruderschaft* (Brotherhood), founded in Hamburg in 1949, and in the early 1950s, he was a member of the *Herrenklub,* which had connections with Werner Naumann's circle. On 19 August 1958, a West Berlin denazification court fined him 35,000 deutsch marks, a lenient sentence, the court affirmed, because Axmann had been a supporter of national socialism from "inner conviction" and not from "base motives." At that time, Axmann was described as an industrial salesman, and in the 1960s he was in partnership with his brother Kurt, also a former high-ranking HJ leader, in an export business in West Berlin.

6.   AXTMANN, Heinz
Gauführer of East Saxony in 1931, Axtmann was born in Chemnitz on 4 July 1903, and joined the NSDAP on 1 February 1931, number 422798.

7.   BACH, Alfred
He was born on 1 March 1896 in Glückstadt, Schleswig-Holstein, and joined the NSDAP on 13 December 1927, number 71930. Following his expulsion from the HJ and NSDAP in 1930 (see chapter 4), he rejoined the party on 1 October 1931.

8.   BARTELS, Willi
      Born on 6 February 1895 in Magdeburg the son of a factory owner, Bartels was educated at the universities of Berlin and Munich, and joined the NSDAP on 1 May 1933, number 2753880. In 1933, he was appointed *Oberbannführer* of Schleswig-West Holstein. In 1939, he was apparently a member of the *Deutsches Arbeitsfront*. He served in the armed forces and was decorated for bravery. After 1945, he set up business in Hamburg.

9.   BARTH, Wilhelm
      Barth was born on 24 December 1908, in Hof-Saale. After joining the HJ on 1 March 1928 and the NSDAP on 1 March 1929, number 121815, he was HJ *Oberführer* of Franconia 1930–31; HJ Reich Propaganda Leader 1931–32; and from 1932 until February 1933, he was attached to the *Reichsjugendführung* with the rank of *Bannführer*. He was then a staff member of HJ *Gebiet* Hochland before being transferred in September 1933 to HJ *Gebiet* Franconia as chief of staff of *Oberbann* Upper Franconia. In May 1934, he was named deputy organisation leader of NSDAP *Gau* Bayerisches Ostmark. In 1939, he joined the *Wehrmacht*, and before leaving with the rank of lieutenant in 1942, he was awarded the Iron Cross, Class II. In 1943, he was appointed a member of the Supreme Party Court and a principal *Gau* leader, but in March 1944, he was once again called up to the *Wehrmacht*. He was a holder of the HJ Golden Badge of Honour, and his HJ membership number was 12001.

10.   BAUER, Theodor
      Bauer was born in Munich on 22 January 1896. During the First World War, in which he was badly wounded, he was awarded the Iron Cross, Class II. In 1922, he was a member of the NSDAP and SA; he rejoined the NSDAP on 20 October 1927, number 68993, and after becoming a member of the HJ on 9 November 1928, he became a leader of the Rosenheim branch. His HJ membership number was 15196. In 1930, he was appointed HJ *Bezirksführer* of Chiemgau, and on 30 January 1933, *Unterbannführer* in HJ *Gebiet* Hochland. In 1936, he was promoted to *Bannführer*, and in 1939 held this rank as leader in the youth hostel organisation. He held both the HJ and NSDAP Golden Badges of Honour, and in 1940 was awarded a medal for 15 years' service in the NSDAP. In 1942, he was still an HJ Bannführer.

11. BAUMANN, Erwin

Born on 29 July 1904 in Stotternheim, Erfurt, Erwin Oskar Paul Baumann originally joined the NSDAP on 31 August 1923. He took his *Abitur* at Ilmenau *Oberrealschule* and afterwards trained as a bank clerk. A member of the *Jungdeutsche Orden* in 1922–23, he was active in the *Frontbann* 1924–25 before joining the NSDAP again on 29 May 1925, number 6658. He was an SA member from 1926 until 1931 when he joined the SS, number 17307. In 1933, he was appointed deputy leader of the administration division in the *Reichsjugendführung,* and in January 1934 became adjutant to Chief of Staff Carl Nabersberg. Later that year he was expelled from the HJ. From 1936 to 1939, he was a *Reichsrevisor* in the NSDAP *Reichsleitung* and an honorary member of the SS. In 1939, he became principally active in the SS and SD with the rank of SS-*Hauptsturmführer.* He was subsequently posted to the SD office in Prague where he was responsible to Reinhard Heydrich. From February to July 1943, he led an SS *Einsatzkommando* unit in the Ukraine, and by the end of 1944, held the rank of SS-*Standartenführer.* He was also a holder of the NSDAP Golden Badge of Honour.

12. BAUMANN, Hans

Born in Amberg on 22 April 1914, he joined the HJ in 1932, and the NSDAP on 1 May 1933, number 2662179. He was educated at the University of Berlin, qualified as a schoolteacher, and in November 1933, he became a member of the NS-*Lehrerbund* (Teachers' League). Baumann was celebrated in the Third Reich as a leading poet and writer of the *völkisch*-nationalist stream, writing *Horch auf, Kamarad* in 1936, *Wir Zünden das Feuer* in 1936, and *Kampf um die Karawanken* in 1938. In 1933–34, he was a leader in the *Jungvolk,* and in 1935 and 1938–39, worked in the *Läienspiele* division of the *Reichsjugendführung.* In 1939, he joined the *Wehrmacht,* served for a time on the eastern front, and remained a soldier until 1945. After 1945, he turned to writing children's books receiving the Gerstäcker Prize from the city of Brunswick in 1956, and the *New York Herald Tribune* Prize in 1958 for his contributions to juvenile literature.

13. BAUMGARTNER, Alfons

He was born on 23 February 1907, joining the NSDAP on 22 November 1926, number 49031. The first leader of the Munich HJ (see chapter 8), he left the organisation in 1927 to join the *Schilljugend,* and later was a member of the *Bund Ekkehard* until 1932. He became an SA member on 13 October 1933, but was expelled in September

1934 for homosexuality. Thereafter, he was an NSDAP block and cell leader until he was attached in a minor capacity to the NS *Ordensburg Vogelsang* in 1937.

14.   BEIER, Kurt

He was HJ leader of *Gau* Westphalia-North from 1931 to 1933. Born on 18 October 1910, Beier joined the NSDAP on 1 March 1928, number 77575. In 1933, he was appointed *Gebietsführer* of *Gebiet* Lower Saxony, and on 15 October 1934, he became leader of the Organisation Division in the *Reichsjugendführung*. He left the HJ on 30 September 1936, and in 1937 he was appointed a *Kreisleiter* in NSDAP *Gau* South Hannover-Brunswick. He retained this position until March 1944 when he was transferred to the NSDAP chancellory.

15.   BENNEWITZ, Gerhard

Bennewitz was born on 25 December 1913 in Bantzen, and joined the NSDAP on 1 December 1931, number 823495. In 1932, he was leader of HJ *Bann* Düsseldorf, and in 1933 was appointed chief of staff of *Gebiet* Westphalia with the rank of *Bannführer*. Although he left the NSDAP in 1932, he rejoined on 1 August 1934, number 1876224.

16.   BERGIEN, Oskar

Born in Essen on 10 November 1909, Bergien joined the NSDAP on 1 February 1928, number 75802, and as an HJ member, he joined the NS *Arbeiter-und Bauernjugend* in 1931. He was readmitted to the NSDAP on 1 May 1937, number 5609277.

17.   BICKER, Willi Botho

Bicker was born the seventh child of a factory manager on 6 July 1900 in Gera. At the age of 12, he joined the *Jungdeutschland* movement, and in 1914 volunteered for army service; he was not permitted to join until 1918. As a member of the 2nd Reserve Company Pioneer Batallion II, he was decorated with the Iron Cross in October 1918. In 1919 he joined the *Freikorps Stillfried* and then the *Ehrhardt* Brigade, taking part in the Kapp Putsch, the Ruhr resistance, and the fighting in Upper Silesia. He was arrested for suspected complicity in the murders of Erzberger and Rathenau, but he was not convicted. He joined the NSDAP on 16 June 1921, number 611, but did not rejoin until 1 December 1930, number 391661. From 1928 to 1930, he was an NSDStB member, and joined the HJ in 1930. From October 1932 until December 1934, he was Reich organisation leader in the *Reichs-jugendführung*. On 1 January 1935, he joined the SS and was attached to the *Reichsführung;* the same year, he was expelled from the NSDAP, but was allowed to rejoin in 1937. In 1939, he was still active in the SS *Reichsführung* with the rank of SS-*Sturmbannführer*.

18.   BISSINGER, Edgar
Born on 25 May 1912 in Erfurt, Bissinger joined the NSDAP on 1 May 1931, number 525723, and in 1932 was HJ press chief.

19.   BLOBEL, Herbert
Born on 30 September 1907 in Berlin, he joined the NSDAP on 1 June 1930, number 254846, and in 1932 was appointed leader of HJ *Bann* Lower Silesia.

20.   BLUM, Gunter
Blum was born on 8 July 1905 in Krefeld, and became an NSDAP member on 1 March 1930, number 210167. A former member of the *Fichtebund* and the *Jungnationaler Bund,* he was *Gebietsführer* of *Gebiet* Hochland 1931–32; leader of *Gebiet* Mittelland in 1932; and in 1933, he was named *Gebietsführer* of *Gebiet* Thuringia. In 1936 a secret NSDAP report bitterly criticised Blum's character, but he was allowed to retain his post in the HJ, despite being expelled from the party in 1937 as a result of this report. In 1939 he joined the *Wehrmacht;* in 1942 he was expelled from the HJ for failing to honour debts, and as a member of the *Wehrmacht,* he was killed in the closing stages of the war.

21.   BOHNENGEL, Oskar
Born in Würzburg on 1 August 1907, he joined the NSDAP on 3 April 1925, number 3006, and shortly thereafter became an HJ member. He was *Gauführer* of HJ *Gau* Lower Franconia in 1929–31. In 1934, Bohnengel joined the NS *Volkswohlfahrt,* and in 1939 he was a division leader in the *Deutsches Arbeitsfront.* He was the founder of the HJ in Würzburg.

22.   BOLM, Hermann
Bolm was born in Brunswick on 7 July 1912. He was press leader of HJ *Gau* South Hannover-Brunswick 1930–31, and on 1 May 1931,

he joined the NSDAP number 537626. After 1933, he worked for a period in the NSDAP chancellory; in October 1943, he was transferred to NSDAP *Gauleitung* Wartheland as a division leader, but early in 1944, he returned to the party chancellory.

23.   BORMANN, Albert

Born on 2 September 1902 in Halberstadt, Bormann joined the NSDAP on 27 April 1927, number 60507, and the SA. From 1929 to 1931 he was HJ *Gauführer* of Thuringia. He joined the NSDAP *Reichsleitung*, Hilfkasse division, but a few months later, in October 1931, he was appointed to Hitler's private chancellory, of which he became leader in 1933. He retained this post until 1945; in addition, he was appointed adjutant to Hitler in 1938 and also retained this position until 1945. He was an SS-*Standartenführer*, and NSKK-*Gruppenführer*, and a Reichstag member.

24.   BOY, Rolf

After joining the NSDAP on 1 August 1929, number 143591, Boy became leader of the Trades School Cell Organisation of the Berlin HJ in 1930. He was born in Berlin on 1 November 1911.

25.   BRASCHE, Kurt

He was born on 13 June 1912 in Nörten, and on 1 November 1928 joined the HJ, number 23043, as branch leader of Thiede. On 1 March 1929, he was appointed HJ *Bezirksführer* of Wolfenbuttel, and from 1930 to 1932, was secretary of HJ *Gau* South Hannover-Brunswick. He was later awarded the HJ Golden Badge of Honour. From 1932 to 1933, he was a member of the Bremen police, and from 1933 to 1937, was a junior officer in the *Wehrmacht*. On leaving the army, he was a division leader in HJ *Gebiet* Nordsee with the rank of *Bannführer*, and was later attached to the staff leader's office in the *Reichsjugendführung*. From 1939 to 1941, he was a lieutenant in the *Wehrmacht*, and from 1941 to 1943, he served on NSDAP *Gauleitung* South Hannover-Brunswick. In 1943, he was awarded the NSDAP Golden Badge of Honour, having joined the party on 1 July 1930, number 265007. After another short period of service in the *Wehrmacht*, he was appointed on NSDAP *Kreisleiter* in *Gau* South Hannover-Brunswick in November 1943. At the same time, Brasche was an SS member, number 470562, and in June 1944, he held the rank of SS *Hauptsturmführer*.

26.   BREUNSBACH, Albert
Born on 22 April 1913, he joined the NSDAP on 1 July 1931, number 570395, and was appointed *Schar* leader of HJ *Gau* Cologne-Aachen the same year. A former member of the *Artamanen* movement, he left the HJ in 1932 to join the *Reichswehr*.

27.   BRIEGER, Curt
In 1932, Brieger was advisor for *Jungvolk* questions in the HJ *Reichsleitung*, and in 1932 also, he was appointed *Bundesführer* of the *Jungvolk;* he was expelled from this post shortly afterwards (see chapter 4).

28.   BRINKMANN, Willi
Born on 25 October 1889 in Düsseldorf, he served in World War I as a lieutenant and was awarded the Iron Cross, Class II. He joined the NSDAP on 1 December 1931, number 752757, and the same year was named leader of HJ *Gau* Düsseldorf. He became a member of the SS on 1 August 1940, number 361260, with the rank of SS-*Hauptsturmführer*. He was previously a police commissioner.

29.   BRÜSS, Hans
Brüss was born on 13 January 1912 in Dresden, and joined the NSDAP on 1 June 1930, number 266694. He was named leader of the HJ Border Land Office in July 1931; he was appointed HJ *Gebietsführer* Ausland on 1 January 1932; on 11 July 1932 he was appointed an HJ *Bannführer*. During the war he joined the *Wehrmacht,* and was killed on 3 February 1944.

30.   BUCHHOLZ, Hans
After joining the NSDAP on 2 November 1925, number 21823, Buchholz was leader of HJ *Gau* Danzig from 1929 to 1931. He was later awarded the NSDAP Golden Badge of Honour.

31.   BURCHHARD, Walter
He was born on 20 April 1908 in Hamburg, and was a member of the *Deutsche Pfadfinderbund* from 1919–28 before joining the NSDAP and SA on 1 March 1928, party number 85844. He was HJ *Gauführer* of Weser-Ems 1929–31; in 1929, he was also *Gauführer* of Lüneburg-Stade; on 15 November 1930, he was named HJ *Oberführer*

North West; and in April 1931, he was appointed HJ *Gruppenführer* North. He was expelled from the HJ and NSDAP in 1931 (see chapter 4). In 1933, he was active as a minor leader in HJ *Gau* Weser-Ems. On 3 December 1937, he was allowed to rejoin the NSDAP, but when he applied for the NSDAP Golden Badge of Honour in 1941, he was refused. In 1969, Burchhard was a *Bürgermeister* in a town in Schleswig-Holstein.

32. BÜRGER, Karl Heinz

Born in Güstrow on 16 February 1904, Bürger became an NSDAP member on 13 December 1927, number 68902. He was also an SA member in 1923 and 1928–30. He was a leader in *Geusen* before he joined the HJ in 1930, and the same year was appointed HJ *Gauführer* of Mecklenburg-Lübeck and HJ *Oberführer* North. On leaving the HJ, he was again active in the SA 1931–32. On 30 January 1933, he joined the SS, number 156309, and by 20 April 1944, he had attained the rank of SS-*Oberführer*. From 1940 to 1943, he served with a *Waffen*-SS unit in Russia, and on 30 October 1944 was awarded the Iron Cross, Class I. He was a holder of the NSDAP Golden Badge of Honour, and of the *Blutorden* for having participated in the 1923 Hitler putsch.

33. CERFF, Karl

Born on 12 March 1907 in Heidelberg, Cerff joined the NSDAP and SA in 1922; he rejoined the NSDAP on 17 February 1926, number 30314, and took part in the 1926 NSDAP *Reichsparteitag* in Weimar. In 1929, he joined the HJ in Heidelberg, and from 1931 to May 1932, he was press and propaganda leader of HJ *Gau* Baden. From 1933 to 1939, he was leader of the radio division in the *Reichsjugendführung*, attaining the rank of *Obergebietsführer*. On 30 January 1939, he joined the SS, number 323782, with the rank of SS *Oberführer,* and from 1940 to 1942, he was on active service with the *Waffen*-SS. He was then leader of the Cultural Division in the NSDAP Reich Propaganda Office, and he retained this post until 1945. On 30 January 1943, he was promoted SS-*Brigadeführer,* and was a holder of both the NSDAP and HJ Golden Badges of Honour.

After 1945 Cerff was a conspicuous figure in neonazi and extreme nationalist movements, including the *Deutsche* Union, and *Arbeitsgemeinschaft Nationaler Gruppen*. Cerff was also a leading figure of the SS veterans' association, *Hilfsgemeinshaft auf Gegenseitigkeit der ehemaliger Angehörigen der Waffen*-SS (HIAG), and in 1962 he was elected one of its directors. Cerff also was a businessman in Heidelberg.

34.   DENGLER, Fritz
Born on 2 May 1901 in Straubing, Bavaria, he joined the NSDAP on 8 August 1925, number 14737, and was HJ *Gauführer* of Lower Bavaria-Oberpfalz 1930–31. After 1933, he was awarded the NSDAP Golden Badge of Honour.

35.   ERLMEIER, Josef
He was born on 18 September 1897 in Landshut, originally joined the NSDAP in 1922, and joined again on 8 August 1925, number 14291. From 1916 to 1918 he served in World War I, and afterwards was a member of the *Freikorps* Passau. From 1922 to 1923 he was a member of the *Stahlhelm;* he joined the HJ in 1926; and from 1928 to 1929, he was HJ Gauführer of Lower Bavaria-Oberpfalz. He also joined the SS in 1926, number 475, and remained an SS member until 1945, ultimately with the rank of SS-*Sturmbannführer.* He spent short periods working in the NS Factory Cell Organisation in 1932, and the *Deutsches Arbeitsfront* 1934–36. He also served in the Wehrmacht 1939–40. He held the *Blutorden* and the HJ and NSDAP Golden Badges of Honour.

36.   ERNST, Gustav
He was appointed chief of staff of HJ *Gebiet* Kurmark in 1933 with the rank of *Oberbannführer.* In 1945, he led HJ *Gebiet* Hesse-Nassau as *Hauptbannführer.*

37.   ETZEL, Richard
He was born in Munich on 12 March 1910, and joined the NSDAP on 16 October 1929, number 156006, and the HJ on 15 March 1930, number 15383. A minor HJ leader in Munich before 1933, he was *Jungvolk* leader of Munich from 1933 to 1934; leader of the Education Division of HJ *Gebiet* Hochland 1934–36; and commissioner for *Jungvolk* affairs in *Gebiet* Hochland 1936–39. In 1939, he joined the *Wehrmacht,* but remained active in the HJ and DJ until 1945. His last known rank was that of *Oberjungbannführer* in the DJ in 1941. He held the HJ Golden Badge of Honour.
     In 1949, Etzel organised the radically nationalist *Jugendbund Adler,* and remained its leader until at least the late 1960s. In the 1950s, he was also deputy chairman of Karl Meissner's extreme right-wing German Bloc.

38. FEHR, Josef

Born the son of a shopkeeper on 21 March 1909 in Munich, and a primary schoolteacher by profession, he was secretary of HJ *Gau* Munich-Upper Bavaria, and advisor for *Jungvolk* affairs in the HJ *Reichsleitung* in 1932.

39. FISCHER, Ernst

He was *Gauführer* of HJ *Gau* Breslau in 1931, and in 1933 was appointed *Bannführer* of *Oberbann* Middle Silesia. In 1934, he was promoted to *Oberbannführer* and named leader of the press division of HJ *Obergebiet* West. In June 1934, however, he was appointed leader of the propaganda division in the *Reichsjugendführung,* and he was also active as editor of the *Westdeutsche Fanfare.*

40. FÖRSCHLE, Erwin

Born on 26 June 1909 in Colmar, he joined the NSDAP on 16 August 1927, number 66486. From 1930 to 1932, he was secretary of HJ *Gau* Baden, and in December 1932, he was named *Bannführer* of *Bann* Hesse-Darmstadt. In 1933, he was appointed *Oberbannführer* of *Oberbann* Brandenburg-South, but was expelled that year from the NSDAP. In 1938, he was an *Oberbannführer* in the Reich Administrative Leaders' School in the Saar. In August 1943, he held the rank of HJ *Hauptbannführer.*

41. Von FRITSCH, Freiherr Thomas

Born on 7 November 1909 in Chemnitz, von Fritsch joined the NSDAP on 1 April 1929, number 123982. He joined the HJ on 6 June 1930, and from 30 March to 31 July 1932, he was HJ Reich propaganda leader. On 27 October 1932, he joined the SS, number 45163. In 1937, he was appointed SS-*Obersturmführer,* and after serving in the *Wehrmacht* from 1939–41, he was promoted to SS-*Hauptsturmführer* in 1943. In October 1944 he was in the *Waffen*-SS and was awarded the Iron Cross, Class II. He also held the HJ Golden Badge of Honour.

42. FRONJA, Ludwig

Fronja was born on 4 October 1908 in Beuthen, Silesia, and joined the NSDAP on 1 June 1931, number 544169. In 1932, he was leader of HJ *Bann* Upper Silesia, and in 1933 he was chief of staff of *Gebiet* Silesia with the rank of *Oberbannführer.* He still held the latter position in 1937. Having previously left the NSDAP, he was allowed to rejoin on 1 May 1937, number 5784899.

43.   GADEWOLTZ, Robert
Born on 30 October 1905 in Berlin, he joined the NSDAP on 17 May 1926, number 36798, and participated in the 1926 NSDAP *Reichsparteitag*. He was HJ *Gauführer* of Berlin-Brandenburg 1928–31, and HJ *Oberführer* East 1930–31. By 1939 he had attained the rank of SA-*Obersturmführer*, but joined the *Wehrmacht* that year. He became an *Oberleutnant*, and was decorated with the Iron Cross, Classes I and II. He also held the NSDAP Golden Badge of Honour. In 1969 he was a district chairman of the rightist German Freedom party.

44.   GEISSLER, Balduin (Bun)
Geissler was born on 26 January 1907 in Altenburg, Thuringia, and became an NSDAP member on 1 July 1930, number 273797. He was HJ *Gauführer* of Thuringia in 1931; leader of the *Deutsches Jungvolk* in 1932; and in 1933, he became leader of HJ *Bann* East Holstein. The same year, he was attached to the *Reichsjugendführung* with the rank of *Gebietsführer*, and he still held this rank in 1942.

45.   GLASHAGEN, Heinz
He was born in Danzig on 16 August 1911, and joined the HJ on 1 January 1930 and the NSDAP on 1 October 1931, number 637437. In 1933 he was appointed leader of HJ *Oberbann* Danzig-West Prussia with the rank of *Oberbannführer*. He was active thereafter in the HJ until called up to the *Wehrmacht* in December 1942. In June 1944, he is known to have been a member of the unit *Standarte Feldherrnhalle*. He held the HJ Golden Badge of Honour.

46.   GOERENDT, Werner
Born on 10 March 1908, he joined the SA on 1 October 1926, and the NSDAP on 1 February 1928, number 75417. He was HJ *Gauführer* of Hesse 1929–30, and in 1939 was editor of the *Schwarzwälder Tageblatt*. He held the NSDAP Golden Badge of Honour.

47.   GRAMKE, Ernst
Gramke was born on 19 May 1912 in Köslin, Pomerania, and became an NSDAP member on 1 April 1931, number 516099. He was

leader of HJ *Bann* Pomerania-East in 1932, and also in 1933 when it was raised to the status of an *Oberbann*. In 1942, he was a division leader in HJ *Gebiet* leadership Hamburg with the rank of *Hauptbannführer,* but the same year he was killed as a member of the armed forces.

48. GROSSE, Artur
He was born on 13 July 1906 in Berlin; he joined the NSDAP on 7 December 1926, number 48406, but left it on 31 August 1928. After joining the HJ from the *Jungnationaler Bund* in 1929, he soon became education leader of the HJ *Gau* Berlin-Brandenburg-Ostmark, and a member of the HJ *Reichsleitung.* He became deeply involved in social revolutionary activity and left the HJ in 1930 (see chapter 4).

49. GRUBER, Hans
Born on 30 March 1906 in Plauen, he helped his brother Kurt to build up the HJ; his HJ membership number was 2. He was also an SA member 1923–31, and an NSDAP member from 10 June 1925, number 7303. In 1926 he was leader of the sports division in the HJ *Reichsleitung,* and in 1931 was treasurer of HJ *Gebiet* Saxony; he held this position in 1936 with the rank of HJ *Oberbannführer.* On 1 October 1940, he joined the *Waffen-SS,* and in 1944 held the rank of SS-*Unterscharführer.* He held both the HJ and HSDAP Golden Badges of Honour.

50. GRUBER, Kurt
He was *Reichsführer* of the HJ 1926–31 (see chapter 1). On leaving the HJ in October 1931, he was immediately attached to the NSDAP *Reichsleitung* as a youth advisor, but in 1932 he was transferred to NSDAP *Gauleitung* Saxony where he became secretary in the Communal Politics Division. In May 1939 he was appointed leader of the latter office, having also been active as an NSDAP speaker and writer, and from April 1935 as an honorary town councillor in Dresden. On 24 December 1943, he died of an apoplexy in Dresden while still leader of the Communal Politics Division. At the time of death, he was also an SA-*Standartenführer* in the staff of SA *Gruppe* Saxony, a holder of the HJ and NSDAP Golden Badges of Honour, and of NSDAP medals for 10 and 15 years of party service. In recognition of his work for the HJ and the national socialist movement, he was given a full ceremonial burial. He left a wife and four children.

51.   GUGEL, Rudolf
   Gugel was born in Nuremberg on 14 February 1908, and joined the NSDAP on 1 May 1928, number 87373. He was HJ *Gauführer* of South Franconia 1929–30; leader of the HJ *Untergau* South Franconia-East in 1931; leader of *Bann* Middle Franconia in 1932; and in 1933, was appointed *Gebietsführer* of *Gebiet* Franconia. He was promoted to HJ *Obergebietsführer* on 20 April 1937 while holding the latter position. In July 1939, he joined the *Wehrmacht* as a junior officer, and was killed in action later in the war. He held both the HJ and NSDAP Golden Badges of Honour.

52.   HAEFKE, Ernst
   Born on 25 July 1913 in Güstrow, he joined the NSDAP on 1 December 1931, number 805733. Before joining the HJ in 1928 he had been a member of the *Wandervogel* from 1924–27 and the *Bund der Kaufmannsjugend* 1927–28. He was HJ *Gauführer* of Lower Bavaria 1929–30. In 1933 he was *Jungvolk* leader of *Gau* Lower Bavaria-Oberpfalz, but left the HJ that year. In 1935, he was active in NSDAP *Kreisleitung* Landau, but was expelled from the NSDAP on 2 August 1937 after a civil court had convicted and sentenced him to 18 months' imprisonment for homosexual offences. At the time of expulsion, he was *Kreis* secretary and organisation leader in NSDAP *Kreis* Landau.

53.   HALLER von HALLERSTEIN, Kurt
   Born on 24 January 1913 in Elberfeld, he had been a member of the *Jungstahlhelm* since 1923, and the SA and NSS before joining the HJ in 1929. In August 1932 he was appointed HJ *Gebietsführer* of *Gebiet* Hochland, but was shortly dismissed (see chapter 4). He joined the NSDAP on 1 May 1935, number 3624748, and the SS in June 1933, number 102343. In September 1943 he held the rank of SS-*Sturmbannführer,* and from 1942 until 1945 saw uninterrupted service in the *Wehrmacht.* He was badly wounded, and was one of the few survivors of Stalingrad to escape back to his own lines. He was awarded the Iron Cross, Classes I and II, and finished the war with the rank of lieutenant. He also held the HJ Golden Badge of Honour.

54.   HAVERBECK, Werner
   He was born on 28 October 1909 in Bonn, and joined the NSDAP on 1 August 1929, number 142009. He was an NSDStB member 1928–29, and an SA member 1928–31. Before joining the HJ in 1931, he was

a leader of several small *völkisch* youth groups, including the *Nörd-ischer Jugendring* and the *Arbeitsgemeinschaft deutscher Jugend*. In 1932 he was appointed leader of the temporary Cultural and Educational Division in the *Reichsjugendführung*, having previously worked in the Cultural Division of the NSDAP *Reichsleitung*. In 1933 he worked on Rudolf Hess's liaison staff and in Hitler's private chancellory. At the same time, he was active in the development of *Volkssturm* work, and in June 1933 was appointed leader of the Reich Office for NSDAP *Volkssturm* affairs, which was part of the NSDAP *Reichsleitung*. In August 1933, he founded the *Reichsbund Volkssturm und Heimat*. In May 1934, he joined the SS, number 277529, but left in 1938 with the rank of SS-*Untersturmführer* for a post in the Reich Peasant Organisation. In 1941, he is known to have been a member of the German diplomatic staff in Buenos Aires.

55.   HECKEROTH, Hans
He was advisor on defence sport in HJ *Gebiet* Greater Berlin 1931–32, and in June 1932 was appointed temporary leader of *Gebiet* Berlin-Brandenburg. He joined the NSDAP in the early 1930s, number 278318.

56.   HEINRICH, Hermann
Born on 15 September 1911 in Halle, he joined the NSDAP on 1 June 1930, number 257843, and in 1932 was leader of the Material Office in the HJ *Reichsleitung*. He left the NSDAP in May 1934, but rejoined on 16 March 1936.

57.   HEMPEL, Georg
Born on 29 October 1907 in Chemnitz, he joined the NSDAP on 5 March 1926, number 31593, and the HJ the same year. He was HJ leader in Kiel in 1930, but left in 1933 while an HJ *Oberbannführer* in Schleswig-Holstein. He was an SA member from 1928 to 1933. In 1934 he taught at the *Nationalpolitischen Erziehungsanstalt* (NAPOLA) in Berlin, and in 1935 joined the NS Teachers' Association. In 1936 he joined the SS, number 277398, and in 1941 held the rank of SS-*Hauptsturmführer* while teaching at a NAPOLA centre. In 1942 he went on active military service, and in 1944 was on the southeastern front, still as an SS-*Hauptsturmführer*. He held both the HJ and NSDAP Golden Badges of Honour.

58. HENGST, Ferdinand

He was born on 2 January 1905 in Leipzig. A member of the *Deutschvölkischer Jugendbund* as early as 1920, he took part in the 1923 Hitler putsch as an SA man. In 1926 he founded the HJ in Halle; in 1929 he was HJ *Gauführer* of Halle-Merseburg, and later the same year, leader of the sports division in the HJ *Reichsleitung*. He joined the NSDAP on 1 February 1929, number 113620, but was expelled from the HJ and NSDAP in 1929 and 1930 respectively (see chapter 4). In 1933 he was again active as an HJ leader in Halle, but was shortly expelled once again from both the HJ and NSDAP for assaulting five Hitler youths. In 1937 he was pardoned and allowed to join the NSDAP for a third time.

59. HENNIES, Werner

Hennies was born on 10 August 1910 in Sarstedt; he joined the NSDAP on 1 August 1928, number 96157, and the same year was leader of the HJ in Hannover. In 1929, he was appointed leader of HJ *Bezirk* Weser-Leine, but in October 1929 joined the *Reichswehr*. During a pause in his army service, which continued until 1937, he was staff leader of HJ *Oberbann* East Hannover in 1933. In 1937 he was named an HJ *Oberbannführer,* but shortly became active in the Organisation Division of NSDAP *Gauleitung* East Hannover. He was expelled from this office in 1938, and in September 1939 joined the *Wehrmacht.*

60. HEUBLEIN, Albin

He was born in Grafenthal on 12 May 1906, and became an NSDAP member on 13 May 1925, number 4620. He was an SA member 1927–30, and joined the HJ in 1930. In 1932 he was named leader of HJ *Bann* Thuringia, and in 1933 leader of HJ *Oberbann* South Thuringia. He held this position as an *Oberbannführer* in 1939.

61. HILSCHER, Lothar

Born on 12 June 1909 in Danzig, he joined the NSDAP on 25 July 1927, number 70025. He was branch leader of HJ Lübeck 1928–29, and HJ *Gauführer* of Mecklenburg-Lübeck from 1929 until his expulsion in 1930. In 1933, he was arrested by the Gestapo and held in a concentration camp until 1934. After his release, he sought once again to gain a foothold in the HJ, and was appointed to work on the staff of HJ *Oberbann* Mecklenburg-Lübeck by its leader, Walter Unger. In 1935, however, HJ Chief of Staff Lauterbacher forbade Hilscher from having anything more to do with the HJ, and he was dismissed. Before 1939, Hilscher was active in Schleswig-Holstein as a speaker and propagandist of the *Volksdeutsch im Ausland* organisation.

62.   HOFMANN, Karl

He was born on 24 February 1903 and joined the NSDAP on 14 December 1926, number 48585. He was HJ *Gauführer* of Rheinpfalz 1929–33. A holder of the NSDAP Golden Badge of Honour, he was active as a party member in the Saar in 1940.

63.   HOGREFE, Lühr

Born a farmer's son on 26 January 1900 in Nöpke, he was a physical training teacher in Osnabrück 1922–28. He joined the NSDAP on 1 December 1930, number 383895; he was HJ *Gauführer* of Weser-Ems in 1931, and *Gebietsführer* of Nordsee in 1932. He joined the HJ in 1930, having previously been a member of the *Jungdeutsche Orden* since 1925. He became a member of the NS Teachers' Association in April 1932. In 1933, he was named HJ *Gebietsführer* of *Gebiet* Nordsee, and still held this post with the rank of *Obergebietsführer* in 1942. On 13 February 1942, he was killed as a member of the *Wehrmacht* on the eastern front. He held both the HJ and NSDAP Golden Badges of Honour, the latter awarded in 1938.

64.   HOHOFF, Heinz

He was born on 8 December 1910 in Gelsenkirchen, joined the SA in 1928, and the NSDAP on 1 February 1930, number 192982. In 1933, he was appointed leader of HJ *Oberbann* Brandenburg-North with the rank of *Bannführer*. In 1935 he was leader of *Jungvolk Gebiet* Kurmark, and was a speaker for the NSDAP Reich Propaganda Office. In 1936, he was appointed adjutant to Staff Leader Lauterbacher, and in 1937 he was named deputy leader of HJ *Gebiet* Middle Rhine. On 20 April 1938, he was promoted to HJ *Gebietsführer* and given responsibility for *Gebiet* Cologne-Aachen. In 1943, he was appointed HJ *Obergebietsführer,* but was reported missing after Stalingrad. He was awarded the NSDAP Golden Badge of Honour in 1939.

65.   HOLLATZ, John

He was *Gau* secretary of Hamburg in 1930, and HJ *Gauführer* of Hamburg in 1931. Born on 16 September 1907 in Hamburg, he joined the NSDAP on 22 April 1926, number 34712, the SA on 13 October

1926, and the HJ on 30 December 1926. After 1933, he was awarded the HJ and NSDAP Golden Badges of Honour.

66. HÜNGER, Heinz

Born in Schwarza-Saale on 15 November 1911, he was a member of the *Jungstahlhelm* before joining the NSDAP on 1 January 1930, number 181787, and the SA the same year. In 1932 he was HJ *Gauführer* of Upper Franconia. In 1934, he was a *Truppführer* in the SA, but in 1936 he worked as a journalist on the *Völkischer Beobachter*. In 1940, he joined the *Wehrmacht*.

67. JACOBS, Walter

Jacobs was born on 24 February 1912 in Brunswick; he founded the HJ there in 1928; in 1931 he was leader of HJ *Berzirk* Brunswick, and in 1933 leader of *Bann* Brunswick with the rank of *Unterbannführer*. He joined the NSDAP on 1 October 1931, number 671551, and in 1939 was an HJ *Bannführer*. He also held the HJ Golden Badge of Honour.

68. JAENISCH, Rolf

He was born in Bremen on 14 August 1909, and joined the HJ on 1 May 1930 and the NSDAP on 1 November 1931, number 708901. In 1932 he was leader of HJ *Bann* Cologne-Aachen, but after having been awarded the HJ Golden Badge of Honour, he left the organisation in October 1935. In 1938 he joined the SS, number 307975, and in November of that year was promoted to SS-*Obersturmführer*. In March 1942, he joined the *Wehrmacht*, but was reported missing in action two months later.

69. JAHN, Erich

Born on 23 July 1907 in Berlin, he joined the HJ in Berlin in 1928 and the NSDAP on 1 February 1931, number 452201. A former *Bismarckjugend* member, he led the HJ Peasant Office 1928–30; in 1932 he was appointed leader of HJ *Bann* Berlin II, and in 1933 *Gebietsführer* of HJ *Gebiet* Berlin. In 1939, he was active in the *Deutsches Arbeitsfront* and NS *Volkswohlfahrt*.

70. JOHN, Heinz Hugo

John, born on 10 April 1905 in Erfurt, was educated at the Arndt *Gymnasium* in Berlin and the *Realgymnasium* in Ballenstedt am Harz until 1921, after which he studied agriculture for two years. In 1923 he joined the NSDAP, spent a short period in the *Reichswehr* in 1924, and on 27 March 1925 rejoined the NSDAP, number 1335. He became a member of the SA at the same time, and did not leave it until February 1932 when he was appointed adjutant to the *Reichsjugendführer*. In 1932 he was also appointed leader of the Personnel Office in the *Reichsjugendführung,* and he retained this post until 1940. From July 1932 until June 1944 he was Reichstag member for Düsseldorf-East.

In the 1930s, he became an honorary member of the SS, number 454401, and in 1943 he held the rank of SS-*Obersturmführer*. In June 1937 he was promoted to HJ *Obergebietsführer,* and in 1938 was made responsible for planning the curriculum of the new HJ Reich Leaders' Academy at Brunswick. From September 1939 until February 1941, he served with the *Wehrmacht,* earning rapid promotion to lieutenant, and winning the War Service Cross, Class II with swords. In 1940, he was also appointed leader of the Organisation Division in the *Reichsjugendführung.* A holder of the HJ and NSDAP Golden Badges of Honour, he joined the 12th SS panzer division *Hitler-Jugend* on 10 January 1944, and was killed on 5 June 1944.

71.   JORDAN, Martin
Born on 17 October 1897 in Markneukirchen, he was originally an NSDAP member in 1922, rejoining on 19 June 1925, number 8207. In 1928, he was appointed HJ propaganda leader and deputy *Reichsführer*. He left the HJ in 1929 and became active as an NSDAP *Kreisleiter* in Saxony. He was a Reichstag member for Chemnitz-Zwickau 1932–45, and held the NSDAP Golden Badge of Honour.

72.   JUNG, Carl
Born on 2 October 1907 in Osnabrück, Jung attended the *Real-gymnasium* in that city, and in 1924 joined the *Kampfbund Friedericus Rex.* Joining the HJ in 1928, he was at first a sports leader, but in 1930 was appointed press and propaganda leader of HJ *Gau* Weser-Ems. He was HJ leader of Bremen 1931–33, ultimately as *Ober-bannführer*. He joined the NSDAP on 9 April 1927, number 59364, and was later awarded the NSDAP Golden Badge of Honour. In 1943 he was still a member of NSDAP *Gau* Weser-Ems.

73.   JUNG, Jacob
Born on 27 October 1895 in Rückweiler, Saar, he joined the NSDAP on 29 November 1926, number 47852, and he was HJ *Gauführer*

of the Saar 1929–30. After 1933, he was awarded the NSDAP Golden Badge of Honour, and was active as an NSDAP *Kreisleiter* in the Communal Politics Office in Saarbrücken.

74. JURZECK, Wilhelm

Leader of HJ *Bann* East Hannover in 1932 and of *Oberbann* East Hannover in 1933, he retained the rank of *Oberbannführer* until 1945. After the war, he was actively involved in nationalist politics, and in 1950 helped to organise a Third Front which aimed at German neutrality in foreign policy.

75. KAEBISCH, Wilhelm

Kaebisch was born in Breslau on 5 September 1910, and joined the NSDAP on 1 February 1929, number 113515. He was HJ *Gauführer* of Breslau in 1930, but died in December 1931.

76. KARBACH, Jacob

Born in Bad Ems on 9 April 1908, Karbach was the leading HJ figure in the Koblenz-Trier area from 1931 until 1945. He was HJ *Gauführer* of Koblenz-Trier in 1931; leader of *Bann* Koblenz-Trier in 1932; and in 1933 was appointed *Gebietsführer* of Gebiet Westmark. He joined the NSDAP on 7 August 1925, number 13213, and also the SA. In 1942 he was promoted to HJ *Obergebietsführer,* and in 1945 was leader of HJ *Gebiet* Moselland. He held the HJ and NSDAP Golden Badges of Honour. After 1945, he established a furniture factory in the Koblenz area.

77. KAUL, Walter

Born on 30 January 1903 in Naumberg, he was a member of the *Reichswehr* 1923–32 before joining the HJ. In 1933, he was appointed staff leader of the HJ and deputy of the *Reichsjugendführer,* having joined the NSDAP on 1 March 1933, number 1429257. In 1934 he held the rank of *Gebietsführer.* In 1935, he was fined and sentenced to seven days' imprisonment for currency offences, but *Uschla* proceedings against him concerning this matter were abandoned in 1936.

78. KAYSER, Wilhelm

Kayser was HJ *Oberführer* Rhein-Ruhr 1930; HJ *Gruppenführer* North West 1931; and HJ *Gauführer* Cologne-Aachen and *Gebietsführer* North West, November 1931–April 1932.

79. KELLER, Christian

Keller, born in Nuremberg on 6 March 1891, was awarded the Iron Cross, Class II in World War I. Joining the NSDAP on 1 August 1930, number 277777, he was appointed head of the Index Division in the HJ *Reichsleitung* in February 1932. In July 1944, he was working in the NSDAP Reich Propaganda Office, and in 1945 was conscripted into the *Deutscher Volkssturm,* Germany's last source of manpower at the end of the war.

80. KEMPER, Friedhelm

Born on 24 November 1906 in Pyritz, Pomerania, Kemper joined the NSDAP in 1923, and again on 26 July 1926, number 41016. He was a party speaker and an NSDAP *Kreisleiter* in Mannheim 1927–30. He joined the HJ in 1931, and in 1932 was appointed *Gauführer* of Baden; in 1933 he was named HJ *Gebietsführer* of *Gebiet* Baden. He retained this post until 1945, and in 1943 was promoted to *Obergebietsführer.* He held the NSDAP Golden Badge of Honour. In 1954, he was involved in the *Notgemeinschaft der ehemaligen Besatzungsinternierten* (Emergency Society for Former Internees of the Occupation) in Baden, which was organised by former national socialists who had been imprisoned after the war by the French forces of occupation.

81. KIELMEYER, Bernhard

Born on 23 June 1899 in Frankfurt-Main, he joined the NSDAP on 2 June 1925, number 5305, and in 1931–32 was HJ *Gauführer* of Hesse-Nassau-South.

82. KIENAST, Theodor

Born on 7 October 1905, he was a member of the *Grossdeutsche Jugendbewegung* in 1924 and an NSDAP member on 1 March 1926, number 31166. In 1930 he was leader of the *Schar* Office in the HJ *Reichsleitung,* and in 1930–31 was HJ *Oberführer* Middle.

83. KLEEBERG, Hans

Born on 10 June 1908 in Ströhen, Kleeberg was an SA member 1930–31 before joining the HJ. In 1931 he was leader of HJ *Bezirk* Northeim; in 1931–32, organisation leader of *Gau* South Hannover-Brunswick; and *Gauführer* of that *Gau* in 1932. In 1933, he was appointed leader of HJ *Oberbann* Hildesheim with the rank of *Bannführer.* In 1936 he was an HJ *Oberbannführer,* and in May 1937 joined the NSDAP, number 4863339. In December 1943, he was named head of the Legal Division in the *Reichsjugendführung*, and he retained this position with the rank of *Hauptbannführer* until 1945.

84. KLEIN, Emil

He was born in Oldenburg on 3 December 1905. He was leader of HJ *Gau* South Bavaria 1928–31; *Gauführer* of Munich-Upper Bavaria 1931, HJ *Oberführer* South 1931; *Gebietsführer* of Hochland 1931–32; and was reinstated in the latter position in 1933. After 1933, he was promoted to *Obergebietsführer*, and during the war, he was staff leader of the Bavarian State Ministry for Education and Culture. He joined the NSDAP on 25 September 1925, number 47014, and held the HJ and NSDAP Golden Badges of Honour.

85. KLÖPPER, Heinrich

Born in Düsseldorf on 27 February 1909, he left the HJ to become a social revolutionary leader in 1931. He joined the NSDAP on 1 July 1928, number 91911; after his expulsion from the HJ and NSDAP, he was nonetheless readmitted to the party in October 1931. Awarded the NSDAP Golden Badge of Honour after 1933, he is known to have been a corporal serving with the *Wehrmacht* in Russia in June 1944.

86. KNÖPKE, Horst

Knöpke was born in Leipzig on 6 September 1907, and joined the NSDAP on 1 August 1930, number 295928. Appointed leader of the *Deutsche Jugendverlag* in 1933, he was expelled from the HJ on 14 July 1934 for publishing secrets of the movement.

87. KÖHLER, Alfred

He was born on 15 February 1909 in Plauen, was leader of the Economics Office in the HJ *Reichsleitung* in 1930, and joined the NSDAP on 1 May 1930, number 244345.

88. KÖHLER, Fritz

Born on 9 September 1909 in Zeitz, he was a member of the *Jungsturm* Adolf Hitler in 1923, and of the *Frontbann* 1924–26. As an SA member, he founded the first HJ group in Zeitz in 1926, and he was HJ *Gauführer* of Halle-Merseburg 1929–30. In the 1920s, he was also a member of the *Artamanen* movement, and joined the NSDAP on 19 February 1927, number 56950. In May 1931, he joined the SS, number 10348, and in 1939 held the rank of SS-*Sturmbannführer*, working in the SD section. He was a holder of the NSDAP Golden Badge of Honour.

89. KOHLMEYER, Wilhelm
He was born in Hamburg on 12 March 1907, and joined the NSDAP on 11 November 1925, number 23494, and the HJ in 1928. In 1932, he became leader of *Bann* Hamburg, and in 1933 was appointed leader of *Oberbann* Hamburg with the rank of HJ *Oberbannführer*. In April 1942, he was promoted *Obergebietsführer* with responsibility for *Gebiet* Hamburg. He became a member of the *Waffen*-SS in February 1943 with the rank of SS-*Obersturmbannführer*, and was killed on the Russian front on 12 December 1943. He held both the HJ and NSDAP Golden Badges of Honour.

90. KONDEYNE, Karl Walter
Kondeyne was born in Pobethen, Sarnland, on 14 July 1903, and qualified as a doctor of medicine in 1929. A former *Freikorps* and Black *Reichswehr* member, he joined the SA medical branch in 1929, and in 1932 was doctor to NSDAP *Bezirk* Kreuzberg. He was appointed leader of the Medical Division in the *Reichsjugendführung* as an HJ *Oberbannführer*. In 1938 he was an HJ *Gebietsführer*.

91. KÖRBER, Willi
Born on 12 May 1911 in Springe, he was educated at the *Realgymnasium* in Hameln and at the University of Munich, where he studied national economy and state education, and joined the NSDAP on 1 September 1929, number 152642. As an NSDStB member 1930–31, he wrote for the national socialist academic weekly *Der Bewegung*. In October 1931, he was appointed leader of the press and propaganda division in the HJ *Reichsleitung*. In 1933 he was promoted *Obergebietsführer* as leader of this office. At the same time he was personal advisor to the Reich radio commissioner.

92. KOSIEK, Theo
He was appointed HJ *Gruppenführer* South West in July 1931, and leader of HJ *Gebiet* South West in November 1931.

93. KRÄFT, Kurt
Born in Magdeburg on 16 April 1907, he was HJ *Gauführer* of Magdeburg-Anhalt 1931–33, and in 1933 was appointed to lead this area as *Gebietsführer*. He joined the NSDAP on 30 March 1926, number 33241.

94. KRAUSE, Fritz
He was born in Berlin-Charlottenburg on 7 November 1906. He was secretary of HJ *Gau* Berlin-Brandenburg in 1931, advisor on social questions in the *Reichsleitung* in 1932, and the same year was appointed chairman of the *Deutsches Jugendwerk e.V.* In 1933, he was a peasant youth welfare officer in Mecklenburg. He joined the NSDAP on 1 September 1930, number 336756.

95. KROLL, Hugo
He was HJ *Gauführer* of Württemberg 1927–29, and had formerly been a leader in the *Schilljugend.*

96. KROLL, Karl
Born in Essen on 7 November 1909, he joined the HJ in 1926 and the NSDAP on 13 December 1927, number 71898. He was an HJ *Scharführer* and propaganda leader of *Gau* Rheinland 1927–29; in November 1929 he joined the HJ *Reichsleitung* as an editor, and in May 1930 was appointed leader of HJ Greater Plauen. Shortly afterwards, he was expelled from the HJ and NSDAP (see chapter 4). After 1933, he joined the *Reichsverband deutscher Schriftsteller* (National Association of German Writers), and tried repeatedly, but unsuccessfully, for readmittance to the NSDAP. In 1944 he was finally refused on the grounds that he did not have the best interests of the movement at heart. In 1936, he was arrested for oppositional activities, but was not convicted.

97. KRUTSCHINNA, Horst
Born on 31 May 1909 in Masusen, East Prussia, the son of a schoolteacher, he studied German, history, and philosophy at the University of Königsberg, where he was also an NSDStB leader in 1931. He joined the NSDAP on 1 June 1929, number 135821, and in 1933 was appointed personal adjutant to von Schirach. In 1936, while still holding this position with the rank of HJ *Gebietsführer,* he was involved in a duel with an SS man. As a result, Krutschinna was forced to

resign, and became a personnel leader in a steelworks. Shortly after the war, he was killed in an accident at work.

98.   KUHNT, Werner
Born on 9 June 1911 in Ostrow, East Prussia, he joined the NSDAP on 1 June 1929, number 135664, and the HJ in February 1932. In 1932, he was leader of HJ *Bann* Middle Silesia. In 1933, he was appointed leader of HJ *Gebiet* Kurmark with the rank of *Oberbannführer,* and in January 1934 became *Gebietsführer* of *Gebiet* Wartheland. While holding this post, he was promoted to *Obergebietsführer* on 20 April 1942, and retained both rank and post until 1945. In 1942, he spent six months in the *Luftwaffe.* More recently, Kuhnt is known to have been a member of the *Nationaldemokratisches Partei Deutschlands* (NPD) and a district chairman of the party in Stuttgart. He was also campaign leader for NPD Baden-Württemberg in the federal German elections in September 1969 and in November 1972.

99.   LANGE, Lothar
Born on 19 February 1894, he was HJ *Gauführer* of Schleswig-Holstein 1929–31, and HJ *Gruppen-* and *Gebietsführer* North 1931–32. He joined the NSDAP on 1 May 1928, number 87109, and after 1933 was awarded the NSDAP Golden Badge of Honour.

100.   LAUTERBACHER, Hartmann
Lauterbacher was born the son of a veterinary surgeon in Reutte, South Tyrol, on 24 May 1909. From an early age, he was actively involved in the extreme nationalist youth movement. He was a founding member in his Kufstein *Gymnasium* (Austria) of the nationalist *Jungen Gemeinschaft* in 1923. In 1925, he was also a founding member and leader of the pronational socialist *Deutsche Jugend,* which joined the Austrian branch of the HJ in April 1927.
He joined the NSDAP in 1927, number 81603, but it was not until his studies took him to the Brunswick Druggists Academy in 1929 that he became concerned with the HJ in Germany. He was appointed HJ branch leader of Brunswick in November 1929; HJ *Bezirksführer* Brunswick in February 1930; HJ *Gauführer* South Hannover-Brunswick in March 1930; HJ *Gebietsführer* of *Gebiet* Westphalia-Lower Rhine in April 1932; and HJ *Obergebietsführer* West in July 1933. He was awarded the *Führerausweis,* No. 1 of the HJ in tribute to his outstanding work for the organisation.
From 22 May 1934 to August 1940 he was chief of staff in the *Reichsjugendführung* and von Schirach's deputy. A member of the

Reichstag from *Wahlkreis* South Hannover-Brunswick since 1936, he succeeded Bernhard Rust as NSDAP *Gauleiter* of Hannover in December 1940, and Victor Lutze as *Oberpräsident* of Hannover on 1 April 1941. He retained these offices until 1945. He held the HJ and NSDAP Golden Badges of Honour. He was an honorary member of the SS, number 382406, holding the rank of SS-*Obergruppenführer* in April 1944.

On 29 May 1945, Lauterbacher was arrested and imprisoned, but after being tried in Hannover by the British Supreme Military Court on charges of war crimes, he was found not guilty and released in July 1946. He was the chief defence witness for von Schirach at Nuremberg. He was freed by an American military court in 1947, and when threatened with an eight-year sentence by a German court in 1949–50, he fled to Italy, and lived under the name Johann Bauer. Faced with arrest and deportation from Italy for alleged neofascist activities, he fled to West Africa where he remained for a number of years. He returned to Germany in 1956, and until 1960 was employed as an export salesman. In the 1960s he was a public relations executive based in Munich.

101. LENHARD, Bruno
Education leader of HJ *Gau* Rheinpfalz in 1932, he was born on 25 May 1904.

102. LENK, Adolf
Born in Munich on 15 October 1903, Lenk was leader of the *Jugendbund der* NSDAP 1922–23 (see chapter 1). When he abandoned youth work in 1925, he had nothing more to do with the national socialist movement until he joined the NSDAP on 1 March 1932, number 1011998. On 17 May 1933 he joined the SA as a troop leader in SA *Gruppe* Hochland, and from 1935 to 1941 he was a staff member of the NSDAP *Reichsleitung*, quartermaster's division and organisation division. On 30 January 1940, he was awarded the NSDAP badge for 10 and 15 years' party service, but on 4 April 1941 he was expelled from the NSDAP after having been found guilty of wearing the *Blutorden* when not entitled to, of slandering colleagues, and of peculating a large quantity of notepaper while working in the *Reichsleitung*. In 1938 he held the rank of SA-*Sturmführer,* and spent short periods of service in the *Luftwaffe* in 1939 and 1941. In 1943 he reapplied unsuccessfully for party membership.

103. LEONHARDT, Bruno
He was born in Gnovien on 9 December 1893, joining the NSDAP on 4 July 1925, number 9260. He was HJ *Gauführer* of Mecklenburg-Lübeck in 1927, but was expelled from the NSDAP on 1 February 1928, and refused readmittance in 1933 and 1938.

104. LIEB, Franz
Lieb was born in Aschaffenburg on 31 July 1906, and joined the NSDAP on 1 August 1930, number 278761. A member of the *Freikorps* Oberland 1922–25, he also joined the SA and HJ in 1930. In 1932, he was HJ *Gauführer* of Lower Franconia, but shortly joined the SS, number 13249. In 1939 he was an SS-*Oberscharführer,* and in 1942 an SS-*Untersturmführer.*

105. LINSMEYER, Max
He was born on 1 January 1907 in Gammelburg-Lower Franconia, and joined the NSDAP on 12 February 1926, number 30349. He became an SA member in December 1930, and was immediately given the rank of SA-*Standartenführer.* In 1931–32, he was HJ *Gauführer* of Danzig. Appointed an SA-*Oberführer* in 1933, he earned rapid promotion; in November 1938 he was named SA-*Gruppenführer* of SA *Gruppe* Lower Saxony. He held the HJ and NSDAP Golden Badges of Honour, and was killed as a lieutenant in the *Wehrmacht* in France on 14 May 1940.

106. LÖNNECKER, Wilhelm
Born in Flensburg on 5 February 1905, he joined the NSDAP on 14 August 1925, number 17046. A former leader of the *Grenzland-schutzbund Germania,* he was leader of *Gau* Schleswig-Holstein 1927–28 and the Flensburg HJ 1930–33, and continued in this role in 1933 with the rank of HJ *Bannführer.* He was a member of the *Wehrmacht* 1939–40, was wounded, and in 1940 was appointed a local NSDAP official in Schleswig-Holstein. He held the HJ and NSDAP Golden Badges of Honour.

107. LOOSE, Alfred
Loose was born in Cöpernick, near Berlin, on 15 August 1908, and educated at the Berlin *Realgymnasium.* Previously active in the youth movement, he was advisor for Jungvolk questions in HJ *Gebiet* Greater Berlin 1931–32. In 1933, he was named leader of the Treasury

and Administration Division in the *Reichsjugendführung* with the rank of *Obergebietsführer*. He was expelled from the HJ in 1934 while holding this post, and interned in a concentration camp. In 1936, he was expelled from the NSDAP and entered the party's "Black List."

108. LORENZ, Fritz

Lorenz was born in Saarbrücken on 26 February 1919, and joined the NSDAP on 1 March 1930, number 210414, and the HJ on 1 August 1930. He was HJ *Gauführer* of the Saar in 1931. In 1934, he was transferred to Heiligenstadt as *Bannführer,* and in October 1935 was named leader of HJ *Bann* Wunstorf with the rank of *Oberbannführer.* In October 1937 he was appointed leader of HJ *Gebiet* Lower Saxony, but was expelled in July 1938 for allegedly embezzling HJ funds. Although he was expelled from the NSDAP at the same time, he was allowed to rejoin the party on 28 June 1939.

109. LÖWER, Lorenz

Born in Bochum on 11 April 1900, Löwer was HJ leader of Westphalia 1928–34, ultimately as *Gebietsführer* of *Gebiet* Westphalia. An NSDAP member since 1 August 1928, number 96382, he was a member of the Prussian *Landtag* in 1932; he left the HJ in 1935, and was appointed an NSDAP *Kreisleiter* in Breslau. From 1937 to 1938, he was an NSDAP *Gau* inspector and *Gau* division leader in Silesia, and from 1938 to 1944 held the same positions in NSDAP *Gau* Westphalia-South. In 1944, he was transferred to the Sudetenland to take over the leadership of the Office for Resettled Persons, but in 1945 he was again active in his former posts in Westphalia.

110. LÜER, Heinrich

Named assistant adjutant to von Schirach in 1933, Lüer was born on 20 January 1907 in Wendhausen, and in 1931 was a member and leader of the Lower Saxony branch of the NSDStB. In November 1935 he was promoted to HJ *Obergebietsführer,* and in 1940 drafted the Severe Punishment Order of the Hitler-*Jugend* for the Duration of the War. On 20 April 1942, he was appointed Reich commissioner in Riga.

111. LUTZ, Günther

He was HJ *Gauführer* of Pomerania 1927–30. Born on 31 January 1904, he joined the NSDAP on 1 May 1933, number 2295591.

112. MAGES, Hans

Born on 20 October 1903 in Reichenthal-Bohemia, he joined the NSDAP on 6 March 1926, number 31637, and the SS in September 1926, number 630. From 1928 to 1931, he was also a member of the HJ, serving as *Gauführer* of Hesse-Nassau 1929–31. Thereafter, he made his career in the SS. In November 1933, he was appointed SS-*Obersturmführer,* and in 1939 was an SS-*Hauptsturmführer.* A holder of the NSDAP Golden Badge of Honour, he was a member of the *Freikorps Oberland* 1922–25.

113. MATERNA, Hans

HJ *Gauführer* of Mecklenburg-Lübeck 1928–29, he was born on 20 April 1905 in Berlin, and joined the NSDAP on 10 June 1926, number 37945. A schoolteacher by profession, he also became a member of the NS Teachers' Association in April 1931, and was an SA man 1926–1931. In 1934 he was a school inspector and NSDAP *Gau* education leader in Mecklenburg. He held the NSDAP Golden Badge of Honour, and in 1943 he was a member of the *Wehrmacht.*

114. MERTINAT, Max

Leader of HJ *Bann* Essen in 1932, he was born on 3 May 1895 in Essen and joined the NSDAP on 1 April 1929, number 125626.

115. METZKE, Franz

Born in Glogau on 24 March 1880, he served in World War I from 1915–1918, leaving the army as a lieutenant in 1920. In 1927–30 he was HJ *Gauführer* of Silesia; 1927–28, an SA leader in Berlin-Steglitz; 1929–30, an NSDAP cell leader; 1930–31, an NSDAP branch leader in Berlin; 1931–32, an NSDAP *Kreisleiter* and *Gau* speaker. In 1933, he joined the *Deutsches Arbeitsfront,* and was still an NSDAP member in 1941.

116. MÖLLER, Albrecht

Appointed HJ *Gebietsführer* of *Gebiet* Ostsee in 1932, he was born on 3 June 1911 in East Prussia, and joined the NSDAP on 1 June 1930, number 250233.

117. MORENGA, Paul

Born on 27 March 1904 in Schloss Baruth, he was a member of the *Stahlhelm* 1925–26, and joined the NSDAP on 1 June 1928, number

89690, and the SA at the same time. In July 1931, he joined HJ *Gau* Schleswig-Holstein as organisation leader and *Schar* leader, and in 1933 was appointed HJ *Bannführer* of *Bann* Schleswig. In 1932–33, he was also *Landesleiter* Schleswig-Holstein of the *Deutsches Jugendwerk e.V.* In March 1933, he left the HJ to rejoin the SA. By 1940, he had attained the rank of SA-*Obersturmbannführer,* and in 1941 joined the *Wehrmacht.* He held the NSDAP Golden Badge of Honour.

118.   MORISSE, Heinz

HJ *Gauführer* of Hamburg 1929–1931, Morisse was born in that city on 26 August 1905, and joined the NSDAP on 13 February 1926, number 30037. In February 1932, he was appointed NSDAP branch leader of Cuxhaven, and from 1933 to 1945 was an NSDAP *Kreisleiter* in Hamburg. He was a holder of the HJ and NSDAP Golden Badges of Honour.

119.   MÜLBERT-SCHÄFER, Hugo

Born on 13 October 1904, and an NSDAP member since 15 December 1925, number 25281, he was HJ *Gauführer* of Essen in 1931, and in 1933 was chief of staff of HJ *Obergebiet* West with the rank of *Gebietsführer.* He retained this rank until 1943 when he joined the *Waffen-*SS as an SS-*Untersturmführer,* and was badly wounded as a member of a panzer division. In February 1944, he was expelled from the SS and tried before a civilian court for malicious slander against a former administrative leader of the Reich Leaders' School. He held the NSDAP Golden Badge of Honour.

120.   MÜLLER, Ferdinand

He was propaganda leader in 1931 and deputy HJ *Gauführer* in 1932 of Rheinpfalz. Born in Landau on 5 February 1909, he was appointed leader of *Oberbann* Rheinpfalz in 1933 with the rank of *Bannführer,* and in March 1937 was promoted to *Oberbannführer.*

121.   MÜLLER, Rudolf

Born on 7 November 1907, and an engineer by profession, he was *Schar* leader of HJ *Gau* Rheinpfalz in 1932.

122.   MÜNCHHOFF, Erich

HJ *Gauführer* of Thuringia 1928–29, he was born in Erfurt on 6 October 1904, and joined the NSDAP on 29 May 1925, number 6728.

123. NABERSBERG, Carl

Born the son of a Krefeld shopkeeper on 11 July 1908, he belonged to a nationalist youth organisation in his home town before he joined the NSDAP on 20 December 1925, number 26269, and the SA at the same time. As a law student, he organised the first NSDStB branch in Cologne, and in 1928 was an ASTA (student association) member at the University of Berlin. While an NSDStB leader, he founded the NSS in Halle-Merseburg, and became a member of the NSS *Reichsleitung* and leader of NSS *Gau* Berlin-Brandenburg-Ostmark. In November 1931, he was appointed HJ Reich Organisation leader.

In April 1933, he was appointed deputy chairman of the *Reichsausschuss der Deutschen Jugendverbände* and leader of the Foreign Division in the *Reichsjugendführung* with the rank of *Obergebietsführer*. From January to May 1934, he was HJ chief of staff and deputy of von Schirach. In 1936 he is known to have been a member of the Index Division of the *Reichsjugendführung*.

In October 1956, a West Berlin denazification court fined him 6,000 deutsch marks for having been an active promoter of national socialism, and for having been responsible for the nefarious ideological training of youth in the Third Reich.

124. NEFF, Oskar

Born on 8 January 1906 in Munich, he originally joined the NSDAP on 1 September 1921, number 4123, and later received the *Blutorden* and the NSDAP Coburg Badge. He rejoined the NSDAP on 21 April 1925, number 739, and also joined the SA. He joined the HJ in 1928, becoming *Schar* leader of HJ *Gau* South Bavaria in 1930, deputy *Gauführer* of Munich-Upper Bavaria in 1931, and *Gauführer* of Swabia in 1932. In 1933, he joined the staff of HJ *Gebiet* Hochland, but until 1939 he was principally active in the SA; in 1939 he was an SA-*Hauptsturmführer*. A holder of the HJ and NSDAP Golden Badges of Honour, he joined the *Wehrmacht* in 1939, participating in the French campaign, and thereafter fighting on the eastern front. He was awarded the Iron Cross, Class II.

125. NIEKERKEN, Karl

HJ *Gauführer* of East Hannover 1930–31, he was born in Eissendorf, Hamburg, on 16 March 1908, and joined the NSDAP on 26 June 1926, number 39666, and also joined the SA. He joined the HJ in 1929, and the *Deutsches Arbeitsfront* in December 1933. In 1936, he was a *Bezirk* education leader in NSDAP *Gau* East Prussia, and on April 1937 was named leader of the Communal Politics Division of that *Gau*. He later joined the *Wehrmacht*.

126.   NIKOLEIT, Alfred
Treasurer of HJ *Gau* Berlin-Brandenburg 1930–31, he was born in Berlin on 11 October 1905, and joined the NSDAP on 30 August 1926, number 43587. A holder of the NSDAP Golden Badge of Honour, he was in the SA in 1936.

127.   NÖTHLICHS, Richard
Born on 16 April 1904, he joined the NSDAP on 1 June 1928, number 90534. In 1930–31, he was adjutant to *Reichsführer* Gruber, and in 1931 *Oberführer* South West-HJ, and leader of the *Schar* Office in the HJ *Reichsleitung*. On 11 November 1931, he resigned from the HJ to take up a civilian post in Mecklenburg.

128.   OLDIGS, Lühr
A former *Artamanen* member, he was born on 14 February 1907 in Neuburg, East Friesland, and joined the NSDAP on 10 October 1927, number 68614. In January 1933, he was appointed leader of HJ *Bann* West Holstein, and in July 1933, HJ *Gebietsführer* of *Gebiet* Nordmark. In October 1940, he was apparently secretary of the educational division, NSDAP *Gau* Wartheland.

129.   OTTO, Paul
Otto was born in Esslingen on 19 October 1903, and joined the NSDAP on 6 August 1925, number 12874. A former leader in the *Schilljugend,* he succeeded Hugo Kroll as HJ *Gauführer* of Württemberg and served in that position from 1929–31. After 1931, he was active in the SA, and following the *Machtergreifung,* was secretary of NSDAP *Gauleitung* Württemberg.

130.   OVENS, Bov
Born in Hamburg on 6 October 1913, Ovens was leader of HJ *Bann* Mecklenburg-Lübeck 1932–33, and in 1933 was appointed leader of *Oberbann* South East Holstein with the rank of *Oberbannführer*. A member of the NSDAP from 1 April 1936, number 3558322, he was attached to the *Reichsjugendführung* 1938–41. In June 1941, he was appointed a division leader in NSDAP *Gauleitung* South Hannover-Brunswick, and in March 1944 was named NSDAP *Kreisleiter* of Hannover.

131.   PATABEL, August
A member of the *Jungstahlhelm* before joining the HJ in 1928, Patabel was born in Insterburg on 30 June 1908. In 1931, he was HJ *Gauführer* of East Prussia, and then *Gebietsführer* of *Gebiet* Ostland. He became an NSDAP member on 1 May 1930, number 241621, and until 1935 when he joined the *Wehrmacht* to do military service, he was chairman of *Uschla* in NSDAP *Kreis* Insterburg.

132.   PESCHKE, Rudolf
Appointed leader of HJ *Gebiet* Ostland in 1933 with the rank of *Oberbannführer,* Peschke was born in Hosena, East Prussia, on 22 July 1910, and joined the NSDAP on 1 November 1930, number 346644. He is known to have been HJ *Gebietsführer* of *Gebiet* Swabia in 1943.

133.   PETER, Herbert
Born on 31 May 1910 in Leipzig, he joined the NSDAP on 1 May 1928, number 87856. He was HJ propaganda leader in early 1931; leader of the Social Politics Office in the HJ *Reichsleitung* later in 1931. Also in 1931 he was in charge of the HJ in Saxony as *Gauführer* as well as the group in central Germany as *Gruppenführer* and later as *Gebietsführer*. In 1932, Peter reverted to his leadership of the Saxon HJ only.

134.   PETERS, Arnold
Born on 30 March 1908 in Hamburg, Peters was HJ *Gauführer* Nordmark 1928–29. He joined the NSDAP on 7 May 1926, number 35582, and after 1933 was awarded the HJ and NSDAP Golden Badges of Honour. In 1931, he joined the NS Factory Cell Organisation, and after 1933 was active in the *Deutsches Arbeitsfront* as a *Gau* division leader. In 1943, he was killed in Russia as a member of the *Waffen*-SS.

135.   PETERSSEN, Adolf
Peterssen, born on 9 January 1912 in Andorf, and an HJ member 1928–31, was leader of the Kiel HJ in 1931. On 12 December 1931, he joined the NSDAP, number 753460, having also become an SS member, number 21357, in March 1931. He was a member of the SS *Leibstandarte* Adolf Hitler 1933–43; as a member of this unit, holding the rank of SS-*Hauptsturmführer,* he was killed on the eastern front in July 1943. He had been awarded the Iron Cross, Class II, and the War Service Cross, Class I with swords.

136. PETTER, Kurt

Petter was appointed leader of HJ *Bann* Weimar-Jena in 1933; in 1939, he was head of the Reich Leaders' School in Potsdam and an inspector of the Adolf Hitler Schools with the rank of HJ *Gebietsführer*. Born in February 1909, he was deputy to Youth Leader Artur Axmann, and head of the Adolf Hitler Schools with the rank of HJ *Obergebietsführer* in 1945.

137. QUITZERAU, Helmut

HJ *Gauführer* of East Prussia 1930–31, he was born on 27 September 1899 in Königsberg, and joined the NSDAP on 1 July 1928, number 91934.

138. RACHER, Karl

Born on 6 August 1907 in Annatzberg, Racher was HJ *Gauführer* of Nassau in 1931. He joined the NSDAP on 1 July 1943, number 1085164, but was expelled in March 1933 for failing "to show interest in the party." He was readmitted to the NSDAP in 1938, number 6140921.

139. RANFTEL, Josef

Born in Graz on 17 January 1904, he was leader of HJ *Gau* Lower Bavaria in 1931. He initially joined the NSDAP on 9 January 1927, number 52572, but subsequently left. He rejoined on 12 January 1932, number 781308. An SA member since 1923 and a former member of the *Vaterländischer Schutzbund,* he was in the SA in 1941, and was an NSKK member 1933–37.

140. RECKEWERTH, Richard

Reckewerth was HJ *Gauführer* of Halle-Merseburg 1930–33. In 1933, he was appointed HJ *Gebietsführer* of *Gebiet* Middle. Born in Oker, Harz, on 22 March 1897, he served in World War I and the *Freikorps*. He was a *Stahlhelm* leader 1922–23, and a *Frontbann* leader 1923–25. He joined the NSDAP on 30 July 1925, number 11711, and also joined the SA. In 1942 he was an HJ *Obergebietsführer* and leader of *Gebiet* Mittelland, holding this rank and post until 1945. In 1942 he was awarded the War Service Cross.

141.   REEPEN, Georg
      Born on 25 July 1902 in Hamburg, he was a leader in the pre-1933 Hamburg HJ; in 1933, he was appointed *Bannführer* and chief of staff of *Oberbann* Hamburg. He joined the NSDAP on 1 August 1930, number 305124, but was expelled from the HJ in 1935 for publishing organisational secrets.

142.   von RENTELN, Adrian Theodor
      Founder and *Reichsführer* of the NSS 1929–32 and *Reichsführer* of the HJ 1931–32, he joined the NSDAP on 1 January 1929, number 109184. In 1929, he was also active as an NSDStB *Gruppenführer*. At the end of 1932 he was named leader of the *Kampfbund des Gewerblichen Mittelstandes* (Fighting League of the Industrial Middle Classes), whose members were largely responsible for the attacks on Jewish stores in April 1938. In May 1933, von Renteln organised and led the *Reichsstand des Deutschen Handels* (National Estate of German Trade), and the *Reichsstand des Deutschen Handwerks* (National Estate of German Handicrafts); in June 1933 he also became president of the German Industrial and Commercial Council. He was a principal figure in the establishment of the NS *Handels-und-Gewerbe* Organisation (NS-HAGO, NS Trade and Industry Organisation), and was involved in many other economic-political organisations and activities.
      He became a leading personality of the *Deutsches Arbeitsfront,* and in January 1935 was appointed its chief of staff. In August 1941, he was appointed general Reich commissioner of Lithuania, and after being on the Russian list of war criminals, he was hanged by them in 1946. He had been a Reichstag member 1932–45.

143.   RENTZEL, Karl
      HJ *Gauführer* of Pomerania 1930–32, Rentzel was born in Stettin on 15 December 1905, and joined the NSDAP on 10 June 1925, number 7356.

144.   RIEGRAF, Oskar
      Born on 19 August 1911 in Fellbach, he was deputy HJ *Gauführer* of Württemberg 1930–32, and joined the NSDAP on 1 May 1930, number 242350. He was an HJ *Oberbannführer* from 1933 to 1938, and after holding minor NSDAP posts 1938–44, he was appointed staff leader of NSDAP *Kreis* Stuttgart.

145. RODATZ, Johann

Rodatz was born the son of a shopkeeper on 4 October 1905 in Hamburg, and joined the NSDAP on 1 January 1928, number 75022. In 1929, he was NSDAP branch leader of Lüneburg, but spent 1930–33 working in Italy and Roumania. In 1932, he joined the SA, and in May 1933 was appointed leader of the *Reichsverband für deutschen Jugendherbergen* (Youth Hostels) with the rank of HJ *Unterbannführer*. He retained this position until 1945, ultimately as *Obergebietsführer*. In 1940–41, he was also HJ *Gebietsführer* of Alsace, and in May 1941 was named HJ plenipotentiary for Holland. He held the NSDAP Golden Badge of Honour, and in 1942 was awarded the War Service Cross.

146. RÖPKE, Johann

Born on 22 December 1905 in Bremen, and founder of the HJ in that city, he joined the NSDAP on 9 May 1926, number 36274, having been a member in 1923. He held the *Blutorden,* and after 1933 was active as an NSDAP and SA leader in *Gau* Weser-Ems.

147. RUSCHEPAUL, Josef

Ruschepaul was born in Cologne on 14 September 1910, and joined the NSDAP on 1 October 1928, number 100321. He held minor NSDAP posts 1928–30; in April 1930, he joined the HJ and was appointed *Gauführer* of *Gau* Rheinland that year. He left the HJ on the last day of 1931, and joined the SS in August 1932, number 45736. In 1939, he held the rank of SS-*Oberscharführer*.

148. SCHÄFER, Karl Georg

Schäfer was HJ *Gauführer* of Lower Bavaria-Oberpfalz in 1932, and later that year was appointed deputy of the *Reichsjugendführer*. Named leader of *Oberbann* Lower Bavaria-Oberpfalz in 1933, he was born in Berlin on 11 June 1900, and joined the NSDAP in 1930–31, number 231809. From July to November 1932, he was an NSDAP Reichstag deputy. He died in Berlin on 10 November 1939.

149. SCHAPKE, Richard

A former HJ *Gauführer,* Schapke was a leading social revolutionary who left the HJ and NSDAP in 1930 (see chapter 4). He was born in Berlin on 16 June 1897, and joined the NSDAP on 1 May 1929, number 127616. He was later executed by the national socialists, probably during the Röhm purge in June 1934.

150. von SCHIRACH, Baldur

The von Schirachs, originally a Saxon peasant family, were raised to the minor aristocracy by the Empress Maria Theresa on 17 May 1776. There was also a pronounced American strain: Baldur's great-grandfather went to the United States in 1855, and his grandfather, Friedrich Karl von Schirach, fought in the Civil War as a major in the Union army. In 1869 Friedrich Karl married into the Norris family, one of America's oldest families. In 1871 he returned to Kiel, where Baldur's father, Karl Baily Norris von Schirach, was born. Baldur's father was an American citizen, and married Emma Middleton Lynah Tillou of Philadelphia in 1896.

Baldur was a member of the *Jungdeutschland Bund* in 1917 and of the small *Knappenschaft* group from 1923–27. Already an anti-Semite after reading Henry Ford's *International Jew,* von Schirach joined the NSDAP on 9 May 1925, number 17251, and also joined the SA.

An unenthusiastic student (see chapter 3), he soon devoted most of his time to politics. He was *Reichsführer* of the NSDStB 1928–31, and a member of the NSDAP *Reichsleitung* from 1928; in October 1931, he was appointed *Reichsjugendführer der* NSDAP with the rank of SA-*Gruppenführer.* On 31 March 1932, he married Henrietta Hoffmann, the daughter of Hitler's photographer, with Hitler and Röhm as the marriage witnesses. On 13 May 1932, he was appointed an *Amtsleiter* on the NSDAP *Reichsleitung,* and on 16 June 1932 he succeeded von Renteln as *Reichsführer* of the HJ. In July 1932, he became a Reichstag deputy and remained one until 1945.

On 17 June 1933, von Schirach was appointed youth leader of the German Reich, a post he held until 1940. In December 1939, he volunteered for army service, participating in the 1940 French campaign as a corporal, but finally as a lieutenant; he was awarded the Iron Cross, Class II. On 2 August 1940, he was named NSDAP *Gauleiter* and₂*Reichsstatthalter* of Vienna; at the same time, he was appointed Reich leader of youth education of the NSDAP and deputy of the Führer for the inspection of the HJ.

He remained in Vienna until 1945, although after a stormy meeting at the *Berghof* at Easter 1943, he had forfeited Hitler's trust and friendship on account of his "un-German" cultural policies, and "liberal" attitudes towards Jews. After the fall of Vienna to the Red Army on 13 April 1945, von Schirach adopted the pseudonym "Richard Falk," and hid in the Alps near Innsbrück before surrendering to the Americans on 6 June 1945; he died in 1974.

A repentant and self-castigating von Schirach was sentenced to twenty years' imprisonment as a major war criminal by the International Military Tribunal at Nuremberg on 1 October 1946. Along with other convicted national socialist leaders, he was interned in Berlin's Spandau jail. In 1952, he fell heir with his elder sister Rosalinde to an American fortune. In 1964 he became blind in one eye. Von Schirach was finally released in October 1966 with Albert Speer.

151.   SCHLADITZ, Heinz

Founder of the HJ in Leipzig and HJ *Gauführer* of North West Saxony from 1929–31, he was born in Leipzig on 9 September 1908. He was a member of the *Schilljugend* in 1927, and joined the NSDAP on 29 July 1927, number 66040. In 1941, he was *Gau* press leader in NSDAP *Gau* Saxony, and a press and propaganda division leader in the Saxony branch of the *Deutsches Arbeitsfront*.

152.   SCHLECHT, Hein

Born in Berlin on 24 June 1906, he joined the NSDAP on 1 December 1929, number 171277. He joined the HJ in January 1930 from the *Freischar Schill,* in which he was *Jungenschaftsführer* of the Berlin branch. He left the *Freischar Schill* because of the equivocal attitude adopted towards national socialism by Werner Lass, leader of the group. Schlecht was leader of the HJ Education Office and HJ press chief 1930–31. After 1933, he was a minor official in the NS *Volkswohlfahrt,* and in 1939 was deputy leader of the Cultural Division in the NSDAP Reich Propaganda Office.

153.   von SCHLEICH, Ritter

He was born in Munich on 1 August 1888, and joined the NSDAP on 1 April 1931, number 483841. In November 1910, he became an officer in a Bavarian infantry regiment, but during World War I he made his mark as a fighter pilot. He was promoted to flight captain in August 1918 after being awarded the Pour le Mérite, the Iron Cross, Classes I and II, the Knights' Cross of the House of Hohenzollern, and other decorations. From 1918 to 1921, he was a liaison officer with the Army Peace Commission, and from 1927 to 1929, was a flight leader with the German Lufthansa. He joined the SS and the NSDAP at the same time in 1931, and in October 1931 was appointed leader of SS Flight Squadron South. In 1933 he became leader of the Flight and Air Training Division of the *Reichsjugendführung* with the rank of *Obergebietsführer*. In 1935 he was a flight major in Thuringia.

154. SCHMALSCHLÄGER, Benedikt

A member of the Flight Division of the *Reichsjugendführung* in 1933, he was born in Munich on 24 January 1890, and joined the NSDAP on 1 September 1929, number 149248.

155. SCHMALZ, Kurt

Born in Frankfurt-on-the-Oder, on 19 May 1906, and an NSDAP member since 10 July 1925, number 9685, Schmalz founded the HJ in Börssum in 1928 when he was NSDAP *Bezirksleiter* of Hannover-Brunswick. After 1919, he was active in several *völkisch* youth groups. In 1926 he was appointed NSDAP branch leader of Cottbus. On 1 May 1928, he was named NSDAP *Kreisleiter* of Wolfenbüttel, and was elected to the Brunswick *Landtag* the same year. In 1932, he was adjutant to the NSDAP *Gauleiter* of Hannover, Bernhard Rust, and in April 1933 he was appointed deputy NSDAP *Gauleiter* of Warthe-land. A holder of the HJ and NSDAP Golden Badges of Honour, he spent 1940–41 in a *Wehrmacht* infantry division.

156. SCHMIDT, Rudolf

Leader of the HJ Border Land Office 1928–31, Rudolf Martin Schmidt was born in Dresden on 3 March 1894, and joined the NSDAP on 10 July 1925, number 9898. During World War I, he was awarded the Iron Cross, Class II, and after 1919 was a member of the *Deutscher Turnerbund*. He joined the SA in December 1930, and in January 1934 was appointed SA-*Sturmbannführer,* but was expelled from the SA that year for homosexuality. In 1936, however, an NSDAP court cleared him of homosexual charges, and he was allowed to remain in the party. In 1941, his application for the NSDAP Golden Badge of Honour was refused on the grounds that he had not been a party member from July 1927 until December 1929; a further application was rejected in 1944. At that time, he was a cell leader of NSDAP branch Litzmann-stadt (Wartheland), and a member of the NSDAP *Kreisleitung* of that area.

157. SCHMIDT, Walter

Born in 1907, and a member of the *Bismarckjugend* from 1923–25, he joined the NSDAP on 1 April 1930, number 226320. In January 1931, he was an HJ-*Gefolgschaftsführer* in Neuenburg, and was HJ *Gauführer* of Württemberg 1931–32.

158. SCHMIED, Georg
    He was born in Munich on 26 October 1894, and joined the NSDAP on 1 March 1930, number 227132. At the time of his death in April 1934, he was an SA-*Sturmführer*.

159. von SCHMIEDEN, Herbert
    Born on 10 June 1910 in Kassel, he joined the NSDAP on 1 February 1931, number 420813, and in April 1932 he was appointed HJ *Gauführer* of Hesse-Nassau-North. Later the same year, he was named HJ *Gebietsführer* of *Gebiet* Hesse-Nassau-North.

160. SCHMITZ, Hans
    In 1931, Schmitz was HJ *Gauführer* of East Hannover; in 1932, leader of HJ *Gebiet* Nordmark and in 1933, leader of HJ *Gebiet* Ostsee with the rank of *Gebietsführer*. He subsequently joined the SS, and in 1944 held the rank of SS-*Obersturmbannführer*.

161. SCHNAEDTER, Franz
    Franz August Johann Schnaedter, born in Wiesbaden on 31 May 1906, began his HJ career as branch leader of HJ Wiesbaden in 1928 after having been a member of the *Bündische* Youth. He was HJ Reich organisation leader 1929–31; leader of the *Deutsche Jungmannschaft* 1929–30; *Gauführer* of Hesse 1930; chief editor of the *Jungfront-Verlag* 1930; HJ *Oberführer* South West 1930–31; HJ Reich secretary 1931; leader of the HJ Social Office 1932; and a leading HJ writer and propagandist from 1930 onwards. In 1933, he was appointed *Obergebietsführer* of *Obergebiet* Middle, and leader of *Gebiet* Saxony. He joined the NSDAP on 29 July 1926, number 41302, and also joined the SA, and after having left the party for a short period, rejoined on 1 September 1928, number 99137. On 5 May 1934, he was arrested and was expelled from the HJ on 1 July 1934. In February 1935, he was expelled from the NSDAP and sentenced to three years' imprisonment by the Saxon Land Court for criminal offences.

162. SCHNARR, Alfred
    Treasurer and secretary of the *Deutsches Jugendwerk e.V.* 1932–33 with the rank of HJ *Unterbannführer,* he was born in Frankfurt—Main on 15 March 1912, and joined the NSDAP on 1 January 1936, number 3706391. In 1942, he held a minor post in the NS-*Volkswohlfahrt* organisation.

163. SCHOLZ, Wilhelm

HJ *Gauführer* of East Prussia 1931–32, Scholz was active in the youth movement before joining the NSDAP in April 1930. He was a member of the *Artamanen* movement in 1927 and *Gruppenführer* of *Gau* Hannover of the *Bund Artam* in 1929.

164. SCHRAMM, Franz

HJ *Gauführer* of Danzig in 1932, Schramm was born on 14 December 1902 in Langfuhr, Danzig, and joined the NSDAP on 1 December 1930, number 400043. A schoolteacher by profession, he joined the NS Teachers' Association on 1 December 1931. In 1934, he was attached to the *Reichsjugendführung* with the rank of HJ *Oberbannführer,* and shortly became a state commissioner on the Schools Administration Authority. In 1945, he was an HJ *Hauptbannführer,* and deputy education leader of NSDAP *Gau* Danzig.

165. SCHRÖDER, August

He was born in Gaben on 17 September 1905, joined the NSDAP on 1 August 1930, number 276755, and was HJ Reich treasurer 1931–32.

166. SCHRÖTER, Gottfried

Born in Dresden on 11 January 1910, he joined the HJ on 27 October 1926, number 3610, and the NSDAP on 1 June 1928, number 89496. He was HJ leader of *Untergau* Dresden in 1930; *Gauführer* of East Saxony 1930–31; and leader of *Bann* Halberstadt with the rank of *Unterbannführer* in 1933. In 1936, he was an HJ *Oberbannführer.* Having been expelled from the NSDAP in October 1929, he rejoined the party in January 1936, number 3704384. He held the HJ Golden Badge of Honour.

167. SCHWANTES, Herbert

HJ *Gauführer* of Danzig in 1929, he was born on 28 June 1904, and joined the NSDAP on 14 November 1925, number 23600. He was expelled from the NSDAP on 1 January 1931 for failing to pay his membership dues, but was allowed to rejoin on 20 October 1934.

168. SEIDEL, Karl Heinz

Appointed adjutant to von Schirach in February 1932, Seidel was born in Leipzig on 24 September 1911, and joined the NSDAP on 1 May 1933, number 1886114.

169.   SELL, Fritz

Sell was born on 5 January 1909 in Wesel, Rhineland, and became an NSDAP member on 1 October 1929, number 176279. He abandoned his study of law, philosophy, and national economy when he became leader of the Osnabrück HJ in 1930. He remained HJ leader there until 1932; thereafter he was principally active in the SA. A former *Front-bann* member, he joined the SA in 1926, and in 1933 held the rank of SA-*Sturmführer*. In 1938 he was an SA *Oberführer* and leader of SA *Gruppenschule* Pomerania; on 20 April 1944, he was promoted to SA-*Brigadeführer*. The same year he joined the *Wehrmacht* with the rank of *Oberleutnant*, and was shortly awarded the Iron Cross, Classes I and II.

170.   SIEBERT, Walter

Born on 4 May 1908, he joined the NSDAP on 1 April 1927, number 61092, and was HJ *Schar* leader of *Gau* Hamburg in 1930. He was killed as a member of the armed forces in April 1942.

171.   SIEMANN, Hans

HJ *Gauführer* of Swabia 1931–32, Siemann was born in Oberbern-bach on 22 May 1905, and joined the NSDAP in February 1926, number 32336. In 1937, when active as a factory cell official of the *Deutsches Arbeitsfront* in Augsburg, he was expelled from the NSDAP because of an impending court case against him. On 22 February 1938, he was sentenced by an Augsburg District Court to six years' imprisonment for homosexual offences. In 1942 he appealed for clemency, but on 1 March 1943 the Reich Chancellory rejected his plea. He held the HJ and NSDAP Golden Badges of Honour.

172.   STAEBE, Gustav

Gustav Lois Erich Staebe, born in Hindenburg, Silesia, on 22 August 1906, joined the NSDAP in 1923, and again on 9 May 1926, number 36247. He was secretary of NSDAP *Kreis* Brunswick-Land 1926–27; NSDAP branch leader of Rathenau 1927; NSDAP *Bezirksleiter* of Barnim 1927–28; acting NSDAP *Gauleiter* of the Saar 1929; NSDAP *Bezirksleiter* of Rhine-Lahneck 1929–30; and *Gau* Propaganda leader of NSDAP *Gau* Hesse-Nassau-South 1930–31.

He was also active as a journalist and writer, founding the national socialist peasant newspaper, *Freiheit und Scholle,* in 1929, and the *NS-Landpost* in 1931, of which he became editor. In 1931–32, he was the agrarian political press chief of the NSDAP *Reichsleitung*. From

1932 to 1933, he was a leading writer on the *Völkischer Beobachter*. As chief editor of the *Bremer Nationalsozialistische Zeitung* and press chief of the *Deutscher Sondergruppen* West, he was appointed leader of the Press Division in the *Reichsjugendführung* in November 1933 with the rank of HJ *Gebietsführer*. In January 1935, he was appointed chief editor of the *Mainzer Anseiger* and *Frankfürter Volksblatt*. An SS member, number 36140, he held the rank of SS-*Untersturmführer* in 1935, and SS-*Obersturmbannführer* in 1938. In 1945, he was an SS leader, HJ *Gebietsführer*, and chief editor of the *Rhein-Mainische-Zeitung*.

173. von STEBUT, Josef

Born on 12 July 1905 in Obelia, Lithuania, and a *Reichswehr* member in 1924, he joined the NSDAP on 1 March 1930, number 202048. He was HJ *Gauführer* of Hesse 1930–31. In 1933 he was an SA-*Scharführer*, and was promoted to SA-*Sturmführer* in 1936. He joined the *Wehrmacht*, and in 1941 held the rank of lieutenant; he was killed in action on 22 January 1944.

174. STEGEMANN, Gunter

Born on 13 March 1907 in Berlin, he was HJ *Gauführer* of Brandenburg 1931–32. He joined the SA in November 1926 and the NSDAP on 1 March 1927, number 57290, but was mainly active in the HJ. He was HJ branch leader of Berlin-Spandau and HJ *Gefolgschaftsführer* Berlin North before becoming *Gauführer* of Brandenburg. In 1933 he was appointed leader of *Bann* Brandenburg with the rank of HJ *Bannführer*, and the same year was transferred to the youth hostel organisation. In 1936, he was an SA-*Obersturmführer* in Berlin, and before 1939 was active in the SA, DAF, NS-*Volkswohlfahrt*, and *Kolonialbund*. A holder of the NSDAP Golden Badge of Honour, he joined the *Wehrmacht* in 1939 and was killed in action in 1940.

175. STEGEMANN, Hartmut

He was born in Niederschönhausen on 14 November 1908, and joined the NSDAP on 19 April 1927, number 59982. He joined the SA in December 1926 but left to join the HJ on 3 August 1928. In 1930 he was secretary of HJ *Gau* Berlin-Brandenburg-Ostmark, and in 1931–32 HJ *Gauführer* of Ostmark. In 1933, he was appointed HJ *Gebietsführer* of *Gebiet* Ostmark; in September 1933, he joined the *Reichsjugendführung* for a short period. From 1933 to 1937, he was an NSDAP *Kreisleiter* and organisation leader of NSDAP *Gau* Kurmark, and editor of the *Märkischer Adler* 1933–35. In 1941, he was appointed SA-*Obersturmbannführer*, and in November 1942, when he was organisation leader of NSDAP *Gau* Mark-Brandenburg, he was promoted to SA-*Standartenführer*. In 1943 he became leader of the Main Organisation Office in the NSDAP *Reichsleitung*. He retained this post until 1945 as well as the deputy leadership of the *Kraft durch Freude* organisation (Strength through Joy).

176. STEINACKER, Erich
     Born in Patschkan on 16 January 1911, he joined the NSDAP on 1 May 1932, number 1145479, and the same year was appointed leader of HJ *Bann* South Hannover-Brunswick. In 1933, he was named HJ *Gebietsführer* of *Gebiet* Kurhessen, but was deprived of this office as a result of *Uschla* proceedings against him. He was disqualified from holding a party office for three years, but appealed successfully against this sentence in April 1938.

177. STEINDECKER, Wilhelm
     Steindecker was born in Dresden on 8 November 1899, and educated at the *Reformgymnasium* and agricultural college in that city. He served in the armed forces 1917–19, was a *Frontbann* member 1924–26, and a member of the *Völkischer Sozialer Wahlverein* 1924–25 before joining the NSDAP on 28 July 1925, number 12619. He joined the SA in 1928; in 1930 he was appointed leader of HJ *Untergau* Vogtland; and in 1931, he was HJ Reich *Schar* leader and head of HJ *Uschla*. In 1932, he was named organisation leader of NSDAP *Kreis* Chemnitz, and was an SA-*Truppführer*. From April 1934 to October 1935, he was a town deputy in Chemnitz, and was promoted in 1934 to SA-*Sturmbannführer*. He held the NSDAP Golden Badge of Honour.

178. STELLRECHT, Helmut
     Born on 21 December 1898 in Wangen, Bavaria, Stellrecht was graduated as a doctor of engineering from the technical high school of Stuttgart shortly after World War I. He served in the war from 1917–19 and was awarded the Iron Cross, Class II. In 1921, he became active in the *völkisch* movement, and in 1922 founded the High School Circle of German Art in Stuttgart. He also joined a *Freikorps* company the same year, and in 1923 fought in the Ruhr as a member of the *Reichskriegsflagge* organisation. Thereafter he was politically inactive until 1 March 1931, when he joined the NSDAP, number 469220, and also the SA.

He founded the SA in Schweinfurt that year, and also joined the NSDAP *Reichsleitung* as an advisor on labour service. In March 1933, he was appointed organisation leader of the Labour Service in the Reich Ministry of Labour, and in September 1933 was named leader of the Training Division in the *Reichsjugendführung* with the rank of HJ *Obergebietsführer*. He held both posts simultaneously until 1939. From 1933 to 1945, he was Reichstag deputy for Potsdam I.

He was the author of several important national socialist ideological works: *Der Deutsche Arbeitsdienst, Arbeitsdienst und National Sozialismus*, and *Die Wehrerziehung der deutschen Jugend*. He served in the *Waffen*-SS 1940–41 with the rank of SS-*Brigadeführer*, and from 1941 to 1945 was chief of staff in Rosenberg's Department of Ideological Education.

Stellrecht was involved in the post-1945 right-wing nationalist movement, and in 1952 he was a leading figure in the attempt to unite all nationalist groups in the *Arbeitsgemeinschaft Nationaler Gruppen*. Cleared by a denazification court in 1947 by using false pretences, he was retried by a West Berlin court in August 1955, fined 22,000 deutsch marks, and deprived of civic privileges for three years. At a third trial in West Berlin in August 1958, he was fined an additional 7,000 deutsch marks. In 1960 he was a textile salesman and resident in Bad Boll.

179.   SZELL, Klaus
HJ *Gauführer* of Lower Bavaria-Oberpfalz in 1931, Szell was born in Ghent on 22 September 1910, and joined the NSDAP on 1 June 1929, number 133517. He was still a party member in 1937.

180.   TEICHERT, Werner
HJ *Gauführer* of Berlin-Brandenburg in 1928, he was born in Berlin on 4 March 1905, and joined the NSDAP on 30 August 1926, number 43573. He left the party on 30 June 1930, but rejoined on 1 January 1933. In 1937 he was an SA-*Sturmführer* in Berlin, and by 1939 was also active in the *Deutsches Arbeitsfront* and NS *Volkswohlfahrt*.

181.   TRAHMS, Karl Heinz
He was born on 6 September 1910 in Bremen. He was press and propaganda leader of HJ *Gau* Weser-Ems in 1930, but left the HJ in 1931. An NSDAP member since 1 March 1931, he joined the SS in 1933, and in 1935 held the rank of SS-*Unterscharführer*.

182. UNGER, Walter

Born in Schwerin on 9 February 1909, he was a member of NSDAP *Gauleitung* Mecklenburg-Lübeck 1928-33. From 1933 until October 1934, he was leader of HJ *Oberbann* Mecklenburg-Lübeck with the rank of *Oberbannführer*. In November 1935, he was appointed NSDAP *Kreisleiter* and *Gau* Inspector of NSDAP *Gau* Mecklenburg, and adjutant to the *Reichsstatthalter* of Mecklenburg. In 1939, he joined the *Wehrmacht*. In 1942 he was named HJ *Hauptbannführer* with responsibility for HJ *Gebiet* Mecklenburg. He was shortly recalled to the armed forces, but after being severely wounded in November 1944, he returned to civilian party work. In 1945 he was inspector of NSDAP *Gau* Mecklenburg, acting leader of HJ *Gebiet* Mecklenburg, and also held the rank of SS-*Obersturmbannführer*. He was a Reichstag member 1936-45, and holder of the NSDAP Golden Badge of Honour.

183. USADEL, Georg

Georg Friedrich Hennig Usadel was born in Gumbinnen, East Prussia, on 14 March 1900; he served in 1918 in an infantry regiment and was later a *Freikorps* member. In 1919, he entered the University of Königsberg to study German, history and religion, and took his doctorate in 1923. An editor of the *völkisch* periodical *Tannenberg* 1924-25, he joined the NSDAP in Insterburg in 1929. Before joining the SA and HJ in 1931, he was active as branch leader, district leader, and finally leader of the cultural-political division of the NSDAP *Gau* East Prussia. When appointed *Gauführer* of HJ East Prussia in 1931, he was a *Standartenführer* on the staff of SA *Gruppe* Ostland. He was leader of HJ *Gebiet* Ostland 1931-32.

In April 1933, he was appointed advisor for the reform of secondary school curriculum in the Prussian Ministry of Culture. In July 1933, he was named head of the Leadership School Division in the *Reichsjugendführung* with the rank of HJ *Obergebietsführer,* and the same month was also attached as a liaison officer of the *Reichsjugendführer* to the Reich Ministry of the Interior. In addition, he was appointed a higher government councillor in the Reich Ministry of the Interior in January 1934. He held the above positions until 4 August 1941, when he was killed at the front. A holder of the HJ and NSDAP Golden Badges of Honour, he was a Reichstag deputy from 1930 to 1941, from *Wahlkreis* East Prussia.

184. WACHA, Hugo

Born in Bosnia on 25 December 1901, he joined the NSDAP on 8 July 1941, number 512752. Until March 1933, he was HJ *Gebietsführer* and organisation leader of *Gebiet* Austria; he was then appointed *Gebietsführer* of Württemberg. In 1937 he was no longer in the HJ. By 1941 he had been active in the *Deutsches Arbeitsfront* and NS *Volkswohlfahrt*.

185. WAGNER, Richard
Wagner was born in Asch, Sudetenland, on 17 January 1896, and as a soldier in World War I was awarded the Iron Cross, Class II. He joined the HJ in 1926, and was HJ Reich secretary 1928–31. An NSDAP member since 1 December 1928, number 108414, he worked in the *Hilfkasse* division of the NSDAP *Reichsleitung* 1931–33, and in its Social Office 1933–45. He held the HJ and NSDAP Golden Badges of Honour.

186. WALLWEY, Albert
Born in Niederstütter on 19 February 1897, Wallwey joined the NSDAP on 28 December 1925, number 26876, and was appointed an HJ *Gebietsführer* in 1932. In 1933, he was appointed *Gebietsführer* of *Gebiet* Middle-Rhine, a post which he retained until 1936. From 1936 to 1940, he was active in the NS-*Volkswohlfahrt,* and in 1940 was appointed an NSDAP *Kreisleiter* in Bavaria. In 1941, however, he was deprived of this office for having misappropriated party funds. He held the NSDAP Golden Badge of Honour.

187. WALTER, Joachim
Walter was born in Berlin on 28 August 1909. A former *Geusen* member, he was HJ *Gauführer* of Berlin in 1931, and HJ Reich education leader 1931–32. He was leader of the NS-*Jugendverlag* from January 1932 until his expulsion from the HJ in 1933 (see chapter 4). An NSDAP member since 1 March 1931, number 479501, he also left the party in 1933, but rejoined in 1939. In 1935 he is known to have been leader of the *Reichsbetriebsgemeinschaft* (Reich Factory Society) in the *Deutsches Arbeitsfront.*

188. WANKEL, Felix
Born in Lahr, Baden, on 13 August 1902, Wankel joined the NSDAP in 1921, and again on 1 October 1926, number 45360. He was HJ *Gauführer* of Baden 1930–32, and Reich organisation inspector of the HJ in 1932; the same year, he was expelled from the HJ and NSDAP (see chapter 4). He was reinstated in the NSDAP in 1939, and in 1940

joined the SS, number 365193, with the rank of SS-*Obersturmführer*. In April 1942 he was expelled by Himmler while working in the SS main office.

189.   WARNING, Elmar

Born in Hamburg on 10 December 1907, he joined the NSDAP on 1 August 1930, number 305128. He was HJ *Gruppen-* and *Gebietsführer* East 1931; HJ *Gebietsführer* of Greater Berlin 1931–32; and HJ staff leader 1932.

190.   WEGNER, Kurt

He was born on 3 March 1910 in Lübeck. Before joining the SA in 1928 and the NSDAP in 1929, he was a member of the youth movement, including the *Lübecker Jugendkorps* from 1922–26 and the *Bund Wiking* 1926–28. He was branch leader of HJ Lübeck 1930–31 and HJ *Gauführer* of Mecklenburg-Lübeck 1931–32. From September 1932 until April 1933, he was staff leader of HJ *Gebiet* Austria with the rank of *Bannführer,* and from April 1933 until August 1934 was leader of *Gebiet* Austria as *Gebietsführer.* He left the HJ in 1934, and in 1935 was SA-*Sturmbannführer* in SA-*Gruppe* Hansa, then SA-*Hauptsturmführer* in SA-*Gruppe* Nordsee. He later rejoined the HJ, and in 1945 was *Gebietsführer* of Pomerania.

191.   WERNER, Gerhard

HJ *Gauführer* of Danzig in 1931, Werner was born in Ohra, Danzig, on 29 October 1910, and joined the NSDAP on 1 January 1930, number 181001, but left it on 1 April 1931.

192.   WESTENHUBER, Max

HJ *Gauführer* of Oberpfalz in 1931, Westenhuber was born in Munich on 5 January 1905. He joined the SA and NSDAP on 1 May 1925, party number 3678. In 1931 he also held the rank of SA-*Truppführer.*

193.   WESTENHUBER, Otto

HJ *Gauführer* of Oberpfalz 1929–30, he was born in Regensburg on 13 June 1909, and joined the NSDAP on 1 February 1928, number 75326. A holder of the NSDAP Golden Badge of Honour, he was later a leader in the *Deutsches Arbeitsfront,* and a *Wehrmacht* officer in 1944.

194.   WEYLAND, Karl
He was born on 26 October 1903, and joined the NSDAP on 1 March 1929, number 114882. He was secretary and treasury leader of HJ *Gau* Rheinpfalz 1931–32.

195.   WILLEMER, Karl
Born in Posen on 12 February 1912, he joined the NSDAP on 1 March 1930, number 210202. He founded the HJ in Naumberg in 1926, and was secretary of HJ *Gau* Halle-Merseburg in 1930. He later joined the SS, number 49187; in 1936 he held the rank of SS-*Oberscharführer,* and in 1942, SS-*Untersturmführer.*

196.   WINKLER, Werner
Leader of HJ Oldenburg in 1931, he was born in Vetschen on 22 August 1908, and joined the NSDAP on 1 November 1930, number 349061.

197.   WOWERIES, Franz
Born in Hannover on 22 June 1908, Franz Hermann Woweries joined the NSDAP in 1923, and again on 27 September 1927, number 68090. Joining the HJ from the nationalist youth movement in 1928, he was HJ Reich propaganda leader 1928–29; HJ *Gauführer* of Thuringia 1929; and HJ *Gauführer* of Halle-Merseburg in 1927 and 1929; and in August 1929, was appointed secretary of NSDAP *Gau* Hesse. In 1930 he was an NSDAP *Bezirksleiter,* and in 1931 was propaganda leader of NSDAP *Gau* Hesse-Nassau-South. In 1932, he became a member of the inspectorate in the NSDAP *Reichsleitung,* and he was a frequent contributor to the party press. In 1934, he became a Reichstag deputy from *Wahlkreis* Hesse-Nassau, which he remained until 1945.
In October 1935, he was appointed a Reich office leader and chief editor of the *Reichsschulungsbriefe der NSDAP,* and the same year, he also joined the SS, number 245547. In January 1938, he joined the Main Education Division of the NSDAP *Reichsleitung* as an office leader. In 1938 he was also promoted to SS-*Hauptsturmführer,* and as a member of the *Wehrmacht* took part in the Sudeten campaign. Although he retained his NSDAP post until 1943, he participated in

the 1940 French campaign as a *Wehrmacht* officer. In February 1943, he joined the state service for a period, but by 1945 he was a Reich office leader in the Political Training Division of the NSDAP *Reichsleitung*. He held the *Blutorden,* and both the HJ and NSDAP Golden Badges of Honour.

198.   WREDE, Franz Otto
    Born in Berlin on 21 September 1912, he joined the NSDAP on 1 May 1931, number 519197, and from 1931 to 1932, he was press leader of HJ *Gebiet* Greater Berlin. In 1945, he was attached to the *Reichsjugendführung* with the rank of HJ-*Hauptbannführer,* and at the same time, was chief of the Foreign Division in the NSDAP Reich Press Office.

199.   ZERRAHN, Wilhelm
    Zerrahn was born in Schleswig-Holstein on 15 June 1904, and before joining the NSDAP on 13 June 1925, number 7643, he was a member of the *Jungdeutsche Orden* in 1923-24. He was an HJ member 1928-31, and a *Bezirksführer* in HJ *Gau* Schleswig-Holstein 1930-31. He then joined the SS, number 11820; in 1936 he was an SS-*Obersturmführer,* and in 1942 an SS-*Hauptsturmführer.* A holder of the NSDAP Golden Badge of Honour, he joined the *Wehrmacht* in 1943, but was reported missing in Russia in 1944.

200.   ZIDAN, Friedrich
    Leader of HJ *Untergau* South Franconia-West in 1931, he was born on 18 December 1909, and joined the NSDAP on 1 April 1929, number 123773.

Reference Matter

The Development of the *Jugendbund der* NSDAP 1922–23

Branch (Ortsgruppe)	Date of Establishment	Branch Leader (Ortsgruppenführer)
1. Nuremberg	15 June 1922	Kurt Ottmar Mintzel
2. Zeitz	8 July 1922	Johannes Saulich
3. Dresden	10 September 1922	Alexander Bettschneider
4. Hanau am Main	12 October 1922	Heinrich Ullrich
5. Stuttgart	15 October 1922	Paul Schlotter
6. Würzburg	15 October 1922	Rudolf Trieschmann
7. Heilbronn	18 October 1922	Karl Drautz
8. Augsburg	18 October 1922	Friedrich Anholt
9. Landshut	20 October 1922	Ernst Berthold
10. Leipzig	22 October 1922	Rudolf Staake
11. Lübeck	25 October 1922	Richard Fellbach
12. Ulm	29 October 1922	Friedrich Laibl
13. Plauen	(?) October 1922	Kurt Gruber
14. Elberfeld	1 November 1922	Robert Schindler
15. Brunswick	4 November 1922	Max Langer
16. Kitzinger	4 November 1922	Heinrich Schwab

Branch (Ortsgruppe)	Date of Establishment	Branch Leader (Ortsgruppenführer)
17. Mainbernheim	6 November 1922	Heinrich Wolfing
18. Freudenthal-Saxony	6 November 1922	Karl Langer
19. Berlin	10 November 1922	Franz Ewald
20. Barmen	11 November 1922	Fritz Vowe
21. Hersbruck-Franconia	12 November 1922	Karl Poppendörfer
22. Herborn	12 November 1922	Adolf Nassauer
23. Eger	14 November 1922	Oswald Jahn
24. Halle-Saale	15 November 1922	Heinrich Kler
25. Trebnitz	15 November 1922	Johann Toller
26. Zuffenhausen	16 November 1922	Oskar Grossmann
27. Dortmund	17 November 1922	Friedrich Bein
28. Ludwigshafen	18 November 1922	Ferdinand Schweitzer
29. Mannheim	18 November 1922	Friedrich Kleier
30. Heidelberg	24 November 1922	Fritz Klein
31. Rosenheim	5 December 1922	Ernst Mengert
32. Bockwitz	10 December 1922	Walter Punze
33. Wünschendorf	12 December 1922	Erwin Neupert
34. Ayltdorf	20 December 1922	Karl Lützsch
35. Schönwalde	22 December 1922	Franz Wischpolt
36. Breslau	22 December 1922	Alfred Klein
37. Görlitz	11 January 1923	Ewald Schneider
38. Hamburg	15 January 1923	Paul Linhard
39. Miesbach	20 January 1923	Johann Kayser

SOURCE: BA: Akte NS 26/333.

APPENDIX II

The Landesverbände of the Jugendbund der NSDAP 1922–23

Landesverband	Date of Establishment	Leader	Number of Branches
1. Bavaria	15 June 1922	Adolf Lenk	12
2. Franconia	1 September 1922	Ludwig Schmidt	6
3. Thuringia	15 September 1922	Johannes Saulich	5
4. Saxony	10 October 1922	Kurt Gruber	8
5. Württemberg	1 November 1922	Oskar Grossmann	6
6. Hesse	1 December 1922	Heinrich Ullrich	5
7. Berlin	15 December 1922	Werner Schütze	6
8. Hannover	15 December 1922	Ludwig Tiedt	4

Landesverband	Date of Establishment	Leader	Number of Branches
9. Silesia	28 December 1922	Alfred Klein	4
10. Sudetenland	28 January 1923	Eugen Weese	9
11. Corinthia	14 February 1923	Walter Proksch	4
12. Vienna	1 March 1923	Walter Gattermayer	3
13. Tirol	1 April 1923	Adolf Bauer	6
14. Swabia	10 April 1923	Josef Eichbauer	5
15. Nordsee	15 April 1923	Paul Linhard	4
16. Danzig	1 June 1923	Karl Besler	1
17. Oberpfalz	1 June 1923	Karl Steininger	7
18. Baden	18 June 1923	Fritz Klein	4
19. Pomerania-Ostsee	4 July 1923	Erwin Bruch	3
20. East Prussia	3 September 1923	Hermann Hesse	1
21. Rheinpfalz	12 October 1923	Ludwig Schweitzer	3
22. Lower Franconia	12 October 1923	Rudolf Trieschmann	5
23. Rheinland	28 October 1923	Theodor Sollseife	6
			117

SOURCE: BA: Akte NS 26/333.

APPENDIX III

The Organisation of the HJ at the End of 1927

Gau	Gau Leader
1. Anhalt	H. Teichmüller
2. Baden	Unknown
3. Bavaria	Paul Neumann
4. Berlin-Brandenburg	Gunther Orsoleck
5. East Prussia	Arno Meissner (?)
6. Halle-Merseburg	Franz Woweries
7. Hannover-South	Unknown
8. Hannover-North	A. Bressel
9. Hesse-Nassau-North	Walter Hoffmann
10. Hesse-Nassau-South	Fritz Geist
11. Lüneburg-Stade	Unknown
12. Mecklenburg-Lübeck	Bruno Leonhardt
13. Pomerania	Gunther Lutz
14. Rheinland	Hugo Maass
15. Rheinpfalz	A. Anschütz

Gau	Gau Leader
16. Ruhr-Westphalia	Robert Grieving
17. Saxony	Kurt Gruber
18. Schleswig-Holstein	Wilhelm Lönnecker
19. Silesia	Franz Metzke
20. Thuringia	Albert Stange
21. Württemberg	Hugo Kroll (?)

SOURCE: BA: ZSg 3/1475.

APPENDIX IV

The Development of HJ Gaue at the Beginning of 1930[1]

Gau	Gau Leader	Remarks
1. Magdeburg-Anhalt	Theodor Hofmann	
2. Baden	Helmut Wetz	
3. Bergisch-Land	Heinrich Reinhardt[2]	At the end of 1930, Reinhardt resigned and this Gau was divided into Gau Düsseldorf under Hugo Maass and Gau Essen under Heinz Mondelt.[3]
4. Berlin-Brandenburg-Ostmark	Robert Gadewoltz	
5. East Prussia	Arno Meissner	
6. Halle-Merseburg	Fritz Köhler	
7. Hesse	Werner Goerendt	
8. Hesse-Nassau	Hans Mages	
9. Lower Bavaria	Ernst Haefke	
10. Mecklenburg-Lübeck	Lothar Hilscher	
11. North Franconia	Wilhelm Stammberger	Franconia was divided into three Gaue in the course of 1930: Lower Franconia, South Franconia, and North Franconia.[4]
12. Hamburg	Heinz Morisse	
13. Schleswig-Holstein	Lothar Lange	
14. Oberpfalz	Otto Westenhuber[5]	
15. Pomerania	Günther Lutz	
16. Rheinland	Hugo Maass	Gau Rhein was set up in

Gau	Gau Leader	Remarks
17. Ruhr-Westphalia		1930 under Josef Ruschepaul. Gau Westphalia was established in 1930 under Lorenz Loewer.[6]
18. Rheinpfalz	Karl Hofmann	
19. Saar	Jacob Jung	
20. Saxony	Kurt Gruber	At the beginning of 1930, Gau Saxony was subdivided into a number of Untergaue: 1) Vogtland; 2) Chemnitz under Willi Steindecker; 3) Zwickau under Willi Künnemann; 4) Leipzig under Dr. Weimert; and 5) Dresden under Gottfried Schroeter. Before the end of 1930, however, these had been replaced by a number of full Gaue: South West Saxony, North West Saxony, Middle Saxony, East Saxony, Greater Plauen.[7]
21. Silesia	Franz Metzke	The Gau was divided in 1930 into Gau Breslau, which incorporated Upper and Middle Silesia under Wilhelm Kaebisch; and Gau Lower Silesia under Walter Lindner.[8]
22. South Bavaria	Emil Klein	
23. South Hannover-Brunswick	Hartmann Lauterbacher[9]	
24. Thuringia	Albert Bormann	
25. Weser-Ems	Walter Burchhard[10]	
26. Württemberg	Paul Otto	
27. East Hannover	Karl Nickerken	
28. Danzig	Hans Buchholz	
29. Austria	Rolf West	

1. Bay. HSA: ASA: Akte NS/1541.
2. SAB: 4/65 781/146.
3. Ibid.
4. SAK: Abteilung 403. No. 16754.
5. SAB: 4/65 781/146.
6. Ibid.
7. Ibid.
8. Ibid.
9. Ibid.
10. Ibid.

APPENDIX V

The HJ *Reichsleitung,* February 1931[1]

Division	Office	Leader
Abteilung 1 A	Reich *Schar* Leader	Günther Kenzler Attached to 1 A were Richard Noethlichs and Franz von Wangenheim, who had special responsibility for field sports.[2]
Abteilung 1 B	Reich Organisation Leadership	Franz Schnaedter
Abteilung 1 C	Reich Education Leadership, which also included the Cultural Office.[3]	Hein Schlecht
Abteilung 1 D	Reich Press Leadership	Hein Schlecht Franz Schnaedter was also attached to this division as a press editor.[4]
Abteilung 1 E	Reich Propaganda Leadership	Herbert Peter
Abteilung 1 F	Foreign Affairs Office	Richard Noethlichs Curt Brieger and all HJ *Oberführer* were also involved in this division.[5]
Abteilung 1 G	Social Politics	Herbert Peter Emil Klein was an assistant in this division.[6]
Abteilung 2 A	Reich Secretarial Office, which included the Personnel Office.	Richard Wagner
Abteilung 2 B	Reich Treasury Office, to which was attached the Revision Office.[7]	August Schroeder
Abteilung 3	Border Land Office	Rudolf Schmidt
Abteilung 4	*Jungfront-Verlag*	Unknown

1. BA: Akte NS 26/370.
2. Bay. HSA: ASA: Akte NS/1849.
3. BA: ZSg 3/3687.
4. Bay. HSA: ASA: Akte NS/1849.
5. Ibid.
6. Ibid.
7. BA: ZSg 3/3687.

APPENDIX VI

HJ Finances: January–June 1931

Gau	Financial Contribution (in reichsmarks)
1. Baden	424.35
2. Berlin	37.00
3. Brandenburg	Not Given
4. Breslau	648.80
5. Danzig	40.05
6. Düsseldorf	232.25
7. Essen	49.25
8. Hesse-Nassau-South	114.80
9. Hesse-Nassau-North	26.50
10. Hamburg	141.80
11. South Hannover-Brunswick	240.00
12. Hesse	132.70
13. Halle-Merseburg	285.85
14. Corinthia	44.15
15. Magdeburg-Anhalt	306.90
16. Mecklenburg-Lübeck	Not Given
17. Lower Austria	30.00
18. North Franconia	110.00
19. Lower Silesia	249.00
20. East Hannover	212.75
21. Ostmark	241.60
22. Oberpfalz	19.95
23. Upper Austria	21.75
24. East Prussia	537.80
25. Munich-Upper Bavaria	233.65
26. Upper Silesia	Not Given
27. Pomerania	669.05
28. Rheinland	408.30
29. Rheinpfalz	450.00
30. Saar	Not Given
31. Saxony	926.65
32. Steiermark	36.55
33. South Franconia	381.40
34. Schleswig-Holstein	546.00
35. Thuringia	759.40
36. Lower Franconia	138.00
37. Weser-Ems	295.30
38. Westgau (Austria)	575.00

Gau	Financial Contribution (in reichsmarks)
39. Westphalia-North	141.25
40. Westphalia-South	469.35
41. Vienna	17.10
42. Württemberg	589.60
Total	11,282.85 reichsmarks

SOURCE: BA: Akte NS 26/339.

APPENDIX VII

HJ *Reichsleitung* Salaries 1931

Name	Position in *Reichsleitung*	Salary prior to 16th March, 1931 (Monthly, in reichsmarks)	Salary after 16th March, 1931 (Monthly, in reichsmarks)
1. Kurt Gruber	*Reichsführer*	108	400
2. Richard Wagner	Reich Secretary	330	330
3. August Schroeder	Reich Treasurer	200	200
4. Franz Schnaedter	Reich Organisation Leader	140	220
5. Herbert Peter	Reich Propaganda Leader	130	170
6. Hein Schlecht	Reich Education Leader	120	200
7. Theo Kienast	Reich *Schar* Leader	180	180
8. Kurt Brieger	Leader of *Jungvolk* Office	None	160
9. Max Lallinger	HJ Index Leader	65	100
Total		1273 reichsmarks	1960 reichsmarks

SOURCE: Bay.: HSA: ASA: Akte NS/1555.

APPENDIX VIII

The Regional Distribution of HJ Membership 1931–32

Gau	1 January 1931	1 April 1931	1 July 1931	1 October 1931	1 November 1931	1 January 1932
1. Baden	498	529	797	1262	1558	1558
2. Berlin	631	602	589	Not Given	Not Given	799
3. Brandenburg	320	402	393	584	706	844
4. Breslau	500	786	985	1305	1280	1586
5. Danzig	45	Not Given	121	156	164	184
6. Düsseldorf	264	348	369	516	557	554
7. Essen	91	Not Given	Not Given	187	345	346
8. Halle-Merseburg	455	591	683	894	925	987
9. Hamburg	172	172	198	248	248	141
10. South Hannover-Brunswick	931	1129	1524	1933	1946	2134
11. Hesse	148	288	Not Given	Not Given	834	1102
12. Hesse-Nassau-North	22	Not Given	Not Given	Not Given	219	337
13. Hesse-Nassau-South	169	120	294	Not Given	Not Given	748
14. Koblenz	322	Not Given	192	319	354	456
15. Cologne	Not Given	236	275	325	354	379
16. Magdeburg-Anhalt	376	339	540	715	656	656
17. Mecklenburg-Lübeck	448	Not Given	540	743	777	802
18. Munich-Upper Bavaria	279	410	400	416	452	612
19. Swabia	Not Given	Not Given	Not Given	Not Given	264	286
20. Lower Silesia	202	327	423	823	743	954
21. North Bavaria	Not Given	Not Given	Not Given	Not Given	Not Given	150
22. Oberpfalz	Not Given	140	105	Not Given	127	146
23. North Franconia	225	267	132	192	292	355
24. Upper Silesia	Not Given	Not Given	Not Given	423	539	712
25. East Hannover	365	481	625	769	754	833
26. Ostmark	388	580	632	1015	1095	1309

Gau	1 January 1931	1 April 1931	1 July 1931	1 October 1931	1 November 1931	1 January 1932
27. East Prussia	528	819	997	1588	1730	1730
28. Pomerania	547	721	852	1208	1306	1591
29. Rheinpfalz	455	480	534	579	596	642
30. Saar	Not Given	Not Given	Not Given	Not Given	Not Given	Not Given
31. Saxony	1428	Not Given	Not Given	2675	2665	3008
32. South Franconia	493	561	469	537	528	553
33. Schleswig-Holstein	531	751	908	1256	1354	1693
34. Thuringia	851	999	Not Given	Not Given	Not Given	2500
35. Lower Franconia	114	145	170	194	195	188
36. Westphalia-North	169	217	267	444	483	584
37. Westphalia-South	461	468	519	747	779	828
38. Weser-Ems	302	448	564	673	799	952
39. Württemberg	380	573	514	514	514	802
40. Corinthia	287	318	369	528	509	501
41. Lower Austria	Not Given	Not Given	598	790	913	618
42. Upper Austria	Not Given	653	810	1000	Not Given	1000
43. Steiermark	197	241	315	340	321	402
44. Westgau	192	257	284	Not Given	312	312
45. Vienna	Not Given	Not Given	429	Not Given	552	350
Total	13,806	15,373	17,902	26,198	28,743	37,304

SOURCE: BA: Sammlung Schumacher: Gruppe VIII, No. 239.

APPENDIX IX

The Development of HJ
Membership 1929–39

Date	Membership
End of 1929	Less than 13,000
1 January 1931	13,806
1 April 1931	15,373
1 July 1931	17,902
1 October 1931	26,198
1 November 1931	28,743
1 January 1932	37,304
1 February 1932	40,129
1 March 1932	43,334
17 June 1932	48,000
30 January 1933	55,365
End of 1933	568,288
End of 1934	786,000
End of 1935	829,361
End of 1936	1,168,734
End of 1937	1,237,078
End of 1938	1,663,305
Beginning of 1939	1,723,886

SOURCE: G. Kaufmann: *Das kommende Deutschland* (Berlin, 1940), p. 39. The figures 1933–39 are for the HJ proper, and do not include the DJ, BDM, or JM.

APPENDIX X

The Organisation of the
Reichsjugendführung: July 1933

ADOLF HITLER

REICH MINISTRY
OF THE INTERIOR
DR. WILHELM FRICK

YOUTH LEADER OF
THE GERMAN REICH
BALDUR VON
SCHIRACH

REPRESENTATIVE
& STAFF LEADER
WALTER KAUL

PERSONAL
ADJUTANT
HORST
KRUTSCHINNA

ASSISTANT
ADJUTANT
HEINRICH LÜER

ABTEILUNG I	ABTEILUNG II	ABTEILUNG III	ABTEILUNG IV	ABTEILUNG V	ABTEILUNG S.P.
Organisation Education Equipment Defence Sports Cultural Activity Einsatz	Personnel Discipline Law & Legal Protection Medals and Decorations	Youth Welfare Hygiene Labour Service	Administration Treasury Material Office Index	Medical Service	Education Cultural Work Educational Camps Propaganda Press Archives Deutsche Jugend-Verlag
Gebietsführer WILLI-BOTHO BICKER	Obergebietsführer HEINZ HUGO JOHN	Gebietsführer ARTUR AXMANN	Obergebietsführer ALFRED LOOSE	Oberbannführer KARL WALTER KONDEYNE	Obergebietsführer WILLI KÖRBER

ABTEILUNG A.R.	ABTEILUNG F.M.R.	ABTEILUNG F.S.	ABTEILUNG J.B.	ABTEILUNG St.	ABTEILUNG J.V.	ABTEILUNG H
Foreign and Colonial Youth Work	Flight Training Reich Air Schools Glider Training Motorised Units Riding Units	Leadership Schools Reich Leaders' School of the HJ	National Socialist Youth Factory Cell Organisation (NSJBO) Youth Office of the German Labour Front	Student Affairs	Commissioner for Youth Affairs	Youth Hostels
Obergebietsführer KARL NABERSBERG	BENEDIKT SCHMALSCHLÄGER	Obergebietsführer GEORG USADEL	Gebietsführer HEINZ OTTO	Bundesführer (NSDStB) OSKAR STABEL	Obergebietsführer KARL NABERSBERG	Unterbannführer JOHANN RODATZ

Note: Also attached to the staff were: Obergebietsführer Ritter von Schleich, Gebietsführer Bun Geissler, and Gebietsführer Ottokar Lorenz.

Source: BA: Akte NS 26/338

Bibliography

Unpublished Sources

(1) *Bundesarchiv Koblenz*

  (a) From the former Hauptarchiv der NSDAP:
    Akte NS 26/
      Folder 325: SA. *Die Stennes Meuterei.*
      Folder 331: *Jugendbund der NSDAP.*
      Folder 332: Adolf Lenk, *Gründer der HJ.*
      Folder 333: Adolf Lenk: *Das Werden der HJ.*
      Folder 334: *Grossdeutsche Jugend.*
      Folder 335: *Reichsführung der HJ* (Kurt Gruber).
      Folder 336: *Das Werden der HJ. Reden des Reichsjugendführers.*
      Folder 337: *Reichsjugendführung-Verschiedene Rundschreiben,* 1931–33.
      Folder 338: *Reichsjugendführung. Entwurf einer Dienstvorschrift für die HJ.*
      Folder 339: *Reichsjugendführung-Stabsführung 1931–34.*
      Folder 340: HJ *Gebietsführung. Korrespondenz 1931–32.*
      Folder 341: *Personelles—Werner Schütze (Jugendführung).*
      Folder 342: *Reichsjugendführerschule. HJ Schulung.*
      Folder 344: *NS Schülerbund 1930–33.*
      Folder 345: *Bund Deutscher Mädel-Allgemeines 1932.*

Folder 346: *Hitlerjugend. Eingänge/Schulangelegenheiten-Massregelungen.*
Folder 347: *Hitlerjugend. Terrorfälle.*
Folder 348: *Hitlerjugend. Hilfe/Schulangelegenheiten.*
Folder 351: *Bericht der HJ Saarpfalz.*
Folder 352: *Versammlungen der HJ 1929.*
Folder 353: *Jungvolk, Werbung-Allgemeines.*
Folder 354: *Andere Bünde.*
Folder 355: HJ *Presse. Propaganda-Schulung.*
Folder 356: HJ *Presse.*
Folder 357: HJ *RJF (Reichsjugendführung).*
Folder 358: HJ *Presse und Propagandaamt.*
Folder 359: HJ *Propaganda-Statistik 1935.*
Folder 360: HJ *Verschiedenes.*
Folder 361: Hitler Youth von Willy Körber [in English].
Folder 362: HJ *Organisation und Tätigkeit des Gaues Branden-burg, 1930–33.*
Folder 363: HJ *Nassau-Bericht über die Entwicklung 1925–31.*
Folder 364: HJ *Südwest-Korrespondenz 1931–32.*
Folder 365: HJ in *Fürstenfeldbruck.*
Folder 366: HJ *Gau München-Oberbayern.*
Folder 367: HJ *Reichsjugendtag in Potsdam.*
Folder 369: HJ *Gefallene und Tote.*
Folder 370: HJ *Grenzlandamt (Allgemeines Korrespondenz),* 1928–29.
Folder 371: HJ *Grenzlandamt (Allgemeines Korrespondenz),* 1929, 1931.
Folder 372: HJ *Grenzlandamt (Allgemeines Korrespondenz),* 1930, 1933.
Folder 376: *Entstehung und Gründung der NSDStB.*
Folder 383: NS *Hilfkasse-Allgemeines 1929.*
Folder 825: *Bismarckjugend.*
Folder 845: *Deutschvölkische Jugend.*
Folder 868: *Völkische Jugend.*
Folder 1264: Von Schirach: *Korrespondenz und Dokumente,* 1930–36.
Folder 1366B: Baldur von Schirach.
(b) NS 22: *Akten des Reichsorganisationsleiters der NSDAP.*
(c) Sammlung Schumacher:
  Gruppe VII   : Nos. 199–209.
  Gruppe VIII   : No. 239.
  Part II   : Nos. 374, 389, 404.
(d) Zeitgeschichtliche Sammlung.

(2) *Bayerisches Hauptstaatsarchiv: Allgemeines Staatsarchiv, Munich*

(a) Sonderabgabe I; *Akten des Generalstaatskommissars:*
Akte NS/
1508: NSDAP und *verwandte oppositionelle politische Verbände.*
1534: NSDAP: *Nationalsozialistische Kinderspeisung.*
1535: NSDAP: *Politische Betätigung der Schuljugend.*
1536: NSDAP: *Verein Deutsches Jugendwerk, e.V.*
1537: NSDAP: *NS Schülerbund.*
1538: NSDAP: *Jugendbund der NSDAP.*
1539: NSDAP: *Jungvolk.*
1540: NSDAP: *Hitlerjugendbewegung München, 1930–32.*
1541: NSDAP: *Hitlerjugend.*
1542: NSDAP: *Bund deutscher Mädel-NS Schülerbund.*
1543: NSDAP: *Hitlerjugend nach der Auflösung, 1931–32.*
1544: NSDAP: *Hitlerjugend Bayern etc.*
1555: NSDAP: *Verordnung des Reichspräsidenten-Auflösung der Hitler-Jugend.*
1556: NSDAP: *Auflösung nationalsozialistischer Verbände, 1932, I.*
1557: NSDAP: *Auflösung NS Verbände, II.*
1756: NSDAP: *Allgemeines 1923–26.*
1776: NSDAP: *Pläne für den 13.3. 32. HJ.*
1803: *Nationalsozialistische Kindergruppe, 1931.*
1804: *Nationalsozialistische Deutsche Arbeiterjugend, 1926.*
1805: *Jugendbund der NSDAP.*
1816: *Auflösungsmaterial 1932: SA, SS, HJ.*
1817: *SA 1932.*
1818: *Der Deutsche Jugendbund Bismarck.*
1819: *Freischar Schill, 1925–31.*
1820: *Nationale Jugendbünde, 1922–33.*
1824: *Adler und Falken, 1925–30.*
1834: *Kampfgemeinschaft revolutionäre Nationalsozialisten.*
1849: NSDAP: *Vordrücke, SS, SA, HJ. Befehle 1930–32.*
1854: NSDAP: *Sterbekasse 1930.*
1870: NSDAP *Hilfkasse.*
1874: NSDAP *Hilfkasse.*
1880: *Völkische Jugendbewegung.*
(b) Akten des Staatsministeriums des Innern:
71799: *NS Sportbewegung Hitlerjugend, 1928–36.*
73437: *Parteien und Verbände: Jugendbewegung.*

(3) *Bayerisches Hauptstaatsarchiv: Geheimes Staatsarchiv, Munich*

Akten des Staatsministeriums des Aussern:
MA 100 425: *Nationalsozialismus 1922–31.*

(4) *Bayerisches Hauptstaatsarchiv: Staatsarchiv für Oberbayern, Munich*

Aktenabgaben des Landratsamts Aichbach:
Akten Fasz. 10/68: *Nationale Volkserziehung 1934–35.*
Akten Fasz. 10/70: *Beteiligung von Schülern der Volks-und Berufsschulen an Vereinen 1924–35.*

(5) *Berlin Document Center*

Personal Files of NSDAP and HJ members.

(6) *Forschungsstelle für die Geschichte des Nationalsozialismus, Hamburg*

Miscellaneous material relating to the NSDAP, SA, and HJ.

(7) *Landesarchiv Schleswig-Holstein, Schleswig*

(a) Regierung Schleswig: Abteilung 309:
No. 22571: NSDAP 1930–31.
No. 22576: *Schwarzes* Front-Otto Strasser-1930–31.
No. 22584: *Politische Tätigkeit vor 1933.*
No. 22668: *Landvolk-Bewegung.*
No. 22700: NSDAP, SA; *Allgemeines.*
No. 22864: NSDAP und SA; *NS Arbeiter- und Bauernjugend.*
No. 22996: *Parteien, Versammlungen.*
No. 22998: NSDAP, SA, HJ: *Allgemeines.*
(b) Oberpräsidium Schleswig-Holstein: Abteilung 301:
Nos. 4555–4564: *Parteien 1925–33.*

(8) *Staatsarchiv Bremen*

Polizeipräsidium: Nachrichtenstelle 4/65:
(a) 179/27, NSDAP Bremen 1922–26.
(b) Polizeipräsidium Berlin: Lageberichte 1674/279 to 1693/285.
(c) Lageberichte 1919–31: 1557/253 to 1567/255.
(d) Lageberichte Hamburg: 1587/259 to 1591/260.
(e) Staatskommissar: Lageberichte: 1627/268 to 1627/288.
(f) Lageberichte: Baden-Württemberg: 1751/298 to 1762/301.

(9) *Staatsarchiv Koblenz*

Bestand 403/16754: *Hitlerjugend, Studentenbund u.a.*: Band I, December
   1929–July 1931.
Bestand 403/16755: *Hitlerjugend u.a.*: Band II, July 1931–September 1933.

(10) *Archiv der Deutschen Jugendbewegung, Burg Ludwigstein*

Miscellaneous documentary records, books, and other literature on the
German youth movement, 1919–33.

(11) *Institut für Zeitgeschichte, Munich*

Zeugenschriften (Witness Accounts).

Published Sources

(1) *Newspapers*

(a) Hitler Youth Press
   Hitler-Jugend-Zeitung. Selections from 1928.
   Junge Nation. Bundesblatt der Hitler-Jugend. 1933.
   Der Junge Sturmtrupp. 1932, 1933.
   Sturmjugend. Kampfblatt Schaffender Jugend. Selections from
      1927, 1930, 1931.
(b) NSDAP Press
   Hakenkreuzbanner. Pre-1933 extracts.
   Hansiche Warte: Hamburger Tageblatt. 1928–32.
   Illustrierter Beobachter. 1928–33.
   Nationalsozialistische Briefe. 1925–26.
   Niedersachsen-Stürmer. 1930–32.
   Völkischer Beobachter. 1921–34.
(c) Non-NSDAP Press
   Berliner Morgenpost
   Berliner Tageblatt
   Berliner Volkszeitung
   Bodensee Rundschau
   Braunschweigische Länderzeitung
   Der Danziger Vorposten

Deutsches Nachrichten Büro
Hamburger Fremdenblatt
Lübeckischer Anzeigen
Münchner neueste Nachrichten
Neue Berliner Illustrierte
Preussische Zeitung
Schlesische Tagezeitung
Vorwärts

(2) Periodicals

Das Junge Deutschland, Amtliches Organ der Reichsausschuss der deutschen Jugendverbände 1925–32.
Das Junge Deutschland, Amtliches Organ der Jugendführer des Deutschen Reiches 1933–35.
Das Junge Volk, 1930–31.
Der Zwiespruch, Amtliches Nachrichtenblatt der deutschen Jugendbewegungsbünde, 1929–31.
Deutscher Freischar 1929.
Die Deutsche Zukunft, Organ der Nationalsozialistischen Jugend, 1931–32.
Die Junge Front, Führerblatt der Hitler-Jugend, 1929–30.
Die Kommenden 1928–33.
Nationalsozialistische Monatshefte 1930–39.
Wille und Macht, Führerorgan der Nationalsozialistischen Jugend, 1933–43.
Wille und Werk, Pressedienst der deutschen Jugendbewegung 1926–33.

(3) Documentary Material

Anacker, H. *Die Trommel, SA-Gedichte.* Munich, 1932.
Brennecke, F., ed. *Vom Deutschen Volk und seinem Lebensraum. Handbuch für die Schulungsarbeit in der HJ.* Munich, 1937.
British Foreign Office. *Germany, Basic Handbook.* London, 194?.
British Government. *Who's Who in Germany and Austria 1945.* London, 1945.
Degener, H. A. L., ed. *Wer Ists?* Berlin, 1935.
Deuerlein, E. *Der Aufstieg der NSDAP 1919–1933 in Augenzeugenberichten.* Düsseldorf, 1968.
——. *Der Hitler-Putsch. Bayerische Dokumente zum 8/9 November 1923.* Stuttgart, 1962.
Deutschen Demokratische Republik. *Braunbuch: Kriegs- und Naziverbrecher in der Bundesrepublik.* Berlin, 1965.
Dörner, C. *Freude, Zucht, Glaube: Handbuch für die kulterelle Arbeit im Lager.* Potsdam, 1937.

Espe, W. M. *Das Buch der NSDAP.* Berlin, 1934.

Fanderl, W., ed. *HJ marschiert! Das neue Hitler-Jugend Buch.* Berlin, 1933.

Feder, G. *Das Programm der NSDAP und seine weltanschauliche Grundgedanken.* Munich, 1932.

Heyen, F. J. *Nationalsozialismus im Alltag.* Boppard, 1967.

Hofer, W., ed. *Der Nationalsozialismus, Dokumente 1933–45.* Frankfurt, 1957.

Jacobsen, H. A., and Jochmann, W., eds. *Ausgewählte Dokumente zur Geschichte der Nationalsozialismus.* Bielefeld, 1966.

Jochmann, W. *Nationalsozialismus und Revolution. Ursprung und Geschichte der NSDAP in Hamburg 1922–33. Dokumente.* Frankfurt, 1963.

Müller, H. *Katholische Kirche und Nationalsozialismus. Dokumente 1930–33.* Munich, 1963.

Nationalsozialistische-Jugendverlag. *Nationalsozialistischer Jugend-kalender 1932.* Munich, 1932.

NSDAP. *Das Deutsche Führerlexikon 1934–35.* Munich, 1934.

Orientalischen Cigarreten-Compagnie. *Männer im Dritten Reich.* Bremen, 1934.

Pross, H., ed. *Die Zerstörung der deutschen Politik. Dokumente 1871–1933.* Frankfurt, 1959.

Reichsjugendführung der NSDAP. *Aufbau, Gliederung und Anschriften der Hitler-Jugend.* Berlin, 1934.

Reichsjugendführung der NSDAP. *Bekleidung und Ausrüstung der Hitler-Jugend.* Berlin, 1934.

Reichsjugendführung der NSDAP. *Blut und Ehre: Liederbuch der Hitler-Jugend.* Berlin, 1933.

Reichsjugendführung der NSDAP. *Deutscher Jugenddienst.* Potsdam, 1933.

Reichsjugendführung der NSDAP. *Die Werkarbeit im Kriegseinsatz der Hitler-Jugend.* Berlin, 1942.

Reichsjugendführung der NSDAP. *HJ im Dienst: Ausbildungs-vorschrift für die Ertüchtigung der deutschen Jugend.* Berlin, 1940.

Reichsjugendführung der NSDAP. *Jahrbuch der Hitler-Jugend 1934, 1935, 1937, 1938, 1939.* Berlin.

Reichsjugendführung der NSDAP. *Unser Dienst: Aufgabe für die neuen Einheiten der Hitlerjugend.* Berlin, 1941.

Remold, J. *Handbuch für die Hitler-Jugend.* Munich, 1933.

Schnabel, R. *Das Führerschulungswerk der Hitler-Jugend.* Berlin, 1938.

Schwarz, M. *Biographisches Handbuch der deutschen Reichstage.* Hannover, 1965.

Siebecke, H. *Hitlerjugend. Eine Dokumentation über Jugenderziehung im Dritten Reich* (phonograph record). Gütersloh, 1964.

Trial of the Major War Criminals before the International Military Tribunal. *Proceedings,* Vols. 1–23. *Documents in Evidence,* Vols. 24–42. Nuremberg, 1947–49.

Tyrell, A. *Führer befiehl . . . Selbstzeugnisse aus der "Kampfzeit" der NSDAP. Dokumentation und Analyse.* Düsseldorf, 1969.

Verlag Neues Leben. *Zur Geschichte der Arbeiterjugendbewegung in Deutschland: ein Auswahl von Materialien und Dokumenten aus den Jahren 1904–46.* Berlin, 1956.

(4) *Memoirs, Diaries, Speeches*

Baynes, N. H., ed. *The Speeches of Adolf Hitler, 1922–39.* 2 vols. Oxford, 1942.
Bolm, H. *Hitler-Jugend in einem Jahrzehnt. Ein Glaubensweg der niedersächsischen Jugend.* Brunswick, 1938.
Calic, E. *Ohne Maske. Hitler-Breitung Geheimgespräche 1931.* Frankfurt, 1968.
Dietrich, O. *Mit Hitler in die Macht. Persönliche Erlebnisse mit meinem Führer.* Munich, 1935.
———. *12 Jahre mit Hitler.* Munich, 1955.
Goebbels, J. *Kampf um Berlin.* Munich, 1932.
———. *Vom Kaiserhof zur Reichskanzlei.* Munich, 1934.
Hanfstaengl, E. *Hitler. The Missing Years.* London, 1957.
Heiber, H., ed. *The Diary of Josef Goebbels, 1925–26.* London, 1962.
Hoess, R. *Commandant of Auschwitz.* London, 1959.
Hitler, A. *Mein Kampf.* New York, 1939.
Jochmann, W. *Im Kampf um die Macht. Hitlers Rede vor dem Hamburger Nationalklub von 1919.* Frankfurt, 1960.
Klöss, E. *Reden des Führers. Politik und Propaganda Adolf Hitlers 1922–45.* Munich, 1967.
Krebs, A. *Tendenzen und Gestalten der NSDAP. Erinnerungen an die Frühzeit der Partei.* Stuttgart, 1959.
Lochner, L. P., ed. *The Goebbels Diaries, 1942–43.* London, 1949.
Ludecke, K. *I Knew Hitler.* London, 1938.
Maschmann, M. *Account Rendered.* London, 1964.
Meissner, O. *Staatssekretär unter Ebert-Hindenburg-Hitler.* Hamburg, 1950.
Prange, G. W., ed. *Hitler's Words, Speeches 1922–43.* Washington, 1944.
Rauschning, H. *Gespräche mit Hitler.* Vienna, 1940.
———. *The Revolution of Nihilism.* New York, 1939.
Röhm, E. *Die Geschichte eines Hochverräters.* Munich, 1928.
Rossbach, G. *Meine Weg durch die Zeit. Erinnerungen und Bekenntnisse.* Weilburg, 1950.
Von Schirach, B. *Ich Glaubte an Hitler.* Hamburg, 1967.
Schmalz, K. *Nationalsozialisten ringen um Braunschweig.* Brunswick, 1934.
Speer, A. *Inside the Third Reich, Memoirs.* London, 1970.
Strasser, G. *Kampf um Deutschland-Reden und Aufsätze eines Nationalsozialisten.* Munich, 1932.
Strasser, O. *Hitler and I.* London, 1940.
Taylor, T., ed. *Hitler's Secret Book.* New York, 1961.
Thyssen, F. *I Paid Hitler.* London, 1941.
Trevor-Roper, H. R. *Hitler's Table Talk, 1941–44.* London, 1953.

(5) *Secondary Sources (selective)*

(a) The Youth Movement (including the HJ)
Ahrens, H. *Die deutsche Wandervogelbewegung von den Anfängen bis zum Weltkrieg.* Hamburg, 1939.

Aley, P. *Jugendliteratur im Dritten Reich*. Gütersloh, 1967.

Axmann, A. "Hitler-Jugend 1933–43. Die Chronik eines Jahrzehnts." *Das Junge Deutschland* 1/2 (February 1943).

——. *Der Reichsberufswettkampf*. Berlin, 1938.

Bach, A. "Gestaltung und Zielsetzung der Hitler-Jugend." *Nationalsozialistische Monatshefte*, January 1930.

Bartelmäs, E. F., ed. *Das Junge Reich, Vom Leben und Wollen der neuen deutschen Jugend*. Stuttgart, 1935.

——. *Unser Weg, Vom Werden einer Hitlerjugend Schar*. Stuttgart, 1933.

Beard, C. "Education under the Nazis." *Foreign Affairs* 14 (1936): 437–52.

Becker, H. *German Youth. Bond or Free*. London, 1946.

Bergmann, W. *Evangelische und NS Jugendführung*. Magdeburg, 1933.

Blüher, H. *Wandervogel. Geschichte einer Jugendbewegung*. Berlin, 1912.

Borinski, F., and Milch, W. *Jugendbewegung: The Story of German Youth, 1896–1933*. London, 1945.

Brandenburg, H. C. *Die Geschichte der HJ*. Cologne, 1968.

Brandt, L. *Warum? Nationalsozialistischer Schülerbund!* Munich, 1931.

Dähnhardt, H. "Wandlungen in der bürgerlichen Jugend." *Das Junge Deutschland* 8 (August 1930).

Dingräve, L. *Wo steht die Junge Generation?* Jena, 1931.

Ebeling, H. *The German Youth Movement*. London, 1945.

Ehrenthal, G. *Die Deutsche Jugendbünde*. Berlin, 1929.

Fick, L. *Die Deutsche Jugendbewegung*. Jena, 1939.

Fischer, E., ed. *Die Junge Kamaradschaft*. Berlin, 1935.

Fischer, J. "Die Nationalsozialistische Bewegung in die Jugend." *Das Junge Deutschland* 8 (August 1930).

——. "Entwicklung und Wandlungen in den Jugendverbänden im Jahre 1929." *Das Junge Deutschland* 1 (January 1930).

——. "Entwicklungen und Wandlungen in den Jugendverbänden im Jahre 1931." *Das Junge Deutschland* 2 (February 1932).

Fouret, L. A. "Pédagogie Hitlérienne." *Revue des deux Mondes* 24 (1934).

Von Galéra, K. S. *Das Junge Deutschland und das Dritte Reich*. Leipzig, 1932.

Gretz, H. "Der Kampf um die Hitlerjugend." *Nationalsozialistische Monatshefte*, January 1930.

Griesmeyer, G. *Wir Hitlerjungen, Unsere Weltanschauung in Frage und Antwort*. Berlin, 1936.

Grosse, A. "Die Hitlerjugend. Bund deutscher Arbeiterjugend." In *Handbuch der deutschen Jugendbewegung*. Edited by K. O. Paetel. Flarchheim, 1930.

Grube, K. *Zur Characterologie der deutschen Jugendbewegung*. Magdeburg, 1930.

Gründel, G. *Die Sendung der Jungen Generation*. Munich, 1932.

Günther, K. *Neues Deutschland, Ein Erinnerungsbuch für die Jugend an das Erwachen des Deutschen Volkes 1933*. Breslau, 1935.

D'Harcourt, R. "Jeunesse Hitlérienne." *Revue des deux Mondes* 18 (1933).

Haufer, H. *Kampf. Geschichte einer Jugend*. Jena, 1934.

Haverbeck, W. "Aufbruch der Jungen Nation. Ziel und Weg der nationalsozialistischen Volksjugendbewegung." *Nationalsozialistische Monatshefte*, February 1933.

Helwig, W. *Die Blaue Blume des Wandervogels*. Gütersloh, 1960.

Hemm, L. *Die Unteren Führer in der HJ*. Leipzig, 1940.

Hempel, G. *Die Kieler Hitler-Jugend*. Lübeck, 1934.

Henrich, F. *Die Bünde katholischer Jugendbewegung*. Munich, 1968.

Holzapfel, O. "Politische Bildungsarbeit in die Jugendverbände." In *Gesellschaft, Staat, Erziehung. Blätter für Politische Bildung und Erziehung*. Edited by F. Messerschmid and F. Minssen. Bonn, 1966.

Homburger-Erikson, E. "Hitler's Imagery and German Youth." *Psychiatry* 4 (November 1942).

Hubben, W. *Die Deutsche Jugendbewegung*. New York, 1937.

Hymmen, F. W. "10 Jahre Hitler-Jugend." In *Die Junge Kamaradschaft*. Edited by E. Fischer. Berlin, 1935.

Jantzen, W. "Die soziologische Herkunft der Führungsschicht in der deutschen Jugendbewegung, 1900–33." In *Führungsschicht und Eliteproblem*, Konferenz der Ranke-Gesellschaft. Düsseldorf, 1957.

Jovy, E. M. "Jugendbewegung und Nationalsozialismus." Ph.D. dissertation, University of Cologne, 1952.

Jung, W. *Deutsche Arbeiterjugend: Auslese, Förderung, Aufstieg*. Berlin, 1940.

Kater, M. H. "Die Artamanen-Völkische Jugend in der Weimarer Republik." *Historische Zeitschrift* 213 (1971): 577–638.

Kaufmann, G. *Das kommende Deutschland, Die Erziehung der Jugend im Reich Adolf Hitlers*. Berlin, 1940.

Kempkens, K. "Die politische Bewegung in den Jugendverbänden." *Das Junge Deutschland* 6 (June 1930).

Kiel, W. "Der Weg der Jugendbünde zum Nationalsozialismus." *Nationalsozialistische Monatshefte*, January 1930.

Kindt, W. "Bund oder Partei in der Jugendbewegung?" *Das Junge Deutschland* 12 (December 1932).

———, ed. *Grundschriften der deutschen Jugendbewegung*. Düsseldorf, 1963.

Klemer, G. *Jugendstrafrecht und Hitler-Jugend, Stellung und Aufgaben der HJ in die Jugendstrafrechtspflege*. Berlin, 1941.

Klönne, A. "Die Hitlerjugendgeneration." *Politische Studien* 106 (February 1959).

———. *Hitlerjugend. Die Jugend und Ihre Organisation im Dritten Reich*. Hannover, 1956.

———. *Gegen den Strom*. Hannover, 1957.

Klose, W. *Generation im Gleichschritt*. Gütersloh, 1964.

Klotz, H. *Wir gestalten durch unser Führerkorps die Zukunft*. Berlin, 1931.

Kneip, R. *Jugend zwischen den Kriegen*. Heidenheim, 1967.

———. *Wandervogel–Bündische Jugend. 1909 bis 1943*. Frankfurt, 1967.

Kneller, G. F. *The Educational Philosophy of National Socialism*. London, 1941.

Körber, W. *Das ist die HJ*. Berlin, 1935.

Korn, E., ed. *Die Jugendbewegung, Welt und Wirkung*. W. Berlin, 1963.

Laqueur, W. Z. *Young Germany: A History of the German Youth Movement*. London, 1962.

Von Lersner, D. *Die Evangelischen Jugendverbände Württembergs und die Hitler-Jugend 1933–34*. Göttingen, 1958.

Littmann, A. *Herbert Norkus und die Hitlerjungen von Beusselkietz.* Berlin, 1934.

Loewenberg, P. "The Psychohistorical Origins of the Nazi Youth Cohort." *American Historical Review,* 76 (1971): 1457–1502.

Massmann, K. *Hitlerjugend—neue Jugend!* Breslau, 1933.

——. *Wir Jugend! Ein Bekenntnisbuch der deutschen Nachkriegsgeneration.* Berlin, 1933.

Mau, H. *Die Deutsche Jugendbewegung 1901 bis 1933-.* Munich, 1949.

Miller, J. W. "Youth in the Dictatorships." *American Political Science Review* 32 (1938): 965–70.

Möller, A. *Wir werden das Volk, Wesen und Forderung der Hitlerjugend.* Breslau, 1935.

Mushardt-Tietjen, A. *Staatsjugendtag, Idee und Gestaltung.* Leipzig, 1934.

Nasarski, P., ed. *Deutsche Jugendbewegung in Europa.* Cologne, 1967.

Nationalsozialistische Monatshefte. "Die gegenwärtige Hitler-Jugend." January 1930.

Nationalsozialistische Monatshefte. "Die Hitler-Jugend." January 1930.

Neesze, G. *Brevier eines jungen Nationalsozialisten.* Oldenburg, 1933.

Nöldecken, W. *Die Deutsche Jugendbewegung.* Osnabrück, 1953.

Orlow, D. O. "Die Adolf-Hitler-Schulen." *Vierteljahrshefte für Zeitgeschichte* 13 (1965): 272–84.

Paetel, K. O. *Das Bild von Menschen in der deutschen Jugendführung.* Bad Godesberg, 1954.

——. "Das geistige Gesicht der nationalen Jugend." *Das Junge Deutschland* 6 (June 1929).

——."Die deutsche Jugendbewegung als politisches Phänomen." *Politische Studien* 86 (July 1957).

——. "Die heutige Struktur der nationalen Jugend." *Das Junge Deutschland* 6 (June 1929).

——. *Die Jugend in der Entscheidung 1913–33–45.* Bad Godesberg, 1963.

——. "Jugend von gestern und heute." *Neue Politische Literatur* (1964).

——. *Versuchung oder Chance?* Berlin, 1965.

—— , ed. *Handbuch der deutschen Jugendbewegung.* Flarchheim, 1930.

Priepke, M. *Die Evangelische Jugend in Widerstand gegen das Dritte Reich von 1933 bis 1936.* Frankfurt, 1960.

Pross, H. *Jugend. Eros. Politik.* Bern, 1964.

Raabe, F. *Die Bündische Jugend, Ein Beitrag zur Geschichte der Weimarer Republik.* Stuttgart, 1961.

Ramlow, R. *Herbert Norkus? Hier! Opfer und Sieg der HJ.* Berlin, 1933.

Randel, E. *Die Jugenddienstpflicht.* Berlin, 1942.

Rodatz, J. *Erziehung durch Erleben.* Berlin, 1936.

Rosenberg, A. "Rebellion der Jugend." *Nationalsozialistische Monatshefte,* January 1930.

Roth, B., ed. *Kampf: Lebensdokumente deutscher Jugend 1914–1934.* Berlin, 1934.

Roth, H., ed. *Katholische Jugend in der NS-Zeit.* Düsseldorf, 1959.

Sautter, R. *Hitlerjugend. Das Erlebnis einer grossen Kamaradschaft.* Munich, 1942.

Schierer, H. *Das Zeitschriftenwesen der Jugendbewegung.* Berlin, 1938.

Von Schirach, B. *Die Fahne der Verfolgten.* Berlin, 193?.

———. *Die Hitler-Jugend: Idee und Gestalt.* Leipzig, 1934.

———. *Revolution der Erziehung.* Munich, 1938.

———, ed. *Das Lied der Getreuen 1933–37.* Leipzig, 1938.

Schmidt, U. "Die Jugendbewegung und Ihre Nachwirkungen in die Hitler-Jugend." Unpublished manuscript, Hochschule Bielefeld 1960.

———. "Uber das Verhältnis von Jugendbewegung und Hitlerjugend." *Geschichte in Wissenschaft und Unterricht* 1 (January 1965).

Schneider, B. *Daten zur Geschichte der Jugendbewegung.* Bad Godesberg, 1965.

Seidelmann, K. *Bund und Gruppe als lebensformen deutscher Jugend.* Munich, 1955.

Siefert, H. *Der Bündische Aufbruch 1919–33.* Bad Godesberg, 1963.

Siemering, H. *Deutschlands Jugend im Bevölkerung und Wirtschaft.* Berlin, 1937.

———. *Die deutschen Jugendpflegeverbände.* Berlin, 1918.

Sommer, K. "Glaube, Wille, und Tat der deutschen Jugend. Erscheinungsformen des nationalsozialistischen Jugendführers." Ph.D. dissertation, University of Düsseldorf, 1938.

Tetzlaff, W. *Das Disziplinarrecht der Hitler-Jugend.* Berlin, 1944.

Überhorst, H., ed. *Elite für die Diktatur. Die Nationalpolitischen Erziehungsanstalten, 1933–45.* Düsseldorf, 1969.

Ütrecht, F. E. *Jugend in Sturm: Ein Bericht aus den schicksalsschweren Jahren 1917–33.* Berlin, 1936.

Usadel, G. *Entwicklung und Bedeutung der NS-Jugendbewegung.* Berlin, 1935.

———. *Zucht und Ordnung.* Berlin, 1935.

Uweson, U., and Ziersch, W., eds. *Das Buch der Hitler-Jugend. Die Jugend im Dritten Reich.* Munich, 1934.

Vesper, W., ed. *Deutsche Jugend. 30 Jahre Geschichte einer Bewegung.* Berlin, 1934.

Walker, L. D., *Hitler Youth and Catholic Youth 1933–36.* Washington, 1971.

Wolff, G. *Die Deutschen Jugendbünde.* Plauen, 1931.

Wrede, F. O. "Eine Geschichte der Hitlerjugend." *Nationalsozialistische Monatshefte,* September 1934.

Zahn, K. F. *Kirche und HJ.* Berlin, 1934.

Zentralrat der Freien Deutschen Jugend. *Deutschlands Junge Garde, 50 Jahre Arbeiterjugendbewegung.* Berlin, 1954.

(b) General

Abel, T. *The Nazi Movement, Why Hitler came to Power.* New York, 1965.

Allen, W. S. *The Nazi Seizure of Power.* London, 1965.

Angress, W. T. "The Political Role of the Peasantry in the Weimar Republic." *Review of Politics* 21 (1959): 530–49.

Anschütz, H. "Die NSDAP in Hamburg. Ihre Anfänge bis zur Reichstagswahl 1930." Ph.D dissertation, University of Hamburg, 1956.

Arendt, H. *Elemente und Ursprünge totaler Herrschaft.* Frankfurt, 1962.

Aronson, S. *Reinhard Heydrich und die Frühgeschichte der Gestapo und SD.* Stuttgart, 1971.

Bennecke, H. *Hitler und die SA.* Munich, 1962.

Benz, W. *Süddeutschland in der Weimarer Republik.* Berlin, 1970.

——, ed. *Politik in Bayern 1919-1933.* Stuttgart, 1971.

Berghahn, V. R. *Der Stahlhelm. Bund der Frontsoldaten 1918-35.* Düsseldorf, 1966.

Besson, W. *Württemberg und die deutsche Staatskrise, 1928-33.* Stuttgart, 1959.

Bleuel, H. P., and Klinnert, E. *Deutsche Studenten auf dem Weg im Dritten Reich.* Gütersloh, 1967.

Bloch, C. *Die SA und die Krise des NS-Regimes 1934.* Frankfurt, 1970.

Bracher, K. D. *Die Auflösung der Weimarer Republik.* Stuttgart, 1957.

——. *Die Deutsche Diktatur.* Cologne, 1969.

——. "Stufen totalitärer Gleichschaltung. Die Befestigung der NS Herrschaft, 1933-34." *Vierteljahrshefte für Zeitgeschichte* 4 (1956): 30-42.

—— et al. *Die Nationalsozialistische Machtergreifung. Studien zur Errichtung des totalitären Herrschaftssystems in Deutschland 1933-34.* Cologne, 1962.

—— et al. *1919-69. Parliamentarische Demokratie in Deutschland.* Bonn, 1970.

Bramsted, E. K. *Goebbels and National Socialist Propaganda 1925-45.* London, 1965.

Broszat, M. "Die Anfänge der Berliner NSDAP 1926-27." *Vierteljahrshefte für Zeitgeschichte* 8 (1960): 85-91.

——. *Der Nationalsozialismus.* Hannover, 1960.

——. *Der Staat Hitlers.* Munich, 1969.

——. "Soziale Motivation und Führer-Bindung des Nationalsozialismus." *Vierteljahrshefte für Zeitgeschichte* 18 (1970): 392-409.

Bullock, A. *Hitler, A Study in Tyranny.* London, 1952.

Burden, H. J. *The Nuremberg Party Rallies 1923-39.* London, 1967.

Carsten, F. L. *The Rise of Fascism.* London, 1967.

——. *The Reichswehr and Politics: 1918 to 1933.* Oxford, 1966.

Cecil, R. *The Myth of the Master Race. Alfred Rosenberg and Nazi Ideology.* London, 1972.

Conway, J. S. *The Nazi Persecution of the Churches, 1933-45.* London, 1968.

Conze, W. "Bruenings Politik unter dem Druck des Grossen Krise." *Historische Zeitschrift* 199 (1964): 529-50.

——. "Die Krise der Parteienstaates in Deutschland 1929-30." *Historische Zeitschrift* 178 (1954): 47-83.

——. "Zum Sturz Bruenings." *Vierteljahrshefte für Zeitgeschichte* 1 (1953): 261-88.

Dahrendorf, R. *Society and Democracy in Germany.* London, 1968.

Diehl-Thiele, P. *Partei und Staat im Dritten Reich.* Munich, 1969.

Diehn, O. *Der Kirchenkampf, Evangelische Kirche und Nationalsozialismus.* Hamburg, 1970.

Dorpalen, A. *Hindenburg in die Geschichte der Weimarer Republik.* Berlin, 1966.

Eilers, R. *Die nationalsozialistische Schulpolitik.* Cologne, 1963.

Eschenburg, T. "Die Rolle der Persönlichkeit in der Krise der Weimarer Republik." *Vierteljahrshefte für Zeitgeschichte* 9 (1961): 1-29.

Eyck, E. *A History of the Weimar Republic.* London, 1964.

Fenske, H. *Konservatismus und Rechtsradikalismus in Bayern nach 1918.* Bad Homburg, 1969.

Fest, J. C. *Das Gesicht des Dritten Reiches.* Stuttgart, 1963.

Feuchtwanger, E. J., ed. *Upheaval and Continuity. A Century of German History.* London, 1973.

Flechtheim, O. K. *Die KPD in der Weimarer Republik.* Offenbach, 1948.

Franz, G. "Munich. Birthplace and Center of the National Socialist German Workers' Party." *Journal of Modern History* 29 (1957): 319–34.

Franz-Willing, G. *Die Hitler-Bewegung: Der Ursprung 1919–1922.* Hamburg, 1962.

Gallo, M. *The Night of the Long Knives.* London, 1973.

Gamm, H. J. *Der Braune Kult.* Hamburg, 1962.

Gay, P. *Die Republik der Aussenseiter. Geist und Kultur in der Weimarer Zeit, 1918–1933.* Frankfurt, 1970.

Gerth, H. "The Nazi Party: Its Leadership and Composition." *American Journal of Sociology* 45 (1940): 517–41.

Gies, H. R. "Walther Darré und die Nationalsozialistische Bauernpolitik in den Jahren 1930 bis 1933." Ph.D. dissertation, University of Frankfurt, 1966.

Glum, F. *Der Nationalsozialismus.* Munich, 1962.

Gordon, H. *Hitlerputsch 1923. Machtkampf in Bayern 1923–24.* Frankfurt, 1971.

Görgen, P. "Düsseldorf und der Nationalsozialismus." Ph.D. dissertation, University of Cologne, 1969.

Hallgarten, G. F. *Hitler, Reichswehr, Industrie.* Frankfurt, 1955.

Heberle, R. *Landbevölkerung und Nationalsozialismus. Eine soziologische Untersuchung der politischen Willensbildung in Schleswig-Holstein 1918 bis 1932.* Stuttgart, 1963.

——. "Zur Soziologie der nationalsozialistischen Revolution." *Vierteljahrshefte für Zeitgeschichte* 13 (1965): 438–45.

Heiden K. *A History of National Socialism.* London, 1934.

Hermens, F., and Schieder, T. *Staat, Wirtschaft, und Politik in der Weimarer Republik.* Berlin, 1967.

Hertzmann, L. *DNVP, Right-Wing Opposition in the Weimar Republic 1918–24.* Lincoln, Nebr., 1963.

Hildebrand, K. "Hitler's *Mein Kampf,* Propaganda oder Program? Zur Frühgeschichte der nationalsozialistischen Bewegung." *Neue Politische Literatur* 14 (1969): 72–82.

Hofmann, H. H. *Der Hitlerputsch. Krisenjahre deutscher Geschichte.* Munich, 1961.

Höhne, H. *Der Orden unter dem Totenkopf. Die Geschichte der SS.* Gütersloh, 1967.

Holborn, H. "Origins and Political Character of Nazi Ideology." *Political Science Quarterly* 79 (1964): 542–54.

——. *Republic to Reich: The Making of the Nazi Revolution.* Washington, 1972.

Horn, W. *Führerideologie und Parteiorganisation in der NSDAP.* Düsseldorf, 1972.

Hüttenberger, P. *Die Gauleiter, Studie zum Wandel des Machtgefüges in der NSDAP.* Stuttgart, 1969.

International Council for Philosophy and Humanistic Studies. *The Third Reich*. London, 1955.

Jäckel, E. *Hitlers Weltanschauung*. Tübingen, 1969.

Jasper, G., ed. *Von Weimar zu Hitler, 1930–33*. Cologne, 1968.

Jones, L. E. "The Dying Middle. Weimar Germany and the Fragmentation of Bourgeois Politics." *Central European History* 5 (1972): 23–54.

Kaiser, K. *Braunschweiger Presse und Nationalsozialismus*. Brunswick, 1970.

Kater, M. H. "Zur Soziographie der frühen NSDAP." *Vierteljahrshefte für Zeitgeschichte* 19 (1971): 124–59.

Kele, M. H. *Nazis and Workers. National Socialist Appeals to German Labor 1919–33*. Chapel Hill, N.C., 1972.

Koehl, R. "Feudal Aspects of National Socialism." *American Political Science Review* 54 (1960): 921–33.

Kühnl, R. *Die Nationalsozialistische Linke, 1925–30*. Meisenheim, 1966.

Layton, R. V. "The *Voelkischer Beobachter*, 1920–1933: The Nazi Party Newspaper in the Weimar Era." *Central European History* 3 (1970): 353–82.

Lebovics, H. *A Socialism for the German Middle Classes: Anti-Capitalist and Anti-Marxist Social Thought in Germany 1914–33*. Princeton, 1969.

Lewy, G. *The Catholic Church and Nazi Germany*. Lincoln, Nebr., 1964.

Lingelbach, K. C. *Erziehung und Erziehungstheorien in nationalsozialistischen Deutschland*. Weinheim, 1970.

Lohalm, U. *Völkischer Radikalismus, Die Geschichte des Deutschvölkischen Schutz-und Trutz Bundes 1919–1923*. Hamburg, 1970.

Loomis, C. P., and Beegle, J. Allen. "The Spread of German Nazism in Rural Areas." *American Sociological Review* 11 (1946): 724–34.

Maser, W. *Die Frühgeschichte der NSDAP*. Frankfurt, 1965.

Matthias, E. "Hindenburg zwischen den Fronten 1932." *Vieteljahrshefte für Zeitgeschichte* 8 (1960): 75–84.

—— and Morsey, R., eds. *Das Ende der Parteien 1933*. Düsseldorf, 1960.

Meinecke, F. *The German Catastrophe*. Boston, 1963.

Micklem, N. *National Socialism and the Roman Catholic Church*. Oxford, 1939.

Milatz, A. *Wähler und Wahlen in der Weimarer Republik*. Bonn, 1965.

Morsey, R. "Zur Geschichte des 'Preussenschlags' am 20 Juli 1932." *Vierteljahrshefte für Zeitgeschichte* 9 (1961): 430–39.

Mosse, G. L. *The Crisis of German Ideology*. New York, 1964.

Neumann, F. *Behemoth: The Structure and Practice of National Socialism*. London, 1942.

Neumann, S. *Die Parteien der Weimarer Republik*. Stuttgart, 1965.

Nichols, A. J. and Matthias, E., eds. *German Democracy and the Triumph of Hitler*. London, 1971.

Noakes, J. "Conflicts and Development in the NSDAP 1924–27." *Journal of Contemporary History* 1 (1966): 3–36.

——. *The Nazi Party in Lower Saxony 1921–33*. Oxford, 1971.

Nyomarkay, J. *Charisma and Factionalism in the Nazi Party*. Minneapolis, 1967.

O'Neill, R. J. *The German Army and the Nazi Party 1933–39*. London, 1966.

Orlow, D. O. "The Conversion of Myths into Political Power: The Case of

the Nazi Party, 1925-26." *American Historical Review* 72 (1967): 906-24.
——. *The History of the Nazi Party 1919-33.* Pittsburgh, 1969.
——. *The History of the Nazi Party 1933-45.* Pittsburgh, 1972.
——. "The Organisational History and Structure of the NSDAP, 1919-23." *Journal of Modern History* 37 (1965): 208-26.
Peterson, E. N. "The Bureaucracy and the Nazi Party." *The Review of Politics* 28 (1966): 172-92.
——. *The Limits of Hitler's Power.* Princeton, 1969.
Phelps, R. H. "Hitler and the Deutsche Arbeiterpartei." *American Historical Review* 68 (1963): 974-86.
——. "Hitler als Parteiredner im Jahre 1920." *Vierteljahrshefte für Zeitgeschichte* 11 (1963): 274-330.
Pridham, G. *Hitler's Rise to Power. The Nazi Movement in Bavaria, 1923-1933.* London, 1973.
Rohe, K. *Das Reichsbanner Schwarz-Rot-Gold.* Düsseldorf, 1966.
Roloff, E. A. *Braunschweig und der Staat von Weimar.* Brunswick, 1964.
——. *Bürgertum und Nationalsozialismus, 1930-1933.* Hannover, 1961.
Sauer, W. "National Socialism: Totalitarianism or Fascism?" *American Historical Review* 73 (1967): 404-24.
Schäfer, W. *NSDAP, Entwicklung und Struktur der Staatspartei des Dritten Reiches.* Hannover, 1956.
Schieder, T., ed. *Beiträge zur Geschichte der Weimarer Republik.* Munich, 1971.
Schildt, G. "Die Arbeitsgemeinschaft Nord-West: Untersuchungen zur Geschichte der NSDAP, 1925-26." Ph.D. dissertation, University of Freiburg, 1964.
Schoenbaum, D. *Hitler's Social Revolution: Class and Status in Nazi Germany 1933-39.* London, 1969.
Schön, E. "Die NSDAP in Hessen." Ph.D. dissertation, University of Mannheim, 1970.
Schüddekopf, O. E. *Linke Leute von Rechts.* Stuttgart, 1960.
Schumacher, M. *Mittelstandsfront und Republik, 1919-33.* Düsseldorf, 1972.
Shirer, W. L. *The Rise and Fall of the Third Reich.* London, 1960.
Sinzheimer, H., and Fraenkel, E. *Die Justiz in der Weimarer Republik.* Neuwied, 1968.
Snell, J. L., ed. *The Nazi Revolution: Germany's Guilt or Germany's Fate?* Problems in European Civilization Series. Boston, 1966.
Sontheimer, L. *Antidemokratisches Denken in der Weimarer Republik.* Munich, 1962.
Stachura, P. D. "The Ideology of the Hitler Youth in the Kampfzeit." *Journal of Contemporary History* 8 (1973): 155-67.
Stern, F. *The Politics of Cultural Despair: A Study in the Rise of the Germanic Ideology.* Berkeley, Calif., 1961.
Stockhorst, E. *Fünftausend Köpfe.* Gütersloh, 1967.
Stolleis, M. "Gemeinschaft und Volksgemeinschaft: Zur juristischen Terminologie in Nationalsozialismus." *Vierteljahrshefte für Zeitgeschichte* 20:1 (January 1972): 16-58.

Stoltenberg, G. *Politische Strömungen im Schleswig-Holsteinischen Landvolk, 1918–33.* Düsseldorf, 1962.

Tauber, K. P. *Beyond Eagle and Swastika: German Nationalism since 1945.* Middletown, Conn., 1967.

Thoma, P. *Der Fall Otto Strasser.* Cologne, 1971.

Trevor-Roper, H. R. *The Last Days of Hitler.* London, 1947.

Turner, H. A. "Big Business and the Rise of Hitler." *American Historical Review* 75 (1969): 56–70.

Vogelsang, T. *Reichswehr, Staat, und NSDAP. Beiträge zur deutschen Geschichte 1930–32.* Stuttgart, 1962.

Vogt, M. "Zur Finanzierung der NSDAP zwischen 1924 und 1928." *Geschichte in Wissenschaft und Unterricht,* April 1970.

Volz, H. *Daten der Geschichte der NSDAP.* Berlin, 1943.

Waite, R. G. L. *Vanguard of Nazism. The Free Corps Movement in Postwar Germany 1918–23.* Cambridge, Mass., 1952.

Werner, A. "SA: 'Wehrverband,' 'Parteitruppe,' oder 'Revolutionsarmee'? Studien zur Geschichte der SA und der NSDAP 1920–33." Ph.D. dissertation, University of Erlangen, 1964.

Whiteside, A. G. "The Nature and Origins of National Socialism." *Journal of Central European Affairs* 17 (1957): 48–73.

Wilson, L., ed. *The Road to Dictatorship: Germany 1918–33.* London, 1962.

Winkler, H. A. *Mittelstand, Demokratie und Nationalsozialismus, Die politische Entwicklung von Handwerk und Kleinhandel in der Weimarer Republik.* Cologne, 1972.

Wörtz, U. "Programmatik und Führerprinzip. Das Problem des Strasser-Kreises in der NSDAP." Ph.D. dissertation, University of Erlangen, 1966.

Zeman, Z. A. B. *Nazi Propaganda.* Oxford, 1964.

Zipfel, F. *Kirchenkampf in Deutschland 1933–45.* Berlin, 1965.

Index

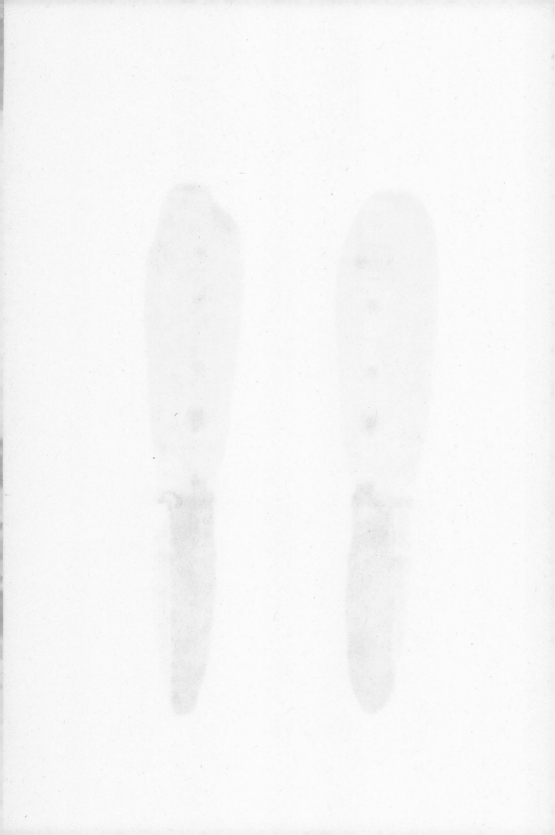